ALL

LOVE

COMES

HOME.....

A PROMISE OF TRUTH

By

GENE FISCH

Published by GM Sto Lat Publishing Company

www.GMStoLat.com

ALL RIGHTS RESERVED
COPYRIGHT © 2012 GM Sto Lat Publishing

ISBN: 978-0-578-11518-4
Library of Congress Control Number: 2012921072

All Love Comes Home...
A Promise of Truth

Written by: Gene Fisch.
www.eugenefisch.com

FIRST EDITION/FIRST PRINTING

GM Sto Lat Publishing Company
340 Liberty Street
Syracuse, New York 13204
315-214-3915
InTruthStoLat@yahoo.com

Printed in the United States
Fundcraft Publishing, Inc.

Minsha's reminder for us all

Despite not anyone, and do not deem anyone unworthy of consideration, For there is no man that not have his hour, and nothing that does not have its place.

ACKNOWLEDGEMENT

This Polish story is dedicated to Bronislawa and Andrew Fisch who conducted their lives in an honorable way...... mothers and fathers who resisted oppression, destruction and annihilation while sustaining a journey of the heart, keeping faith in God, country, home and family.

The beauty of truth is inside the pages of this novel that is a slice of the "Whole Picture" of 20th Century's greatest struggle for freedom of the soul and mind. The story returns back home from history's mistruths to a family who endured and then prevailed....

And thus with special thanks to Bronislawa and Andrew Fisch for the thoughts that give eternal truth ... a full flight of a priceless heritage; minds and souls that triumphed in the greatest struggle in history's most devastating times. To my beloved sister, Longina, may her memory be a blessing; and to Monika and Dominik, who landed at the shores of New York with honor, then traveled forward where all love does come home. To my sons who are closest to my heart: Gene Fisch, Jr and Matthew Ronsheim, the bright stars with their great thoughts and shining futures.

I am sharing my Trilogy with you in the truest sense knowing full well that the greatest tragedy of the 20th Century was witnessed by my family in a place of history that was overlooked. BOOK ONE and TWO are based on their personal experience, at a most disastrous time, when one out of three Polish citizens unnaturally disappeared from the author's beautiful land.

I had written over thirty thousand pages, badly in need of revision, and am truly grateful to Myrna Jacobs for her superbly edited work, to Peter Lubrecht for the final touches, to Rosalyn Synakowski for her devoted administrative work and the typing of twelve thousand hand written pages, and to the late Dr. Lala Dunbar for feeling the love of my work and giving clarity and meaning to Book One in the kindest ways. Many thanks to Heather Caines of the New York City Public Library for the most thoughtful application of resources in order for me to keep my promise alive...*A promise of truth that now is enshrined forever...* The bookends have been sealed.

Gene Fisch

INTRODUCTION

The time has come to turn the page on history's greatest struggle in a part of the world that had its hour of choices ....either a path of self destruction with the forces of hatred, or a journey of the heart ...

A mother's voice is the unheard bit of life, the remaining connection that is the whole truth of the Christian genocide of 20th century, and the compelling secrets of the most disastrous era in all of western civilization....over one hundred million Christians and six million Jews systematically mass murdered in three decades of War. And my family was right in the center of it all.

The world remained silent, cloaked in secrecy, but at this hour, we have the historic moment to right course. People don't want to believe it,but it is true back then, and it is true now, and my eternal hope ..is For ALL Love to return Home

Book-One is bound to open the world's eyes to a tragedy and providence never before thoughtfully discerned. Within the walls of Communism and Nazism beckons the emergence of truth. Some people may think it incomprehensible to redress the sequence of history, though it is replete with misdeeds, but there are many facets to the knotty tragedy of war, each needing and deserving the right of presence and authentic discussion.

My family survived five occupations, but sustained a free mind against the innermost truth and meaning of 20th Century's hatred and love. If Bronislaw and Andrew Fisch could render a greater service today, it is for the love of life not to vanish like the piles of body dust scattered namelessly in the wind. For not one being, leaves the field of war unaltered and without a footprint of suffering on their soul. For this alone, we must never allow the presented remnants of war to serve as the buried fabric of truth.

The scope of misdeeds dwarfs all disasters of history, but much of the truths were swept aside. More than sixty million dead in silent graves were left behind from August of 1939 to 1945, shrouded in secrecy for two generations. The only witness to these heinous crimes was the reticent, pervasive darkness which created a cruel injustice, a loss of love of higher ideals, family and home.

AUTHOR'S REASON TO LIVE

I was born in war-torn Polesie in eastern Poland. My mother, who at all times was the embodiment of unconditional love, felt there was every reason to live, and in a lonely field, bit off the umbilical cord. In the presence of evil, death and the worst and best of humanity, she did not dismiss a newborn as another life lost and overlooked, but welcomed me so I might have a chance to survive and prosper.

In my story, I have much to share with you, but most worthwhile of all, is the great love of mother and father. When in times of intense struggle, separation became a devastating end to many, yet Andrew and Bronislawa remained as "one great love" and wherever they found their home, Andrew neatly planted a rose that was always compatible with beauty attributed to what was on the inside of the home,a love of family that remained intact always as one.

Thus, when I look back, I wonder how we survived at all? I am thankful that my family and I are the beneficiaries of my mother's and father's life values and that I had a chance to live them out. Gratitude is truly good for the soul and can make the seemingly impossible--- possible.

Book One and Two unravels a life-long theme expressed best in this family's testament to the strength of Polish character and an abiding love of a future   as a way of life from where we've come, and what we've become. This story is a rarity for us all, the World War Two truths never voiced before today.

My professional career was once described by a reporter as a "rags to riches" story, a Polish immigrant who won public acclaim as a *"survivor of the worst of Europe's horrors" who went on to apply the best of the "old world traditions of discipline, integrity and sacrifice to excel, first in athletics, then in government and academia, and finally in the business world."*

I graduated with distinction from New York University BS- Economics/MBA, and have integrated my past while continuing to embark on new thoughts……and doing the *right* thing at this moment in time, that is seeking truth and meaning … a kind of reflection of my family's life against the backdrop of deep-seated hatred.

Book One way of life is the opening of a rose that needs to bloom naturally, and honestly and to preserve the legacy of 20th century's greatest courageous spirit of the heart, always extolling the beauty of trust.

GENE FISCH, Author

PROLOGUE

Marianne Krull, after years of travel and war, was dying slowly. Her Polish hard ducha had worn her down and the end was near. Her three children only had flashback of memories of dirt and muddy, dark smelly earth. Their Mother had delivered the last boy by herself, in a furrowed field in Eastern Poland. There had been no one else, no Doctor, Nurse or Mid-wife to help her. The world had exploded into a war. Somehow, the family survived. Poland was left bloodied and wounded in cruel debris as the fire of conflict smoldered for decades of death and destruction in and into the blaze of World War 2.

Somewhere, buried deep in her memory, was the recollection of dark faceless figures dragging her children screaming onto the night. They were crying for her before, during and after they were tortured as they endured the resulting searing pain. The treatment left scarred bodies and minds. Even though her family had escaped to America, they struggled with their past, their pursuit of truth and its revelation became an obsession. For years, Marianne would not talk of her part in the fight against an inhuman enemy, but now, and only as she felt herself crumble, as all men must at one time or another, did she believe that she could reveal her part in the history of the continuing fight for humanity and its values in the midst of an ongoing evil. One key to her past was a small snapshot of six Jewish children smiling into the sun behind the old Brownie camera, which was buried deep in her drawer. On the back in a foreign looking hand was written Aaron, Tamara, Yari, Seth, Seymour and Myrna Dorovitz-"Aby outher Mama. Dziękuję." Proudly, she once told her children that Aaron was a famous Rabbi in New York, and that the youngest Myrna Dorovitz –Jacoby taught History in London. However, at that point she said only that they were friends of the the family in Poland in another time.

Rabbi Dorovitz had returned to her with the object, which lay in the drawer next to the pictures carefully tied and wrapped in brown paper. While on a search for ancient Talmudic manuscripts, housed in Russia, he was able to revisit a hut in Polesie in Poland. It was deep in the woods, where Polish patriots hid from the Russians and then later from the Nazis. It was marked by a crude natural altar near Janow. Marianne's father built that altar and her husband Andrew and family lived in that small hovel. The center of their faith was in that patch of woods. They survived there as the saviors of many, and God's instruments of vengeance to others .After finding the right hovel, Rabbi Aaron was able to get through the undergrowth to a door stuck into the sod of the ground, which he forced open and in the small space inside he found the central hearth made of flat stones. Under the center stone was a wooden icon, a copy of the Black Madonna of Częstochowa.

The hidden compartment inside this icon contained Marianne's wartime diary and a single film canister. If it had been found when written, it would have meant death to all of them. When they were forced to leave their home in the woods, it was hidden in an old green tin radio container under the fire pit. They had wanted to reveal to the world what had happened during those years in Polesie, and when they had fled, they thought it lost forever. Aaron had returned the Madonna to Marianne, complete with the trick catch that opened it when the halo on the Christ child was pressed. It had been beautifully carved and created by Marianne's husband Andrew, truly a work of love. Inside there lay, carefully tied with wool yarn, a packet of letters in Polish, written in a small close hand on all different kinds of paper, along with an aged roll of thirty five millimeter film and a single negative.

The tiny, fine educated Polish script was almost completely faded; however, Marianne re-examined these notes, and was able to translate and transcribe a good part of the story. She had cried openly when she saw the Madonna again, for to her it contained the souls and hearts of those who survived.

Here is her story.

I

Krakow was home, near the Polesie plain. The city suffered terribly from1915 to 1949 when armies invaded and stamped out every vestige of life. Millions lay dead, on the plains among the trees, their deaths shrouded in secrecy. Three generations had been cut off from their heritage and their country. There were no witnesses. The center of Marianne's life was her Tata (Father) Ludwig, who never allowed fear to dictate the course of his life. He knew, and taught his child, that the harsh reality of living included having a hard ducha, (a yearning heart) on which all love centers and which returns home after great struggles.

Wadeslaw Ludwig lost his wife during the birth of their second child; however, his daughter miraculously survived, and he was left to raise the little ones by himself. He missed his Anna very much, as she had been the love of his life. The Doctor and midwife were unable to save her from post-partum fever; and had to find a way to raise the baby to childhood. The little girl named Marianne after his Mother , blossomed into a precocious beautiful child, and he kept her close to him, loved her and taught her very much at a very early age.

When she was three, Marianne did something to make the family housekeeper Pani Kowalska very angry, After soundly spanking her, Pani lumbered all the way up the hill to Ludwig's factory, dragging Marianne behind her. Red-faced and furious, she said to an alarmed father, "Do you know what this one did today when I am supposed to be through at noon? After the babka went into the oven, I went to give her some lunch and what did I see? She broke all the eggs, one after the other all over the floor in my nice, clean pantry. Tata, asked: "Marianne, why would you do something like that?"

The small child explained, between sobs, that she wanted a baby chick, and that she didn't make a mess; the eggs were broken over the wood box and she thought after waiting long enough, the baby chicks would emerge. She was still puzzled why there were no chicks.

Her father laughed and, hugged her and said, "Is that all?"

Pani Kowalska stomped angrily towards the house alone. She knew better than to stand up to both of them. From then on, "is that all" became a personal phrase shared by father and daughter. "Small steps lead to big steps," he continued, "Once you break the egg, only God can put it back together. "Is that all?"

One of her earliest memories was waiting in the garden for Tata to pick her up as he usually did. She was wearing her favorite pink ruffled dress. When he arrived she ran to him and hugged him tenderly. He gently took her hand and led her down the winding path, past the fountain, to their field filled with wildflowers and dotted with fruit trees which were scattered amid the occasional oak. The path ended at an old weathered iron gate that had been standing open for so long that a blooming apple tree had grown up in front of it. Wadeslaw Ludwig and his little girl sat down on their favorite bench. Seven-year-old Marianne had been badly frightened when he told her that her grandfather had died last week saving others. The Germans WW1 released a new yellowish-green poison gas in Bromilow, his hometown, that looked like mist, and which permeated every nook and cranny killing anyone who was exposed to it. While they experimented with the new gas in his town, Grandpa, who owned a factory refused to leave, but ran from hut to hut getting his employees to evacuate the area. At that moment the winds changed and blew the gas into the houses. The 18,000 poison gas shells released by the Nazis were directed at Russian troops on the outskirts of Bromilow; however, the gas outside the houses died off in the cold weather, but if it reached the interior of the warm house it killed the occupants. People running for shelter were the most affected. Grandfather had tied a wet cloth over his mouth, and gasping for air, clutched the hand of one of his workers, determined to lead him out of the factory. Three days later, they were both found in the tangle of corpses. The gas had burned the victims' faces; blistering their eyes and throats. "Your grandfather was identified by the engraving on this his pocket watch." Tata said lovingly as he touched his father's shiny watch.

Marianne remembered the words clearly, and when she was older she realized that this event was the beginning of the conversion of Poland into a wasteland. Three imperial armies converged on ancient towns like Rawa Ruska, Podgórze, and Przeherśl. The desolation had occurred on a grand scale.

She was growing up in the midst of a terrifying war against the Union of Soviet Socialists Republic, which to her family was the most evil government in the world. She often knelt in church and prayed for the soldiers, and for the suffering people of Poland. The family was devout, trusted in a kindly God and in a service to Jesus by helping others who were less fortunate .Papa had said that the brave soldiers had never faced a battle of greater importance than the Battle for Warsaw.

2

Tata explained, as best he could to a child, that they were dealing with Bolsheviks who wanted to expand the revolution from Russia into all of Europe. "They believe that we are too weak to defend ourselves; therefore, they want to unite the lower classes to revolt against the educated, intellectuals, and professional people. In the Eastern parts of Poland ancient cities are being destroyed, while its citizens are being tortured, murdered and starved. Resistant Christian farmers and laborers had their villages burned to the ground."

As difficult, it was for a young girl to understand, Ludwig Krull believed that this bright star in life had the capability, even then, to comprehend the forces in the world around her. He called the Bolshevik leaders the "Inner Circle of Evil", who created an atmosphere of fear, operating on a system of reprisals and rewards based on citizen reports of supposed offenses to the leaders in return for rewards of position and power. The war had begun after the May Day Revolution of 1905, which led to the Revolutions of 1917 and 1918. The atheistic Bolshevik drive for extreme power in 1918 not only destroyed the lives of the anti–Communists and Christians of the USSR's Republics' people, but also included a fanatical fervor to murder tens of thousands across the Russian borders into Germany, Poland, Hungary, Rumania, and Czechoslovakia. The design was to produce a terror so great that no religious person could continue to be a believer. Christians were the target because they comprised the largest group of people in Europe who were unified by the tenets of their faith.

Marianne learned much of Polish history in Ludwig's library, which she loved as much in her memory as when she was actually there. It was a large room, oak paneled with high ceilings and very high bookshelves, each section covered with its own glass-fronted door. There was a big central table with green glass shaded "captain's lamps", and two large podiums, one held a dictionary, and the other a Bible. She loved to touch the leather bindings of the books and feel the almost harsh texture of the pages with her fingertips. Tata had collected all kinds of literature in different languages. He was a classical scholar who had studied at Jagiellonian University. Therefore, the works of Plato, Aristotle, Dioscorides, Herodotus, Sophocles and Aeschylus, all in Greek, were next to Caesar's "Punic Wars", and the works of Horace, Ovid and Plutarch, all in Latin. Dr. Wadeslaw Ludwig read several languages easily, and he had collected the German classics of Goethe and Schiller, with the philosophy of Nietzsche and even the "trashy" American Western novels, in German, by Carl Mai. He had given the works of the great Polish writers, Jan Dlugosz, Gallus Anonymous,

Wincenty Kadlubek, Jan Kochanowski, Jan Polocki and the others their own bookcase in the center of the room. Most importantly ,however, were the different editions of the Holy Bible prominently displayed on the central table, including the King James English version, the Latin Vulgate, the English Douai Bible, Martin Luther's Bible, and most prominently Wladysław Nehring's Psalterii Florianensis pars Polonica, Poznań, .

Marianne read Rousseau's Social Contract, Adam Smith's Wealth of Nations, and the works of John Locke. She would often spend long hours in the room, curled up on a cushion near the large window reading about history. Like her father she was a polyglot, and languages came easily to her. As she grew, her interest in history sprouted into a passion, and she and her father often discussed issues long into the night. They dissected Edward Gibbon's *Decline and Fall of the Roman Empire*, which Ludwig had read four times. Years later, she treasured the memory of her night owl father, small enough to sit with his heels up on the same chair seat that he occupied, drinking a nightly glass of milk and eating a midnight snack, while relating the history of the early Byzantine Empire. He revered the classics, and often told her that he saw her someday as a young Joan of Arc, albeit with a better end. He also reconstructed the day's political activities, for he had great concerns about the future of intellectuals and the educated in the days to come. He was deeply religious as well, and during the course of Marianne's Catholic upbringing, they would often quibble about the Bible and spirituality, still ending with "Is that all?"

The intelligentsia and the religious leaders were seeking a way to answer and fight against the Soviet menace. Every Tuesday, therefore, prominent Polish leaders, gathered at the Ludwig home in the library. At first,Tata allowed young Marianne to sit quietly in the back chair while these men discussed politics and philosophy. Discussions ranged from Nietzsche's concept of an anti-Christ glorification of man exemplified by the Nazi Troops on the Polish border, to the coming threat of a Moscow centered communism. Poland, they believed, was being squeezed in the middle of these two powers. Unfortunately, as they poured over the foreign newspapers, they began to realize that the truth was being carefully hidden. The world journalists reported the Bolshevik directed situation in Poland as "civil strife." The foreign mercenaries sent by the Soviets were depicted as young idealists. Gradually Poland was being used as a source of propaganda, and the reality of their situation for whatever reason the Western press had, was being selectively and carefully hidden from the world.

This gathering gave the teenager an inside view of the Polish opposition leadership against the Bolsheviks , led by the Polish President, who in the 1917-18 Polish War led his country to victory against them. Alongside of him, at Ludwig's large round library table sat Count Zamolenski who had been an extraordinary and effective leader, who had helped to save Europe and Poland from the Communist march through them.

Zamolenski, a great big man with a bushy mustache, seemed to be eight feet tall to Marianne. He usually spoke about the coming conflicts in a loud booming voice. "We shall never close our eyes to the Communists. here or anywhere else! We must never forget that history's greatest evil is at our borders ready to strike at any moment!" he declared.

On one occasion, he described the crimes committed against Polish border guards. "The Communists invaded our territory, captured our guards, and with Polish collaborators, stripped them, hung them upside down, beat and cut them, until they died, while the Bolshevik observers relished and smiled at the torture. He had photographs of the event. The images frightened, while at the same time hardened the young observer, Marianne.

He continued with a plea to defend the borders against the Soviet Union. "The Soviets were attacking schools and villages and blaming it on Ukrainians and Jews. No doubt, they were the foreign agents, NKVD. These mass murderers had faces and names, and he went on to count them off on his fingers Lenin, Stalin, Trotsky, Mikoyan, Vyshynsky, Kanganovich, Beria, Frenkel, Berhman, Mecklis and Khrushchev. These men are the architects of trouble and terror in our world."

"On the other hand," he said, the Nazis are crusaders, and they preach their belief. They will march across the strategic territorial corner of the world claiming that Poland was Prussian and should be returned to the Aryan empire. In order to complete that task they would destroy our most precious values: love of faith and country. Then they will march east to fight Communists!"

Zamolenski inspired the young girl. How could she join this fight? She did not want others to suffer. Not everyone was the enemy. Her Christian upbringing led her to the decision of caring for the people in need.

Zamolenski's inspiring speech went on, as Marianne wondered what a young woman could do to join in the fight. "Polesie is about three

5

hundred miles from Warsaw; it has a rich history of heroes and defeat of invaders. Strategically eastern Poland, particularly Polesie, was an easy conquest that had humbled Sweden's Charles XII when he invaded Russia in the 17th century and Napoleon during his disastrous winter retreat from Moscow. It was the battleground between the Germans and Russians during the Great War of 1914-1918. We were alone and forgotten, and yet, we supplied food and wheat for Poland and most of central Europe."

"If the Soviet evil is crossing our borders, it is because we are not doing anything about it. It is a threat to every citizen of our nation, and we need to root out any plotters in Poland. We do not need to hurt others. I want to save lives. I want to give everyone a chance to live….even the traitors to our country."

Marianne, however, was not at all convinced that the next speaker in this one particular meeting belonged there. Dumblosky and his brother, political activists and Bolshevik supporters, spoke angrily and usually with the same repetitive philosophy. "There is hatred against Jews, and today we must do something about it." Ludwig had included him among the decision-makers of Krakow, she discovered later, in an effort to seek reconciliation between cultural and political differences. His credence was minimal, since he was viewed by most as a "servitor" for the Bolsheviks; Lenin had called him a "useful idiot." Ludwig told Marianne one night "Put your enemies where you can see them."

Krakow's Bishop Krakowski, General Pilsudski, and Mayor Blaski, were "regulars" at these meetings and all agreed that something needed to be done but how?

One day, well into over a year of these meetings, they turned to Marianne still sitting quietly, but hoping someday to be heard and decided that they needed a new generation of voices in Poland and why not start with the bright young girl sitting in the corner. She had blossomed into an elegant, beautiful young woman, a fact not lost on the men in the room, and the Bishop looked at her and said: "Marianne, you will be a teacher! We will get you into St. Paul's Seminary, where you will make history as the first woman to teach there! That may be difficult for a lone woman among men but I do believe in miracles and will follow up personally".

The Bishop recommended her to Jagiellonian University (Uniwersytet Jagielloński).He said that "her love of country would lead to teaching history."

Marianne, therefore, was sent into the world of men. She wanted desperately to teach, and particularly about the story of Poland. Her first step was to finish her schooling, and once finished the Bishop found a position for her at St. Paul's Benedictine Seminary for priests, as he had promised.

II

She began in the Seminary, in September 1929, teaching contemporary history. At first the school was a lonely place. Marianne diligently prepared lessons echoing her family's teachings of love of neighbor, of Christian ethics, of the love of truth, of home, and of country. During this time fear and hatred were the enemy. Marianne yearned for the comfort and closeness of family; however, the seminary allowed few chances of finding love or even companionship.

She struggled with the teaching of Christian principles amidst the political chaos of the day. It was difficult to   interpret Christian doctrine amid the horror from 1917 thru July 1929 caused by the emergence of the Soviets, whose trail of hatred and terror created Europe's deadliest place in history. She tried to keep to the principle of love and truth even though the eastern border Poland was a graveyard of murdered Christians; engineered by Lenin, Stalin, and the Communist party faithful.

These mass murderers, however, had been held "blameless" by the world's leaders. The Western press, often through the eyes of Walter Durante, of the New York Times, ignored the truth. The field was soaked with blood and was now littered with graveyards, resulting from the mob violence and Bolshevik order. Thirty million souls had perished. As she prepared her lessons, Marianne wondered how all history teachers could show the truth to young people facing a very dangerous and uncertain future and who could alternatively turn to fear and hatred by those who" hated" as a way   life. They killed those who love. How could she demonstrate the belief that violence, fear and hatred could be overcome by love?

The other "godless" menace was growing in Germany under Adolph Hitler causing a press of power on both sides of Poland. The seminarians' faith would probably carry them through the impending disaster; however, how could she teach love of the homeland to people who were facing its destruction?

On her first day of class, Marianne wept as she walked through the gate at St. Paul's and up the long stairway; she cried because she was so scared. Even later in life, she would remember the large white-washed room at the end of a long marble corridor, filled with robed young men who stood silently, waiting to formally greet her with the traditional Dobry Rano Nauczyciel . She said "Dobry Rano klasa ".They sat down.

She barely remembered, in later years, the blur of her first words or the first lesson However, she knew that she started with a lesson on love of country, family, and home, and the problem of teaching the younger generation philosophy based on love, when hate was the easier path. She recalled saying "If hate overpowers our love of country and our faith, we will have an unprecedented disaster for our nation, and also for Europe as well. The responsibility of this rising generation of priests, our future leaders, to spread this love must not fail."

"You are young men. It is up to you to promote reconciliation of faith and let all faiths move on with life." she said. " Four million Jews live in our country, and this nation made the difference between life and death for them. We were the first and only nation in Europe, to provide freedom of religion to Jews, as the constitutional right that every human being is equal"

She connected to them the American President Thomas Jefferson's writing of: We hold these truths to be self-evident that all men are created equal to the sixteenth century Polish philosopher, Tomas Glowacki. "Time is our enemy. The stakes are high for Poland. There are no easy choices. The way ahead will be very hard, but not hopeless. How do we win and unite the hearts and minds of all Polish citizens?" During her lecture, it was clear to see that the class of seventy seminarians were so focused on Marianne's every word, no longer caught up with the idea of a woman teacher. Her first lecture was over and indeed, very liberating.

However, as the lessons continued, twenty-one year old Marianne was captivated by a handsome blond student in the third row, fourth seat from the right.and she had a difficult time trying to ignore him. The seating chart listed him as Andrew Krull; he had a quiet confidence that reminded her of her father's seriousness. His eyes twinkled with flashes of blue and his warm smile quickened her pulse. Although men had been a part of her life, not one of them appealed to her, nor did she care. Now in her new life, she wanted a priest! It was a strange feeling. The seminarians looked very much the same in their robes to her; except for Andrew. He appeared, special, a bit older, and very aware of self and his surroundings. He was an active participant in her class, and as the days progressed the attraction between them grew stronger. Marianne forced herself to believe that it was only intellectual and philosophical, but then she started to be overly aware of his physical

9

presence and appearance. He radiated an optimistic view of the future, and apparently was hiding a difficult past, a past that drove him into the seminary.

Eventually, their relationship came to a point of no return. One day, in the sunset's quiet presence, they arranged to meet on the long pathway at the far end of St. Paul's. Excited with anticipation, she rushed to join him. As they came closer, the physical attraction was magnetic, and as if rehearsed, he kissed her. The kiss lasted only a few seconds, but the warmth reached deep inside and filled them with the most exhilarating sensation they had ever known.

From that moment on, they would usually slip away and walk to the garden under the willows to touch and hold hands in a private world. With each secret meeting, the passion became more intense.. As it did, confusion grew for both of them. Was his faith strong enough? He needed the comfort of St. Paul's, he felt, but not if it meant betraying his heart ---surely he must explore and examine his life. She began to see the enormity of their actions as a mortal sin committed by succumbing to physical desire. Could he make the difference in her life? Could he leave the priesthood?

Eventually, they confessed their love for one another, even though that declaration led to further uncertainty. " I have always lived for this moment", she gently confided. "Forever be there to caress me, to make my body dance and my heart sing. You Andrew, are the love of my life, my heart and soul. Bear with me at every turn. I shall see you again." Andrew squeezed her hand, leaned his head close to her heart, firmly believing what they were solemnly promising. However, could he suddenly break away from a life committed to the priesthood? Andrew finally said "We cannot have happiness if we thoughtlessly pursue our passions. My feelings for you are true but I also need to prove my worth and not impulsively leave my life's work to love someone selfishly." Without saying a word, she gently kissed him good-bye outside the walls of St. Paul's. They would have decisions and critical choices to make, but at the moment, she could only think of his handsome face, with the wavy blond hair falling across his eyes and that special smile that ignited her passion.

As she left the western gate of St. Paul's, she realized that the lasting impression she had made at the seminary was not the kind her father would have expected. She had violated the seminary code, and would never be able to set foot there again. Guilt surfaced as the thought of her home in beautiful Krakow. Her roots were precious and nothing could be more devastating than tarnishing the good name of Ludwig with an illicit love affair; however, her heart was pounding with longing and the fear of never seeing Andrew again. Along with her thoughts was the feeling that she had violated Bishop Krakowski's trust. He had brimmed with pride at her being the first female teacher in a seminary, and now she was leaving.

III

After verpers, Andrew slipped out a side door into the stately gardens of St. Paul's to his beloved flower gardens. All his life he loved flowers, and as a boy learned how to nurture and cultivate them. At St. Paul's, he found his skill led to peace and contemplation, and the delicate white begonias, brilliant blue irises, and climbing roses were flourishing. Andrew was happiest in the flower garden, where he felt close to his Creator, but tonight he was filled with sadness. His thoughts were only about Marianne Ludwig. He saw her beauty, again and again, in his mind's eye, her large amber colored eyes and her long raven hair that framed her face. Sick at heart, resting on the cool stone bench, he came to what seemed to be an inescapable conclusion. He owed the seminary everything, yet now he thought of turning his back on it.

Andrew was four when his mother had died in Scepnica, Austria, a region that had been Polish before the 1870 partition. An influenza epidemic rapidly took the lives of many families, often three or four of them at a time. The suddenness of the blow, which caused the death of three older children as well, destroyed his father, who irrationally blamed little Andrew for the deaths. Grief- stricken, he packed up his wife's clothing, and gave it to the church. Then, almost as an afterthought, he delivered his son to a farm couple, the Brozeks. They had agreed to feed and clothe Andrew, with the understanding that when he was old enough he would work for them. Their farm, in an isolated area about thirty kilometers from Krakow, consisted of a cow, a few pigs, some chickens, and in the fields, uneven rows of potatoes, beets, cabbages, and the remains of the summer corn. It was a far cry from the tidy home Andrew loved, with its gingerbread trim, surrounded by his mother's autumn sunflowers and chrysanthemums smiling up from the yard. He remembered the orderliness of the home and his mother instilling in him the love of God and nature. This was an ugly, unkempt place, and he couldn't imagine why his father had brought him here.

"Is this where they are keeping Mama?" he wondered, looking around hopefully, his eyes fixed on the door of the small gray house. But instead of Mama, an old woman and man appeared. The lady jerked him out of the carriage and set him down roughly in the yard. He recoiled from her cold eyes and her horrible smell: a combination of onions, old sweat, and the thick cloying odor of homemade brandy. Andrew's father dropped his bag down on the ground with a thud and picked up the horse's reins.

"Tata!" the boy called out, scrambling to his feet and grabbing onto the carriage wheel as he realized what was happening. His father looked back for a moment. His eyes darted around desperately, as if he, too, was hoping to see Mama somewhere. His gaze returned to the little boy, who was the mirror image of his mother. That decided it.

Shaking his head, he quietly announced, "It's for the best. A man can't raise a child by himself and work all day too. It just can't be done." Cracking the whip to his horses, he sped away. Andrew, hysterically, chased after the carriage, screaming and calling out, but his father never looked back. The Brozeks grabbed Andrew's bag and returned to the house without uttering a single word. The little boy lay in the dirt and sobbed until tired and spent. He fell asleep in the yard like a stray dog. It was not until morning when he saw the Brozeks again, and it would be a long, long time before Andrew cried again. The young boy developed a "hard ducha", a heart suffering silently that eternally nourished his soul.

The next night Pani Brozek tossed a rough woolen blanket into a corner of the barn, and then she disappeared. Andrew did not see his bag again, nor did he ever find out what was packed in it. As the months went by, he would dream of recovering it in some secret hiding place and maybe a picture of the golden angel who had been his mother. In his dreams, she would pull him out of his nightmare by singing and rocking him the way she had before, but he always awakened to the scurry of rats and the stink of chicken droppings. After a while, he stopped dreaming of her at all.

For nearly six years, at least once a week, usually on Sundays, Andrew was hung from the rafters of the barn and beaten mercilessly with a belt until his back bled. He never understood the exact reason for this, only that the Brozeks fully expected their due in return for sheltering him. They always felt they had been somehow cheated, because for the first three years or so, Andrew was too small to do heavy work. No amount of beating or cajoling could get his little body to grow fast enough to suit their purpose.

"I will break you eventually," the old man would grunt as he wiped his brow with satisfaction.

For him it would be well worth the effort if he trained the boy as one would a dog. The image of Brozek's broad sweating face with the low brow and square jaw was burned into Andrew's memory, as was the overwhelming sensation of helplessness he felt when roped up for a beating.

His only recourse was to withhold the one reaction that they wanted. No matter what they did to him, if they starved him or beat him or refused to let him relieve himself, he would endure the pain and shame with no expression whatsoever. He would bite his tongue until it bled to keep from crying out, and the only sound they ever heard from him was the whoosh of his breath as they knocked the wind out of him. With no one else to encourage him, he would congratulate himself on surviving another day.

Each night, he would pray to God and make the same promise, "No matter what they do tomorrow, they will not break me".

Andrew's most persistent source of hope and inspiration was his relationship with nature, with the nearby streams, wild flowers and animals. To him, the forest had a dazzling radiance with the birds singing and the grass humming. He sought comfort in observing the natural order of God's great design and the cycle of give and take that sustained all of life since time began. He marveled at how a certain flower was shaped perfectly to feed a hummingbird, or that a poisonous mushroom was bright red, as if to warn people from eating it. At sundown, he would take a rosebud, place it in a container of water and let it open, and because the bloom was his and his alone, and an object of beauty, he felt comforted.

The Brozeks rarely included him in their family meals, so he ate what the forest provided and developed a remarkable ability to hunt and fish. He could prepare a sling, load it with a stone, aim it carefully and make a bird fall instantly. Quickly removing its feathers and cleaning the bird, he would cook it over an open fire for his meal. He fit easily into the world of the forest and began to look forward to each day, especially in summer when the sunlight filtered through the trees, the blossoms were at their peak, and if he was silent, he could hear birds and the wind.

As it happened, fate turned in his direction, when Father Baron, a regional priest of the Benedictine order, heard of Andrew and the abuse the Brozeks were heaping upon him and every few days he would stop by to see him. Andrew would happily run toward the priest walking down the road. The young boy had not known warmth and kind gentleness since the death of his mother; even the Brozeks would not dare cross or argue with the priest. Soon arrangements were made for Andrew to leave the Brozek's farm for more pleasant conditions. The new foster parents quickly insisted upon his labor, but treated him decently and took him to church with them on Sundays. Father Baron taught Andrew to read, write, and do arithmetic. Soon he became an eager student and studied hard. For the first time, he learned to realize that there was a world outside of the forest and the brutality of his private hell. The priest felt a natural kinship towards the young boy for he had also endured a difficult childhood and told Andrew of his own struggles. Like Andrew, he had been abandoned prior to entering school. He considered himself blessed because of it.

"The light of God shines forever," he advised Andrew, "but some of us only see it when the world is first darkened. If one endures and trusts in God, the result is an inner strength one cannot earn in any other way."

As Andrew listened to Father Baron, he began to understand those simple words from the Bible, "I am the way, the truth and the light." He saw that the world of man could be as beautiful and ordered as that of nature. Quite simply, one had to make that choice. He discovered that like the elements of nature, the Holy Mother and God could be his constant companions.

"Heaven is full of my friends," he would say to himself.

He began to treat life as a happy adventure. No matter what challenges lay ahead, he earnestly believed that God meant for him to experience each moment not in anger but in the true joy of living. He wrote fervently of his maturing faith. "The angels will take care of me," Andrew believed. "If I live my life to follow in Christ's footsteps, I can walk up the mountain to touch the hand of God. It all depends on the destination and the true joy and triumph is to get there".

On his eighteenth birthday, Andrew was granted permission to leave his foster parents' home for a school operated by a religious order of brothers in the town of Pavlov. He remained there for five years, and then he served two years in the military. At 25, he was finally able to enter the seminary. There, everything was ordered and clear, as blissful an existence as he could ever have hoped for; however, when he found Marianne, his world changed.

He would never forget her inner glow. When she entered the room, he felt an excitement of such enormity that he could not describe it even to himself. He felt that he was approaching the most important decision of his life. Although he did not know what was coming, he wasn't afraid. Rarely do heaven and earth meet, but when they did, for

15

him, "It's here, it's now, in a place such as this: the beauty of the garden." It had never occurred to him that he would ever leave the seminary once he had entered it, but after endless soul searching, he finally reached his decision. He desired Marianne's love and wanted to make himself worthy of her.

The next morning, he sought out Father Baron. "I have a fire within me," Andrew said, his voice quavering. "I've never known a woman, but I think I would like to now!" He blurted out this last part, deeply embarrassed. "She's brilliant. She is tall, has beautiful brown hair. I look at her with a burning desire. She is kind and considerate. There is such gentleness in her smile that I melt at her sight. She is so intent on doing good things, and has the soul of an angel."

Father Baron chuckled at Andrew's enthusiasm, "She gives you that tingling sensation, and I believe I know who she is. Anything else?" he asked.

"She has changed me. I'll never be exactly the same. My emotions are stirred, and I can't stop myself. Her skin is as smooth as a rose petal. Her eyes are amber. Her hair is twisted like fine spun silk into a little precious knot."

Andrew was out of breath when he finished and relieved that he had gotten it all out. "Father Baron, I have a longing for this woman that cannot be explained. I never meant for it to happen, and before this, I had not paid much attention to women. I'm afraid …"

Father Baron finished his sentence, "…. that the determination to become a priest has somehow faded? There is a desire for love in you that has never been fully realized. For some, the need for love can be fulfilled in the priesthood by serving mankind. For others, the need is somewhat more personal and can only be satisfied by the one God has chosen. I believe you may be of the latter type. I'm afraid that what brought you here was more a fear than a vocation, and now that you have healed the wounds of your past, perhaps it is time that you move on. Don't look so surprised, my son; it is not God's will that you walk the earth alone. Why else would he have sent you Marianne Ludwig?"

"This way of life is no longer right for you. It pains me to tell you this, but Andrew, St. Paul's is not a place to escape fears, but to find your faith. In that, I think we have not failed you. You have tapped into your real feelings, and your eyes have been opened. Your belief in God is strong and always will be. Do not feel ashamed because you are thinking of dropping out of the seminary. Your whole life is ahead. Go out into the world, find faith in yourself, and live it fully. There's no avoiding the moment, just acknowledge it, my son!"

Andrew choked back his tears. "Once I leave there is no return," he said. "I wish…"

Father Baron interrupted him, "You may wish all you want, but God decides. Make your choice and accept what comes. In some ways, you're actually luckier than most. At a time when you were at your most helpless, you somehow endured the worst of all humanity. Now that you are strong enough to live with yourself; it will all come together, be assured. Few have earned living by not surviving."

The next morning Andrew rose before dawn and packed all his belongings in a single suitcase. Father Baron accompanied him through the seminary gates. "I have no idea where to go," Andrew said.

"Go to Krakow. When you are ready, let Marianne know that you're nearby."

As he made the sign of the cross on Andrew's forehead, he said, "God be with you." Then he reached into his pocket. "Here is five hundred zloty. Take it. I guarantee you will need it. Write to us. Promise to be in touch every three months so I don't worry."

"I promise and thank you with all my heart. Goodbye Father Baron," Andrew said as the kindly priest turned to enter the seminary. Andrew stood on the threshold of the garden watching the gentle sweep of the Father's robes as he made his way down the path.

"Goodbye, Tata," he called out. The ground was still damp with the morning dew, and as he stepped off the soft lawn of the seminary onto the pavement, he left wet footprints that grew fainter and faded as he walked away.

IV

Back home in her beloved Krakow, Marianne walked slowly on the cobblestone road leading to the Bishop's house. Could she muster up the courage to face this man and tell him of her longing for a seminarian? After two years of dogged determination, the Bishop, her advocate, overcame the hurdles of a woman teaching at St. Paul's. Her thoughts dwelled on the disfavor she may have cause the seminary by resigning.

She entered and was escorted down the long foyer into the study. The kind, silver haired Bishop greeted her warmly and quietly asked, "What's going on, Marianne?"   "St. Paul's was a mistake. My decision is to resign immediately. I am resolved to got to Polesie."

"There are no mistakes" said the Bishop, his eyes unwavering. .

"I introduced you to St. Paul's. Your teachings there truly inspired the young men. You made me proud. That means a lot more than anyone dares to admit. Life is filled with choices but should also be about love and humanity."

His comforting words touched the young teacher. "Please accept my apologies for hurting your feelings, and even compromising St. Paul's reputation. I would never betray your trust and confidence." she said. "And there is a man in my life", she blurted, sobbing at the same time.

"There is no need to apologize. You are near to the end of your first journey. You have much to contribute by going to Polesie. There are possibilities, opportunities, and a network of schools there and these children have been abandoned for too long." He gently touched her arm and then asked, "Is it a seminarian, this new man?"

She nodded yes. She went on: "The moment our eyes met, instinctively I liked him, and before we knew it we were both sharing the same feeling. Bishop, love does not come and go! My feelings for him are still intense; however, I am determined to teach the children and to work with Zamolenski to help save Eastern Poland from a very clear evil."

"Tell me now, who is this young man?" The Bishop said.

"Andrew!" she exclaimed.

"Oh, I thought so. Father Baron has often spoken of Andrew, and is quite fond of him. Your Tata always knew that one day he would approve of the man who captures your heart. It's not shameful that you

18

are in love, or that you are physically attracted as well! We are all entitled to have fulfilling lives. Tell your father nothing about St. Paul's except that you are seeking out your destiny. You are twenty-one. Those children in Polesie have great needs, and I know Zamolenski will welcome you warmly, and Ludwig will feel great pride. Go to Polesie with my blessing. Set up your schools. I will contact the Franciscans and Benedictines, and who will help you get started."

Holding back tears, she said softly, "I have learned so much from you, Bishop, and from my Ludwig. My love for St. Paul's will be part of me forever. Now, I must say confession, " Bless me Father for I have sinned."

With a straight face and an inward chuckle, the bishop replied, "Say ten Hail Marys!" She then knelt down and kissed his ring as he placed the sign of the cross on her forehead. She came to terms with the magnitude of her decision.

Five days later, Marianne arrived in Polesie and immersed herself in her teaching. Her life was centered on the children, but the image of Andrew tugged at her heart daily. Miraculously, he found his love at the very place he would never dream of: the seminary.

Once he made the decision to leave, he knew that he had to declare his love for the woman he left, if ever he could find her again. He spent hours combing each street, making inquiries at school after school where she might be teaching. Remarkably, his trail led him to her older sister, Stephany, who was teaching at a Catholic grammar school near the seminary. She liked him immediately, and cheerfully provided Marianne's address. For Andrew, the search had ended and there was no longer a hopeless dream to follow, but maybe there was a new life ahead. He wrote to her regularly for two years; she kept and cherished his notes, remembering their times together.

He told her in one letter, that he worked as a gardener, to help him get in touch with his soul and to allow him to think of his departure from the priesthood. His life was like a garden, he explained. Stooping to weed it is one chore, but for him rising above the weeds, was the establishment of a family with happy children, framed with blessings of a mother and father. In a later note, Andrew told how he became a cabinet maker in Krakow as well, sometimes working two or three jobs at a time. He was driven by the thought of bringing joy to her life. Nothing could please him more. He poured his heart and soul into his creation of shaping wood into graceful cabinets and furniture, creating a variety of ornamental pieces.

He proposed in his last letter which struck to the core of Marianne's hopes and dreams; "The objects I created are only as good as the effort I put into them with a determined heart and soul". He wrote, "No longer do I wish to be the best cabinetmaker, but I am now the best. Now will you have me?" She accepted. "Yes, of course I will," she wrote back "but we must go slowly for my mission in life to build schools in Polesie. It has been my dream to do good works here."

Andrew wanted to look forward and try to forget bad experiences of the past. He had been in the military for two years, and often while working, vivid images would spring into his head. They were like "day mares" intruding on his consciousness. He had been a border guard with the Marshland Company near Pinsk, a town once part of the Russian Ukraine. Polish troops were assigned to operate outposts every half kilometer along the border and sentries regularly patrolled the distance between them. The Soviets then, were located behind the slim strip of a no man's land that separated the frontiers. Moonless and stormy nights were always a problem, for they were used by Communist partisans or NKVD thugs, to slip into Polish territory to create as much sabotage, polarization, and fear as possible among the Polish, Jewish and Ukrainian villagers. Then they retreated before the early hours of dawn. These raids were a common occurrence, and what Andrew witnessed he would never forget. He had not told Marianne about them, even in letters, and when she accepted his proposal, he hoped that after a while, when they settled down, the horrible images would subside.

One winter's day, the Communist NKVD (The People's Commissariat for Internal Affairs (Народный Комиссариат Внутренних or ел Narodnyy Komissariat Vnutrennikh Del), entered a Polish village just after midnight, killing the soltys (mayor), by cutting off his head. What they did to the Catholic priest was even worse. When Andrew and his comrades arrived in the village, long after the partisans had left, they found the priest's body in the sacristy of his church, shot and mutilated. He was clad in the brocade silk vestments usually reserved for Easter and other holy days. The thugs had apparently made him dress like this before killing him. They had also opened the tabernacle and sacrilegiously urinated on the consecrated bread.

However, after these experiences, which he never told to anyone, including Marianne, Andrew had become the best and most imaginative cabinet maker in the factory. The owner, ironically Wadeslaw Ludwig, decided to publicly recognize his achievements. Normally, acknowledging employees for performance was an annual event, usually just before Christmas when Pan Ludwig would issue bonus zloty for making the year successful. However, Pan Ludwig wanted to reward Andrew with a special summer bonus for outstanding service. Andrew was a fine example to the others, inspiring them to give their very best to a common cause. Ludwig promoted him to factory manager, and arranged for a large luncheon and award ceremony in his honor. Andrew was delighted.

When Andrew saw Marianne seated alongside her father, and learned that she was Ludwig's daughter, he could only stare in disbelief. He went forward to accept the letter of recognition and the two hundred zloty.

"I can't believe I'm finally here beside you," he said. They held hands, slowly moving to the far end of the room to Ludwig.

"Tata" she said", " I met Andrew at St. Paul's and someday I will tell you the whole story. For two years, we were separated, but he has remained close to my heart. Although my days have been busy and full, my thoughts have been only of him. He was the Brother that sat in the third row, right aisle in my class. I shall never forget those moments."

Ludwig smiled. He knew that he had not heard the whole story; however. He was pleased that a man had finally captured her heart, especially since she seemed so much in love with him.

"And I suppose", he went on, "that you left the seminary because you found a more compelling vocation?" Ludwig asked.

"I was torn between my loyalty to my beliefs and her love," Andrew replied. "I love what I do, particularly when it is alive with excitement."

Ludwig smiled, but did not miss the deep blush coloring both of their faces as they rushed away.

"My father holds you in high regard,"she told Andrew. "Occasionally, he spoke to me of Andy, the cabinet maker, but I never dreamed that it was you. Your letters to me said that you were a woodworker, who listened to the hearts of little children, and that you were determined to be the best worker, who created the most imaginative carved artistry."

Andrew answered her. "It all seems unreal to me. Sometimes I woke up in the middle of the night and thought, "Has this truly happened?" I used to rush around the room, collecting your letters and poems as some sort of evidence." They both laughed. "It just never occurred to me that someone as wonderful as you could ever think I am wonderful too. Do you understand, Marianne?" "You are my only true love" she replied. "It is time for me to go now. There will be much more to say tomorrow"

She left, and Andrew drew a deep breath and looked around the room for Pan Ludwig. When he found him, he went to him and said, "For the past two years I have been in love with Marianne. I filled my days with hard work and at night yearned for her. Starting with nothing, I struggled to earn a position from the day I left the seminary. Now it is time to share it all. Your daughter is beautiful, and it is a privilege that she wants me. I will do whatever it takes to make Marianne happy and comfortable. It is my hope that I'm deserving of her now."

Pan Ludwig was slightly surprised by the news. He had long admired Andrew as a man who possessed a strong character, was self-sacrificing, who worked hard at what he loved, a true embodiment of a Polish heart! Ludwig understood that his daughter had made a choice, and it was a wise one. "There are no barriers in our home, Andrew. The door is always open to people of good will and genuine human spirit. Surely, you are bringing excitement to her life and our home. Besides, when you pursue the right path, all remains positive and individual dignity prevails. You have endured a great deal in your life, and you have an obvious moral strength."

Andrew grinned, and said stiffly "With your permission, sir, I would like to court your daughter with the intention, if she is willing, of making her my wife."

Pan Ludwig said, "Naturally, it pleases me; however when it comes to marriage, only the two of you can make that decision. You know that she is a hard woman to hold for two years. She seems to have deep feelings. I saw the glow in her eyes, her arms around you. It isn't secret; you are always welcome at our home."

Andrew came calling many times thereafter, always welcomed warmly by Tata. The two men spent hours in each other's company. The day finally came when they clasped hands, raised their glasses of wine jubilantly, as Tata toasted: "May Ludwig and Krull join as one, now and forever!"

Within a year, Andrew and Marianne were married in a Polish Catholic ceremony. Marianne stood tall in her Mother's traditional white dress, which had been carefully preserved by Ludwig, and the new bride and groom celebrated happily with friends and family. Fifteen months passed, and a son, Stefan was born, and eighteen months after that, a daughter Maria. The family settled in a beautiful house in Janow in the Province of Polesie, bordering the Soviet Union.

The nearby Zamolenski estate was a backdrop for them, with its winding formal gardens and decorative ponds. Life could not have been more idyllic or perfect in this picturesque setting. Andrew gazed at their happy children playing in the rose garden and at the herds of cattle and deer slowly grazing across the broad field beyond. However, the country and the good life was soon threatened by the sounds of war from the Nazis and by the Soviet presence on Polesian soil as Communist NKVD troops were on the march once again. As Marianne feared for the family's lives and safety, she resolved to also accept the high-risk consequences of working with the Polish government, and in doing so she would try, she thought, to define the Soviet enemy and its ensuing horror more clearly. She so desperately loved her land and its people in addition to her own family, that despite the major risk to the family, she hoped that she could help stop a war on Polish soil and try to save millions of lives. Marianne kept at her household chores, and Andrew worked hard at his job; however, the approaching news of the impending invasions and possible war kept growing in intensity. She became obsessed with the future, partially because of her need to safely raise her children in an environment of love, morality and understanding, but also to answer her deep attachment and love for her country. The emotions caused by daily world news ate at her soul and psyche. Finally, she realized that she had to talk to Andrew about it, who, although he understood her concerns, was content with enjoying his children's growth and planning on a rosy future.

Andrew knew that something was bothering Marianne, but he also realized that when she was ready she would confide in him. They were walking through a field near the house, sunlight on their faces, looking at the rolling fields thick with bluebonnets and buttercups, among the pines that edged the pastures. Andrew asked, "What is bothering you, Marianne? You've been preoccupied, and, at times quite angry. We need to talk.. There is a frightening world out there, and only together can we face it." He watched her intently, looking for a response.

23

Marianne, as much as she loved and trusted him, could not bring herself to answer. Perhaps he guessed her concern, or more likely he had understood her growing restlessness. As his expression became cold and unsettling, fearful thoughts flashed through her mind.

She finally spoke, almost thinking out loud, "The uncertainty of what lies ahead is terrible. I love you more than any woman could ever love a man, but we are no longer just two cultured people walking in the flowered fields. Citizens are being killed around us, and schools are being set on fire in and around Vilnius. There could be blood at our doorsteps any moment."

She went on to explain. "There are new atrocities every day; people are being hanged in public squares and armed foreign agents are staging attacks and parading with the results of atrocities supposedly caused by others."

Andrew had not been aware that she had been still attending the meetings at her father's house on a weekly basis, partly because of her concern for her widowed father and his welfare, but more so, for the information on the impending Soviet and Nazi attacks on her homeland.

As predicted, the depths of the Soviet's merciless liquidations, hatred, and brutality were not being condemned by anyone. Sixty-million people had been slaughtered in Russia the past two decades, yet the world remained silent. It was this acceptance of horror that bothered her the most. She could picture deep in her mind's eye, the destruction of her beloved country, and a sweeping holocaust that would destroy her and the children as well. She knew that Andrew would be content to pray and have faith in an avenging or forgiving God. She felt that he represented so many Polish people, who would accept conditions imposed by others rather than fighting against them. "We can pray and die," she finally said, " or we can pray and act."

Andrew grasped her hard by the shoulders. Suddenly, this tall stately, beautiful mother of his children, and the love of his life was showing a side that he had never seen before. It was something akin to a mother bird protecting her young and nest. She seemed resolute, and hardened to the task at hand. She wanted, she said, "for the world to see the atrocities, and rape directed at the Polish people and its soil for the last twenty years" and she was resolved, not only to do so but to prepare to fight the invaders.

"I believe," she continued to a shocked Andrew, "that if the world had knowledge of the Soviet horrors, its opinion would be swayed.

Darling, the Nazis and Soviets have always felt that Poles know how to die for their country, but not how to live for it. Ludwig is doing his part in the west, Zamolenski in the east. How are we helping?"

Haltingly, she proposed a part of her solution "I was asked to go to Moscow and see for myself. A while back, a man named Dumblosky and I had an encounter at one of our Tuesday Roundtable sessions. He is a puppet controlled by the Soviets in Krakow. Ludwig and Zamolenski think that I need to leave for Moscow since I could still travel more safely than they can. The Soviet horror is at our doorstep. I feel it. Ludwig does too. We have to do something!!"

She continued pleading with him that action had to be taken before tanks and planes roared into Poland.. "Ludwig feels that if we can find a way to truthfully report the Soviet's terror apparatus, its organizational structure and methodology, we may possibly influence world opinion, perhaps allying with Germany to fight the Communists! But when I return, the risk for my family; will be greater. We will probably have to leave our home here, and move to fight another battle somewhere else. The children will be heartbroken."

"We are trying to avoid disaster, and the terrifying prospect of protecting our families from the Soviet agents invading every corner of our world. Our children look to us for their comfort and safety. How long will it take to disappear? How long before they lose us, or we lose them? We have a struggle ahead, but I need to do what is right for us and the country; I must go to Moscow."

Andrew's response showed for a moment how there were parts of him that she did not know. She had been afraid of telling him about the meetings with Zamolenski; however, she realized how well he knew her. His grim face and quiet voice was assuring. "You need not be afraid. We cannot turn away from disaster, and there is no time to spare. I believe that the Soviets will use deception and terror to wage war against Poland's civilians. They are going to murder, plunder and kill and then retreat back across the border to safety. Our world is getting darker daily, but we must have faith that there is light at the end, and Poland, is the last best hope for Europe. We may be broken and confused now, but we need to proceed knowing that our greatest strength is the bond between us. Marianne, if they decide that you are a Polish agent, you will be targeted for a bullet in the back of the head. Our preparation for the worst starts today. I know what you need to do, however, you and the children are everything to me. I would rather die than have harm come to you. I will never walk away."

V

Count and Anna Zamolenski's family roots went back to King Sobieski, in the 16th century Polish empire which stretched across most of Europe. The gardens of the Zamolenski mansion where the Polesian children often played were settled on eighty acres of park land, with sloping lawns and shaded walkways. The main house had a wide front entrance; behind it herds of cattle and deer sheep grazed. These herds fed half of Polesie, much of Belorussia and Polish Lithuania. People prospered there because the Zamolenskis cultivated the land efficiently and effectively; he employed Mazowszia's citizens to build schools, roads, bridges and to provide postal service, as well as telegraph and telephone lines. Zamolenski was connected to the Polish government and General Rückemann, who provided "tulnovs" or defensive troops. Communist and Socialist political activists regarded the Zamolenskis, the Ludwigs, and now the Krulls, as the selfish landholders, part of the intelligentsia with" clean hands". This slogan inferred that workers had the preferable "dirty hands" of laborers. The Communists and Socialists issued propaganda calling the Zamolenskis the worst land holders living in eastern Poland since the Turks invaded in the 16th century.

Marianne and Andrew packed the children and the family dog Basha, into their horse- drawn buggy and rode toward the estate. The Count's help was needed for the trip to Russia. As they approached the drive to the house, three armed horsemen rode up, former cavalry men, part of the Count's private security force of about 150 men who patrolled the main road and the perimeter of the Count's large estate. Marianne and Andrew, with their children, were given a cursory glancing by the troops, and they continued on to the main house, where the buggy stopped at the front door. It was opened by Zamolenski himself who grabbed Andrew's hand in greeting, as Anna hugged Marianne. "We are so happy to see you." she said

The Count wasted no more time on niceties; he turned to Andrew and said: "I know you are afraid about her trip to Moscow; however, with communication lines between most of the Eastern European countries destroyed, we will need to find information somehow. Marianne is the perfect cover; a young woman visiting a dying relative in Moscow. We paid a good deal of money to buy the right officials, and she has been cleared to go. I hope that she will return with an observation of what is occurring in Moscow, so that no one needs to rely on the Communist propaganda coming from there. The risk she is taking is enormous, since if caught, or even connected with one of us, she will be marked on her return. None of our group can go without being shot or worse. We need information to help us deal with the coming menace."

The party walked through the entrance to a sitting room, bedecked with huge mirrors in gilded frames hanging over the large marble fireplaces. The mirrors, a sign of wealth in 18th century Europe, reflected statuary, sculptures, and life- size portraits of Kosciuszko, Zamolenski's great uncle Sobieski along with other members of the family. Gleaming chandeliers, carefully polished, hung overhead. The ornate cushioned chairs they settled in, faced toward floor to ceiling windows which revealed a spectacular view of the formal gardens. The contrast between the east side of the panorama was the winding road leading to the Soviet- occupied western Ukraine, an unpublicized war zone for twenty-five years. Marianne thought how unbelievable it was that evil men could succeed and then threaten the peaceful world. Maybe, she thought, the world could be saved and a new genocide against a Christian population, one that was ignored for a quarter of a century could be avoided.

Zamolenski, a tall, elegant broad shouldered man, stood tall in the middle of the opulence of the room and said: "I can't believe that you were only seventeen years old when I first met you, and even then, you knew about these awful cruelties. We all have learned since those days; however, the world has not seen the images of people with pleading eyes and desperate faces for the past ten years, caused by murders, deaths, hunger and cold. New York Times' correspondents, honored for their reporting out of the Moscow Bureau, have hidden these events and the reality of horror and death from their readers. The systematic mass starvation of 14 million Orthodox Christian Ukrainians never appeared in any report. The Times star reporter Walter Durante reported that the death of fourteen million people in the Ukraine was a good fortune for the depopulation of the area."

"The Soviets are plunging a dagger into the heart of Europe, with Poland, at its center." The Count warned, "No report has been made to the world. Soviet propaganda is now as effective as the trail of blood that they are leaving behind."

"If you can succeed in getting a clear picture of what is happening to the people of Moscow, we can prepare for the difficult days ahead. Love of country is what the Soviets loathe most." he concluded.

27

All were silent for a moment. Zamolenski's speech sounded very much like a need to get the ideas out in the open, as if their airing made them clear to the people in the room. He spoke passionately of the Nazi's and Communist's expansionistic plans and their vision of Poland as the link to Europe, trapping thirty-four million people between the Soviets and the Nazis. Zamolenski saw both countries as major threats to Polish freedom, and hoped that a preparation for war against both enemies was being made. Hitler's ideal was of marching eastward, to fulfill the Nazi dream of Lebensraum (Living Space) allowing the German troops to goose step across Polish soil. "If both sides attack us," he continued "we'll be permanently crushed. We are heading for a prolonged war, which I do not think will have a decisive victory. The United States of America will enter the war on the Soviets' side. Roosevelt's political considerations and The New York Times will see to it. Mass genocide on our soil will be inevitable." he finished sadly.

Zamolenski continued to say that her trip would be a sure sign to the world if her findings on a personal level were made public amidst the cacophony of rhetoric and saber rattling surrounding their Motherland. "What else could we do" he asked. Marianne and Andrew were silent knowing that this meeting and the support of Zamolenski had sealed their fate…whatever it was.

"We are on the right track for the sake of our country and maybe even our world. Good Luck!" he said.

The topic of Polish survival vanished during the elaborate dinner prepared by the Zamolenskis. They served estate wines and traditional Polish food: hot borsht, pierogi, golabki, and then a special Gorzka cordial to mellow the taste of the venison that followed

The children, not forgotten at this dinner, finished with the sweets of chrusciki , and when they were apparently full, they were given paczki to nibble on the trip back home. This would be the last taste of the good life for a long while. Good- byes were said and Zamolenski called out a loud "Good Luck! Have a safe trip. Z-Bogiem" as they departed in the carriage.

Marianne resolved, "I shall return from Moscow. That is not all."

MAY 24, 1039

Marianne, wearing a plain dress and coat, with a small hat perched on her dark hair, rode one train east towards Pinsk, then north to Minsk, and one more to Leningrad and Moscow. She couldn't get the

Soviet's depravity and violence out of her mind. The peaceful countryside contrasted starkly with the images of horrors that flashed through her mind, thoughts she felt were branded into her brain forever.

She tried very hard to understand, and to seek an underlying motivation for the two decades of silence about Moscow's political maneuverings. She thought of many questions as the train chugged fiercely on the tracks toward Moscow. She imagined hand lettered banners hanging throughout the country because the authors could no longer speak from starvation and weakness, reading "Tell the world. Europe is in peril." She pictured innocent civilians being murdered; Parents and their children imprisoned for months, waiting only to die behind barbed wire fences; thin, hungry orphans with gaping sores, in empty fields and in railroad stations begging for food with skeletal hands.

Marianne was dozing off to the rhythm of the train; however, as she awoke she left the dream world for the real one. The train entered into Soviet controlled land, and the appearance of the landscape changed drastically, when and if an occasional house came into view, it appeared abandoned, or deserted, and then a small puff of smoke or a raggedy wash line appeared showing these hovels to be inhabited. If the Bolsheviks were fostering this life style, which Marianne believed they did, how could they hide it from the world? She suspected that they were killing and murdering, under the protective covering of a growing German menace, and therefore, no one on the world scene was paying attention to them, but rather to the return of the evil Huns.

MAY 25, 1939

The next morning Marianne, changed trains with an NKVD escort, and they picked their way through the worn, shattered dirty and hungry terrified souls who were strewn on the dirty cement of the well-patrolled platforms, visible to all passing as the trains traveled through. The magnitude of the atrocities in this moment became real to her. The NKVD guard hurried her through the crowds of dirty and hungry people; she was not supposed to notice the beggars, hungry children and dead bodies propped against the station wall. After she boarded her train, she stared out the window at the country side, where numbers of people were living in damp filthy dugouts. They all were being worked to death, as part of land reformation, collective farming, or slave labor under the barbed wire of gulags. This, she thought, was a deliberate, wholesale massacre and execution of innocent Christian people! The world must fight back.

As her emotions churned from anger, to despair to painful sympathy, she turned from the window toward the sadly frozen expressionless faces of those sitting in her compartment. She tried sipping a cup of tea, and closing her eyes; however, she kept seeing the horrible images of badly treated people in her mind's eye. About an hour from Leningrad, a middle-aged Soviet colonel sitting opposite her in the compartment started to stare at the beautiful young woman seated across from him. He tried to talk to her several times, but halted and looked away. Something about her gave him the confidence to finally speak. His tone was condescending, as if he was a superior, and he said, "Would you like to know who I am?"

Marianne, now alone with this man in the compartment, wondered how to respond. Why was this man talking to her? "Yes, if you wish to tell me," she finally said. She was frightened because maybe he was part of the military arm of the NKVD. The man, however, awkwardly introduced himself as Colonel Friedman. Marianne sensed his need to talk in the grisly lighted railway compartment, which now appeared other- worldly and even resembled the close quarters of the confessional.

Colonel Friedman had a powerful physical presence. He had grown up in the Jewish shtetls of Pinsk, he explained, where poverty and poor treatment in the ghetto caused him to become a true follower of the Bolsheviks.

His life was first dedicated to First Comrade Kanganovich, but at the present he was serving First Comrade Vishinsky. Striking his hand angrily at the wall, he bent down nervously and told her how his family originally moved from Germany to the eastern Ukraine to escape vicious anti-Semitic acts and condemnation. "The Communists attracted many Jews, about ninety per cent of the NKVD is from the poverty stricken Pale of Settlement Region and about thirty per cent were in leadership of the Communist Party."

He adjusted his thin wire framed glasses, and he continued with his own cathartic confession "They promised us land, our own homes and upward mobility for our children if we joined the Red Revolution."

As he tried to rationalize his own commitment to mass murders, in terms of the Biblical eye for an eye, the train compartment became more and more surreal to Marianne. She kept thinking of his motives for telling his life story to her. He told of his family, and how his mother, father and sister were murdered while he was away fighting the "Whites" near Minsk in 1918. The White Russians, mostly Orthodox Christians, came to every Jewish house in his shtetl of sixty or so souls, and shot them all. "Everyone!" "At eighteen, he had joined the Russian cavalry, fought with the Reds, then against the Poles in 1920, knowing all along that he was paving the way for his own downfall. His confession became more intense and rushed and Marianne became even more frightened. "The leaders were men and women who prospered from their heinous crimes! During the early days of the second Revolution, they killed all that was dear to me. I decided to fight with the "Reds" and with Kanganovich. I murdered thousands of people figuratively, and severed the heads of our opponents, mostly Christians and Nationalists, hoping I would live long enough to secure a position in Moscow next to him. However, the authorities now say that I know too much. They have transferred me to Vishinsky who heads the military arm of the NKVD."

Friedman, looking for even the smallest absolution for his crimes, was confessing openly to a stranger, not caring if he lived or died. Marianne realized that her identity did not matter to him; however, his early Jewish tradition of atonement for sins had surfaced, although he had long forgotten how to go about it. He went on to say that he had outlived his usefulness, and along with thousands of other loyal Communists, was being replaced by more energetic younger men and women.

"The point is," he said "they must kill to get ahead. Andziej Vishinsky is now in charge of the purge of his own former followers. I am in the midst of a personal struggle. I pursued a madness of revenge, and was little concerned with morality, justice or truth. We in the Red Movement wanted revenge. Our concern now is for survival. I have to believe that everything I say or do is overheard. You and I are candidates for assassination if someone were to be listening to us. I was a believer in the Party, and would understand what was expected---kill to gain power. It was all about survival. This may possibly be my last train ride because they are transferring me from the NKVD to another assignment over my objections. These officials cannot be trusted and they do not trust me. When they transfer one from one leader to another, the new official questions your loyalty. I have seen it before. Now it is my turn."

The dark wood paneling, and the yellow wicker of the seats in the small closed compartment, took on a grimy glow as the hours went by. This Russian Colonel leaned over and softly said: "I believe it might have been the Reds, particularly the ones who survived, – Stalin,

31

Kanganovich, Beria, Frenklin, Berman, Padek, Zinoviev, Kanenev, and Mechtlis who had the Jewish villagers shot in order to angrily divide the Christians and create an opposition against the Whites to attract young Jews to Bolshevism."

Colonel Friedman paused for a moment, and said. "They are capable of such tactics. Everyone, including my family, is dead now. And when I think of who I was, what I was, at twenty-five, or thirty-five years old , and what I have become, I remain marked for the rest of my life. Having started as a killer, I am finished as a killer. I keep waiting for my life to end at any moment, or with each passing hour. My soul was lost a long time ago when I became part of the Communist Movement. My crimes were crimes against humanity, but no one will ever know. We were always silenced. At least now I have peace of mind because my murdering days have finally come to an end."

Tugging at his gun, he whispered nervously, "You don't need to say anything to me, but too many have already died needlessly at my hands. Now it is over, and I am very, very tired.

"I have buried thousands of bodies, and now you know."

Marianne had no answers. Was he realizing the end was near? He broke into her reverie saying "What do you think?"

She stood up and glanced out the window. She was left alone as he started to leave the compartment; maybe this was the beginning of her own end. Marianne thought that she would not at all be surprised if he committed suicide after killing her as the recipient of his confession. However, he blinked his eyes and asked "Who are you, anyway?"

"My name is Marianne Krull., my Mother was a Russian and my Father Polish, and I am going to visit a very sick relative in Moscow."

He lowered his voice and murmured, "There is no need to say anything further. You do not belong to our party. That much I can tell. You are not a spy."

He slowly sat back down, and looked at this young woman sadly. Be careful," he said ominously. "you know what that means?"

"No, what does it mean?" Marianne leaned forward to ask him to explain;

He whispered "We are in Leningrad," as the train noisily pulled into the station. He nervously glanced out the window, and then he placed his hand on his medal- covered chest "It is all over now. And

32

what that means is that you are lucky to be alive, and as long as you are, let the truth come out, but that's only if you leave Moscow alive. Be careful."

He stood up at attention, as if his moral burden was lifted from him by his recent confession. He said good-bye, and slowly walked toward the exit door of the car, through the smoke, and out on to the platform, where he was surrounded by the NKVD. Within minutes, there were sounds of gunfire outside the window as the Colonel started to run frantically and Marianne saw him, stopped by a hail of bullets fired repeatedly into his body. He had outlived his usefulness; unable to escape from the cycle of fear and destruction he had come to his own final peace. She said a silent prayer for his soul, as people on the platform scattered everywhere, some diving to the ground, and others hiding under benches. In direct contrast to this fear, the remaining train passengers sat quietly, hardly reacting to the horror that has just transpired. They were numb to the acts of Soviet barbarism at the hands of officials which they had seen so many times before. As the train pulled from the station, the Colonel from the compartment, lay on the gray pavement . As his blood oozed into a giant puddle, passersby made a large path around him without even a glance at the murdered man. He was sprawled flat, arms out appearing as if he had been crucified; Marianne prayed that he had found his own atonement and peace, and sat silently folded back into her seat in the compartment thankful to be alive.

MAY 26, 1039

New York Times reporter Durante wrote an article six years earlier saying "Any report of a famine in Russia is today an exaggeration or malignant propaganda. The food shortage, however, which has affected the whole population in the last year and particularly in the grain-producing provinces--the Ukraine, North Caucasus, and the Lower Volga--, has, however, caused heavy loss of life. It is conservative to suppose that in certain provinces with a total population of over 40 million, mortality had "at least trebled."

Marianne, now less than an hour from Moscow, kept hearing Friedman's last words;" be careful" echoing in her mind. There was a chill in the air the moment the train arrived in Moscow. Armed guards boarded the train, as others patrolled the corridor outside of each compartment. Vigilant NKVD men and women were obvious in their leather coats as they mingled among the passengers. No one was above suspicion. They were looking for "enemies of the people". At the first checkpoint, just below the ever present portrait of Josef Stalin, a guard demanded Marianne's passport. As he read it, he loudly bellowed: "Polish!" She dared not look at him as she answered "YES!" The eyes of everyone present were focused on her as her identity papers were carefully scrutinized. The NKVD guard looked at her up and down and said, "At the next stop we'll do a better job of interrogating you."

Marianne's first reaction was to run, and to get out of this place, but she was ordered to present her passport at two more checkpoints; she was forced to answer a barrage of questions regarding her reasons for visiting Moscow. Finally, a guard waved his arm and shouted, "Enjoy your stay in Moscow. Your papers are in order."

She had just survived the first of many nightmares to come. Now in Moscow, there was the distinct impression and eerie feeling of being constantly watched. Men and women shuffled their feet, whispered, and kept a grim watch on each other. As she started a slow walk to her hotel, Marianne noticed that people were crowding into small spaces, apparently heated by a single coal stove; the small overcrowded houses had holes in the roofs and the walls, which must have allowed the frigid air to come in. They had to suffer through treacherous winters cold and frostbitten.

Since the forests were nationalized, and therefore, properties of the state, anyone who had the strength of will to cut a branch or plug the holes in the dwelling was punished by death. Closer to the edge of Moscow sleeping rooms were available only on a quota system, which were heated with drops from kerosene lamps made of pottery. A swarm of informants had accused the poor potter who made these makeshift heaters of speaking freely, and then declared him an enemy of the state. His art came to an abrupt halt. The NKVD murdered the elderly man, enabling their own families to take possession of coal, his utensils and his furniture. The lower echelon of workers could not go outdoors, because there was a shortage of clothing, including hats and shoes. These people too were silenced, constantly monitored by their own informers: NKVD regulators and secret servitors murdered others in order to survive. These servitors, in turn, were rewarded with the illusion of living, but inevitably, their own day of reckoning came as well.

The grocery shops in Moscow carried a few selected items at times- radishes, or some bushels of cucumbers. The local citizenry had to rise at dawn in order to wait hours on line for the few meager items available. The elite Party members, however, shopped at exclusive "designated stores" stocked with a variety of food selections. There was no rationing for the servitors, now officially called Regulators. They stolc it all. The NKVD officials and their immediate families had full stomachs. This was Durante's reported food shortage.

Their clothing, coats, boots and fur hats, were made by slave labor, forced to use the skins of animals usually used to clothe themselves, for coats and hoods for the NKVD, which left the local people freezing as well as hungry. The symbol of power for the NKVD men and women was the sable hat. The regulators, servitors, and NKVD's children wore fur suits and mittens which commanded immediate attention, signifying that their clothing came from forced confiscation. Marianne saw a noticeable contrast between the richer and poorer people in the city.

Moscow Square was the symbol of Russia in 1939, where ornate Byzantine architecture, originally designed to indicate a separation from the outside world, housed the seat of the government, the Kremlin, the ancient fortified section of the city where Joseph Stalin lived. Located inside its walls, to the west of Moscow Square was a building named "People's Commissar of Internal Officers" (Народный Комиссариат Внутренних Дел Narodnyy Komissariat Vnutrennikh Del or NKVD). It housed a secret military system which spied on those who were not part of the Communist elite. The rest of the Square's buildings were used to enclose the offices of Stalin's inner circle.

Each day as Marianne walked through the city, from her shabby "elite" hotel to her supposed "sick " relative, really a Polish spy, all she saw was oppression, deceit and destruction. She kept a record of what she saw on thin tissue writing paper, rolled tightly into her underwear. After a fitful first night, she welcomed the early light of dawn and went to the hotel store reserved for the regulators, the journalists, and the VIP tourists. Although she had been given privileges as a visitor, she only bought two apples for breakfast.

The Muscovy River overflowed from the driving night rains; therefore, the odor of excrement filled the city air. The gusting winds spread the stench into every doorway and corner, as Marianne walked past the doors of the U.S. Embassy, wondering why Ambassador Davies had not spoken about the Russian atrocities to the free world, especially since America was that this was her last day in Russia. Homesickness overwhelmed her, as she longed to hear the voices of her children, Maria and Stefan and her husband Andrew.

A peasant woman sat down besides Marianne on the bench. Though she was probably about forty, her deeply wrinkled face made her

35

appear much older. The woman was shivering from the cold and whispered, as she held back tears, "You are Polish. I can tell. Are you here collecting information on how "not to live?"

Marianne offered her the one remaining apple, for she knew that the woman was hungry. "What will happen when it's discovered that you are spying for the Polish government?" The lady whispered as she slid the apple into her sleeve to hide it.

"They will probably shoot me," Marianne muttered back.

"It was not my intention to scare you."

"Well, you certainly did,"

"I can tell that you are not a government KGB agent, for you don't have the fur hat and leather jacket but you are not silent! Surely you have seen much."

Her face looked battered. She trembled slightly as she leaned forward placing her hands on Marianne's. She confided to her that her entire family was gone, leaving her alone for the last seven years

."I was right. You are Polish, aren't you?"

"Yes"

"I, too, am Polish. My love for my country is deep; however, in 1924, a young idealist, I came here to join the Revolution. Fifteen years later, I am now among the walking dead, also scared of living."

She was cold and shivering. Her obvious pain moved Marianne who took off her sweater and offered it to the old woman, who put it on. The eyes in her drawn face reflected fear.

"This is not a good year for Poles. Please, you must escape from Poland. There will be great danger there for you. One only has to listen on the streets in Moscow."

"If you stay, the Communists will eventually get you. You are part of the "intelligentsia", a teacher, correct?"

"How could you tell?"

"My Bolshevik training has made me very aware of features, and distinguishing characteristics. Pani, you have soft hands that do not know hard, dirty work. Your second finger has a callus and a swelling from writing. More importantly, you have kind eyes. "I remained here after Lenin died. It was the worst decision I ever made .I had graduated from the University of Warsaw and could have been somebody; however, my intellectual life was divided between Poland and Communism. I became an NKVD agent after eagerly joining the Party. As a reward, my husband and two boys were executed two years ago for not being "pure" enough. My devotion and loyalty to the Communists ended on the day they were killed. You are Polish intelligentsia; you are a woman with clean hands and an inquiring mind which marks you as a distinct threat to the Soviets."

The two women, one old and dirty, the other composed and well-dressed sat and cried together.

"We have lost our souls. It is no secret that the NKVD are monsters. They will burn down schools to prove their power, and rid their world of educated people who would later be a threat. They are waiting at the edge of the Polish borders, now, ready to strike, targeting Poles for execution right now. They burn schools with children and teachers locked in them. I am ashamed to tell you this because I fear for you; you look too Polish. These men know who you are. You are going to die."

Marianne answered her "I cannot leave Poland; but you could return there quickly. Your voice could save the lives of many people. "

"Nobody has called me "Pani" for twenty years," she said as tears flowed down her cheeks.

Marianne hugged her and a faint smile appeared. The lady bit hungrily into the apple, then stared across Moscow Square.

"It frightens me to think about Poland from so far away. I feel cold and lifeless now, but can only imagine how it might have been if I had stayed."

"Then you should understand. My love for my family is deeply rooted, and I must return to them. Why don't you come back with me and tell the truth? I will arrange for you to cross the border and I will pay your way."

"No, it is impossible Pani," she moaned quietly. "War in Poland has already started. All you need to see is the invisible, tattered poor; those who are loyal to the men and women in power get clothes and food. They cheat and lie to live one more day. I am now battered, having been there but I am surviving. I am ready for my end, but I must look like a survivor, downtrodden, beaten, only to live one more day. "

. "Where are you staying?" Marianne asked her.

"Most nights I watch Moscow Square, looking for strangers like you. My daily pay is a dish of potato soup and a bonus of two slices of bread if I inform on anyone who appears to be suspicious."

"I am glad you told me. I wish you would return with me."

As Marianne hugged the skeletal woman she said, "It is my hope that you don't earn any more bonus pieces of bread."

"I am so sorry, she said softly. "I am better off telling you what is happening. It is my way of finding forgiveness for what I have done. There isn't much time. You have to leave Moscow and Poland immediately!"

Marianne reached into her pocket and gave the tattered old Polish woman a few rubles, then left her standing, hopeless and forlorn, in the center of the street. For a moment, Marianne thought that she was again confronted by another repentant sinner, condemned to a living in Hell on earth, and who needed to suffer, it seemed, in a private purgatory in Moscow, in order to find absolution in her own way.

More than ever, it was Marianne's determination and naiveté, which led her to try to reveal to the world the immorality of Communism, and more so, to save her beloved country from tragedy. Waiting for tomorrow was not an option. If she were to be killed, all her information would be lost forever. She rushed back to the hotel, locked herself in her room, and started to write. Kill me, she thought, but not the truth. The urgency of her report became a priority. She thought, in her innocence, to send it to Defense Minister Smiglia, Foreign Minister Beck and Counsel to the Government Wadeslaw Ludwig, immediately. Her fear was that if she knew about them, they would know about her. Three hours passed since she talked to the tattered woman. The thought haunted her, that the old lady was a paid informer; however, she appeared to be genuinely sincere. Marianne was frightened, aware that her life was in danger, and that she should probably leave Moscow immediately. She rapidly and hurriedly started to write:

JUNE 5, 1939

To:
Wadeslaw Ludwig,
President Ignacy Mościcki Foreign Minister Józef Beck
From: Marianne Krull

The Living Definition of Evil

38

The Bolsheviks slaughtered seventy million people over the past two decades in Russia. Twenty million souls lie dead in the Ukraine alone; Two million in Kahkistan. The rest of the population is imprisoned, awaiting and suffering a slow death. The world, however, is silent. My heart goes out to the Soviet citizens of the Republics, that I have seen: People lining up for food that wasn't there; a murder of a political adversary first hand; the dying, lining the alleys of Moscow, homeless, and starving. I was not supposed to see any of it at all. I was closely guarded on my visit, and these atrocities were to be hidden from my sight, just as these acts are to be hidden from the free world. Now that I have been here, and observed far too much, my life, too, is in danger. I have been told that I have been "marked" for death.

The political leaders of the world must repudiate this terror before this evil empire expands to Poland and beyond. Men with honor and integrity must take a stand, to lead effectively and to defend, or be destroyed. Great Britain has already yielded. The Bolsheviks are responsible for allowing and also forcing the rise of Nazism in Germany as a reaction to the fear of Soviet invasion through the geographical buffer of Poland.

The directive for mass murder comes from the inner circle of nine leaders inside the security buildings. They have butchered millions of men and women prior to today. If Poland should lose the fight and be annexed by the USSR, the shape of the future is clear: genocide shall embrace and destroy our people, and we will be liquidated.

The true character of Josef Stalin must also be shown. Military bases on the borders of eastern Poland have experienced more recent attacks than any place in Europe. Eventually there will be an act of war and the inevitable collapse. We are alone in the fight against an enemy that doesn't believe that they can conquer us. Time is pitifully short. Poland is the central battlefield in a war that started in 1917, and we are about to have 34 million people trapped between Germany and Soviet Union.

The American, English and French embassies are closing their eyes, and ignoring the Soviets' monstrous acts. We must mount a furious charge to negotiate with the Nazis.

We cannot leave our people between two evils and then rely on France and England to come to our defense and somehow call it a triumph. We must start now to mobilize and plan for a decisive strike.

I believe in you, most honorable ministers, my dear father, and my beloved country, forever my home!

Respectfully submitted,

Marianne Krull.

Marianne focused on reaching Janow safely; since exposure to this Bolshevik society increased personal paranoia. Her shivering Polish woman companion had been carefully watched, she thought. Even if she had not disclosed the conversation, the fact that she spoke to Marianne at all, would raise serious suspicion; better to leave as soon as possible, so she sewed the single sheet of her report into the side compartment of her suitcase, and then tore the remains of the scribbled notes into shreds, lit a match to them and flushed the ashes down the toilet.

At four o'clock the next morning, there was a soft tapping at the door. A frightened Marianne asked who it was. A man identified himself as a friend of the woman in the park. Cautiously she opened the door. A tall, young soldier spoke through the slight opening she had allowed, and said: "The woman you met yesterday asked that I drive you to the train station. She is my friend. You will be safe with me for the moment, so hurry."

"Thank you," said Marianne and opened the door all the way. "How is our friend doing? Is she all right?

"I was told that she had been arrested," he said gravely.

"On what charge?" Marianne asked, almost afraid to know.

He replied: "Two years in the gulag for stealing an apple, but be aware that she did not disclose anything. Luckily, you met her, because undoubtedly, she saved your life, but honestly you are a marked woman for the rest of your days in Poland. Two men from Krakow named David and Jacob Dumblosky have joined the NKVD, and will be operating there, and they connected you to this visit to a supposedly "sick" friend.

Our friend made me promise to take you to the train station before the secret police have had a chance to think about your whereabouts. There is no time left to talk. We'll take the side streets."

Marianne, already packed, grabbed her suitcase and then checked her documents.

"Time is short. We must leave, Pani Krull. Hurry!"

Her heart racing, she clutched her suitcase tightly. They rushed through the back streets before climbing into an auto parked in an alley three blocks from the hotel. The soldier assured her that everything would be all right once they got past the first screening near the railroad station.

"Your papers are in proper order," a guard declared loudly, as they stopped at the first checkpoint outside the train station. Her documents were carefully examined and studied three times; answers were demanded quickly, and her eyes were watched as she answered

Hesitantly, she asked, "When do I get the train?"

"No guarantees," the guard replied. She noticed that her mysterious savior had disappeared. The lobby was filled with men and women in uniform, moving constantly to and fro, cradling machine guns or automatic rifles pointed at the people. Marianne just wanted to return home as soon as was possible. After a two hour wait, a voice announced, "Train 301 to Smolensk!"

"May I catch the train--west?" she asked politely.

A woman guard, answered. " Follow me. It will cost you five rubles for me to get you safely to your seat." Marianne pulled five rubles out of her pocketbook and gave them to her.

She was bound west to Poland. Once in her train's compartment, her heart pounded furiously. With tears in her eyes, she looked westward toward Poland. Moving closer to the window, she whispered to herself, "Truth is my refuge. Never will I give in to their way of life." She wondered how much time they all had left. How will we meet our fate? Stefan is only seven, and little Maria is only four, she thought.

The name Polesie derives from a Slavic root and loosely translates as "woodland". This area was acknowledged by scholars as the oldest remaining parts of preserved ethnography and culture of the Eastern Slavs. Marianne arrived there from the darkness of Moscow via Smolensk through Pinsk, on mid-morning of June 18, 1939. She finally saw the sign of "Janow", Polesie on the train platform. After two days of traveling, her body ached with the tension caused by seeing the violent Communist crimes. Her rage at the atrocities simmered beneath the surface of the face that she presented to the world. A few agonizing minutes passed before the train stopped, the doors opened and she saw Andrew and her children. Little Maria was holding flowers and when she rushed out to her children and husband, they all hugged hard and long. Stefan and Andrew took her luggage as Maria handed her the flowers. She whispered to Andrew, "We are together again so everything is better today. For the first time in twenty- four days, I feel real peace."

Andrew drove past St. Stanislaus Church on the way to Zamolenski's front gate where they were greeted. Anna flung her arms around her, "Marianne, you will never know how delighted we are to see you. You are finally home safe. Thank God. We were so worried." Zamolenski asked excitedly, "Marianne, tell us the details of your report. What did you see and hear in Russia? Who are the culprits?"

She had wanted to tell them everything immediately, since news leaked slowly out of the Bolshevik world; therefore, she outlined the definition of the enemy, and the mobilization of troops in the Urals, Georgia, Mongolia, eastern Ukraine, and Russia. If an open war broke out, these divisions would be the front line troops, but they wouldn't strike first unless Germany did

Zamolenski was shaken and thinking out loud, asked Marianne a "what could be done?" Marianne, never afraid to offer an opinion, told them that the country should enter into an arrangement with Germany and then immediately mobilize its forces and consolidate them against the Bolsheviks.

"Crush them before they crush us. We can deal with Germany on our terms, but first we need to focus on the Soviet Union. They are desperate, lacking food, and supplies; the leadership will sacrifice its people. They are purging the old guard and reaching out to new young followers, like the Dumbloskys. Their empire is in shambles, totally out of control. War is their salvation if they are ever to unite. Right now, Poland is their target "

Zamolenski said. "All we can do is to try to get what you wrote to the right people, and hope that there is an ear to hear what is going on."

Mail was being censored so he took Marianne's suitcase and ripped out the concealed compartment containing the tissue papered writings. They rushed to a "code transcriber" hidden under the kitchen stairs to send her letter off without fear of discovery. As Zamolinski's ticks and taps of transmission seemed to grow louder each minute, all they had now was hope and prayer.

The founder of the Soviet secret police, Felix Dzerzhinsky, had expressed the guiding principle of the Cheka in 1918: "We represent in ourselves as organized terror -- this must be said very clearly."

On July 25, 1939 Marianne was standing in the Janow Market Square, looking at the Chief Constable, whose strained face and labored breathing showed his fear and anger. The Janow police were keeping a watchful eye on the Citizens' Guard station which was a one-story brick building located in the center of the town. The banners reading "DEATH TO POLES" were displayed in front of a podium. Soviet agents, disguised as peasants, had attacked villagers, radio stations, and cut telegraph wires. "This man- made catastrophe threatens us all," Constable Nowatzki said loudly, "Those Soviet bastards have struck."

The day was a nightmare. The NKVD, armed Soviets and secret foreign agents had crossed into Poland and started, as they were trained, to stir up insurrections, and to organize networks of anarchists and terrorists. They condemned Polish officials and assassinated potential leadership in preparation for a takeover of the country. It became painfully clear to all the people that the Soviets were trying to politically destabilize the governments of eastern Poland. There were some in Janow who joined them, a carryover from the Marxists who sided with the Soviets in the 1920 war, later forgiven, free to roam Poland. In addition, now, after more than fifteen years of harmony in Polesie, homes and schools were being threatened.

"Mobs have struck central Baranowicie." said the constable," The Janow Police Office confirmed that there had been fatalities.....sixteen people were mutilated, mostly Citizen Guard members."

He looked at the crowd, composed of Jewish, Orthodox Christian, Ukrainian, and Polish Catholics, and said with conviction, "We'll get them. We are activating the Guard and mobilizing border patrols to move into that area. The NKVD walked across our land; surviving witnesses found a rock lettered with blood of the victims...'Death to Poland'. Then they killed again in Slonim and in Hornsby. Children pleaded for their lives; eighteen free citizens were murdered. Now only the forest bears " silent witness." Nowatzki caught his breath for a moment and then continued in an even louder voice. "Streets in Lwów were sealed off in a predawn raid by men dressed in hoods, as if they were the Citizens' Guards. The NKVD organized it.. "Lwów's large Jewish population suffered as the Soviets abducted rabbis to torture them, blaming the Polish Catholics to cause an anti-Catholic backlash among the world-wide Jewish community."

Nowatzki, he alone, had to read the very bad news to the public. "We caught them infiltrating the Citizens' Guard. This time we caught them in the plot, but they will be back"'"

Marianne looked at the square's large crowd. They gathered regularly, some from wealthy homes, others from thatched roof shacks, while some came from their shops in town, all diverse peoples joined together. They bought fresh produce, exchanged thoughts and greetings, and then would go back to their homes freely and safely. However, now the crowd was frozen, huddled, and frightened about the approaching terror. Nowatzki finished his report on the number of deaths blamed on the Soviet insurgencies, and then shook his head, wiping his face with trembling hands. "We must stand united and join hands in our fight against the Soviets."

Marianne closed her eyes for a moment. Her emotions and thoughts went wildly in different directions, and she hardly knew what to think. What was the answer to all of this? Could there be a new order or would Polesie itself explode into anarchy? Jewish scholars and workers, along with their rabbi, were standing together quietly, acknowledging the horror that threatened all their lives. Marianne looked at them, and with faint hope finally spoke to all around her : "We must act together."

The old Rabbi said, "There is no surprise that the NKVD resurfaced in our midst. Communism is the invention of the devil. I am sorry that we as Jews have been connected to the Bolsheviks and that some of our working community still support them. We need to unite against both the Communists and Nazis; the only result will be a violent passionate backlash for all enemies of humanity."

"The Nazis are coming from the west and the Communists from the east. During the next thirty days, we will be trapped if we do not take action." Marianne said.

The Rabbi gave her a faint smile, and then said "The hardest thing to learn in life is which bridge to cross. May we rest in peace, *wieczny odpucynek,,* as our source of strength. We are all Polish; hart *ducha,* the hard spirit and the living soul." His voice trailed off as he and the Jewish community walked away.

Marianne turned her eyes toward her home on the hilltop and wondered. Does everything happen for a reason? We are all at war, threatened by informants, NKVD secret police, in the darkest and loneliest spot on earth. The Rabbi said it best in Ukrainian … *dushegubka*….it means soul-breakers….the Ukrainians know who has crossed the bridge of life….leaving all homes unsettled….some to burn and over fourteen million Ukrainian lives lost forever….and the beginning of endless hatred of the Bolsheviks.

We are trapped, she thought; however, there are ways to find our exit before our soil is soaked in blood. In the end, we may be scarred and drained, but our children have to survive torture, cold, hunger and always be on a vigil against the loss of their soul, and those whose only purpose is to break the human will.

The so-called Kasprzycki-Gamelin Convention, signed May 19, 1939, in Paris, (named after the Polish Minister of War Affairs General Tadeusz Kasprzycki and the commander of the French Army Maurice Gamelin) obliged both countries to provide military help to each other in case of a war with Nazi Germany. In May, Gamelin promised a "bold relief offensive" within three weeks of the Nazi's attack. Distant agreements and conversations did not affect the people of Janow, as the sun was slowly rising over the Krull orchard at five thirty A.M. Marianne lay awake and stared at her Andrew and thought of the challenges ahead. She was deathly afraid. We would not recover, she thought.

At 7:00 A.M, one of Zamolenski's guards rushed to their front door, and knocked loudly. When Andrew opened it, he saluted. His message, from Zamolenski, was short:" The Government of Poland is confident that England and France will live up to the promise of "full protection". Germany and the Union of Soviet Socialists Republics will abide by the Treaties of Non-Aggression of 1936 and 1938" Marianne realized then that her trip to Moscow was a useless exercise, and that her message either never reached the proper people or it was being ignored. Almost as an afterthought he added ,"Please expect a telephone call from Wadeslaw Ludwig at 11A.M. at Zamolenski's home"

She was stunned and outraged. At this moment, she thought her heart would break. Four hours later, she was with Andrew, Anna and Jan at their home, sitting anxiously in the library, seriously thinking there was something wrong with their logic, and as a result, they would all be vulnerable to an all-out destruction on their own soil. The phone rang once, then twice, and Anna handed it to her. It was Ludwig: "I'm deeply sorry," he said faintly. "Beck and Smiglia had read your report and assessment. They appreciated it very much, but the Polish Government would not press the issue with Germany and would not take a preemptive

45

strike against the Soviet Union. They do not want to disrupt a strategic relationship with France and England, but they have not ruled out military action if Germany and the Soviet Union do not halt their provocations."

Then Ludwig apologized for what he called a horrible lapse in judgment. He indicated that the men in power felt that a woman's appraisal of an international situation was presumptuous, "I want to make it clear that everything you wrote is true, and I am deeply saddened and sorry about the outcome. The Soviets have hurt many people. I care very deeply about our good citizenry as I do for the safety of our family. I wish I could have done more," he said softly, his voice cracking. "We all want our country to survive. Whoever wins will create massive hatred…that's Moscow's strategy and its worldwide propaganda is very effective. We are heading for a very long struggle. Marianne, Andrew and my dearest friends the Zamolenskis, look to the future, but watch your back. The Soviet's Secret Police have penetrated every ministry, bureau and provincial department in our government. In Eastern Poland, Communists have infiltrated the Citizens' Guard. Marianne, your name has been noticed and Soviet surrogates have been assigned to monitor your movements. Rest assured you will be harassed relentlessly." Ludwig's voice was trembling with indignation. "If it is any consolation, the head of the Defense Ministry, Smiglia, referred to your report as "very impressive" and a "brilliant analysis." The Polish nation extends their gratitude to you. They are hoping that with Zamolenski as the head of the Provincial Government in Polesie and Field Marshall General Rückemann in charge of the twenty thousand military forces in Eastern Poland, we will be triumphant in the end."

Then, there was an uneasy silence. She said goodbye to Ludwig for now, and went into the quiet study. Marianne felt betrayed, and above all her fear that the squeeze on Poland would kill them all.

Marianne wrote to her father:

My Dearest Father:

You taught me to hold to truth as an objective, and you gave me many wonderful memories; however, right now, all I can think of is thirty-four million Poles buried in one long graveyard. I know that my life will never be the same after this coming conflict. You nurtured me, preparing me for life's awful events. But I will never give in.

. What is going to happen to my family and to the people of Eastern Poland? There is little chance for honor to survive, and if the Soviet evil does succeed, the world will have lost its entire honor.

There is no better time than now to keep working harder than we already have, to fight, because the love of home and country are at stake. We must all find a refuge.

Your loving daughter,

Marianne

She was very anxious to send her note, for it told Ludwig, between the lines, in invisible ink, that the her family would leave their beautiful home on the hilltop, for a safer place in the Pripet Marshes, nearest to Russia's border. They would hide there as their ancestors did.

With the Zamolenski's help, Andrew and Marianne had decided to leave their home. They knew they were in danger and clearly saw its presence in their lives. The engines of war were steaming, and streaming, across Europe during these August days, just as they had in August of 1914. The events mirrored an ironic "deja vue". French and British neighbors were preaching "Peace at Hand," instead of "Peace in Our Time." As if nothing for the past twenty years, including the desperate cries from inside the Soviet Union had happened, Roosevelt inched closer to a far greater evil, and from the printing presses, Soviet mistruths were coming forth. Men were hanged for a single iota of truth and being punished in the gulags for telling it. People of faith and religious credos were in for a more horrible end.

Anna said softly to all of them as they sat in the Zamolenski parlor, "We are in a great struggle that may have no end. We must think of what is right for our home and country. How can we go forward? How do we keep the children of Polesie as free as possible, how do we reeducate them to prepare for the enemy we will be facing. How then do we continue with everyday living? Andrew, Zamolenski, Anna and Marianne explored every possibility, hoping that their children would understand why they decided to leave their comfortable homes and go eastward to a village a few miles away from Pinsk at the Soviet border, within the forests, marshes, and ponds of Pripet. They decided that they wanted the children to live there. It is where their ancestors had grown up, and the four adults trustingly believed, out of their own deepest conviction, that the move and the radical decision would be right for them.

Andrew saw the move as a message from God, which would assure a future, and retained the Christian philosophy of "love thy neighbor". Marianne saw her husband's incredible past as a gift from God, allowing their survival. Andrew said that he regarded the agony and solitude in the forest of his earlier life as a savior from evil and he began to pray silently.

The deeply rooted Christian tradition of Poland was being squeezed on both sides by destructively evil forces, both of whom followed the mantras of demonic leadership. Josef Stalin's credo was that "one death is a tragedy, a million is a statistic"; and that "true solidarity is found in the cemetery." He believed that death "solves all problems - no man, no problem." The founder of the Soviet secret police, Feliks Dzerzhinsky, expressed the guiding principle of the Cheka in 1918: "We represent in ourselves organized terror -- this must be said very clearly."

Marianne returned to her desk as a school administrator in Janow. Her job was unusual in the sense that it was usually held by a man. Over time, and with experience, her firm dignity and educational advantage led her to this position in the local schools. She knew she would soon have to give it up, for schools were not part of either Nazi or Bolshevik tradition. She could not imagine teaching Nazism in every sentence or for that matter having a large portrait of Josef Stalin staring at her from the classroom wall daily.

Every morning, Marianne looked at children, fearing the worst of the terrible struggle ahead. She knew that the Soviets were absolutely certain to destroy their home and the smiling faces of all children of Polesie. She was very worried that as an NKVD target, she would injure her family. Her fear turned to terror when she received a note from Janow's Constable Nowatzki, an old family friend in Janow.

Marianne:

Two people were charged with spying, and their throats were slit in front of a crowd as being "enemies of the people." The mayor spoke, then, against Communism. He was muzzled, and his body was axed as if Jewish peasants did it. The first ax blow was not stuck near the heart, so the peasants could hear the gigantic moans on the platform. Later, dozens of Ukrainian peasants attacked Jewish villages near Hrodna. Not all escaped the attack. The Jews cursed the Poles furiously. They will make sure world reporters write about what Poles did to the Jewish villagers. Evil Bolshevik tactic! Don't you agree?"Constable Nowatski

The defining, heartbreaking moment arrived for Marianne when seven-year-old Stefan came to her, after school , in tears, holding broadsides that had been handed out reading "Death to the Poles." and "Landholders-- get what they deserve — an ax across the head."; and "Death to Poland". "The Russians are coming!" She could only hold him, and cry with him, as this incident solidified the decision to leave. How else could any child survive this horror?

Every day for the past two weeks, she had agonized over the decision: "Life is pitifully short for all of us. We need to save our children. It is painful for us to have to choose to leave at the precise moment, but if we are to save the lives of many children of Polesie, we must last as long as we can. She set a mental timetable for the family's departure and waited for Andrew to come home to make preparations and careful plans.

Marianne was sure that provisions had to be made for educating her children, as well as all Polish children. The Soviets and Nazis would control it. Hitler imprisoned teachers who did not follow doctrine in the classroom, while Stalin publically said, "Education is a weapon whose effects depend on who holds it in his hands and at whom it is aimed."-

As she readied herself to complete her housing and moving arrangements, Marianne heard very bad news of Soviet actions in Poland, all of which sped up her preparations.

"Thousands of Soviet insurgents had chanted, "Death to Poland", Nowatski wrote, "They are eager to cause destruction to Polesie, Vilnius, Lwów, Slonim, Pinsk, and Hrodna. Everyone needs to consider the serious situation, before the Soviets establish a foothold as the buffer between Germany and themselves. By August 10th, the situation in eastern Poland has gotten worse. The Soviet NKVD created a reign of terror, leading armed mobs to attack schools. Conflicts between the Jews and the Ukrainians are increasing at an alarming rate. Seven fifteen year old boys and five girls of a Ukrainian Orthodox School, St. Jadwiga's, were beaten severely. One of the teachers had said ," Bolshevik Jews!" It is just the beginning. It was a terrible crime and bound to stir awful reactions among the villagers. What will our lives be like?

Violence breeds violence. Polish patriots, including every Jew, Ukrainian, Byelorussian, and Lithuanian usually responded with terrible fury. Ten Polish border guards were executed in a brazen NKVD raid, in the Pripet Marshes near Pinsk," he continued. "In Hrodna, fifteen Citizens' Guard were blindfolded and executed by Beria's trademark: a bullet in the back of the head. Five Catholic boys from an area outside of Janow, across from our beautiful St. Stanislaus Church, were killed, while a crowd of men yelled religious insults and one shouted, "I hate Catholics and   Death to the Poles!" According to the Constable, they were NKVD agents that had been coming to Janow. A Catholic classmate reported the horror …the bodies were half-decapitated, and lay bleeding to death in the gloomy darkness of the school's soccer field. "

For this reason Constable Nowatzki urged Marianne to close the local schools. He said that it is simply too dangerous to keep them open.

The news got worse. The next morning, in the village of Knew, fifteen miles away, a close knit, peaceful Jewish community was in a state of siege. Two hundred or so, angry Catholic peasants armed with axes and bricks, were retaliating against the Jews. They were kicking them to death; stripping and beating them. No military presence was there; this was an explosion of blind rage; shacks were burned. Some people, after being murdered, were hung from trees and others were tortured and maimed for life.

Marianne saw, during these awful moments, that Polesie, the unprotected front line of Eastern Poland was under attack. Unless protection arrived or something was done, Poland, before harvest and when winter set in, could expect a mounting slaughter rate, and within three months, a larger number of slow deaths by starvation and freezing.

Each morning, for the past ten days, Marianne traveled from one school to the next. She visited three schools in a day. The teachers' faces seemed gloomier than usual, and the students' bright eyes, a little sadder as she went by.

By August 16,   the Soviet invasion was on the mind of every citizen of Polesie. The violation of human rights was a reality and. Marianne had to close twelve of the schools that she oversaw. It was heartbreaking. Polish leaders and patriots were part of the population of .Catholics, teachers, land owners with military backgrounds, and also members of the upper class, which made them potential enemies of the Soviet System. They had to hide.

Andrew set a five day time table to manage his factory, and together with Zamolenski, made final details for his family to depart secretly for a mysterious place close to the Russian border. They would have to leave their household goods and possessions behind. Marianne had finally closed the last four schools, including her prized model school, St. Andrew's. She didn't want to frighten her children, but all Catholic children were in peril during this violent "intelligentsia cleansing". The Bolsheviks expected to remove the leadership, and consequently bring disaster to the families and their country. Marianne's thoughts about her precious children were dominated by the question of the harsh reality of the possibility of a bullet in each of their heads.

Early one day in August, in the midst of her very jarring reverie, the bedroom door flew open and her children came running in. There were hugs and the happy barking of their dog Basha, who snuggled next to Andrew. Each morning the family joined together in prayer. Andrew had carved a copy of the Black Madonna of Czestochowa, an icon centered on the small family altar, which he had framed so elegantly with his remarkable carvings and embossed with gray figurations along its edges. The icon had special meaning for them since the Bishop of Janow blessed it last year. "Today we pray for a safe country and for all love to come home," Andrew began softly as Stefan and Maria knelt on a cushioned kneeler, their eyes focused on the Black Madonna, "Mama and I have not made a final decision yet as to when, but starting today we are getting ready to leave our home. We prayed that this would not happen, but it is now necessary to prepare. Stefan and Maria, always remember, though we'll be in a different place, the heart of our home shall never leave us." The two candles on the altar flickered. The children's faces became sad and tearful as they sensed danger.

"Why are we going to leave our home?" Stefan asked.

Andrew tried to explain the situation simply to the children." Mama went to the Soviet Union to learn about good and bad people. She gave the government a report about those who are trying to hurt us. We need to make sure we stay together no matter how difficult it gets. I learned my lesson of good and bad when I was a little boy, alone at the age of four. You will never be alone. If you sense danger, remember that your mother and I will always be there for you, ready to bring sunshine to your day. Do you understand?

Maria asked, "Who is going to hurt us, Mama?" Marianne kissed her forehead and Stefan cuddled next to her, as they held each other tightly.

"We live here in our country, and another country is planning to hurt us. We believe in God; they do not. These bad people make bad things happen for they want to harm our bodies, minds and souls. Adults call them Communists and Bolsheviks. Because our countries have very different beliefs, they may attack our schools and villages, jump out, waving clubs and guns. Some will be wearing red armbands. We will be strong and brave, always trying to do the right thing. We will protect you and all the children of Polesie, so that everyone will be safe from their terrible ways."

"I am afraid of monsters, Mama," Stefan said "I hate Russians. Does that make me bad?"

Andrew shook his head in dismay. "You shouldn't hate. Most Russians are good people. It is not the Russians, but it is the Soviet leaders who are bad. They send soldiers and NKVD monsters who may try to harm us."

Stefan replied, "I'm not afraid. I'll be brave." Little Maria tenderly kissed her mother on the cheek.

Andrew had the children help start the packing for the coming journey, while Marianne headed for St. Francis in the village of Tylicz. When she arrived, she was greeted by polite, well-scrubbed youngsters, all anxiously awaiting the final ceremony. The proud parents had seen easily, the progress of their children in reading and writing and above all the Polish culture.

Marianne had been called upon to give a short, final speech to the graduates. She was being held up as an example of an elegant, educated woman and she had been flattered by the invitation. As she entered the school's assembly hall, she was greeted with enthusiastic cheers and tears welled up in Marianne's eyes. After a while, the children settled down and she began to speak.

"We are all blessed. Our Polish heritage shines on us like a bright light. That is reason enough to live. It is a firm steady promise. Thank you, teachers and parents, for your devotion and commitment. You have contributed so much to so many, not because you have to, but because you want to. We have perilous times ahead, but together we shall overcome them. You are all very important to me; I will miss you terribly. We shall unite in strength, always very proud of today, from this time forward."

Principal Stanislaw Lukasz spoke next: "There is no greater devotion than what you see in this assembly hall. What's deep inside each and every one of us will never be lost or betrayed. We have been taught well at St. Francis'. I believe that with all my heart. Thank you!"

Marianne took one last look at the children and Principal Lukasz, knowing that they may not see each other again. As the assembly ended, an unfamiliar woman sitting in the first row caught her attention. She appeared intensely nervous and her face was pale with fear. She approached and spoke softly to Marianne in Ukrainian accented Polish. "I need to see you privately. It is important and serious."

The woman grasped her arm and rushed her to a secluded corner of the room.

"Pani Krull, I am Ilana. My last name is not important. You do not know me, but I know who you are. I drove for two hours to give you these roses here at St. Andrew's. I have come to warn that you are in grave danger. You must leave Poland immediately!"

"Pani Ilana, We are all in grave danger. What really brings you here?"

Anxiously, she moved closer and whispered "We come from two separate worlds: You are Catholic and Polish. I am Jewish and Ukrainian. We are political opponents. You provide leadership and love your birthplace: Poland. My husband and I are Communists. He is an important politician, which means he knows exactly what is going to happen in Polesie. There are massacres and there will be more."

"You live in fear. I feel sorry for you. Sixty million Christians are dead. Your husband is following Stalin. To me, you are an accessory to mass murder and ultimately you will all share the fate of war's victims." Marianne said flatly.

The woman stood absolutely still and tugged at her hair nervously: "We make our choices, and mine may be an awful one. It was an agonizing decision for me to come here. They will shoot me if anyone finds out that I am with you, and then my six children will be without a mother. I discovered yesterday that your family and others are marked for death even before the invasion. David Dumblosky, a native Pole from Krakow is part of a Special Operations Unit directed by Behrman, Beria, Lazar Moiseyevich Kaganovich and Vishinsky. It has been newly organized to take over Eastern Poland. His brother Jacob is assigned to a special KGB unit aimed at creating chaos and fear by assassinating Polish intelligentsia and potential leaders from Vilnius, Brest and Pinsk. Bolshevik leaders see Polesie as a buffer between Germany and the western Ukraine. They view Count Zamolenski as an effective leader. Polesie, whose produce feeds thousands of people, is the right place to set up a regional defense command. Both Germany and the Soviet

Union want to occupy Poland after the war starts and after the harvest. They are ready to divide the country in half and have already agreed to do so in principle. The Soviet government wants to occupy Eastern Poland, and use it as bargaining chip with the Nazis. Their strategy is to use the land east of Warsaw and the food supply from it, leaving thirteen million people starving. Your name has been discussed at the highest levels and you have been targeted as an enemy of the people.

You must trust me. Although we may all die before this is over, we could possibly survive as well. Operation *Clean Hands* is coming. The Soviets are sending 20,000 NKVD troops to organize the Communist Revolutionary Committees, identified as Lists of Workers to administer the government after the anticipated successful Russian and Nazi invasion. Their mission is to use terror and identify potential "enemies of the state" whose backgrounds are counter to Soviet intentions. These so-called enemies will be executed before and after the takeover. You, Pani Krull, will be eliminated."

Marianne looked straight into her eyes and said, "We well know that the Nazis and Soviets have targeted 34 million lives simply because they are Polish, Christian, anti-Communist and anti-Nazi? What do you want me to do?"

The woman stared for a moment, took a deep breath, and then rapidly spit out a desperate warning. "I am talking about the next three weeks! Pani Marianne, enemies of the people and other counter-revolutionaries are targeted by the Soviet: Operation Cleansing of our Hands plan. They know that if they kill the educated patriots of the intellectual class, the whole structure crumbles, and the Polish society would be undermined. Marianne grabbed her arm and pleaded. "Please tell me as much as you know"

"Pani Krul, your remaining schools will be targeted. They know all about your Moscow visit and report. They also know that you, personally, called our leadership "the most evil men on earth" and "a threat to humankind". They are sending out assassins for you, as you are now a marked woman whose voice is dangerous to their plans. Please hide, escape. Do not risk your life and that of your family's. If you decide to stay here, you should disguise yourself. Hide for the next three months. No one who shows love of country is safe in Poland. The schools are in danger and need to be warned. There's no telling if the children will be harmed, but I do know there is great danger when you return to these schools. "They" are waiting at St. Paul's, St. John's, St. Joseph's as well as here St. Andrew's. Close them now!"

Marianne told Ilana that it took courage to alert her, but either way they both can't hide. "The schools are being closed. We have requested cavalry for protection and all we have left to do is to pray." Marianne added the words: "and ask for forgiveness" internally. She felt yet again that a "deathbed confession" of a suffering soul had just come her way, as it had with the Colonel in the railway car.

Ilana had stopped, turned back around and said quietly: "I have always wanted to meet you. We have one important thing in common – a deep love of family. I am a mother who bears a great sense of guilt. We Bolshevik Jews are despised. We are sinning by willfully consenting to mass murder as allies of Nazis. I teach my children good values. I don't want them to have twisted minds"

She looked at Marianne and cried softly "Pani Krull, believe me. I did everything humanly possible to warn you."

"No, forget about me. You are betraying your country and the love of your homeland. You need to denounce your husband and everything that he stands for. How can you still commit these awful crimes knowing your children are in the same home where their father, your husband, is taking orders from Moscow? Think of your children," she desperately demanded.

"You must drop out of sight, Pani Krull. I am pleading with you!" she said. "It is horrible, but I have to deal with it. There will be no escape, but perhaps my children can be saved. I suspect that somehow you, Pani Krull, will make it through this hell on earth. Perhaps there will be a day for repay by saving the souls of my children."

"Pani Ilana, We will meet again, I'm sure"

"May God be with you always, Pani Krull. Before leaving for St Andrew's, please read this". She then slid a dirty piece of paper into Marianne's hand, and quietly slipped out the back door for her long road home. Fifteen minutes later, Marianne was with Pani Lukasz telling her to spread the word that the danger of the Bolshevik "invasion" they had all feared was happening now, and also for her to tell Zamolenski to send his horsemen to each of the schools.

"I will call Father Zajac to let him know you are coming. What else should I do?" she whispered.

"Bravely go on. The Soviets have arrived and more will be here in force. We will need to notify as many people as possible. God bless you, Principal Lukasz."

Marianne was seriously shaken by Ilana's warning; however, the realization was still there that it was issued by one of "them"no matter how sympathetic Ilana seemed. The information, she thought, needed to be shared immediately with Ludwig and Zamolenski.

Ilana's scrap of paper contained a memorandum reporting on a successful "demonstration" in Slonim. It included descriptions of men carrying flaming torches, the beating of teachers and priests with clubs, the firing of shots, and the indiscriminate rape of young girls by bands of Soviet NKVD roaming the countryside. "Death to the teachers!" was their rallying cry.

Marianne ran to her automobile parked outside of the school. She had gotten the machine from her father, and with Andrew's expertise held the car together. It was a 1933 Fiat, dark brown, with a clutch that only Marianne seemed to be able to master. The top of the car was tarred yearly to keep the elements away from the cloth surface. Marianne turned it over and pushed and bumped her way to St. Andrews over the hole- dotted roadway. Her auto shuddered forward and entered a narrow winding road, which led to the entrance of the school. As she got out of her car, the Franciscan monk, Father Zajac, his face white with agony, huddled among the children; he grabbed her hand while Pani Novak tearfully greeted her. "This is just wrong! Very wrong!" he repeated loudly and sadly.

A little ragged boy in baggy trousers stood directly in front of Marianne. His name was David; she found out from the Father; he was eight years old from nearby Slonim. Silently, he was beating both fists onto his chest in repeated stabbing motions.

"I'm afraid. I am so afraid, Pani Krull. They killed my uncle!" he sobbed.

Marianne hugged him as she thought Oh Lord, please let these precious children and teachers survive the nightmare. Father Zajac held on to her arm and sadly spoke quietly and bitterly: "Pani Krull, four teachers were tortured and butchered in the Town of Slonim and the children were forced to watch. David's uncle was one of them. Little David had seen these monsters stab his Uncle and Aunt after they had set his two cousins on fire." Marianne could not understand this inhumanity and cold relentless destruction of human life and she started to sob as well.

"Which teachers were killed?" she asked Father Zajac.

"Pani Kulska, Mikulska, Bartoska, and Pan Kowa, the very same ones that you and I recruited and trained have disappeared one by one. My God. Why?" Wiping her tears, Marianne sadly called out, "These innocent victims were our teachers, so decent and good. My heart bleeds for them'.

Father Zajac cried, "I am not supposed to hate, but I despise them! May they all burn in hell."

Marianne pleaded, "Father, we have to finish the school year. We cannot let them win. These children need hope and we must show them that we are not helpless. Please, keep the parents away; and have the teachers continue with lessons on what is right. I will join you at graduation, but only with some help to protect us."

Soon Pani Nowak gathered the students and announced, "Let us honor the brave teachers. We shall never forget this hour. We must remember their names forever. Come children, we are going to sing for Pani Krull." They started:

"We are the children of Poland.

Alive and free

Not lost, as long as we are here with thee"

The National anthem resounded loudly throughout the halls, the children's voices singing with the passion only a child can produce. The adults quietly wept.

Poland was being squeezed by two major powers. Hitler saw Poland as the birthright of Nazis everywhere. To them, it was not an Aryan land. Poles were "untermensch", "inferior people," only good as slaves or corpses. After the dismemberment of Czechoslovakia, Hitler ordered his general staff to draw up plans for the invasion of Poland. The Nazis would invade from the West, the Soviets from the East, and divide the country along previously agreed upon lines.

Marianne prayed that the decision to finish the school year at St. Andrew's was the right one. She had spent an anxious, sleepless night and had grave misgivings that another disaster was in the making. Zamolenski told her, the day before, that no protection in the form of guards or security was available at St. Andrew's, since it was needed for the town and for his own protection. Father Zajac and the children were in immediate and serious danger. Since Ilana had assured: her that a death warrant for her life had reached the highest levels of Moscow, she felt alone, isolated and unprotected.

Clouds swirled outside her window as violent blasts of wind filled the air making the trees hiss. There was emptiness outside the home, coupled with a tension inside, She finally got out of bed, fell to her knees and prayed to God to grant courage and strength for the teachers and Father Zajac to make it through the day, because tomorrow, twenty- thousand NKVD agents would cross the Polish borders. The woman, Ilana called it: "Operation Cleansing Hands!" However, it was really an invasion and an act of war!

At 4:45 a.m., Andrew gently placed a hand on her shoulder. Although he looked outwardly calm, Marianne could feel the knots in his stomach muscles caused by panic as they made the final preparations for their secret departure. They were anxiously waiting for "proper" identity papers, forged and designed to change their name from Krull to Ludwig, in order to disappear without a past. Every day that they remained visible, they jeopardized their survival with the massive terrorist attacks and selective murders that appeared to be imminent.

At 5:30 A.M. the bedroom door slowly opened. Maria tiptoed across the room and Stefan joined her on the bed with their parents. They too were wound up with excitement and anxiety. Marianne and Andrew hugged their children as Marianne asked her son:

"What's your name?"

"Stefan! Stefan"

"How old are you?"

"I am seven."

"What is your father's name?"

"Andrew Ludwig"

"What is your mother's name?

"Marianne Ludwig."

"What does your father do?"

"My father works with his hands. He is a woodworker."

"Do your mother and father go to church? Are they Catholic? Are they Polish?"

"I don't know ma'am, but I go to church."

"They don't go to church, but you do?"

"Ma'am, I go to festivals, picnics, races, and play with my friends in the fields. We go to village dances, do the polka and the church is our playground.

"Where are you from?"

"A small farm near Masowsie (Masovia). We have lots of festivals."

"Do you know the name of the village? Do you know who Stalin is?

"No, ma'am!" "Did your mother ever talk about Stalin?

"No,ma'am."

"Do you know Zamolenski?"

"No,ma'am."

"Do you know how you get your food?"

"No,ma'am. Well maybe."

"How?" said Andrew.

"From the ground, sir."

"What kind of home do you have?"

"It's a nice home. We have a kitchen, bedroom and an outhouse."

"Do you help your father work?"

"Yes,ma'am! I have a pitchfork, shovel and lots of mud. We raise grain, barley oats and potatoes."

"What kind of clothes do you wear?'

"Pants,shirts and wooden shoes."

"Do you go to school?"

"Yes, I went to kindergarten and first grade. Now, I work on my father's farm and look forward till tomorrow's sunrise."

"Is your mother a teacher?"

"I am not sure what she does."

"Fine, you are a good boy. Now, my new friend, are you telling me the truth?"

"I do not lie ma'am. My mother tells me never to lie."

"Where is your Mama?"

"She's helping my father on the farm and with his woodwork."

"Good! Remember when nice boys grow up, they become Communists. They respect Stalin, and only obey government leaders. Mama and Tata will not live if you don't obey Stalin."

"Ma'am, will you let me grow up? I wish you good-bye."

Little Stefan turned to Marianne seeking a hug of approval. He looked straight into her eyes and for the first time, said, "Stalin's bad police will never catch me."

"I love you, my son. You have learned so much in such a short time, but you shall learn even more! We are off to a good start. Now scoot. Mama and Tata need to have some time to ourselves."

"All right, Mama." Stefan answered as he ran outdoors.

As daylight peeked through the curtains, a glint of sunlight brightened the room. Andrew asked hesitantly, "How do you think the children are doing?"

"They are actually doing quite well, considering all the frenzy around us."

"Andrew", Marianne said, "Hold me close. I need your love more than ever," her voice cracked. Without a word, he pressed his body next to hers. Their passion and physical need erased their fears for a moment. Warm and satisfied, they finally, lay in contented silence; the only sound was Andrew's peaceful breathing.

Her lingering pleasure was abruptly interrupted by fearful thoughts of what would happen at Father Zajac's school. Andrew spoke hopefully, "I know you want to keep your promise, but you can't go to that school alone." He reached into the bedside desk and took out his gun. "You will need some protection. I want to go with you with this in my hand. Danger is out there for all of us."

Marianne insisted. "No! You cannot come with me. Why risk everything? A gun exerts more pressure on me. For every gun we bring, they will have ten, in addition to pitchforks, axes and plenty of hate! I would rather use my wits. That's my only weapon!"

"Marianne!" he said, "There is greater danger than you could imagine out there. Three schools have been attacked. You may need your wits, courage and a gun; otherwise, you should not go, or I'll have to go with you."

"Absolutely not!" she stubbornly answered. Marianne's greatest failing, if she had one, was stubbornness. Once she latched on to an idea she did not let go. "You have too much to do right here. We must not break from our daily routine, since we are being watched every moment. We have no choice, my love. I must go to St. Andrew myself to honor Pani Nowak and Father Zajac for their defiance and bravery, and most importantly, for not yielding to fear. I will take the gun."

Andrew gave in, then showed her how to use it and the safety catch, and said:" You are loaded for eight shots. Should the worst happen, aim straight at the leaders, nobody will move unless the leaders give orders. They do not want a martyr. As you say, they are cowards, not human beings, who will not move an inch forward out of fear for their lives. The leaders do not want to commit suicide. Their existence is based on surviving one event at a time."

"Let's hope you are right. I love you so much...don't worry. No one bullies me."

Andrew's face showed his unhappiness as he got up and slid into his leather boots. "There is no need to talk about it anymore. It is your decision. Here, take the rosary. Say some prayers along the way". They kissed and then Marianne sadly wished her children goodbye amid hugs and tears.

The car was packed with clothes and food for the children at the school. As she started her drive, Zamolenski's eight house guards appeared, who were armed and mounted. The leader told her that they could only go with her for about twenty miles since they had been instructed to collect supplies from the Cavalry unit that had been ordered to Vilnius to curtail the immediate threat of invasion. Zamolenski had tried to stop the order, but it was too late.

As the horsemen rode off, she drove up the road. Eventually, as promised, the guards vanished from her rear view mirror. She patted the gun under her blouse, hoping its presence would give her reassurance. She arrived on the grounds of St. Andrew's in time, and safely for the celebration of the end of the school year and graduation of the upper form. At the end of the long pathway, Father Zajac and Pani Novak were waiting to greet her. She was escorted to the auditorium by the little boy whose uncle was killed a week earlier, and who came forward with a dozen roses. The students broke into applause on her arrival. There was a celebration, Marianne said to the students gathered in front of her "Today we are together in joy. We have food, good company, and you have all worked hard to get to this moment. "

On the teacher's cue, the children began to sing patriotic songs of their homeland; ironically, the festivities were short lived; they were ended by a deafening explosion. The screaming began after confused silence and shock. Pani Novak was exceptionally calm when she told the assembly that a bomb had been thrown near the building's entrance. Marianne was horrified as the terrified children started to cry and stumble in to each other in efforts to escape. The panic increased as the screaming and wailing got louder and louder. "They are in front of us!" Marianne screamed. "We can try to hold them off. Get the children out, one group at a time." Pani Novak had the children hold on to each other's hands and led them to the back entrance of the school.

The screaming soon started again. Marianne marched resolutely to the front door. She couldn't do more than react and be angry. Her hands shook as she opened the entrance door. There was a mob approaching, men and women, wearing red arm-bands, carrying axes, pitchforks, and guns. They were waving banners lettered with hateful slogans, including *Down with Cleansing Hands.* Marianne slammed the door shut, leaned against it, took the gun out of her blouse, and held it tightly. Instead of obeying her impulse to fire into the crowd, she began to pray asking for God's help. Andrew's words rang in her head: "Aim the gun straight at the leader. Remember, a coward always fears for his own life. Outwit him! Do not kill him. Strike fear in his and all their eyes."

As her body trembled and her knees shook, she wondered. "How long will I be able to hold out?" She opened the door to face the oncoming crowd, she noticed, as people do in times of crisis, the darkening clouds above the heads and flags of the mass of people in front of her. She held the gun in both hands with her finger on the trigger. The leader stepped forward. The mob shouted in cadence, "Kill Krull!" Suddenly, the leader cried out, "No! Not yet! Do not kill her."

An agent wearing a red bandana and red armband stepped out of the crowd shouting, "Listen! Listen! Wait! Hear what she has to say."

Marianne responded: "If you move just one inch, I will pull the trigger and you will be done! I hate you all and really do want to kill all of you. Try me!

"You will die, the children will die," the leader answered.

The mob surged forward and closer as if it was one person. Marianne fired a single shot over their heads, and tentatively they retreated, not daring to rush onward for fear of being the first one shot.

"You will die! You will die! Your brains will be blown out if you come one step closer!" Marianne shivered as her hand tightened around the gun pointed at their heads.

"Down with landowners!" They chanted loudly. A moment later, an NKVD agent shouted, "We will kill everyone with clean hands!" Another leader cried in Russian, but his heavily accented Polish accent gave his true identity away. "Krull! Your days are numbered!"

"You'll never get me before I get you, you bastard! My gun is aching to blow your head off." Marianne felt that she was losing control, and instead she directed her rage at the two leaders while her gun shook slightly as she pointed it at them.

She fired another shot over their heads. The mob stomped their feet and chanted wildly again and again, "Kill Krull!". Suddenly their screams were silenced by a blast which detonated inside the building. Windows were shattered. The children inside were screaming. The mob surged forward, as Marianne screamed, "I'll shoot anyone who tries to pass me!"

"But we will spill your blood on the doorsteps of this school! Marianne Krull is an enemy of the people".

She pointed her gun at the Krakow traitor. "You will be the first to die if you take one step forward. I will outlive you!"

They looked confused. "You cannot escape, Marianne Krull!" A voice, which she guessed was David Dumblosky barked from within the crowd. She fired again. "David Dumblosky," she cried, "need I shoot you?"

She continued to stare defiantly at the agent in the red bandana. He glared back at her furiously. Finally, with cold expressionless eyes, he turned to the crowd and bellowed "It's over! Enough for now! There will be other times, Marianne Krull; my comrades will burn you alive. I will personally rip your heart from your chest".

"Someday, provided you are not dead first!" She fired a shot in the air. "Get out of here! Better be looking over your shoulders the rest of your life".

As they turned away, a thunderclap sounded loudly in the sky, and a torrential rain fell. It was miraculous! Father Zajac ran out into the drenching, pouring rain and knelt in the mud facing the persecutors. Marianne was struck by the biblical scene of the drenched cleric, with hair and beard plastered to his face, talking loudly to his Lord and thanking Jesus for the rain. He was lit sporadically by lightning, and his serene ignorance of the danger of the storm only underlined his holy intent. The mob could only stare, torn between their furor, and the pious priest, who triggered long forgotten religious memories somewhere deep within them. Soon, as if to bring all of them back to reality, someone in the mob shouted in between the thunder and lightning. "For you, Krull, there will definitely be another time, and another place of our choosing. You will not live long." Marianne's gun and Father Zajac's prayers had had an effect on many in the crowd. They started to leave. Rocks and clubs were dropped in front of the school. One desultory member suddenly rolled the stone he was carrying, at Marianne's feet and then quickly ran away.

Marianne shouted after them, as much to warn them, as to assuage her own anger: "Some of you will die at your own hands tomorrow. Remember, Communists kill their own. You are as good as dead! Let that be a reminder for any Polish traitor. Many thousands of you will die."

The St. Andrew's siege was over. Marianne knelt down in the wet mud with Father Zajac to thank God for their safety and blessings. She finally started to breathe evenly again and decided that she had to go back to the children. She bent down and picked up the stone at her feet, and discovered a note tied to it. Cautiously, she removed the paper: it read:

"Marianne Krull, you are dead" was scrawled in jagged letters. She stuffed the note into her pocket and when Father Zajac asked to see it, she simply said it should not concern him or the others. "I am aware of the threats, but don't need to be reminded of them. God watched over us today, so let's pray He always will." She realized that she had better leave the area sooner rather than later, and turned toward the school and entered the building.

The children began to return from the back entrance to their rooms and soon everyone was accounted for. She looked at the teachers and children beginning to gather around her, and wanted to hug every one of them. "You are a symbol of triumph. *Z bogiem!* May God bless you always!" The good Father blessed each child with a sign of the cross on the forehead. He turned to Marianne and said, "My dear Marianne. I saw it with my own eyes. Praise God for putting you on this earth. You saved our lives. You alerted us to what was ahead. The children prayed on their knees. They screamed, but did not panic and even little David got through it. Bravely, we shall move on."

As the rain tapered off, on her ride home, Marianne's heart sank as she saw the roadside littered with mutilated human bodies. She recognized a colleague, Father Alfred Kolonowski, lying dead on the ground, shot in the back of the head.

"This was the work of the devil" she thought. There were about twenty mutilated naked bodies! Some were hung, others were butchered like animals, or beheaded. There was a pregnant woman with her neck slit open; children's eyes had been gouged out; women were stabbed, their breasts sliced off and left beside them. At the end of the road, as she approached the little town of Katrynia, residents were on their knees weeping and praying. She cursed Dumblosky under her breath. There were signs with the now familiar slogan: *Death to all Poles with clean hands!* This day of violence had left her numb. Ludwig's timeless wisdom, which was always with her, came to her mind: "Provide us strength and infinite capacity to move on. At the end, there is always light from God. Our faith will give us courage today and tomorrow. We will prevail."

When she arrived home, she threw herself into Andrew's waiting arms. They went to the little chapel in the corner, took the children, and knelt down to pray.

AUGUST 22, 1939

On this day, Hitler authorized his commanders to kill "without pity or mercy, all men, women, and children of Polish descent or language, to achieve German living space [lebensraum] we need". Heinrich Himmler was quoted as saying, "All Poles will disappear from the world. It is essential that the great Nazi people should consider it as its major task to destroy all Poles."

In the shimmer of morning light, Andrew and Marianne faced the darkness of eastern Poland. Amidst the growing tension, they left

65

their beautiful home for the last time .They knew the decision to leave was the right one. Their house on the hillside had always been a happy haven, surrounded by the beauty of the forest, the sweet scent of the pines, and bright sunshine. Suddenly and violently, forces stronger than them, all had rudely interrupted their lives.

The scenes of horror at Katrynia haunted Marianne: entire families tragically erased in an instant while the children were forced to watch. The shocking event at St. Andrew's was also engraved into her consciousness. They had promised the children a place to play and a different but nice new home. They would leave under the cover of darkness, wearing tattered clothing, to Zamolina, the small town near Pinsk, a major railroad center connecting Moscow to Poland. Zamolenski had given them an old hunting cabin located on the edge of a forest, about four hundred yards from the village Square, along with a plot of six hectares, which was one hectare above the Soviet standard for a rich peasant. His thinking was that they could negotiate downward a hectare, if at some point they were given the choice of remaining on the land or being deported to Siberia. The new property had two deeds: one in the name of Ludwig, the other in the name of Krull. Ludwig was used in the event the Soviets first occupied eastern Poland: Krull would be used if the Nazis were to occupy all of Poland.

At six-thirty a.m., Andrew, feeling a deep sense of loss, headed to the factory where he told Foreman Kowal, his best artisan, and the forty workers with him to prepare for war. After marrying Marianne, Andrew had formed his own business, and now after years of nurturing his dream, there was nothing left but good-byes. Despite the anguish, he faced his workers and Joseph Kowal. "I must say good-bye now my dear friends. No one loved this place more than I did. Together, we produced jewels that spread across Poland's cathedrals, from a factory not just of brick and mortar, but also of real people. However, sadly, today I must shut the door so you can return to your families and pursue the right course. For consolation, if there is one, you will each receive one head of cattle, two weeks' pay and my eternal gratitude for your work so creatively produced, but above all, respected. My sorrow will never end, but perhaps we will have another chance to build jewels that are even more beautiful when the war is over."

After teary embraces and solemn farewells, Andrew sadly bolted the factory doors. He brought home a battered old farm wagon, drawn by two bay horses that Zamolenski had given to him from his own estate. His days with the Fiat were over.

66

He pulled the wagon to the front of the house and parked the Fiat closer to the side of it. After hesitating for a moment, Andrew rushed upstairs into the bathroom and shaved all his blond hair off until he was bald. He went to the barn, slaughtered three sheep, squeezed the blood into a bucket, heavily salted the carcasses, and placed them in the wagon. He took the sheep's blood and spattered it over the patio, bathroom and bedroom.

"We are starting a new life," Marianne solemnly announced and quietly asked the children to put on the clothes prepared for them the night before. Stefan balked at wearing the wooden shoes "Just put the shoes on, tie them with the ropes. Take Maria and find a spot outside under the tree and wait for Mama and Tata!"

Andrew and Marianne tore the window shutters off the hinges, and Andrew poured blood in the drawing room. They ripped up the sofa, and broke the other furniture into pieces, and finally threw contents of the drawers onto the floor, all with the intent of creating a lasting impression of NKVD savagery. They buried some of their treasures in little hiding places that Andrew had prepared in the slim hope that someday they might return. The glass china closet in the corner tumbled forward and shattered into fragments. Clothes were dumped in jumbled heaps. Dishes were thrown about and wine bottles broken. Marianne's desk was left open with the lock broken, and papers were tossed all over the room.

Marianne tore the curtains off the rods, and stained them with the blood of the carcasses. Finally, after all the devastation, they stood in silence for a brief moment just inside the doorway to make sure all personal notes, identification and pictures were burned or buried. Andrew turned to her, ""We'll make it! God! How I loved this home!"

After taking one last look at their house, Andrew lit a match to a long cord, which had been soaked in kerosene. It should smolder for about an hour and then reach a full bucket at approximately ten o'clock, giving them enough time to be far away and out of sight. The fire on the cord would start slowly and then erupt into a brighter flame taking the house and the car with it, and more importantly unusable evidence for the NKVD. . Zamolenski was to sorrowfully announce that the Krulls were dead."

Marianne and Andrew packed the wagon and then began the journey, as the children huddled in the front seat with their parents who recited the rosary, one bead at a time. "Our Father, Who art in heaven…"

followed by "Holy Mary, Mother of God, Pray for Us." With each ten Hail Marys, Andrew turned to little Maria and Stefan and said aloud, "God Almighty, watch our children each day. Tomorrow, bring us a brand new sunshine in all its truths. Give us the morning star heading directly eastward towards the border, and best of all, let us be together in the joy of family." Stefan pulled close to Andrew, his voice sadly crying out, "I don't want to die Tata." Andrew reached over, placed his arm on Stefan's shoulder, reassuring him that they intend to outlive the NKVD with all their strength. Then he added, "Mama and Tata are working hard so you and Maria will have a happier tomorrow. No one will harm you, my son. No one! We'll enjoy Zamolina side by side, shoulder to shoulder." For the moment at least, their son was a little less fearful.

They had to pass through Katrynia, where a march honoring the tragic victims was in progress. Anna and Jan Zamolenski were in front of men and women, young and old, bravely chanting, "Long Live Poland!" Another soaring display of patriotism, Marianne, thought, surely a scene that would make the NKVD bristle with rage. Marianne's thoughts were abruptly interrupted when Jan, on horseback, suddenly cut off the wagon, and angrily announced to Andrew and Marianne that Germany and the Soviet Union had reached a Non-Aggression Pact, which meant a disaster for Poland. Outraged, Marianne told him, "They will steal the country before our very eyes because people in authority cannot make bold decisions. We are at war, How many lives must be lost before they come to the obvious conclusion that the Soviets much be crushed? After yesterday's bombing and massacre, we can no longer be paralyzed with indecision. The Communists have shown themselves for what they are for the first time in their twenty year history. The world shall finally see clearly the conspiracy of the two evils." Marianne grew more excited and continued, "Maybe we could gain world opinion and U.S. approval, and then negotiate for peace with Germany against the Soviet Union."

Zamolenski just stared at her. Her argument made perfect sense to anyone willing to see it. However, could these ideas be communicated to a higher level? Zamolenski promised to rush a telegram off to General Ruckemann, and Foreign Minister Josef Beck. He would try to work through channels of the upper diplomatic core. Jan Zamolenski still had connections at those levels, and with the extensive information Marianne supplied, maybe immediate action could be forthcoming.

"General. Rückemann is a brave man, a patriotic Pole," Zamolenski exclaimed, "and he may have the strength of numbers to face the enemy. We will be in touch. We are at the beginning of a great struggle that has no end." He waved good-by to Marianne, Andrew, and the children.

"God be with you always! *Sto Lat!* Never forget you have a Polish heart!"

The memorial procession had stopped at the edge of Katrynia, directly in front of the village bell. The huge crowd was singing *"Święta miłość kochanej ojczyzny"* (Sacred love of the beloved homeland) and Mazurek *Dąbrowskiego* (Poland is not yet Lost). One of the peasants approached the wagon and yelled, "Long live Poland!" as tears streamed down her cheeks. Marianne's heart pounded with each step and bugle call.

Marianne, too, had been transformed. Her once auburn hair had been dyed a dirty dank brown and fell on her face as she sat next to a bald farmer with two ragged children. . The Krulls were gone; the Ludwigs had emerged carrying two flickering fish oil lamps, dimly lighting the road leading east, closer to Pinsk, and much closer to the Soviet- occupied Western Ukraine border.

Stefan clutched Andrew but made no sound. Maria was snugly curled up in Marianne's arms. The dog Basha barked as she zigzagged around the wagon before settling down next to Maria, licking her face as if to make the little one more secure. Maria fell asleep. The wheels of the wagon began to grind slowly.

The transformed peasant family now owned two work horses named Sasha and Tasha, two heads of cattle, four sheep, two goats, a dog, a quilted comforter, two barrels of honey, and Andrew's wood-working tools. Hidden in the comforters and quilts, under the seats and in the wagon bed, were a pair of binoculars, three salted sheep carcasses, one thousand zloty, a compass, peasant clothing, ten fish-oil lamps, one hundred candles, soap, salt, dry sausages, and two sets of identity papers. Inside a third barrel were six guns with one hundred eighty-four rounds of ammunition, along with twenty-two watches, twenty bottles of vodka, and ten thousand rubles. A fourth barrel was filled with lard soap, rock candy, twenty rings of kielbasa, brightly colored folk clothing, and two metal containers, which could be used as stoves, but were stuffed with bullets to use in battle if need be. In the wagon, led by Sasha and two lighted lanterns, they slowly vanished into the darkness.

As the sun rose, Andrew handed the reins to Stefan, whose eyes brightened as he began to direct Sasha. Stefan stood up to see where their home would be. Andrew exclaimed, "We should hurry. There, at the edge of the forest is our home." Maria's blue eyes were alive with joy. Stefan stopped the wagon. Marianne looked at their thatched-roof home.

AUGUST 23, 1939

Von Ribbentrop in the Nazi high command wrote a memo:

VERY URGENT

Moscow, August 23, 1939-8:05 p. m.

No. 204 of August 23

Please advise the Führer at once that the first three-hour conference with Stalin and Molotov has just ended. At the discussion, which moreover, proceeded affirmatively in our sense, it transpired that the decisive point for the final result is the demand of the Russians that we recognize the ports of Libau and Windau as within their sphere of influence. I would be grateful for confirmation before 8 o'clock Nazi time that the Führer is in agreement. The signing of a secret protocol on delimitation of mutual spheres of influence in the whole eastern area is contemplated, for which I declared myself ready in principle.

RIBBENTROP

He received a positive response from the Fuhrer. Toasts in Moscow were being given to Molotov and Stalin for the development in favorable relations between Moscow and Berlin. Stalin wrote to Hitler that the Soviet Government took the new Pact very seriously and that he could guarantee, on his word of honor, that the Soviet Union would not betray its partner.

In the glow of mid-morning sunlight, the Ludwig wagon of hope slowly followed the curling picturesque, winding road to Zamolina, amid the rich fields of barley, potatoes, and wheat mixed with beets and beans. The ox and horse-drawn wagons, belonging to the approximately 650 villagers, stood by the wayside of thatched roof shacks. These dirty grained peasant workers from the field, their muddy, tattered clothes hanging in rags on their bodies, presented a striking portrait of survivors in their final struggle, living on tenacity from season to season.

They were good, decent people who lived on despite a harsh existence. They rose at dawn to the tolling of the village bell and began a day of hunting, fishing, and exhausting labor in the mud. Most followed the natural flow of sunrise, sunset, seasons and festivals without the benefit of clocks. The regional priests, landholders, and mayors, "solty, " presided over school sessions, church meetings, celebrations, and alerted the villagers to dangerous events.

These were people set in their ways, with conflicting political and religious opinions because of the diverse ethnic, political, and religious mix of Polish, Ukrainian, Byelorussians and the minority of Jews who comprised the majority of the Bolshevik leadership. They lived the way they had lived for centuries with no note of the animosities of the present.

Marianne explained to her children how to welcome these good people into their lives.

"When you shake their hands, the customary greeting is "Z-Bogem— God be with you."

The arrival of a "new" family, however, upset the daily routine. In most small European villages a new arrival is an event. One man, usually a self-appointed town crier, spreads the news. However, this wagon- load of a family appeared to be different to the native populace. Something in their manner did not speak of country folk. There was still a bit of polish in stance and gesture as they rode along. Men with wrinkled, weathered faces gave them cold stares. The wagon slowly passed a bearded old-timer, who asked gruffly, "Where are you going?"

Andrew turned on his broadest" hail friend" grin and said "To our new home, over there at the edge of the forest."

The old farmer looked them over suspiciously. Stefan stood up on the wagon seat and with the innocence of youth: "It's nice here. I smell the grass and hear the birds singing. We want to be your friends."

The old man stared at him. Most of the local children weren't this precocious, but were instead shy and a bit withdrawn. The man laughed, finally, liking the serious little boy and said "Good boy. I like that. We need to go fishing when you settle down."

"I love fishing, but I must help Tata do some farming first," answered Stefan.

A short, stocky, crinkly- faced woman with sunburned cheeks and missing teeth called out from the field a bit further off, as they passed her, "Who are you?"

"We are the Ludwigs from west of Warsaw and have come to live here," Andrew proudly answered .Stefan jumped down from the wagon to shake her hand, and little Maria eagerly introduced herself, "Hello…I am Maria. I am three years old. We are happy to meet you."

The woman eyed them suspiciously, but disarmed by the children's easy warmth and respect, she looked straight at Andrew and Marianne, then said loud and clearly, "*Z Bogiem* -May God be with you." Turning to her neighbor, she announced, "It's a nice family." The neighbor promptly rushed off bursting to share the news.

Further down the road, they saw the first home about seventy yards from the village center. This beautiful old, ornate structure sat among stately trees on a well-kept lawn. Marianne whispered to Andrew, "They are the landholders, and in this time of fear and hate, they are probably wary of strangers. Why don't we just wait awhile? I have a feeling they'll come out and welcome us."

A few minutes later, a man and a woman opened their door, and walked cautiously towards the wagon. "So you are the new neighbors. We are Barbara and Wladek Pasternak. We heard about your arrival. Welcome to our village!" Andrew jumped out and shook Pasternak's hand. "I am Andrew Ludwig. My wife is Marianne Ludwig. These are our two children, Stefan and Maria. We are pleased to meet you and be your neighbors."

Pani Pasternak was about forty years old, tall with wavy blond hair and alabaster skin. She looked at Andrew guardedly, taking notice of his aged, work- worn appearance. Marianne got a vague sense that she was threatened by their arrival, yet there was compassion in her deep-set eyes. Pan Pasternak had a powerful physical presence, a thick mustache, a full set of bright white teeth and a deep resonant voice. His hair was the color of straw, and he appeared to be in his mid-forties. At first glance, it seemed strange that he was wearing a heavy jacket on this hot summer day, but upon a closer look, the bulge of a gun was visible in his pocket.

"You are from the Warsaw area." Pani said in a low voice. "I can tell by the hand- woven design on your dress. You will not find anything remotely like central Poland in this region either in its landscape or its people." Pan Pasternak then exclaimed, "It's not every day that we get new neighbors in Zamolina."

"We came here to escape from the Nazi invasion of western Poland," Andrew told him. "We are taking advantage of land that was given and deeded to us out there at the edge of the forest. We may be safer here."

The man looked at Andrew for a moment, obviously struggling to decide how much to reveal. "They are everywhere. The Bolsheviks are up to their usual tricks. We can deal with the Nazis because they are very open, declaring what they want to, with the military; however, the Communists are the real enemy; they have infiltrated our country and then look for ways to slaughter innocent people. We are suspicious of strangers, although they say they are strangers often they masquerade as patriots, and then commit murder. The Bolsheviks are cutting the telegraph wires, and since they have crossed into our country and violated our borders, it is an act of war.! Are you Bolsheviks? he said threateningly.

"No! No! We are Polish Catholics and patriots," Andrew said proudly. "The Communists are worse than the devil. They are Atheists. I saw them murder when I was a border guard so I know what they can do"

Pasternak was enraged by the acts of internal NKVD terrorists and explained, that in a village about 25 kilometers northwest of Pinsk, the Communists murdered the mayor a day before the "Luwigs" arrived. . Lewandowski, a close friend , never had a chance. They found his bloody body in a ditch, with an ax through the center of his skull. He had a note stuck to his chest saying: ENEMY OF THE PEOPLE! He was a Polish patriot, fierce anti-Communist, and landholder and that is why they killed him. Also a week ago, the mayor of Zamolina, Kowalski, delivered a speech to the peasants, which the Communists immediately deemed treasonous. He was named "an enemy of the people" and given a warning. Mayor Kowalski swiftly went into hiding, but he was found several days later, executed with the same note pinned to his chest. Pasternak went on to say, "These are two ugly episodes in a short 48-hour period that should tell you much about how safe our village is. You would be safer with the Nazis than living here among the Bolsheviks. There are also reports of Communist activities east of Janow. Katrynia was attacked, schools burned, and teachers butchered from Vilnius to Groden."

Marianne began to think of her own note. Had that been the mob's intention outside the school? How desperate were these activists? The note, she realized, was meant to be pinned to her bloodied blouse.

Pasternak's voice jolted her back to reality. "Your lives are at risk here. We are near Pinsk, a center of Communist activity. They kill peasants as routinely as they kill landholders. You were safer in central Poland. We are on the main road to Moscow, an important route for them. The Soviets have invaded Poland, which is an act of war, and what are those bastards in Krakow, France, Britain and Warsaw doing about it? Nothing! They have abandoned us. We have no choice but to fight our battles alone," he snarled. "Can you fight?"

Andrew and Marianne were shocked at such explicit descriptions; the children became very frightened, although Maria, at three, did not understand the words completely, but reacted to the anger and fear of the adults in front of her.

Andrew finally spoke." I have been in the military and even with only farm tools I will defend my home and country".

Barbara recognized the fright of the children and turned to little Maria, who was snuggling close to Marianne. She said gently to her. "My name is Barbara. You are such a sweet little girl. Tell me your name again."

"Maria, Maria Ludwig. I am the daughter of Andrew and Marianne Ludwig. Do you want to ask me more questions?"

"Yes, I do. Your face looks a little dirty, but where did you get those pretty eyes and that wonderful smile?"

"My face is dirty because we drove all night and day. My Mama tells me that I have Tata's eyes and I got his smile too. The rest of me is like Mama. Pani Pasternak broke into a delighted chuckle.

"How old are you?"

"I am going on four."

"You, your Tata, Mama and little brother must come to visit us," Pani said.

Andrew responded, "Thank you. You are welcome to come to our home as well. We look forward to sharing some bread. Marianne makes the best babka in Karpathia."

"Why don't you all join us Sunday, for Harvest Mass at *Towlicza.* A priest will bless our fields for the season, and it will give you a chance to meet some of the community's landholders."

"We would be privileged. May God bless us this week" said Andrew.

"You will certainly need God's blessing, new neighbor. You have a lot of work ahead. That shack used to be a hunting cabin owned by a count. He sold the land and forest to the government so that the people could hunt, fish, trap and settle here. The farmer who lived there left in a hurry about six months ago. His crops could be salvaged, but they do need a lot of care if you want to have some food on the table this winter. It is too far off the road for our workers to have looked after your house, but you do have some good land. No one will bother you. Between the road and your home, there is tall grass for hay, also there is brush that needs to be cleared, but luckily, you have a neighbor, Varya. He has a good plow, and he will help you. He works for Makowski, the largest landholder in the area. Varya's wife, Luba, is our village healer with natural remedies for the sick. Florence Makowski is the mid-wife and caregiver. There is a doctor in Pinsk, which is about seven to ten miles away, but I wouldn't go there. The road is treacherous since Communist agents are on the march and getting help from Pinsk and are alarmingly close to Zamolina. You are coming into their line of fire. Be careful!"

Andrew thanked the kind man for the warning and information, slapped the reins on Sasha's back, and the wagon slowly moved off across the muddy fields and tall grass to reach the family's "new home." From a distance, the "new" house looked like a cozy farmhouse nestled in a field of waving grass. However, as they drew nearer they saw a rundown, shabby, dirty peasant shack, covered with pigeon droppings and dirt and a manure pile next to it.

They carefully approached the old stone house, and Andrew pushed the door wide open. The first room they entered was filthy, vermin- infested and not fit for living. The children started sneezing and coughing, their eyes watering from the stench. The house was over a hundred years old, and had morphed from a farmhouse to a hunting lodge and then to a ruin. Originally, it had been a Polish peasant dwelling, which had the barn attached directly to the living quarters. In the winter, the stabled animals provided heat, and in summer, the earthen floor in the stone barn kept it cool. The living area, in this case, at the far end, had an entry door opposite the main road. Windows were on either side of the house, one of which gave a clear view to the town square of Janow barely 400 meters away across the main road. A firepot, without a chimney, was centered in the original living space. Under the roof, the meat and sausages had been smoked on hooks in the rafters above. Behind the main "room" were beds built into the walls. Hinged wooden doors had once kept the night air out of these small pockets halfway up the wall. Hunters had abused the house for years, so there were bottles and debris everywhere. Mold and mildew were the byproducts of these crude living quarters. Marianne, Andrew and the children, used to middle class comforts and cleanliness, polished floors and curtains, were horrified at the daunting cleanup task ahead.

Andrew, however, was not disheartened, for he had experienced far worse. He sent Marianne and Maria out for a walk around the grounds as he and Stefan started cleaning up the mess. .

"Enjoy the scent of pines and God's gift of nature" he said." Stefan and I have work to do. I will get my tools. Give us a few hours, and you will hardly recognize this place". Andrew kept up his usual optimistic chatter. "We will have a safe, clean home."

Marianne planted kisses on their cheeks and with Maria in her arms, walked off into the forest.. Andrew and Stefan quickly took a shovel and broom, first cleared and spread the manure from the pile outside the door around the garden to the back of the house.

They worked feverishly and when Andrew finally called them back, the little thatched roofed farmhouse had its door attached, and its stone floor cleaned and scrubbed. The hearth around the fire pit had been washed down, and firewood was neatly stacked next to it. Although there was not much that they could do in a short time, plans were made to whitewash the walls and to repair the windows. Andrew said, "Stefan and I have a surprise for you both. We found and planted two rose bushes, one white, one red, the colors of our Polish flag, on each side of our home. Next year, there will be many red and white roses blooming brightly, and two years from now may there be a thousand flourishing in our garden opening their buds to greet us at dawn".

"This is so beautiful, my Andrew and Stefan" Marianne said proudly. "Our new home will bear the hope of tomorrow".

Marianne and Maria had discovered an area with a hidden stream buried from view underneath the tall pine trees in the forest. It had crystal clear cold water. Inside the grove of trees was a bare spot where the light of the sun pierced through the high branches. Feathery ferns lined the natural floor of clearing. They thought that in the evening, it could be a private family place. They all decided to have their first meal as a family under the stars and pines. They brought a blanket, a fish oil lantern and Andrew added cherry flavored vodka to the cold supper that Marianne prepared. .After a quiet and thoughtful meal, far from the starched damask table linens of home, Andrew said, "I am glad that we decided to come here. It is not so much that we chose such an unlikely place in this remote corner of Polesie, but it is our hearts that led us here. There is hope. There is life. It is not just a new home but a new beginning that makes each day even more special".

AUGUST 24, 1939

In a final effort to avoid war, President Franklin Delano Roosevelt sent a personal appeal to Adolf Hitler, asking him to address the Polish issue through diplomatic channels. The British parliament met in a special session and voted the Chamberlain government almost dictatorial powers to deal with the Danzig-Polish crisis. At the same time, British and Polish representatives signed a mutual assistance pact. The British government wanted to demonstrate its support of Poland to deter a Nazi invasion and the Polish government began to call up reserves.

Under Andrew's guidance, daily chores were organized. Other than the morning milking, and water gathering, food had to be produced so weeds were being pulled out and potatoes, cabbage and carrots were carefully cultivated. They created a crude bedroom from the "holes in the wall" and planned to finish a better set of rooms from the existing one in the future. There was a tumbled down old shed and out- house behind the house as well. These buildings needed shoring up; however, with the new work the old appearance of a poor peasant's hovel needed to be maintained to protect the "Ludwigs" from any intruders or "tattlers."

While Andrew viewed the six hectares as if it was his own little kingdom, Marianne planned to stay out of sight so that nobody would recognize her. She hoped to attend a Defense Conference scheduled for late August. Her appearance, as a representative of the educated class, had been arranged as usual by Ludwig, who felt that her presence there would be a voice of the people who could be silenced by either force invading the country. Early in the morning, she continued her cleaning chores aided by Maria, with as much attention as a three year old could generate. Quite suddenly, she became dizzy, with her stomach churning. She ached all over. Nevertheless, she continued to work, but then broke out into a cold sweat, convulsed with pain as if some kind of demon was controlling her body. Feeling horribly weak, unable to take another step, she staggered, then lay down on the floor and began to vomit. At the same time, she had a serious bout of diarrhea. She prayed, "Dear God, please help me."

She called Maria to fetch Tata and begged him to quickly find Varya's wife Luba---the village healer. Maria dashed out; before long, Luba was at Marianne's side. Maria held her mother's hand while Andrew massaged her neck and arms. Luba, the kind gentle woman with the wrinkled cheeks, ordered Andrew and Stefan to return to their chores. "Go back to work. You need to put bread on the table."

Luba warned Marianne, "This treatment may hurt, but believe me, it works. I learned it from my grandfather. It is a virtue to listen to our parents and grandparents." She placed a large rock into the flames, in the fire, and wrapped the heated rock tightly in a wet towel and pressed it to her patient's feet; she then moved it slowly back and forth between her thighs and then to her back and spine. Marianne screamed in pain from the heat, which traveled through her skin. She screamed until finally no sound came out. Luba piled blankets and clothing over her until she started to sweat. Marianne was completely helpless on the farm house floor. Luba washed her with a soft cloth and said "It will be over soon. Tomorrow you will be in less pain." Marianne turned on her other side and pulled herself up as Luba cradled her head as she thirstily drank one cup, then a second and then a third. The cramps in her stomach gradually lessened, yet there was still pain when she tried to stand up. Marianne gratefully said to Luba, "Thank you with all my heart. Gratitude is good for the soul."

"It is a miserable feeling, I know," Luba replied, "you will get better and better each day. Remember, you have a friend here. You are one of us. I'll hold your hand for a few minutes, and then Maria will do the rest." Luba slowly massaged her palms with her work-hardened fingers and then said, "Your hands are so smooth."

After she left, Marianne began to worry that word might travel around the village about the mysterious family that lived in the shadows of the forest, but before very long, she fell into a troubled sleep. Two days later, she slowly began to regain her strength. The herbal vapors that Luba left behind boiled day and night on the fire and they seemed to be a cure- all and disinfectant of the foul air.

By the end of the week, Marianne was able to resume some of her chores. When Luba returned to check on her patient, Marianne asked Luba if there was a way to get the neighbors to help her family build a wall to divide the rear room into two bedrooms, and to help repair the outer shed. Marianne needed to establish a bond and camaraderie with her neighbors, and at the same time she wanted to keep a home, which would appear to be the home of a poor itinerant farmer and although ugly on the outside, would be clean on the inside.

The men of Zamolina had already accepted Andrew as one of their own: a loyal man of the soil, ready with a pitchfork to defy any adversaries or to sling hay into the barn. Andrew's faith in God, his love of his Marianne, and the warmth of a family coupled with his work ethic gave him some of the happiest moments in his life.

*The **London Times:** wrote of* "Herr Hitler's" desire to promote better understanding between Germany, Britain and France as long as they do not get in the way of what he considers to be a "just settlement" in Poland.. The.Tarnow Rail station attack was a bombing by a Nazi agent at Tarnow, Poland. It occurred on the night of August 28,1939, when a time bomb planted by the agent exploded killing 20 people and wounding 35.

On this day, Varya and Adam Makowski visited the Ludwig farm. Stefan was Luba's husband, a Ukrainian Catholic, angular faced, short, stocky, and broad-shouldered. Adam Makowski, a tall man with a pale weathered face, and a large forehead, smiled and welcomed the family. He was the largest landholder in the area,, owning more acreage than Pan Pasternak. Pan Varya was Makowski's loyal foreman and confidant. Ukrainians accounted for approximately 40 % of the village population. They had a bitter past with the Poles over disputed land rights, but remarkably they were living together peacefully in the village. Marianne greeted them, *"Dzien dobry*, Pan Makowski! Wladek Pasternak told us of you and your wife, Florence. Luba worked a miracle for which I am eternally grateful." Andrew then announced that his wife was the best cook a man could ever wish for and Marianne added, "I love to cook and how happy I would be for us to share a good meal." Andrew then invited them to sit down for a drink. They accepted a traditional Likier Truskawkowky (cherry vodka) and before leaving, formally invited the family to the summer village festival. They embraced with affection, and a feeling that trust was developing.

The Warsaw government ordered the Polish army to mobilize. Drastic measures were taken to stop any possible sabotage by pro-Nazis. Foreign Minister. By 4.30 PM., all Polish towns were covered with posters summoning all men up to the age of 40 to report for enlistment.

AUGUST 30, 1939

Andrew awoke with a renewed surge of optimism. He took a deep breath, gazed out at the landscape, looking at the thriving plants surrounded by chirping birds. The same field, just a short time ago, was buried in weeds and rocks, and driven by neglect, showed the fruits of labor and tender care. Long ribbons of potatoes and cabbage plants sprouted above the ground. Although the news of Beck's call up for men for the military had sped through the town, Andrew had served his time, and, furthermore, no longer was registered after the house was burned down in Janow. The major worry now was the preservation of the crops for food. If the Bolsheviks arrived, and the populace was sure they would, strict quotas would be enforced to create a starving and helpless populace. Marianne and Andrew had carefully planned to hide food from the harvest, deep in the swampy woods of Polesie. Fortunately, Andrew's troubled childhood gave him an intimate knowledge of survival and storage in the wild. The careful plans had been made before the fall, and the Ludwigs were going to the village folk festival celebration.

These good people, of this village, still held to the old ways, centuries of celebrating the end of field labor, and knowing that thanks given to God and the Blessed Virgin for the crops will assure bread on the table for the winter. The villagers were to gather in the town square, in traditional costume for *Dożynki*, which would include singing, feasting and drinking. Most importantly, there would be a thanksgiving service for the good crops. Andrew had taken his carved Black Madonna from the family altar and planned to offer it for use in the ceremony. In some parts of Poland woven wreaths and produce would be taken, with pilgrims, to Czestochowa and the miraculous Black Madonna there. Andrew believed that his icon copy of the Madonna would bring prayers to ensure survival in the coming times.

Traditional costume was required, and Stefan and Maria looked skeptically at the old wooden box, which had been brought along from Janow. Maria's dress came first, and Marianne' emotions welled to the surface, as she saw what had been her costume lovingly given to her by her father, which Maria now wore . As she twirled about the room, in her layered red skirt striped with yellow and green, the little girl laughed and posed. Stefan put on a pair of knee pants and a brightly colored vest, over a white shirt and a sash. Marianne had a flowing skirt with a black jacket and a hat, which covered all of her hair, the trailing scarf gave her a very different aspect. She looked like a peasant. "How do I look?" Stefan asked as he stamped his feet, performing his idea of an intricate folk dance.

"You look like a toy soldier," Maria teased.

For the moment, all thoughts of destruction of country were distant. As Marianne looked at her happy children all the misery, poverty and tragic times vanished momentarily into the creation of this fairy tale family.

Andrew, decked out in the traditional men's garb of the Lubin region, took Marianne's hand and murmured, "I love you.".

Happily, the peasant wagon drove the short distance onto a grassy patch near the Village Square. The other families had already arrived, all dressed similarly. The charming folk scene was marred only by a small cadre of Makowski's family guards, lined up on the perimeter of the square. The villagers still eyed the Ludwigs with some suspicion; however, Pasternak and Makowski showed trust. Pasternak led the ceremonies and prayers. There were six families, including the Pasternaks and Makowskis, whose dress demonstrated their position as the ruling elite of the region. At the end of the ceremonies, everyone stood at attention and emotionally sang the Polish national anthem complete with tears of joy:

Poland has not perished yet

So long as we still live

That which alien force has seized

We at saber point shall retrieve

The Makowskis had set a traditional feast, with an abundance of the food of the Polish peasant; whole grain loaves of bread, sausages, and baked goods, traditional dishes, accompanied by vodka, coffees and fresh milk filled trestle tables. The children were happily eating the wonderful desserts while Florence Makowski gave presents to each one. Stefan got a *pilka nożna* (soccer ball) and Maria a colorful doll. Andrew emotionally said: "We are privileged to be in your company."

"It is nice to be in your company, too," Florence called loudly over the beginning of music provided by a village band. Instruments had appeared as if from nowhere, and the musicians, frequently lubricated by the vodka next to their chairs, began to play the happy raucous music of the countryside. Soon everyone was happily singing along. Marianne loved watching the dance that had begun, as her children stamped their feet, and circled along with the others. Barbara was staring longingly. She was quietly weeping. Marianne draped an arm around her and asked what was wrong. Barbara answered quietly "Your children are beautiful, Pani Ludwig. The village is my family for I have no children. Could you please allow Stefan and Maria to visit us?" Marianne assured her that they would.

The town was vibrating with rhythm and joy. Music and laughter were everywhere, skirts were swirling, boots clomping, and polka music reverberated throughout the square. People were sitting with linked arms, swaying and singing along, only to be interrupted by an occasional drink of vodka or homemade beer. Toasts were offered and the happy children danced in small circles.

Pasternak, quite suddenly, interrupted the music and called everyone together. His sad face and grim solemnity was an abrupt reversal of the joy and love that had reverberated through the small square just moments ago He announced, "I want to let you all know what was reported this morning on the telegraph and my wireless". The once warming sun now transformed into a harsh light of reality. The warm peasant colors looked garish and ridiculous in the square. Pasternak continued sorrowfully, "More good voices have been permanently silenced. Here is the latest sad news. Yesterday in a nearby village, over a hundred leading citizens, mostly Polish teachers, priests, doctors and landowners were executed or imprisoned. The NKVD shouted 'Down with Clean Hands.' Friday night, over sixty Polish men and women near Vilnius, were marched before a firing squad and systematically executed while others were 'sent away.' Although mobilization was ordered to protect Poland from attack by the Nazis, I have been advised that eastern Poland is going to be the next target of the NKVD agents. Some railroad centers are now guarded by the border patrols. Most of the mobilization forces are heading westward to defend our western boundaries against Germany; therefore, we are on our own. Several towns and villages near Lwów, Kobryn, Vilnius and Janow, where rail lines and the air force are situated, will soon be under attack. Although, the authorities still call it an internal matter, we are at war with the Soviet Communists!"

Pasternak's voice was angry and tense as he bellowed "It's the Soviet Communists. Let's not lose sight of who the enemy is! It all began yesterday in the west. General Rückemann with his 20,000 soldiers was to protect us here. Unfortunately, we are at war, and no one is doing anything about it."

Marianne struggled to suppress her anger and her intuitive urge to speak out. She was taken by the image of these happy folk celebrating in contrast to the Soviet rape of all that was good and ethical. Although she knew they had violated the borders, and were presently identifying persons to torture, which would lead to the inevitable annihilation of intelligentsia-- soldiers, officers, teachers, intellectuals, professionals, and landowners, she also knew that carrying guns right now would not resolve fears and ensuing danger. She cautiously stepped next to Pasternak, thinking how much of her past could she reveal to these village people? Her resolve to do "something" took over. She said, "We must store food equipment, tools, honey, and warm clothes; our own arms may save more lives. Sir, it will get worse before it gets better. There will be no peace with the Soviet Union. We cannot risk losing our leadership. The landholders have to survive. The loyalty of the peasants and Ukrainians is critical to the security of our nation. We need to survive! Ready your pitchforks to dig in and hold our own ground."

Pasternak said, "We will protect ourselves. We need to act now. Winter is coming and storing food away makes sense." He put his arm around Marianne, who was standing next to him. She felt that a mantle of leadership in this community had somehow landed on her as well as Pasternak. Slowly, the people, including the Ludwigs, drifted off to their houses carrying the burden of a fear-filled future.

On August 31, 1939, a small group of Nazi operatives, dressed in Polish uniforms seized the Gleiwitz station and broadcast a short anti-Nazi message in Polish. Their goal was to make the attack and the broadcast appear to be the work of anti-Nazi Polish saboteurs. They then took an unknown prisoner from one of their concentration camps, dressed him in a Polish uniform, took him to the town and then shot him. The staged scene with the dead prisoner dressed in a Polish uniform was supposed to appear as a Polish attack against a Nazi radio station. Hitler followed this attack with a message that said "all the political possibilities were exhausted to eliminate by peaceful means a situation on its eastern border, which is unbearable for Germany, "I have decided on a solution by using force." He said. "The attack on Poland is to proceed along the lines of the preparations for operation 'White', with modifications resulting from the now almost completed strategic movement of the army. There will be no change in the goal of the operation and the way the tasks are divided. Day of attack – 1 September 1939 Hour of attack – 4:45. This time is also for operations in the Gdingen-Danzig bay and the Dirschau Bridge. In what regards the west, the responsibility for the beginning of hostilities has to be unmistakably placed with England and France.... The neutrality of Holland, Belgium, Luxembourg and Switzerland of which we have been assured, is to be carefully preserved."

Marianne awakened to the sunlight streaming through the one small window of her newly renovated bedroom. She stared at the rough, freshly whitewashed walls inside of the roof beams above her head. The neighbors had helped convert the interior, at least to decent living quarters. They had repaired the outer shed, and an old manure cart that they found. Marianne was thinking of the consequences of her decision to leave today for Zamolenski's Defense Conference. She would need to remain in peasant clothing and would have to use little Maria as a companion and cover for her journey back to Janow, the town in which she supposedly had burned to death. Her father had given her money for travel and bribes, and this was the morning of departure. She feared the onset of Hitler's invasion, but what she feared more, was an unannounced Bolshevik invasion. Maybe she would never see her family again.

She leaned over and softly whispered to Andrew "I love you so much."

She wanted to be held tightly, and feel the comforting warmth of his body. "I need your passionate good-bye," she said as she pulled her night dress over her head. Although still groggy with sleep, he responded. Soon, they were physically devouring each other, sinking into the depths of love, temporarily forgetting their fears. For a wonderful moment, they threw all cares away, passionately proclaiming their bond.

"I'll see you at St. Stanislaus Church my dear Andrew, I am sorry that I have to travel with Maria, but I need to look like any other traveling peasant with a child. I feel guilty using her as cover, and I am very afraid."

"We shall all meet in Janow." Andrew whispered back, "Stefan and I will see you tomorrow at Stanislaus. Nothing will stop us! This coming war will affect children as well so pay no mind to your fears."

. Marianne woke Maria, while Andrew dressed, then went out to harness Sasha to the small manure wagon. Andrew would take the other horse and the wagon. It was less of a risk for them to take separate paths.

She thought of the safety of separate travel and then to meet inside the St. Stanislaus Church the next day at 10:00 AM. for Mass.

"*Z-Bogem*. Be careful. I love you,"

Andrew whispered. "I love you, too. Take care, my little one."

She climbed onto the wagon, waved good-bye, and soon moved into the darkness of early dawn. As Maria pressed close to her, Marianne began to grapple with all that loomed ahead. As the wagon drew up the muddy gravel road, they soon passed into daylight. The old road in front was crowded with automobiles and carts heading eastward. With each passing hour, they saw more and more of them, slowly or as quickly as they could, head eastward toward the Russian border. Polish citizens were fleeing to what they saw as safety in the Soviet Union. Marianne shivered as she thought of the cruel destiny awaiting them as they joined the enemy. They were betraying their country. Marianne became angrier as she neared her destination for she realized that the Communists, no doubt, had knowledge of the time and place of the Nazis attack. These people were deserting the defense of their homeland. An old man, gray-faced, stopped his ragged cart and warned "Go east, Pani, go east! You are heading into disaster if you go to Janow." He waved a sorrowful farewell.

Marianne urged Sasha on as they continued their journey westward. When they finally reached Janow, Maria, very frightened, shrieked, "Oh, No! No! Look there is our old home". They stared at the burnt frame, standing alone on a hill. It was all that remained of their beautiful, treasured home. The child began to cry. A flood of memories sadly unfolded as they both fixed their eyes on the site.

The presence of a ragged manure cart with a woman and child at the Zamolenski estate appeared odd to the armed guards lining the perimeter. So many passersby stopped to beg for food or water; therefore, a patrol halted Marianne and Maria at the edge of the road adjacent to their old house. Landholders from Polesie, Lithuania, and Latvia, were entering with their own guards, followed by a mixture of leaders from Belorussia and western Ukraine, Marianne identified herself and as expected they were sent to the back entrance, where Anna and Jan Zamolenski greeted them. When they commented on the tattered appearance of their visitors, Marianne said: "We may live in secrecy, but we are always together in our hearts. We will do whatever it takes to survive." Zamolenski, not wasting a minute said quietly: "We need to get started. The strain of the past days had to be quite difficult for you and Maria. We will begin the conference when you are ready."

Maria and Marianne circled through the back way, along a garden path, past servants who did not recognize them in disguise. They had to be   constantly alert for the KGB spy system, working with the Nazi Gestapo Secret Police, looking for information on the Zamolenski estate.

Maria was parked contentedly in the kitchen, still in her peasant rags. Marianne entered the immense hall. A man raised his hand in greeting and announced for all to hear, "How proud we are! You kept your promise. You are the hero of St. Andrews."

Marianne was taken aback by the general reception; however, she was the only one living in the "trenches." She could see, from her vantage point in Polesie the advancing Russian Bolshevik menace. The small assemblage of very powerful men asked her to talk about what she saw. Her heart beat faster as the crowd fell silent.

Nervously she began: "We are about to enter difficult times. We must unite for our coming struggle with two rulers who want only our total destruction.   Hitler's message to all, two weeks ago was clear:: 'Kill, without pity or mercy, all men, women and children of Polish descent. Only in this way, can we obtain the "Living Space" we need. Stalin's version here in the east was similar: "There is no Poland, now or ever. All peoples shall be annihilated."

"We are afraid, uncertain, and alone. Where can we hide? A Nazi battleship is docked at Gdansk, ready to fire its guns at innocent civilians. The Soviets have forty divisions ready to strike here in the east."

Marianne continued to describe the Nazi menace, joined with its fear of Communists and Bolshevik Jews. "The Bolsheviks," she said, "would have problems with the deeply religious and patriotic Polish peasants. We have to prevent Poland's destruction. We have to convince the world that it must pursue a policy that will not let the Bolsheviks succeed. Poles can save lives if we stay united, and spread the word of truth to Germany before the devastation is so enormous that it would be too late for our salvation."

"Your friend and colleague," my father once said: 'To live to a noble end is the love of the future, to fight is the honor to achieve a noble victory. There is a noble end. Those who are not willing to die for their country are not fit to lead it. "

Marianne pointed out the need for support from the peasants, who must be armed and fed. She said that the answer for food came from her little farm in Polesie. She saw that a small economic system based on barter already existed within the communities. The woods and marshes of the district were perfect for underground armies and guerilla warfare. She continued with her plan, almost a fantasy, hidden forest centers for schools, food , medicine and supply distribution, and for the salvation of the priests who inspire the minds, hearts, and repair our souls.

Breathlessly, and with no regard for the reaction of the men in the room, Marianne rushed on headlong. She gave an odd appearance of a statuesque peasant woman dressed in rags, yet speaking in the eloquent style of the educated. The room appeared to be larger, and the men in it stared at her, knowing she was speaking the truth and striking at the core of the problem, in a very different way than they had heard in diplomatic circles.

She was not restating the obvious, but putting forth solutions. She suggested a government in exile with Zamolenski as the leader. Since war was moments away, and they were three months from winter, the immediate needs had to be met first to prevent families from starving and freezing to death. An underground government, economic, educational and military system needed to be devised. The tragedy, she went on, would be blamed by world journalists on the eventual Polish demise by natural causes, as Durante of the *New York Times* did with the deaths of peasants in Russia.

Marianne reached the end of her impassioned plea. She not only suggested a solution to the problem, but also a need to cause awareness of the Polish plight to the rest of the world. She finished with a quote from Tata Ludwig: "All knowledge is political. We need to spread the facts worldwide, apply knowledge for good and develop philosophical constituencies."

. Marianne looked around the room at the startled faces, stirred from their complacency, and she was quite relieved to see how frightened they were. These men were heroic, but she guessed many of them would not survive this war.

As the men settled down to talk and smoke cigars, she left to use the telephone to call her father. When she finally reached him, Ludwig sounded somber and sad since he knew that Krakow, one of the most historical and beautiful cultural centers of the world, was the principal Nazi military target. He told Marianne that Stephany, her sister, and Joseph her brother, were considered potential leaders and were marked for extermination by the Bolsheviks. His gallows humor resonated in Marianne's mind as he joked bravely about his own conspicuous presence, "In the end, we are always alone" he said, "for there is no right time to die." She told him of her meeting, and her idea of hidden enclaves to store food and for the creation of a sort of underground resistance movement.

Her father continued, saying that he believed that the Nazi onslaught would come on the next day. The idea of an enclave for a safe haven was good, but underground tactics including guerilla warfare would only be effective after the invasion; The Polish people would suffer from both sides, since the Soviets were aiding the Nazi onslaught.

Sadly and slowly, he said to his loving daughter, "It is too late for me, but I have full faith that we shall meet you, Andrew, Stefan and Maria at the Gates of Heaven."

Marianne could not find words to express her horror and fear. However, her father became serious and professionally directive. He said, "I have been chosen for a special mission. I cannot yet discuss it, particularly on the phone. My code name is "Zebra." Zamolenski will know how to reach me. I am neither a hero, nor a fool, just a human being, who wants to do his best to preserve our country and most of all, our honor. Please take care of my affairs in the event that this is a one-way mission. Stephany and Joseph are joining me here in Krakow. Please remember to tell your children that the fundamental human spirit that lives in all of us, is necessary for a favorable outcome. I will keep your picture close to my heart. Say farewell and love to Andrew, Maria and Stefan. I will think of you all while we battle against the enemy. I love you, Marianne, my dear daughter."

"I love you my father. Is that all?"

"Yes, that is all, Marianne…that is all!"

As he said goodbye to her, she prayed silently: "Oh God, --- please help us. Please help him!" She feared that she might never see him again, and that only God could take care of Ludwig, Stephany and Joseph."

After Marianne hung up the phone, she found a corner of a dark room and started to sob uncontrollably; Dear Tata, she thought. You have given great meaning to my life. You are my treasure. Your soul is my soul. May God watch over you---till we meet again. There is more to tomorrow than the dawn of September 1st."

SEPTEMBER 1,1939

The Nazi SS took twelve prisoners out of Buchenwald Prison Camp, and, drove them to the Polish border where they were dressed in Polish Army uniforms and forced to take poison. The corpses were then shot. An SS Officer, broadcast in Polish to Germany declared that the supposed soldiers had come to invade Germany. The SS fled. Hitler presented the Reichstag with this invasion and responded that the Wehrmacht was returning fire at 5:45 AM. The reality of the response was a carefully planned and highly mobile attack code-named *Fall Weiss* (Case White) which had been planned earlier by General Field Marshall Walther von Brauchitsch, Nazi land, sea, and air forces were moving rapidly into Poland, whose army in 1939 was totally unprepared for the new style of warfare. Poland, like many armies, had large cavalry forces, useless against armored divisions. . What modern aircraft the Polish Air Force had was caught on the ground.

England and France knew that they could not sacrifice Poland as they had Czechoslovakia. On September 3, 1939, the Allies declared war against National Socialist Germany. The declaration did not save Poland. Lodz was about to fall and Krakow fell on September 6. The fort at Danzig fell on September 7, after a week of direct fire from Nazi battleships.

At dawn, Stefan and Andrew perched on the front seat of the wagon. Usually, Stefan and Andrew loved going to Janow. Sundays had been the high point of the week for the family when they lived there. They would join the Zamolenskis, dressed in their best clothing for mass at St. Stanislaus, which, on a nice day, glowed in the early morning sun. The town's market square had a fresh clean look to it, as they walked on the cobbled stone streets to church. However, today was different. Both father and son were dressed in tattered rags.

Andrew, although outwardly carefree, was churning inside for his fear of the family's safety. Nazi mobilization had just begun. NKVD agents were traveling east on the main road on their way to a strategic air force and railroad centers. Stefan had fallen asleep under the comforter in the wagon. As each hour passed, Andrew saw increasing numbers of soldiers in autos heading westward near the town of Ratwyn toward

89

Janow, passing hundreds of civilians riding , walking , pushing carts loaded with household possessions eastward toward the Soviet Union.

At one point Andrew saw red shirted NKVD men and women along the edge of the forest, downing electric poles and slashing wires. When the squads of soldiers arrived, they all scurried towards the forest. "Traitors! Bastards" he thought, watching them in the distance, shaking his head in disgust, wondering how anyone in his right mind could possibly help the Soviets and Nazis undermine the mobilization.

Andrew determinedly continued his journey despite the menacing signs of military vehicles moving in every direction. He finally turned off the main road and followed a well-marked map, showing safe, but icy back roads to Janow.

Marianne, who spent the night with the Zamolenskis, couldn't sleep because of worry. She feared for her father's life, and now, until she met Andrew and Stefan, she feared for theirs. She prayed that nothing would stop Andrew and Stefan from meeting them at St. Stanislaus's High Mass. Nothing! There was a loud knock on her door, and, Anna, still clad in her nightgown, said angrily "WAR! Those Nazi bastards are bombing cities! Polish skies are swarming with thousands and thousands of planes dropping bombs, blasting buildings, bridges and airports. The Nazi troops have crossed the western Polish border. They are bombing Krakow, Warsaw, Danzig, Poznan, and Lodz. The attack started at 5:45 a.m., Danzig time! Innocent civilians were massacred!"

Her knees buckled, and Marianne caught her breath as they both started to cry, holding each other in terror and fear. Marianne sobbed: "Krakow! Warsaw! My Ludwig and Stephany……. They could be lying dead or suffocated under the rubble at this very moment. Please God, watch over them."

A moment of realization brought Marianne back to the tasks.

"Andrew and! Stefan! My God! Maria! We need to go! Anna, please dress her!"

They wakened Maria who sleepily asked: "Mama, why?"

"We need to hurry! Tata and Stefan are expecting us at St. Stanislaus."

"You shouldn't go! The Nazis and the Soviets certainly will bomb the road leading from Zamolina to Janow. It's the mobilization route," exclaimed Anna.

Then, through the large window of the bedroom, they saw a formation of German bombers flying low over the estate. Anna was terrified "My God, they are going to bomb us! You can't go! Those are Nazi planes ready to attack Janow!"

"No! Those are bombers heading to the east of Janow. Andrew and Stefan are on their way to meet us. Maybe they are heading for the central rail station there. "

They hurriedly dressed and rushed out. Maria started to cry and scream "Tata, Stefan!" as she clung to Marianne's dress. "Mama, I am scared!"

Marianne raced to harness the horse to the manure cart, hoping that they could get safely to Janow to meet Andre and Stefan. She prayed hard for their safety. Anna hugged her tearfully as she whispered good bye, and said she would pray for their safety. Zamolenski, meanwhile gave orders for the guards to secure the area. Guests and servants scrambled into basements or any hiding place that they could find. He stopped our wagon, stalled in the chaos of people running." What are you doing?" he pleaded.

"I must meet Andrew and Stefan at St. Stanislaus."

"You can't go! It is too dangerous. Andrew will find his way back here. "You need to get to a bunker."

"Absolutely not!" Maria, terrified, held tightly to her hand.

"Mama, where's Tata? Mama, don't let go."

Zamolenski ordered her to stay.

She replied: "Crossing Janow is a greater risk than remaining here. I must leave. We will meet right at the center of town. It is better than waiting. I will see you in two weeks at Sunday Mass."

Zamolenski gave in: "I'll pray for your safety. God speed!"

"May God protect you. Let Ludwig know that we are safe!" Jan Zamolenski would always remain in her memory as one of the greatest men she had ever known, next to her Ludwig and Andrew.

She took the reins, heaved them against Sasha's rump, and pushed Maria to hide under the front seat of the wagon for safety , as they went out of the gate down the road toward St. Stanislaus.

The images of the ride to Janow would stay with her during odd moments, later in days to come and in vivid nightmares. Bombs were falling on Masowsza village, where her home once was on a hillside. About three hundred yards from there, a farmhouse was in flames. A young boy had blood streaming out of a back wound. He got weaker and slowed down but continued to move forward. His father caught him and held him while he screamed at the planes overhead. The picture of anguish and despair was branded into her consciousness. She could feel the tremor of the battered earth. She could see severely wounded people diving into muddy puddles. The road nearer to Janow was in shambles. Unseen screaming, terrified voices cried out, and people dragged brothers and sisters along the ground begging them to move faster into the safer ditches and trenches.

The rumblings from Janow grew louder. Sirens split the air with a deafening whine. Everything was being attacked. Marianne wept and turned her head steering away from a dead child lying spread-eagled on a roadside. "Why in God's name are they killing civilians?" she thought. Death and destruction arrived very suddenly; every explosion renewed her fear that Andrew and Stefan would be killed at any moment. "Please, Lord. Do not let these creatures destroy the people I love the most." She kept depending on Andrews's strong will and survival skills,

Andrew and Stefan were watching the same bombers as they came lower in front of their route as they began to attack the city. The wagon rocked sideways as the horse was startled by a hissing noise and the thunderous explosives in the distance. Autos and carts had to swerve out of the way of military vehicles speeding by them. The thump of explosions became steadily louder as they approached Janow. Andrew pulled Pasha to the side of the road, grabbed Stefan in his arms, and dove into a ditch. He held his son's face close to his heart, as he burrowed as deep into the damp earth of the ditch as they could go. Waves of aircraft were descending on the city. In the distance, what looked like lightning flashes, blazed low on the horizon, silhouetted by a ridge of trees. Andrew knew at once what he feared most was happening. Fighter planes had joined the bombers and were strafing the roadways to stop military vehicles and at the same time were destroying farmhouses and killing scores of innocent civilians.

"Oh, God spare the women and children. Spare Marianne and Maria! Please, God! Please! I beg of you!" he prayed silently.

Stefan became hysterically frightened as he heard the muffled blasts of the bombs, and felt the earth tremors and eventually heard the screams of the dying and the wounded. Andrew held his head down in the ditch while Stefan pleaded, "Tata, help me." Andrew, tenderly covered Stefan with his coat and looked up towards the sky to see the planes race mercilessly above.

The feared war had arrived, now coming in a torrent of destruction that would ultimately flood and destroy an entire country. As Andrew's heart beat violently in his chest, the bombing stopped suddenly and he saw the planes returning the way that they had come, disappearing high into the clouds. Stefan's face, caked with mud and tears, looked up, as the area was suddenly and strangely quiet. Andrew clutched Stefan's trembling body, and with his voice cracking said, "Pray my son Pray!" Andrew crossed himself, as he held the frightened child as he too prayed for safety. The Lord, he thought, is my refuge and strength...., and with that thought the Holy Psalms came rushing back to him. "Yea, though I walk through the valley of the shadow of death, I will fear no evil: For thou art with ......Stefan asked "Where's Mama? All I can see is smoke and fire."

"We'll find her. Do not worry! We need to hurry, no matter what. We will keep our promise." Andrew climbed carefully out of the ditch grabbing Stefan, then onto the wagon, and held his son close. "We're at war, son...."

"Will the Russians and Nazis come here?" Stefan asked tearfully.

"The Nazis are already here! Those were their planes; Russian's military NKVD is here, too. I saw some men back there cutting telegraph wires, but our army will stop them." He started toward St. Stanislaus with awful images flying through his head.

Andrew and Stefan were miraculously looking directly at St. Stanislaus by mid-morning. On the street, through the smoke, frightened faces stared at them in disbelief, seeing a cart with a father and son on it, riding through the melee, not even attempting to hide. Stefan covered his ears with his hands to drown out the noise of the bombs as best as he could, as they neared the Town Square. The street leading to St. Stanislaus was littered with the residual effects of bombing, cluttering streets with debris, including cars, carts corpses and destroyed building parts. This vision of destruction would become commonplace across Europe for the next few years. People were weeping and running, clinging to their possessions, while others called out for friends and family members. A pale, lovely young girl, perhaps thirteen or so, dressed in a red and green torn dress shivered, shook and wept on the curb. Amidst the screaming voices, she held a wounded, howling dog.

Right before Stefan's eyes, the girl held the trembling pet close to her pale and little body. She, arose and then walked desperately alone, and disappeared into the crowd. Stefan called to her "Don't worry! We'll pray for you."

There was still no sight of Maria and Marianne. Andrew asked himself repeatedly "Are they in St. Stanislaus waiting?" He looked straight ahead at the crushed walls of the cathedral. "Please God, watch over them. Allow them to breathe through the ashes. Let them not be buried in these ruins."

Andrew continued driving the wagon through the streets of the town, searching for the other half of his family. Stefan called out, "Mama! Maria!" repeatedly and tearfully.

Marianne and Maria were nearing Janow when more tragedy and destruction came from the west. The planes were back! She heard the unmistakable sound of machine gun fire as a plane dove down near the wagon. It started to spray the road further ahead. However, Marianne urged the frightened horse forward toward the center of town. Fortunately, the plane was a single one hurrying to join the Luftwaffe formation. Eventually, and thankfully, they arrived at the center of town where they saw the death and destruction that Andrew had witnessed a few moments earlier. By this time, fire raged all around! Men were hurriedly sifting through the debris, tossing bricks, one by one, as they searched for bodies under the rubble, which was still falling with force from the bombed buildings. A piece of cement, seemingly with a will of its own, bounced wildly into the wagon just as Maria looked out from under the seat. It struck her squarely on the forehead. She went limp as Marianne pulled the wagon to whatever safety she could find near a wall. Marianne was terrified, until the child started to whimper then cry. Her arms were scratched and her leg was bruised as well, but thank God, she was able to move and otherwise seemed all right. A woman stopped to help and gently wiped her face with a handkerchief as she smoothed her hair back and cleaned her scrapes and cuts. With tears in her eyes, she said, "You are going to be alright. There, your Mama's holding your hands!"

"Thank you! God, Thank you!" ...as if she ever doubted the good will of the citizens of Janow!

Maria clutched her Mama tightly. Marianne leaned forward and kissed the woman's forehead, "May God Bless you forever. You have truly touched her heart! Thank you. You saved our lives. This we will never forget."

"*Z-Bogem!*"

Cautiously, they continued to search nearer to St. Stanislaus for Andrew and Stefan. Andrew had tied Pasha and the wagon to a water trough at Town Square amidst the scattered building fragments. He feared the worst; he thought that maybe they were trapped by debris, and hopefully they would still be alive. One of the few remaining structures in front of him collapsed and an enormous wall broke down with dust, rubble, bricks and glass falling in every direction. Andrew and Stefan ducked into a side street. As they did, a terrifying sight confronted them. A beautiful woman was sprawled flat on the street. Andrew ran to help her. His mouth dropped open as he stared at her. "I thought you were my wife. Thank God you are alive! May God bless you?"

He pulled the woman out of the debris. She grasped Andrew's hand and with tears in her eyes, thanked him. "You will find your wife, I swear." *Z-Bogiem*! You'll find her." As they continued along the tracks, Andrew determinedly told Stefan, "Don't worry, I promise! We are doing right. Knowing Mama, she will follow the railroad tracks."

Marianne carried Maria around the rubble toward the railway tracks with difficulty. The bombardment had ceased, however, the destruction was still steaming, and small fires broke out seemingly everywhere. The railroad and police center were devastated, as were the government buildings. Marianne fearing the worst, and that any minute she would trip on Andrew's body struggled along as Maria   yelled "Tata! Tata! Stefan! Stefan! Where are you?"

Marianne heard a familiar voice calling her name, and she thought that the situation was playing tricks with her mind; however, there stood a tall man with a shaven head a few yards away. The little boy with him was calling for "Mama and Maria". The scene looked surreal, for there amidst smoking rubble of what had been a familiar landscape stood Andrew and Stefan. Andrew lifted his head, raised Stefan onto his shoulder and ran excitedly toward them.

They were filled with emotional numbness after what the four of them had just survived. They embraced, cried together and started towards Marianne's wagon. Nothing needed to be said. When they reached the spot where she had left it, there stood the horse hitched to a crushed cart. A stone lintel had fallen from the building and flattened it. Marianne thought that had they stayed a moment longer, they too, would be gone; she felt God's hand on her shoulder and knew at that moment she was destined to continue the fight for her homeland, Poland, a battleground for survival during a fight between two powerful agents of Godless hate. Andrew and Stefan stared at the remains of the manure cart and unhitched the horse.

Andrew's horse and wagon, however, were still tied to the water trough. He hitched the other horse to the harness with the other one. They all washed their faces in the dusty water and went inside to the altar of St. Stanislaus, filled with gratitude. Maria hugged Stefan just before they knelt in a family prayer. "I love you and Mama, and Tata." she said. They began a prayer of thanks to God to mourn for the dead and to beg mercy for the wounded.

They returned home on a road spread with holes and craters. As they neared the Town of Ratwyn, Andrew shook his head in disgust. "It is here that NKVD Communists cut telephone and telegram wires. These were not our neighbors or people of good will. They were NKVD agents— Polish born bastards!" he snapped.

At this point, as they were about halfway to Zamolina and with the late afternoon sun peeking behind the clouds, loud screams pierced the silence; near a shell crater, a woman with torn clothing was laying close to the edge. She kept sliding down the muddy embankment as two disheveled little girls tried to help her out. The woman screamed, "Help us, help us, please." Nearby, the remains of a smashed wagon lay on the roadside. Andrew stopped the cart and told Stefan, "Take care of Mama." Then he jumped out and rushed towards the woman. "I see you" he said we'll help you. Don't worry," he assured her.

Andrew lifted her to safety, placed her gently on the soft ground, all the while soothing her and the two girls with his kind words. The woman cried out to Andrew, "My husband and my two sons are gone--- all murdered."

The two little girls sank into Andrew's arms sobbing, one pleading, "I want my daddy and my brothers."

The woman said, "They smashed our wagon, took our horse, threatened to bury the children and me in the crater, then decided to just leave us here to die. My husband is gone. My two sons are gone. We are alone. The NKVD killed them.You are God's blessing. Thank you." She asked, "May I have some water, please? My daughters and I are so thirsty."

Stefan ran back to the wagon took a canteen and a cup and offered it to the woman. She drank and said, "May God bless you. I am Magdalene Kozinska. My two girls are Monika and Franceska. I hope we can become friends."

As the two girls hid their faces and hunched against their mother's side, Magdalene began to tell her story of the past days. "The war for us, started a few weeks ago and ended in the death of my husband and two sons. I am without a husband and the children have no father. "Nazis and Soviets-- evil bastards! Those Bolsheviks! They are evil people! Pure evil! I shall never forget. We lived outside of Ratwyn, about twenty-five kilometers northeast of the Zamolenski Estate. The Bolsheviks, the NKVD were burning villages near Ratwyn, pulling the men and boys from their families and then shooting them as their horrified women and children watched. My husband had been an officer in the Polish army. He loved his country. My two sons were sixteen and eighteen years old and got their papers for the army just two days ago. All three felt their duty was to our country. They were real patriots whose love for freedom was more meaningful than their own safety. The NKVD executed them last night, threw their bodies on the side of the road. I pleaded for them to shoot us, and then I begged to have my husband and sons buried. A big Bolshevik pointed his rifle at me and shouted "We'll kill you too, you fucking bitch, and we'll rape your daughters. His name is Dumblosky! He murdered my husband and two sons. He made fun of the situation saying, "We already shot three animals!" That's when he violently lifted me up and tossed me to the ground."

Marianne was chilled by the now sobbing woman's horrible tale. Moreover, it struck her that this was the same Dumblosky who spoke at her father's meetings in Krakow. She could only grieve from the bottom of her heart that such a violent act was committed by Polish born traitors. Dumblosky, whose father spoke freely and openly on Tuesdays at Ludwig's house, was now living a life of hate and murder. The past crimes at Katrynia and St. Andrew's and the murders of human beings gave her every reason to hate them. Their time shall come.

Andrew took Magdalene in his arms and Stefan gently calmed the trembling little girls. Andrew offered: "We are heading to Zamolina near Pinsk. We will gladly take you to our home."

"My brother's place is near yours. His name is Makowski. He and his family live between Zamolina and Pinsk."

"Yes, we know them as one of the most prominent families in Zamolina; they are people of good will and live about three kilometers from our home. We'll go together. Our wagon can handle it. Use our comforter to cushion the ride for we still have a quite a way to go."

Andrew took the reins. Stefan climbed in next, and Maria sat on her lap. Monika, Franceska and Magdalene settled in the rear. As the wheels turned away from the late sunset of this day, they realized that they were a whole family moving ever so slowly into darkness. They had not yet seen the full extent of the inferno that would burn for years, including mass killings and betrayal. Germany and the Bolsheviks were positioning to crush Poland, bent on destroying the Polish hard *ducha*...the capacity of the heart to rise above the struggle.

SEPTEMBER 3, 1939

Neville Chamberlain, British Prime Minister wrote: "Although this communication was made more than twenty-four hours ago, no reply has been received but Nazi attacks upon Poland have been continued and intensified. I have accordingly the honor to inform you that, unless not later than 11 a. m., British Summer Time, to-day 3rd September, satisfactory assurances to the above effect have been given by the Nazi Government and have reached His Majesty's Government in London, a state of war will exist between the two countries as from that hour."

Franklin Delano Roosevelt the American President wrote*: It is right that I should recall to your minds the consistent and at time successful efforts, of your Government, in these crises to throw the full weight of the United States into the cause of peace. In spite of spreading wars I think that we have every right and every reason to maintain as a national policy the fundamental moralities, the teachings of religion the continuation of efforts to restore peace -- because some day, though the time may be distant, we can be of even greater help to a crippled humanity.*

SEPTEMBER 3,1939

Marianne, in Polesie, was following the world affairs as closely as she could; newspapers had been disrupted, radios confiscated and there were few telephones. However, she had obtained a wireless radio that was stored in an old green tin cover. From the outside, it looked like an old metal tool box, with a cover of rusty screwdrivers and hand tools. Underneath, however, Ludwig had constructed a state of the art wireless radio, and a two- way receiver. It was newly released for commercial use with a magic control and was battery operated. Marianne had to be kept hidden from sight of anyone who might turn her in.

She discovered that France and England had declared war on Germany, but not on the Soviet Union. The population of 34 million people diminished daily while the world stood numbly by waiting for the Soviet Union to launch its military invasion. The ultimate occupation of all of Poland fed on the ambitions of Hitler and Soviets' Inner Circle's lust for power.

By the end of day of September 3, 1939, the extent of annihilation of innocent citizenry was still unknown to those in the east. They knew of the German capacity for the Blitzkrieg. At this point they could hear the sounds of war in the distance. Marianne continued to grieve for the countless people who had met death, and she thought of the many more that were still to come. Her motherly instinct for the preservation of home and hearth had surfaced. She had to bury her own emotions to competently face the coming days and the scores of battles, local and worldwide, still ahead. She knew that staying alive in mind, body and soul was at stake.

After several days, Nazi forces were advancing relentlessly, wreaking destruction and bringing terror. The Bolsheviks too, would soon start to destroy the 14 million people who lived in eastern Poland. Lwów was about forty per cent urban Jewish; Vilnius was thirty per cent Jewish, and Marianne's family was close to Pinsk, which was sixty per cent Jewish. These people had become Bolsheviks and were promised power and success by the Communists. In the area of the peasant and farming population, amid open fields, marshes, ponds, and forest, were rural, conservative Catholics, Jews, and Orthodox Christians, who stood alone and innocent between the Nazis and the Bolsheviks.....something they all understood for twenty years.... death would come to millions of innocent people.

On September 4, 1939: an air raid killed over a thousand Jews among citizens of the Polish town, Sulejow. On September 4, 1939, 180 Jews were shot in the city of Czestochowa for refusing to burn the Torah. The Nazis burned Rabbi Abraham Mordechai instead. On September 5, 1939, the Nazis set fire to a predominantly Jewish section of a Polish town, Sulejow. Six Jews died in flames, five were shot while fleeing.

On September 5, 1939: Germany asked Russia to invade Poland. Molotov replied that they would "at a suitable time."

SEPTEMBER 6,1939

Marianne watched her husband on one side of the house watering the potato crop, while on the other side, hundreds of people were fleeing from the west eager to reach the Soviet border.

Andrew and Stefan were hard at work in the field from dawn to dusk. The only hope that was held out on Polish radio was for General Rückemann's force on the Eastern Border to fend off the Russian troops. But how could twenty thousand repel a million and a half Soviet armed forces? She thought that they all may die in a matter of hours or days. The only question at hand however, was how long would they be able to save crops and find ways to hide the food to save their lives?

Sometimes after a hot bath, when the children were asleep, Andrew would take Marianne to their wooded hiding place. When she was in his arms she knew that love could mean the difference between life and death. She felt weak in contrast to the energy of Andrew's strengths. His love of God was so remarkable and anyone who knew the history of Poland knew that the strength of its people lay in their abiding faith. She felt that she was with the world's most courageous person, whose endless hope never ceased to amaze her, and never ceased to give her strength.

However, on this night, they took their children to the hidden spot in the woods and knelt in prayer. They prayed for Ludwig, Zamolenski, Father Baron, Stephany and Joseph,and all the patriots across the land. They included the Pasternaks, Makowskis, Varyas, and Magdelene Kozinska, who steadfastly held their ground each day. Marianne felt, after absorbing the news of the day and praying to a God who seemed to have turned his head on the Polish people, that they had a chance. As long as they were alive---they were free.

SEPTEMBER 7, 1939

The relentless Nazi advances continued as the naval base at Westerplatte surrendered and the army retreated from the Narew River back to the Bug River. The German 10th Panzer Division captured the village of Wizna, when mounted Polish squads abandoned the village after a short fight and retreated to the southern bank of Narew. Nazi infantry advanced towards Giełczyn, but were repelled with heavy casualties.

Marianne was praying for a miracle in front of Andrew's carved copy of the Black Madonna, Our Lady of Czestochowa, which had been placed on the wall over an ever burning candle in the peasant hut. The real Madonna in Czestochowa had been in Poland for six hundred years and legends traced its origin to St. Luke who painted it on a cypress table top taken from the house of the Holy Family. The icon was credited for the miraculous salvation of the monastery of Jasna Gura from a 17th century Swedish invasion. King John II Casimir Vasa "crowned" Our Lady of Czestochowa ("the Black Madonna") as Queen and Protector of Poland in the cathedral of Lwów on April 1, 1656. Marianne prayed for the same salvation now. She pulled herself to her feet and decided to seek any gossip of Nazi advance from the fleeing people who streamed by on the road past her house daily.

She donned baggy old clothes, pulled the peasant scarf around her head, and set out along the road to seek out every available bit of news. "Poland Is Dying" said some. "Fierce Fighting," said others. "We have no option, but to escape" said still another. She stood as close to the road as she could, eager to hear what was being said. She asked for more information from those fleeing from the Nazis. She had no way of telling them that fleeing toward the Russians made no more sense than fleeing from the oncoming Nazis. They were trapped in either direction.

She turned away only to find Wladek Pasternak standing next to her. As he looked at the passersby he said: "If they want my land, they will have to walk over my dead body. There isn't much time left." He looked at the hordes of those passing. He said bitterly, "They are heading eastward to Pinsk and beyond into Moscow. I am afraid that those fleeing eastward are potential Soviet officials and collaborators. Marianne, they are betraying us openly. They have made their political decisions in the past and failed. I am furious".

Marianne quietly disagreed believing that the migrant's departure was based on fear. She explained to Wladek the importance of the need for Polish unity on all levels. She said that on the roadside, she felt desperation and fear coming from their hearts, and a survival instinct that would go to any lengths to be successful.

Andrew pulled his wagon alongside of them and began to offer food and water to passersby as a gesture of Christian charity. Soon other farmers joined him.

Pasternak and Marianne saw two elderly men slowly making their way along the road. Both had sunburned faces, wore birch-bark sandals and were dressed in ragged, dirty clothing. Each carried a cloth banner on which the name of the Blessed Virgin was embroidered.

Andrew explained that they were pilgrims who were going to the shrine of Czestochowa, high in the Carpathian Mountains on the Jasna Gura promontory near the Czechoslovakian border, to celebrate the nativity of the Blessed Mother, on this September 7. He added that they saw war as a curse in the eyes of God. Andrew explained to Stefan and to the others that these men would go the entire distance on foot, finishing the last part of the journey on their knees. "They believe", he said, "that suffering gives meaning to life. The love they feel for the Virgin Mary leads them every year to Czestochowa to strengthen their faith where they will pray for all those suffering, Our family not only has her on our altar, but we have her picture in our hearts. The Blessed Mother there is the queen protector of Poland."

Andrew told them that as a boy he had made the trip and saw the pilgrims throw themselves on the rough flagstones of the church, lying with their face down weeping and praying aloud for the Blessed Virgin Mary's help.

Marianne thought how much her Andrew resembled the kind Priest that he originally had been. His love of his Savior was so evident in his help for the sorry peasants walking by. He had a calming influence and a spiritual core that she envied. Stefan piped up "Maria and I will pray for them; I know we say the rosary every morning. That's praying for all of us." Wladek Pasternak placed his hand on Stefan's shoulder and then turned to Maria, smoothed her hair and hugged them both.

Andrew and Stefan then left to join the other men working in the field. Meanwhile, Marianne seized the moment to tell Wladek of her own vision. "We must use our strong faith in our country and God to prevent our destruction by the Nazis and Bolsheviks; to do this we should construct a hidden "Cultural Free Zone." We have to create places of refuge within our homeland that will allow freedom for the Poles, and provide food, comfort and education, all of which will certainly be denied by these conquering animals."

"My family has been on this soil for over two hundred years" said Waldek with a heavy heart.

Marianne continued "You need not say more. The Polesian people will starve if we do not have a good harvest; they are not immune to the cold of winter or disease. They are the silent victims of war. We could hide food and equipment in a designated "Liberty Zone," and create a secret Polish Government in Exile here in Polesie, but we will have to act fast. We must start now and work with Zamolenski. We need an underground economic system of trade and hidden caches of armaments, supplies and tools. After the NKVD occupies our land, they will take the entire harvest in thirty days or less. If we could hide a portion of the produce to secretly be distributed for the long winter ahead we have a chance. We only have three weeks...maybe four ...to gather and hide as much food and supplies as we can."

The line of people leaving their homeland on the road in front of them appeared to be a symbol for the choice that they had to make ahead. Is escape a possibility, or a dream? Marianne felt that the only hope for their survival was to deal with the present time and place, even if it eventually meant fighting the oppressors.

Pasternak spoke quietly "Marianne, this land and the people on it are my family. We have been here for eight generations. I have worked our fifteen hundred hectares growing wheat, rye and vegetables since I was a boy. My two brothers were killed in World War One, the youngest of them was tortured to death in 1920 by the Communists, and therefore, I am the sole surviving son carrying the Pasternak name. I cannot do what these people are doing and abandon my family's heritage while everything else is crumbling around us. This discussion must be kept secret, for no one should know of it except for Makowski, Kozinska, and Varya, and those that you will ask for support. I'll let you know which families will prove to be loyal and devoted. I don't think Adam and Florence Makowski will leave here either."

He hugged Marianne and whispered into her ear, as if he was afraid of being overheard in this field. "You are temporarily safe if you operate in total secrecy. Keep as much out of sight as possible for I expect the worst here. Your idea of creating safe refuge and home within the tumultuous world is a good one. I will do everything to support it."

Marianne said as she parted and walked toward her peasant house, "We need to get started."

SEPTEMBER 8,1939

While Marianne was fretting over resistance possibilities, the Nazi 4th Panzer Division reached the Warsaw suburb of Ochota, The Polish garrison commander in Warsaw, General Czuma, broadcast a defiant Order of the Day: "We shall fight to the last ditch!" Some 100,000 Polish civilians in Warsaw were engaged in digging trenches on the city outskirts. Nazi attacks concentrated on Radom, only 60 miles south of Warsaw; and the San River north and south of Przehersl, while in the north the Nazi 19th Panzer Corps (Guderian) attacked along the

103

Bug River to the east of Warsaw. These actions triggered the American President's announcement of a "limited national emergency" due to the war in Europe. On the same day the Russian NKVD caused multiple tragedies including the execution and torture of village mayors, over ninety villages were occupied by Communist's List of Workers. Scores of influential intellectual and military Polish citizens were assassinated, shot in the back of the head. Catholic schools were burned by the NKVD and a few hundred priests had been tortured and shot. Russian agents were infiltrating Polish Lithuania, Estonia, Latvia, Belorussia, parts of Poland, and the western Ukraine. Forty Russian divisions were ready at the border to join Germany to invade eastern Poland.

Marianne had finished cleaning up after breakfast, and as Andrew and Stefan started to leave for the fields, there was a knock on the door. When she opened it, Barbara and Wladek Pasternak, Florence and Adam Makowski, and Magdalene Kozinska were standing there. They looked frightened; however, they were also determined.

Wladek, obviously excited, passed on the usual amenities of morning greetings to get right to the point. He had just received a wireless report that stated Nazi forces were marching on Warsaw, and that an estimated 311,000 civilian casualties were the result. Marianne's face turned chalk white upon hearing the news. She and Andrew sent the children into the yard to play, and pulled the visitors into the room and sat them down at the breakfast table. Marianne's fright and anger always caused her to bustle and move about, as if she could obliterate her feelings. The Nazi invasion, once only a news bulletin was now close to home. She told them all to wait until she served, as if the black tea of Poland would remove the threat.

Wladek continued finally "The Nazi armies are marching on Warsaw. Hitler announced for the third time in four weeks that there would be no pity or mercy for all men, women, and children of the Polish race or language. Warsaw is now being bombed daily with the full force of Germany's Blitzkrieg, although the Polish resistance is providing a stout defense. There can be no retreat. We will have to fight to the last soldier and civilian, and while the Polish resistance is fierce and bloody, it cannot stop the destruction of many major cities, including Gdynia, Poznan, Bydgosch, Kulno, Lodz, Krakow and Warsaw."

Makowski shook his head and said sadly, "This is just the beginning, the first six days of war. What is to come? There obviously will be no help for Poland! France and England will not honor their commitment. Stefan Starzynski, the Mayor of Warsaw appealed to

France and England on the 6th of September. He asked for the promised help. Poland is waiting. The world is waiting. Where is your moral conscience? No answer was returned .From this day on, he noted, we are alone and abandoned."

Marianne's anger faded into anguish and care for her family in Krakow, so she pushed Pasternak further, "What about Krakow?"

Wladek went on to say that there was little to tell. "Let God watch over them. No one knows what has happened to them there. The Mayor of Krakow told every man, woman and child to leave before the old city is destroyed."

Marianne was shaken at the news; she grasped Andrew's hand for support. It would be easy, she thought, just to give in and try to survive within the structure of Nazi socialism or Bolshevik communism. However, that clearly wasn't a possibility with the amoral nature of the invaders, therefore, the only clear path to Marianne and the rest of the gathering around that morning table was resistance. She asked all those present if they could commit to creating an area for freedom and sustenance. She knew that there would be questions, and fear of the future.

Magdalene, started to weep and spoke first, "Could we set up a "Liberty Zone" as a tribute to our love of country and home?"

The rest of them agreed, and noted that time was of the essence. Andrew, walked toward his icon of the Black Madonna, and said that they needed to take a moment and pray for guidance, and to ask for God's help with this dangerous step. Adam Makowski agreed, "Let's pray for God's blessing as the start of better times to come."

They knelt at the small family shrine facing the carved Madonna which would become the center of their world, and fervently asked for aid from the higher power, and as Andrew pointed out, not one would turn his back. "God works in strange ways" he concluded.

Marianne felt better now that the desperate feeling of being powerlessly abused left her for the moment. She gathered everyone at the table, and started them setting forth plans for the creation of their safety net. Andrew pointed out that the Polesian marshes were the safest place to hide food, people, money and freedom fighters. He knew the roads to a safe spot within the swampy territory, and he added the natural surroundings would lend material and food to those dwelling there. They all agreed and Marianne spoke of the need for a governing body;

someone to be in charge. The group decided that as the most educated at that table, she should be the leader. The other deciding factor on the leadership role was the Nazi and Bolshevik attitude toward women. German men actually had a society, at one point, to keep women from voting and taking leadership roles. The Bolsheviks included women, but in a supporting role only; therefore, suspicion of leadership and resistance would not as easily be directed at a peasant woman.

The last pieces of the plan concerned the procurement of guns and explosives, the creation of an educational system, for when the Bolsheviks closed the schools, and most importantly a communication system. The discussion lasted for a while, and finally they saw their idea formulated into reality. The danger was in any transcription or loose talk of the "zone of freedom". They had to find a way to communicate with the local populace. This problem was still to be solved.

Marianne continued by saying that all energies should be focused on the coming harvest before the imminent Russian invasion. After that, she said, there would be a need to keep healthy and energetic with a sufficient supply of food and to create an economic system of barter and trade.

Pasternak, after a moment, spoke emotionally: "The Polish-born traitor Vishinsky was quoted last week in Pravda when he said. "There will never be another Poland."

Everyone was silent. "The sorrows of Poland,' Marianne continued, "will be ever present. We can weep for the citizens and soldiers who in these six days of war gave their lives for their country. However, my father taught me well. Before Andrew and I came here to Polesie his words were: "Prepare for the worst because the Soviets breed misery, unanswered grief and loss. Rise above them. Put faith and spirit above hopelessness! It applies to all mankind, not just Poland! Our Liberty Zone should be a corner of the world where people can pray, be hopeful, and love what the future holds in store. Most importantly, we will need to know whom to trust."

"For now we will put nothing in writing, we will have to hold this in our minds with great care and secrecy for the NKVD/KGB and its spy network will use fear to pit one person against the other. We probably will be targeted for assassination; therefore, we need to keep a mental list of names of people involved and keep leadership secret." she concluded.

Marianne led them to agree that mid-November would be the date for opening their own Sanctuary in the midst of the nearby marsh, which they would refer to as part of the swamp without fear of discovery. They could always say that they were going to: *"Torfowiska Chelmskie"* to gather peat for fuel, and no one would be the wiser. There were few paths to the inner part of the Marsh, and without knowledge of travel to the interior of the region one could really get lost or sunken into the mire.

"Let us call our center Pasternak Sanctuary, and that will be known only to us" said Marianne. "Since we are on a main road between Moscow and Brest, a Regional Workers Headquarters here is very possible." Solemnly they each were sworn to secrecy on Andrew's worn Bible.

SEPTEMBER 10, 1939

Polish armies retreated to defensive positions in the southeast, as the Luftwaffe bombed Warsaw. Nazi propagandists broadcasted false news bulletins announcing the fall of the Polish capital on the same wavelength as Radio Warsaw. In Britain, a special session of Parliament approved Prime Minister Mackenzie King's request that Canada join the war in Europe. The decision, seen by most Canadians as inevitable, came exactly one week after England and France declared war on Nazi Germany. Polish forces counterattacked Nazi troops along the River Bzura near Poznan.

The tension in Polesie grew with each passing hour. The outside world of conflict was drawing closer and closer to the area. Every morning, Marianne and her small group met at the grotto hidden deep in the woods. There they exchanged and discussed the war news and then they planned strategies for their own struggle for survival. They had to hide, they believed, fifteen per cent of the harvest in utmost secrecy before the Soviets would come to power and seize the land, its production, and its homes. The remoteness of Zamolina at the moment was its strength. They were distanced from the Bolsheviks, and their supporters. Peasants, in their view, were not useful or intelligent enough except for hard labor, and the fulfillment of quotas. However, Marianne knew, as did her friends, that what the Bolsheviks feared most was leadership and intellectuals. If they could be able to stir up anger, and hate among the peasants and then shower them with promises, inevitably the leadership would step forth for reward and would summarily have their throats slit. Therefore, on this morning the discussion focused on the apparent presentation of lack of leadership.

Marianne, seated on a rock beneath the statue of the Virgin, talked of emergency plans. She believed that the Communists would set up their regional district in Pinsk, strategically to the north, while the District Commissars would officially settle on principal roads in rural areas in order to have easy access to Moscow from Pinsk, Brest, Litowsks and Warsaw. Brest was the communications center of Eastern Europe; it had a road and rail line transecting Zamolina. She, and the others, carefully considered the possibility that Zamolina would be designated as the official sight for the Commissar's headquarters. They needed to find out for sure. Marianne said that she could imagine long lists and dossiers being collected for liquidation. They were trying to formalize a governing system and safe recruitment methods, she realized that the reality of invasion forced action, and left little time for philosophical discussions of enemy motivations. There was temptation to launch into tirades about the inhumanity of the coming torrent of disaster. However, action had to be placed at the forefront and Marianne had to force herself to avoid excursions into her learned past. She caught herself at one point considering Newton's Law that every action has an equal and opposite reaction, and the Hegelian dialectic about every thesis has an anti-thesis. She pulled herself back, frequently, to the here and now

At the end of each meeting, after each item had been covered, Tata Ludwig's haunting question---"Is that all?" became her mantra. "What are we to do today to have a tomorrow?" The irony struck her that these people despised by the Russians were fighting back with their intellect and their hearts. All the ideas and materials had to be carried in their heads.

Following this particular morning's session, they felt a new sense of urgency, fueled by world events. Varya, Pasternak, Makowski, and Andrew were to gather whatever they could before the "official harvest", then to secretly store bushels in dug-outs in the forest. Magdalene Kozinska, Florence Makowska, and Barbara Pasternak found trusted members to dry mushrooms and make smoked kielbasa. They also gathered medicine, honey, and light farm equipment.

Marianne reported about her journey through the columns of the fleeing on the road. She had seen brave men and women emerging from the shadows of protection only to pay a heavy price for confronting the NKVD, as well as the Nazis. She had seen a courageous Catholic priest, proudly and faithfully still wearing his vestments, not only labeling himself, but in these times, putting himself in mortal danger. He became a target that offered an alternative spiritual vision for the peasants, and, therefore, he would have been treated as an enemy of the state...

The tensions of the day were high. Bloody reports of fierce fighting were reinforced hourly, and ruthless NKVD activities had never been more frequent. Marianne worried, as she traveled this road and sensed from the emotions of the fleeing people that a general feeling of despair and helplessness would sweep across the land, even before the Soviet invasion, which would remove the chances of forming an underground resistance movement in Polesie and across Poland. Those who feel hopeless will never prepare to have a future.

That evening after a full, hard day, Andrew, Marianne, Stefan and Maria found peace and warmth with their family. They sat down to a supper of dried mushrooms, soaked in hot cream, and potato soup. Marianne added whatever meat was left over from another meal and made a stew. The bowl of food was steaming on the table as Andrew asked the blessing when the dinner was interrupted by a loud knock. Andrew cautiously peeked out the window, and then quickly opened the door. A tall, lean priest, dressed in a mud- spattered cassock, stood trembling on the threshold. Andrew recognized him at once, "Father Zajac!" he said as he embraced the priest and welcomed him into their home. After greeting and hugging the rest of the family, the good Father spoke solemnly and slowly. "I am here with a heavy heart and an urgent message from Zamolenski."

"Marianne, I must warn you. Jacob Dumblosky has been reported to be in the Janow area. You knew him in Krakow as the son of a Bolshevik, and he is a very evil man who joined the Soviets. He is among the many traitors who are aggressively attacking Polish priests and leaders. They are desperately looking for you, since they do not believe anyone perished in your house fire. Zamolenski is being watched day and night by informers and collaborators working for the NKVD. So be very careful."

He then took a map of Poland from his pocket, pinpointing spots as he spoke. "The Nazis, however, are leveling villages, towns and cities and are ferociously applying all their killing apparatus with amazing precision leaving toppled buildings and charred bodies. The Polish victims are discovered, hundreds at a time, jammed under clutter or debris, in towns and streets in Krakow, Warsaw, Gdynia, Poznan, and Gdansk. After a concentration of bombing and blitzkrieg fire in Poznan, nine hundred victims in one row of homes were found." He started to cry openly in a combination of anger and sorrow. "These are human beings, people caught under tumbling walls who are marked for death simply because they are Polish. And the war has only just started "

Father Zajac looked at Andrew and Marianne with Maria and Stefan silently huddled close to them. His sad eyes gazed down at little Maria, as he gently took his thumb and crossed her forehead, lips and heart, then he did the same to Stefan. He said as he made the sign of the cross on their foreheads, "Jesus loves you." Both children instinctively clasped their hands and bowed their heads.

"God has created a very special little girl, pretty as can be . Stefan, you are a fine, strong boy," said Father Zajac. "Thank you, Father" said Stefan, his face beaming. Maria smiled, her cheeks flushed bright red.

Andrew stirred the fire and the embers shone brightly. He squeezed Marianne's hand and then said, "Father, please join us at our table."

Father Zajac, said a blessing, then ate the remaining potato and mushroom soup with great gusto, thanking them profusely. After dinner, he stood up, straightened his wrinkled soutane, before looking out the window to the road and trees beyond. "We will talk now, but within the hour I must go back to St. John's in Towlicza where I belong...to do a higher duty."

The children and dog Basha were sent outside to play, in the very manner that parents use when they want to talk about topics not for little ears.

The Father continued. "Two days ago, I traveled to Zamolenski and Towlicza. The countryside was being bombarded by NKVD agents killing Poles. Marianne, you were there at St Andrew's so you know what it is like. It was worse in Janow. Three days ago, I was approached by a group of farmers. They had found two bodies, tortured and left hanging in front of St. John's Church, the most sacred place in Towlicza. A band of men headed by a Jacob Dumblosky had been seen in the vicinity. Some farmers also spotted these same men and women near Janow. They kept repeating – 'Marianne Krull, the teacher from St. Andrew's...Zamolenski's friend and whore. Do you know her whereabouts? 'Later, I traveled to Janow to confront the Chief of Police Nowatzki. He relayed some important information but inquired, "Are the Krulls dead?"

Andrew just stared at him, his face burning. They were after Marianne because of her resistance to the attack on St. Andrews, and for the fear that with her connection to her father, which Dumblosky knew full well, she would be trouble in the future unless eliminated now.

Father Zajac continued "The chief of Police also said, "If they are not already dead, God help Andrew and Marianne Krull!" Father Zajac began to weep, tears coursing down his cheeks. However, he slowly composed himself. "They killed people closest to you both… teachers, postmasters, foremen. Marianne, your childhood friend, a priest, was tortured and murdered because they somehow believed he knew of your whereabouts and that you may have contacted me. A female teacher was riddled with bullets two nights ago at her home. Then, after killing the poor soul, they nailed her hands to the table." Andrew's face turned pale and Marianne's heart sank when they heard the gruesome details. "She was our Helena Nowak of St. Andrew's," said Father Zajac.

"Oh my God!" Marianne cried bitterly as Andrew crossed himself and started to pray silently. "She was murdered for nothing more than being a good teacher and setting the right path for her students."

The Father holding tightly on to Andrew's arm continued. "The postmaster, Zygmund Kalowicz, who delivered your mail, met his death because they thought he knew where you were. They shot him as he lay in bed next to his wife. She wasn't injured, but she hasn't been coherent since. She now hysterically repeats over and over, "Where's Marianne Krull's mail?"

Marianne grasped Father's hand, overcome with deep sadness laced with guilt. "People I loved have died because of me!" cried Marianne.

"We must pray" the Father said as he gently brushed Marianne's forehead. "There is still more. I only wish I could stop here …Edwin Kowal was found dead by Zamolenski's guards. They cut off his head. His body was found in a ditch, his head in the center of a road."

Now Andrew began to weep as well and clenched his fists in rage. "Just four weeks ago, Kowal and I were talking about his family and how glad we'd be if the war would never begin. He truly loved his cabinetry work and life in Polesie! He was killed to give us a message. I want to tear Jacob Dumblosky apart. My foreman, Edwin Kowal, tortured and killed. It is unspeakable."

Father Zajac tearfully said, "We'll pray for them; they all will have peace in heaven."

There was a long silence when Marianne buried her face in Andrew's chest. Father Zajac's voice interrupted her thoughts, "Zamolenski wants you to know that Tomas Dorovitz, the Revolutionary Chief of this area, is a madman, and he, as we speculated, is the husband of Ilana Dorovitz, the woman who alerted you to the St. Andrew's attack! He's expected to be this region's Chief of the Communist Commissar following the invasion and occupation. He and Jacob Dumblosky are the traitors behind these savage atrocities. You already know about Dumblosky, but now beware of Dorovitz. Watch him, and find a way to deal with him before he finds out who you are. The NKVD now know that you are alive, but they have no idea where you are."

"Shortly, after divulging the information, Nowatzki disappeared." Father Zajac added. "There is a desperate search for him. Zamolenski understands that two NKVD agents, including David Dumblosky, have been killed because they allowed you to escape from them at St. Andrew's. The other may be Ilana Dorovitz, but he was not sure. David Dumblosky has been shot by his own people to placate the Christian peasants….a Bolshevik Jew is dead!" Marianne began to think about Ilana and suddenly wanted to be assured of her safety.

They knelt with arms around each other in front of the family's altar. "Father, we are all marked men and women." said Andrew. "I can only close my eyes in prayer and wonder. The lives ended, here on earth, are truly directing the course for others to follow. I am one of those. Stay with us or leave Poland now, the Communists will always fear the church and our soul. It represents a spiritual power they can neither understand nor accept. They will crush the church and kill her servants whenever and wherever they can. We have our own safe spot where the trees touch the hand of God and the earth and sky are one. There will be more joining us in a couple of months. We have laid out our plans carefully."

The Father looked gravely at Andrew, and then met his eyes and replied, "I may do what you ask, but first I must return. One must live for each day. There will always be time enough to die tomorrow. It's in the natural order. I am anxious to serve my flock, and you are a special part of it." He blessed them again.

112

Andrew called to Maria and Stefan. The children rushed in and cuddled up next to their parents. Maria noticed the teary and weeping eyes and was upset.

"No, please, my little one. There's no need to shed tears. Little girls like you are meant for laughter not tears. You are Mama's and Tata's children, but when I ask you whose child are you also, what do you say?"

"I am God's child," Maria replied

"God will watch over you," said the good priest. "I may be back. I pray to God for your safety." Then buttoning his coat, he took leave as quietly as he came. "Goodbye, my friends."

Marianne thanked him for giving them courage to face whatever was ahead.

They all watched as this pious, faithful man of God slowly walked into the night. He was too far away to hear Maria's "I'll pray for you, Father Zajac."

SEPTEMBER 11,1939:

The Nazi forces crossed the River San north and south of Przehersl, in southeast Poland. The Polish force at Radom was destroyed with the Nazis capturing 60,000 men. The Nazi captured the industrial area of Upper Silesia.

Marianne slept uneasily, waking several times in a cold sweat, thinking that maybe it all was just a bad dream. However, the morning brought reports of increasing horror giving them all a sense of dreadful reality. A Polish police constable in Janow was killed, and his body was hung from a lamppost in the town square with a sign pinned to his chest, warning that anyone who removed his corpse would suffer a similar fate. The Polish "solty" in Towlicza, along with his wife and four children, were found shot in the back of their heads in their home.

The small group in Polesie hearing of the tragedies was at a loss of what to do; however, Marianne and Andrew wanted to go to Janow to see of Father Zajak's safety. He had risked his life to identify Tomas Dorovitz as the leading butcher in the region, soon to be appointed Revolutionary Regional Head.

Andrew's was angry, out of character for him, as he volunteered to infiltrate the organization before the military invasion. He had thought of a way to reach Dorovitz. Andrew struck the right chord with the small group of friends and resistors, and gained approval without any

113

objection. Unquestionably, it is the most dangerous assignment, for any mistake meant automatic death for Andrew and his family.

Andrew and Marianne left with Josef Varya in an oxen wagon for the two-hour ride to Towlicza. Maria and Stefan remained behind with Barbara Pasternak. They arrived at about 10:00 in the morning but it was too late. A crowd had gathered by the church and when they pushed their way through to the front, they were horrified to see Father Zajac's body sprawled on the church steps, his limbs viciously torn; his throat had been cut, leaving a gaping wound from which blood was pouring down his white vestment. Andrew was sure that he had been prevented from clasping his hands in prayer. A sign nailed to the door proclaimed that he had been killed for "treachery to the people."

Andrew turned away sickened. In shock, he tried desperately to compose himself and then stood for several minutes in silent prayer. With his voice quivering, he finally said to the Father's body. "You did bring us all together. You will have everlasting happiness in heaven as a martyr and a saint who gave every conceivable gesture of love. Thank you for being in our lives. We will miss and always remember you, our dearest friend." Andrew knew that the Bolshevik's removal of his arms had not stopped the torrent of prayers from him, and he wondered was the Father asking for forgiveness for his torturers just as his Lord Jesus had done.

As they numbly made their way back to Zamolina, Varya said as tears flowed down his cheeks, "He died a martyr. I grieve deeply for our beloved Father, and I have made a silent pledge to avenge his death." He shook his fist at the empty sky and swore: "Jacob Dumblosky and Dorovitz, you will hear from me. We will avenge Father Zajac's death"

Andrew who had been silent finally spoke:" Whatever we are doing now is not enough. We need information that can be used quickly, and Dorovitz can give that to us. Up until now, he has been operating secretly near the Soviet border, and if he is about to become officially the Regional Head of the Communist Party, he may need a local farmer or person to help him run his estate tomorrow and maybe permanently . I know he will be on the alert for his comrades who would betray him, and also for any violent or resistive actions of the locals. He will need assurance from someone that his life and that of his children can be saved." Andrew returned to his thoughts.

Marianne and the family gathered that evening at their altar, where Father Zajak had knelt the night before. Stefan with the unwitting wisdom of a small child broke the silence by saying, "Mama, I want to be just like Father Zajac when I grow up."

Marianne tearfully answered "You picked the best. He was what a hero should be. Love never dies for those special souls in heaven."

SEPTEMBER 12, 1939

Polish forces had some success, pushing the Nazis back twelve miles south of Kutno and recapturing Lowicz; however, the Luftwaffe bombed Krzemieniec, where Warsaw's diplomatic community had sought refuge. Furthermore Germany threatened military action if Rumania gave asylum to Polish officials.

The enemy on the national scale was clearly defined by the ongoing wireless reports to the peasant house in Polesie. Tomas Dorovitz, on the other hand, was a local enemy within. He had been trained by the old Communist system, and taught to develop an intense hatred of Catholic Pole and Orthodox Christian Ukrainians. He trusted no one. His future was based on deceit, hatred and mass murder.

During the night, Andrew dreamed horrible images of Dorovitz's torture of Father Zajac and Dumblosky's murders of Chief Constable Nowatski, Postmaster Kulawich, and Kowal. All the praying he had done had not helped him; however, he felt there was some reason that he had been chosen to right this wrong. Over and over he asked God "Why such evil existed in the world?" and then he came to the conclusion that these evil people were faithless, and held no deity or person above themselves. Maybe, he thought, they held the party leadership as a kind of God because of their control of life and death. The more he thought, the more troubled he became and finally decided that there needed to be ears in the enemy's house. He thought again of the 23rd Psalm, "Thou preparest a table for me in the presence of mine enemies", and connected the present to the times of the Old Testament when forces were constantly fighting God's chosen people.

Early in the morning he decided that he would go to Dorovitz, and make friends with the butcher; Chief Commissar, Tomas Dorovitz would need an innocent person of "low worth" with no previous political history, someone who is not a threat to him, but could be helpful to his family when his day of judgment comes. Andrew thought that in Bible stories, in times of danger, God was always on the side of his people. Andrew's inner conflict was based on Jesus' teaching of "turn the other cheek." He reasoned further in his own mind that there was no other cheek to turn at this point. He decided he could go with God and follow his will,

Andrew sat up in bed at dawn and said to Marianne, "I have decided to go to Tomas Dorovitz, offer my services and pay special attention to his wife Ilana. When she approached you, she said that she needed to protect her children. You mentioned her kindness and her faith in God; therefore she could be our link to information about the NKVD, and of course to Tomas who is in charge. She knows you, but she will not know me. I think I can get close to the inner soul of Ilana Dorovitz. Maybe her need to save the souls of her children, as well as her own, will separate her from her loathsome husband who will continue to terrorize on Polish soil."

"Even though she is following her husband's path, she has no choice, but until the day comes when something inside of her says that her way is wrong, I will do everything possible to get much more out of her than I put in." Andrew finally had a plan and a matching idea. He felt better once he had worked all the thoughts through and finally felt an inner calm.

The old Andrew reappeared momentarily with a big smile and a kiss for Marianne. "Trust me" he said "We'll get it done."

After an early farmer's breakfast, at 7:00 AM, Andrew and Marianne met with the others of the inner circle of the soon to be formed Pasternak Zone of Freedom. They told the group that Andrew had taken on the dangerous mission of infiltrating the Dorovitz compound. He related his plan of infiltration so as to get closer to the enemy. He quietly told them that his second motive was revenge for the deaths of good honest people.

Marianne added, "Jacob Dumblosky is as good as dead. I'll kill them with my bare hands the next chance I get. I'll be looking for him at St. Stanislaus. I want to meet Zamolenski for any kind of information he might have and also to see if he heard from my father and family."

Andrew said that he thought that Marianne shouldn't go alone, and was there anyone who could go with her. Magdalene Kozinska didn't hesitate "I want to go! My daughters and Maria can stay with Florence. I, too, have a score to settle. I want to tear Dumblosky's heart out, not with my hands, but with my teeth." Andrew said, "That is what we all want to do; however, this is not the time for public revenge. We need to keep our cover as ignorant, dirty peasants who fit the Communist and Nazi image of low life".

116

Barbara offered to babysit Maria and Stefan. Stefan could help Wladek conceal the "illegal potatoes" and Maria could help pick mushrooms and chestnuts.

Andrew hitched up his wagon later that morning and put his carpenter's tools in a wooden kit on the seat, as he set out for Dorovitz's farm, about 30 kilometers to the northwest of Pinsk closer to the Soviet border. Dorovitz owned 160 hectares of land near a small lake, where he grew rye and flax like the other farmers in the region. His farm was about six kilometers west of a *shtetl*, an orthodox Jewish village, which ironically was established by Catherine the Great of Russia as a haven from anti-Semitism. Andrew looked at his map, took a deep breath and started on his journey. "This is the way I shall do it," he reassured himself.

Three hours later Andrew reached the perimeter of the farm where a number of horsemen were on duty .Although at first they stared at him suspiciously, not one of them did more than give the dirty peasant a passing glance as he continued on. They may have thought that he knew Ilana, or Tomas Dorovitz, why else would he be on this road to the home of the new Regional Head of the Communist Party. A slight man wearing rimless spectacles appeared at the end of the road. Could this be the terrible murderer of priests and teachers, thought Andrew? He looked like a clerk from a small store. Andrew stopped the wagon; he did not get down, but looked upward at the house next to the end of the path. He guessed that it was more in disrepair than he thought, judging from the warped clapboards and loose roof tiles. His expert eye surmised that the roof leaked.

Dorovitz, did not like strangers who suddenly appeared, even though this one resembled a slow- witted peasant. "What brings you here? I do not know you" he growled. Andrew responded "Not too may people know me. It is better that way. I'm looking for work to feed my family. We were late with the harvest and my children and wife are facing winter. I'm an excellent carpenter and farmer so I am going from farm to farm to try and share my skills to help prepare for winter's cold. You have a big piece of land here and I could be a good worker for you and your family." Dorovitz soon learned that this was a bald woodworker, who, according to his story, helped some Jews escape the Nazi invasion, and had fled to Polesie after hearing of a land incentive. Dorovitz trusted no one, however, this man on the wagon looked harmless and simple enough. In the custom of the Bolsheviks, the assumption was that all the smart people were either dead or gone.

Perhaps he would offer Andrew the job of fixing his roof which leaked into his family bedroom. His wife Ilana had been complaining about it for the five years that they lived here.

Dorovitz thought for a moment, about how someone, anyone, could pass all the guards and be on top of him so quickly without his knowledge. He asked him who he was.

"Andrew Ludwig from Zamolina."

Dorovitz had softened in his approach when it appeared that Andrew was not a threat, at least at the moment.

"Pan Dorovitz, my family is hungry" Andrew replied. "I need the work."

"My instincts tell me that you are fair. You shared your food with refugees from western Poland, when you were hungry."

Andrew thought of a Bible verse again, something that was happening very often lately. "Jesus said what you do for my brother you do for me." Andrew would have had no other way; however, was revenge and murder part of the helping one's brother out of tyranny? Dorovitz had been going on about work, and how tired he and his workers were and how much needed to be done, when Andrew realized that he was offering to have him replace a leaky corner section of the roof. Dorovitz pointed to the barn, and told Andrew that there he would find wood and a ladder that he could use for the repairs.

"I'll take care of it right away," Andrew replied smiling, hoping his expression didn't look false. He was not certain that he could strengthen the relationship. Dorovitz, he realized, had started to speak of his family's need for a dry and comfortable environment .Andrew said that Dorovitz's wife must be devoted to family to come here five years ago.

"Yes, she is." said the little man, "What could one expect her to do?"

"We must live for our families" said Andrew. "I'll do anything to scrape enough bread on the table to keep them safe and healthy Pan Dorovitz."

"Start with the roof" said Dorovitz, "and don't call me Pan, I hate that word. Tomas will do, or Comrade. Next week you must come and fix the windows. All right?"

118

"Good. There is no time to delay." Andrew said that Polish peasants like him could not go to church with all the commotion around, so he would be available for more work on Sunday. "I can do more for you and your family before the storms and winter blizzards are upon us."

Dorovitz agreed, saying he liked that kind of worker.

"Thank you, Tomas. Now, I'll get to work."

From a distance, grim-looking guards continued to scrutinize Andrew. However, suspicions began to evaporate as they watched him work. Andrew repaired the roof in less than three hours. When Andrew finished, he found Dorovitz, stretched out, asleep in a chair on the back porch. His wife Ilana was seated nearby and Andrew hoped that she would not recognize him. He smiled and told Ilana that her husband should let him know on Sunday if the work was not satisfactory. "I'll fix the windows. I am the best around." he said.

She offered him a *zloty*, in payment.

Andrew refused the money, and assured her that his repair of the windows would allow cool air in, while holding the warmth in the house in winter. Ilana was curious about this peasant who had suddenly appeared to do repairs at the house, for she dared not ask her husband how it all came about; however, she liked this quiet man who refused payment because of trust. There was no trust in her world. She felt surrounded by informers, greed and deceit. She asked him his name and he had simply replied "Andrew." In the way that people do, she asked about his family. Andrew had to keep information guarded, and told her only of having a wife and two small children.

Ilana was an educated woman, and this plain, simple stranger reminded her of the romantic communistic ideal of the simple peasant, who followed his labor as the only cause, and rose above the intelligentsia and military by working hard. . He obviously loved his wife and family, and was rooted to the soil, not to advancement up the socialistic ladder. Instinctively, she trusted him and an aura of goodness he carried with him, like a shield in troubled times.

Andrew , on the other hand , after inquiring about her children and family, felt he had made progress in preparing a way for future dialogue; however, his caution could not be thrown away either. He did feel some guilt, as always, for his duplicity of motive. Then he told her, he would return on Sunday to fix the windows, and to prepare her home for the winter. He offered any help that they needed since the Dorovitzes were newcomers to the area, and told her that they could find him in Zamolina at the edge of the forest and were always welcome in their home.

Ilana, seemingly needing a connection told Andrew that she would like to meet his family one day.

"We are all part of the same family, isn't that so? I believe we can be friends in good or bad times" said Andrew carefully. After shaking her hand formally, and leaving the sleeping Dorovitz on the porch, he told Ilana: "I need to be back on the road. My wife always says 'all loves comes home.'"

Ilana returned a warm smile. "Please give her all my good wishes."

Andrew rode back to the farm mulling over his good start with Dorovitz and hopefully a connection with Ilana. Marianne greeted him as he climbed off the wagon onto a carpet of autumn leaves. Later that evening, after dinner, he told her, "Today's task may have been disagreeable, but it may prove to be life-saving."

Marianne thought of the coming plight of Dorovitz's children. If the parents were punished or eliminated what would happen to the innocent little ones? Andrew suggested that they could be responsible for them if need be, and that he would offer that idea to Ilana in the future.

Marianne's worries at the moment however, were about her father and family, facing the ensuing invasion.

September 14, 1939:

As Nazi troops entered Gdynia, the Polish seaport west of Danzig and attacked from East Prussia, then swept around Warsaw and began to close in on the Polish capital, the Soviet Union and Pravda launched an anti-Polish propaganda campaign with a front-page article deploring the treatment of minorities in Poland,

Sunlight was glistening through the trees in Polesie .With a twinkle in his blue eyes and a smile on his lips, Andrew stood in the field gazing up at the mantle of the rainbow on the horizon. He and Stefan were harvesting the cabbage and a potato crop made bountiful by the heavy rains at the end of summer. Soon their baskets were filled to the brim. Marianne and Maria were in the forest collecting berries and mushrooms. At the end of the day, as they returned toward the house,

120

traffic on the road had changed. Military vehicles, filled with retreating soldiers going toward the west, were passing the ragged people heading eastward. As Marianne and Andrew drew near to their home, they spotted a small group of weary soldiers pause at the roadside as the convoy dragged to a halt. The brave men sat down under the shade of a birch tree and placed their rifles on the grass. Marianne and Andrew thought that the Russians may have invaded Poland and that the army could be rushing to join the major force of troops. Even so, they would be sadly outnumbered. These men looked defeated and spiritless from the turmoil of their combat. They were injured and beaten, one had a bandaged head and another had his arm in a blood-soaked sling. The stark reality was that they were ill equipped with arms and food; thin ragged boys dragging guns along with them. Andrew and Stefan hurriedly fetched food and water, as they often did for weary travelers.

The brave, young soldiers, grateful for the food, heartily ate every last bit of bread, mushrooms and potatoes and thirstily drank from the water gourd that Andrew brought. Marianne said, "Thank God you are alive," then always anxious for any scrap of news about her father and family, asked what was happening on the front.

One young looking soldier answered "The war is not going well. We pray for it to end,"

Andrew thought the boy looked not more than fourteen years old. "Where do you come from?"

"From Bydgosz," he said.

"From Krakow," answered a grizzled looking veteran, who was probably the leader of the group.

Marianne told him that they were originally from there as well and the man sad sadly. "It's over for Krakow...perhaps it is already lost."

Marianne, fearing the worst for her family, tried to remain calm at least outwardly, as her insides began to churn.

The soldier continued "The Nazis have taken over control of the city. They didn't have too much resistance after they left to head toward Warsaw. There's still some hope, Pani. Thousands are putting up a fierce fight in Warsaw."

Andrew's quiet strength and calm demeanor drew people out and like a priest in a confessional, he patiently listened to them. The man continued bitterly, "When the Nazis advanced from Silesia and Slovakia to the west, and from East Prussia to the north, we were unprepared,

121

disorganized and demoralized before the battle even started. There was such confusion at Bydgosz; I was part of the rear guard, instructed to delay the Nazi advance as long as was possible. We armed some civilians who volunteered to join us. The narrow streets of this town forced the Nazis to abandon their tanks, and go in on foot. We started shooting at them from windows, doorways, behind walls, and from anywhere we could hide to fire. We held them for most of the afternoon. The Nazis finally stopped their attack. We pulled back leaving some as a rear guard. The next morning, the people who lived in the houses which had housed gunmen were shot."

The captain, who had been at the far end of the row of soldiers, stepped forward and introduced himself as Jan Malinowski, a veteran of terrible battles who had observed multiple atrocities and he vowed to continue to fight on. His lean, strong face was one of courage and quiet dignity and Marianne liked him instantly. She thought how effective he could be as the leader of a secret paramilitary group and his cavalry would be perfect for this terrain. When Marianne suggested he join the resistance movement at Zamolenski's estate, the captain assured her he would certainly give it thought but right now he had a duty to continue the fight with the army. He thanked them for the food and water, and for the hope and encouragement. His final words were "We will hold our ground. *Z'bogem.* Good luck to you." As the soldiers marched up the road towards Pinsk, their rifles slung over their shoulders, they glanced nervously skyward and Marianne thought, "Their battle is not over, nor is ours."

SEPTEMBER 16, 1939

Marianne woke Andrew at midnight, and made him a breakfast of corn meal mush and coffee, made from ground acorns and chicory. Andrew's back ached, and he was tired from the field work the day before. However he was working toward a trustful relationship with Ilana and Tomas Dorovitz, using kindness, conscience, sacrifice, loyalty, and real courage, which was antithetical to the credo that they followed. His life was at risk every time he traveled to Dorovitz's home. Information from them was a desperate need, so Andrew felt pressure to succeed, before Tomas Dorovitz became a First Communist Commissar.

Marianne felt a need also to see Zamolenski; she wanted local war news as well as word about her family. She left the children at the Pasternaks for the day, met Magdalene, and climbed aboard the family's wagon which had a lamp at each side of it to shed some light on the road ahead.

Both women were wearing raggedy, typical peasant attire, dressed in several layers of sweaters and long pants over scuffed, muddy boots. They had applied earth to their usually shining regular features to look like weathered, working women. Marianne was wearing an old ragged topcoat tied with a rope about her waist functioning as a belt and on her head she had a faded babushka Both women carried revolvers, obtained from retreating soldiers, underneath their coats.

The dawn of the day showed the devastation and destruction in the town of Ratwyn as they drove through it. Dead, decaying horses, lay in front of shacks burned to the ground, and in some places all that was left were gray patches of ash on the hillside. Trees were uprooted, and Magdalene grasped tightly on to Marianne when they realized that this was the very spot where she and Andrew rescued her.

Grimly she said "I will never forget the red arm band and the repulsive face spouting obscenities as he tried vainly to hide his Polish accent as he shot my husband and two sons, while they were kneeling and crying "Long Live Poland! I want revenge."

By mid-morning they reached the railroad station in Janow. In the eerie, smoky, surreal silence, the rage on the faces of people was apparent as they walked quickly through the square. The debris had not been touched since the last time Marianne had approached St. Stanislaus Cathedral. The streets leading to the square were spotted with deep craters caused by the bombing damage. They tied the horses to a post near to the Church, and walked quickly into the old building. Magdalene and Marianne slipped silently into the last pew in the rear, feeling connected to the many men and women at mass. They sang emotionally "*My Cheher Bogem.*" (We want God for Home and Country).

Poland is not lost

As long as we are alive.

Poland still is not forgotten

While her sons remain.

Honor out of shame begotten

Let our swords proclaim.

Marianne thought of the long difficult road ahead, and prayed silently for guidance along the way; however, she thanked God for the love in her life, which would survive all the struggles.

123

After Mass, they looked for Zamolenski, aware of their danger in the midst of murderers and traitors who just might be looking in the church for "enemies of the people", and also for the targeted Marianne Krull.

Pan Zamolenski's automobile arrived, closely guarded fore and rear by a car full of armed guards. Marianne had trouble deciding how she, a ragged looking peasant, could approach the elegant looking Zamolenskis without arousing suspicion. Anna Zamolenski was out of the car distributing bread to the hungry people. She looked out of place in contrast to poorly clad worshipers. Magdalene suddenly nudged Marianne to look at a man standing across the street. He was tall, large and well dressed, and he was flanked by two heavy set women wearing sable fur hats. Magdalene tightened her grip on Marianne's arm when she recognized the man as Dumblosky. She wanted to kill him on the spot, but with the NKVD carefully searching the Christian church goers for potential arrests, this was not the time or the place. Marianne sent her to the far opposite side of the square to keep an eye on him.

They had to make contact with Zamolenski; however, the NKVD must continue to believe that these women were Sunday morning beggars. Marianne got at the very end of the line, and when she reached Anna , she said that she felt ill from hunger and "fainted" .Anna knelt beside her As she cleaned her face, she took a closer look and gasped: "Oh, my God ! Marianne! It is you."

Jan, seeing the old peasant woman on the pavement rushed to his wife and the woman. When he realized that it was Marianne, he said," You know we are being watched this very minute so we can speak only briefly,"

They "helped" Marianne down the now empty steps of the cathedral, and Magdalene after signaling that Dumblosky had left, joined them. As the Zamolenskis guided the peasant woman to the street, Marianne introduced Magdalene as her remarkable partner, and sadly told them of the tragic murder of Father Zajac. Anna and Jan, visibly shaken, called him a true martyr. Marianne then went on to alert them of Andrew's infiltration of the Dorovitz farm. Most of all she wanted to know about her father. Zamolenski removed a letter from his pocket and gave it to her

At his car, he opened the trunk, and while ostensibly treating Marianne, now seated on the running board, he gave her a package of medicine, including morphine, iodine, penicillin and aspirin, which she tucked under her voluminous coat. The letter, however, she clutched in her hand.

Jan Zamolenski had little time to speak, or even be seen with Marianne, now partially hidden from sight on the side of his car; he rushed information at her, including the fact that Dorovitz was a trained assassin from Moscow, who came to Polesie some years ago with his wife Ilana and their six children. He continued "the Soviets under General Timoshenko are expected to invade Northern Polish Lithuania and the Polish southwest. General Kovalyov will invade the north via Belorussia. Watch out for them; this General is ready to kill every Pole, Ukrainian, and Byelorussian who may be a threat to the state. I am placed as a leader of the Polish resistance movement. However, the Soviets will see me as the community leader able to amiably settle grievances and political questions."

Zamolenski continued to describe his role in keeping the Polish underground in contact with the rest of the world, and he believed his visibility would protect him as the only leader in Polesie. He would stay in contact with friends in the Polish Government, if it went into exile.

Anna added that she hoped for the success of the "zones of freedom" as a secret haven and network for the starving and persecuted.

Jan felt that they were being watched and had to go, and as Marianne and Magdalene thanked their saviors, he said "We have made our choice to stay. "

Marianne added that if possible, could they meet on October 5, at noon on this corner. "We will need supplies of guns, food, and medicine." She told Jan of Captain Malinowski, and that he may very well fit into her plan to form a resistance troop of militia. As the two women limped and leaned on each other, one clutching a loaf of bread, the car pulled away, and any observer would have thought very little of the event.

They shuffled their way to the wagon, where Marianne removed the packet from under her coat, and asked Magdalene to drive, and stop somewhere safe out of the town where she could read it.

After what seemed like a very long time, she pulled the wagon off onto a side road and brought the vehicle to a stop. She sat quietly looking on, as Marianne carefully opened the brown envelope, and with hands shaking, started to read the letter.

September 9, 1939

My Beloved Marianne,

    Hope you are well. I saw six horror- filled days during the fall of Krakow. Our house, our beautiful house, is now occupied by the Nazi higher officials. It would be dangerous to write where we are living, but we are safe. Many of those who attended our Tuesday meetings have been arrested.

    We have been warned that any resistance against occupational forces will be dealt with by deadly measures. Fifty randomly selected Poles will be killed for each Nazi that falls to a resistance fighter."

Your Pani Kovalska is dead. I know she was your female guiding light and part of our family for thirty-five years. She was shot after firing at the Nazis from her window. She displayed great courage and honor as part of the Ludwig family.

    The streets in parts of Krakow were littered with corpses. Only God knows how many perished across the landscape of Poland. Allied help never came. Where were the British? Where were the French? They betrayed us while they talk of a fraudulent war.

    Eventually I am going to Warsaw to meet Stephany and Joseph and to fight, and to preserve what is worth saving: Polish heritage, character, and justice. We will lead the charge to preserve the Polish heart to the end. Like an old soldier, I prefer to die in battle rather than be led to slaughter. We may be heartbroken and betrayed, but please do not despair.

As we would say," Is that all?

    Now for news for you: be vigilant, Dumblosky knows your identity. He has killed an entire Polish family, taken their credentials and escaped into eastern Poland. He and his two sons are a threat to your life as they work with the Communists. He has changed to blend in with the fleeing refugees, not as a Pole, but as a traitor

    I love you very much. Thinking of you helps me carry on. You and Zamolenski must fight the fight. Farewell, my daughter.

Your loving father,

Ludwig

    Marianne wept as she shared the letter with Magdalene. After a long period of silence, Marianne turned to her as if she was thinking out loud: "Ludwig's spirit in me shall never die before his name. We need the Liberty Zone inside of Polesie more than ever."

They rode silently the rest of the way home. Upon reaching the Pasternak's house where Andrew led the sleepy- looking four children to them, Pasternak and Makowski, looked disheartened and told the sad news that four new families recruited for the "Zone of Freedom" had decided to leave in the middle of the night. One by one, each family picked up, left their property and homes behind to make the difficult journey to Hungary and Rumania, and one family had headed directly to Warsaw. Pasternak said firmly "We are staying and holding our ground."

When the families, gathered together, had eaten, Andrew sent the children out of doors, so that the adults could talk. They had to find a secure place for the new medical supplies, and they were finally hidden under a floor board. Marianne knew that the group present had to agree on a course of action. Ideas were spilling out all over the place. Finally, Andrew held up his hand for silence, and since he rarely chattered on when he spoke, everyone listened intently. He said "We cannot compete with guns and military brutality, but we can live on our terms as a form of resistance. The Nazis believe we only know how to die for our country. The Communists believe, on the other hand, that they can crush our spirit. However, all of us together can build a sanctuary, not only to save our lives and bodies but our souls as well."

Marianne told them of her meeting with the Zamolenskis, and they all started, right there, to formulate their plans for the construction of the zone of freedom in the middle of the marshy forest. First and foremost was the establishment of a secret security system to give information only to the most trusted allies and also to find a way to get news.

The secret enclave in the woods had ramshackle shelters left over from earlier peat gatherers set, almost buried in the earth. In this way, they could remain hidden from invaders who could not navigate the disguised marshy tails without putting themselves in danger. Logistically, everything they needed was within the forest; dried peat could serve as fuel, and the smell of it burning was less obvious than wood smoke. Food could be hidden, cached and supplemented with wild berries and mushrooms, which if harvested and dried properly would offer sustenance. They presented the ruse that they were simple peasants who not only accepted whatever came to rest in Polesie, but also aided them.

Marianne feared that once parts of the Soviet army reached them, and she thought they were probably as close as Pinsk, by now, all the telegraph wires would be cut.

Wladek said that they were grossly outnumbered no matter how many men were coming from any direction. There was no Polish army large enough to stop them. Marianne noted that the Soviets need the harvest; therefore, they cannot be defeated in Polesie. They also talked of Andrew's safety as long as he continued to work for Dorovitz.

Andrew told the little group that the harvest must be quickly finished and hidden away in storage. Building the shelters also needed to be done. They left each other fully aware of the seemingly insurmountable barriers to be overcome. After the women went home, Andrew and Stefan joined the village men to harvest crops during the darkening hours. Haste and long hours were to be a part of their life for a while.

SEPTEMBER 17,1939

Soviet troops entered Poland. After the Nazi attack, there was almost no defense on any front. The Poles had only 18 battalions in the east of their country. The Red Army invaded along the entire 1300 km border, advancing against the surprised Poles; therefore, Soviet forces advanced virtually unopposed. The Polish government fled towards the Romanian border. St. John's Cathedral, in Warsaw was bombed during mass, leaving the dead to be buried in public parks because the cemeteries were full. Although Warsaw was isolated, converging Nazi forces took 40,000 Polish prisoners; however, they stopped because of the Soviet invasion in the east.

At 2:15 a.m. M. Waclaw Grzybowski, the Polish Ambassador to the U.S.S.R., was formally summoned to the Soviet Foreign Office. He was received by M. Potemkin, who informed him that the Soviets considered the Polish Government disintegrated, and therefore, to them, the Polish State had in fact ceased to exist, and all agreements between the U.S.S.R. and Poland were now void. Since Poland was without leadership, he continued, it had become a suitable field for all manner of hazards and surprises constituting a threat to the U.S.S.R. The Soviet Government is indifferent to the fate of kindred Ukrainian and White Russian people living on Polish territory, who were now defenseless.

Therefore Potemkin, continued , the Soviet Government had ordered its troops to cross the Polish border to protect the lives and properties of the populations of Western Ukraine and Western White Russia. He concluded that the Soviet Government would help remove the Polish people from the unfortunate war into which they had been dragged by their unwise leaders; this invasion would lead to a continued peaceful life.

John Gunther, a reporter wrote in London, "This has been a hard day today, a bad day. We've seen something very terrible to watch: The death of a free country - The death of a nation. Poland was killed today, in effect assassinated for the fourth time in its unhappy history, Poland has been partitioned . . . . . for all intents and purposes the Poland we have known these past 20 years has ceased to be."

SUNDAY SEPTEMBER 17, 1939

On a dreary Sunday morning of September 17th, a shaken Pasternak, and all the others of the germinating resistance band were standing at Andrew and Marianne's door. While the dog was barking and the children were screaming and fighting over a toy, he asked them if they had known of the arrival of the Soviet military. He heard on his wireless that they had crossed the Polish border with forty divisions of two million men who were invading the towns in parts of the southeast and northeast. They all realized that the Nazis had cleared the way for the Bolsheviks.

Marianne was still agonizing over the fate of her father and family. She said "We knew it was coming!" At least we are somewhat prepared, that is better than panic or retreat."

Pasternak continued to say that over four hundred fifty thousand Polish Jewish citizens from the western sector joined forces with the Soviet Union, as regulators, Communist Commissars, or joined the List of Workers to secure the transition from a Polish State to Sovietization. Pasternak told of the coming Soviet salvation of the Ukrainians, White Russians and the Polish people announced on the radio that morning.

They stood in numb silence, the children suddenly quiet. The adults were shocked and furious. The need to take some immediate action, even as helpless as they felt, became apparent. Andrew, in his usual fashion led them to the little Altar, now only lit by a votive light, since his carved Virgin had been moved to the forest enclave. He prayed for guidance, help and direction. He said that even if the world knew little of the truth, nothing was hidden from God's eyes, and reminded those present that it wasn't our will but God's that would help them through the worst of times.

They settled down at the table in the one room, and decided to keep a hidden record of this slaughter and above all keep to a survival plan. Anything that they put in writing would be subject to confiscation and remuneration. They vowed, at Andrew's insistence, to keep a unity of faith united against an Atheistic hoard; even in the small world in which they now lived, there was still a voice, although it may not yet be heard.

Marianne commented that a need for paper to write on, once taken for granted in schools where it was thrown away daily, now became magnified. The Bolsheviks saw no need for it, since those able to write would be obliterated. Therefore, they had to plan; they realized everything to the smallest detail. There was no way, she knew now, that mail, letters or information would ever leave the country. Censorship would be more far reaching, and eventually would include verbal expression and then would invade the inner core of the being, causing a docile populace. Marianne's anger surfaced again, knowing that the Soviets were trying to convince the American media that the world war could not be blamed on them. No matter, they realized their home soil would soon be soaked in blood, and locally in   two or three days, Dorovitz would also have power.

WEDNESDAY SEPTEMBER 20, 1939

Prime Minister Neville Chamberlain addressed the House of Commons in London:

"No Threats Will Deter Us: We will fight to eliminate Hitlerism"

"On September 17, an event occurred which inevitably had a decisive effect on the eastern front.

On the morning of September 17, Russian troops crossed the Polish frontier at points along its full length and advanced into Poland.

I cannot say that the action of the Soviet Government was unexpected. Statements had appeared in the Soviet press and on the Soviet wireless, referring to the positions of the White Russians and Ukrainians in Poland, which bore the interpretation that the Soviet government was preparing the ground for intervention.

On September 17, a note was handed to the Polish Ambassador to Moscow to the effect that Warsaw, as the capital of Poland, no longer existed, that the Polish Government had disintegrated, and the Polish State and its government had ceased to exist. In the same way, agreements between Poland and the Soviet government ceased to exist.

Poland became a suitable field for all manner of hazard and surprises that might constitute a threat to the Soviet Union. The Soviet could therefore no longer present a neutral attitude and the Soviet government had ordered troops to cross the frontier and take under their protection the lives and property of the Western Ukraine and Western White Russia. The Polish Ambassador to Moscow refused to accept this note and has since been instructed to ask for his passport. A copy of this message was sent to His Majesty's Ambassador to Moscow with a note stating that the Soviets would pursue a policy of neutrality in relations between the U. S. S. R. and Great Britain.

A similar communication was made to the diplomatic representatives of the foreign powers at Moscow. In view of this situation, His Majesty's Government authorized the issuance of a statement on September 18 that this attack by the Soviet Government upon Poland—at a moment when Poland was prostrate on its face by overwhelming forces brought against her by Germany—could not be justified by the arguments put forward. While the full implication of these events was not yet apparent, nothing had occurred which would make any difference in the determination of His Majesty's Government to fulfill their obligations to Poland and to prosecute the war with all energy until all obligations were achieved.

The effect of the Russian invasion on the hard-pressed Poles naturally has been very serious. The Polish forces are still continuing their courageous resistance............

Let me conclude by quoting the words of the famous Polish general who, in bidding good-bye to the recent Allied military mission, said:" We shall fight. A large part of our country will be overrun. We shall suffer terribly. But if you come in we know that we shall rise again."

SEPTEMBER 20, 1939

Marianne was writing at her table, finding that recording as much as she heard of the invasions increased her sense of hopelessness, but she continued writing; if it weren't for Andrew she wouldn't be able to hold on to each day. It was his inner faith, almost a glow that carried her along. "Only a Pole born and raised on this sacred soil could fully recognize the awful cruelty, the injustices, the mistakes, and the desecration of the beautiful land and its people. She wrote: "The Communists' are transforming Poland into a slave state."

She continued with tales of the barbaric Soviet takeover, and the fact that the Bolsheviks were in Polesie, bringing their cruelty and oppression; supposed traitors were hanged instantly; farmers were shot;

children were mutilated, and above all their movement was to rid the land, closer to home now along the Pripet Marshes towards Pinsk, of educated Polish and Lithuanian Catholic leaders.

Meanwhile, Andrew had to continue to develop a relationship with Dorovitz, before Tomas had realized a false sense of power and achieved a complete destruction of all the families in Polesie. Andrew even went as far as to attend a rally in the square in Pinsk where Dorovitz was speaking. Stefan was aboard as well. When they reached the town, there was Thomas, posturing, gesturing and exploding with power like a strutting rooster. The market square was jammed with trucks waving the Polish flag minus its white bar, symbolizing a "red" takeover. Soviet soldiers lined the streets, wildly celebrating. Several, as if on cue, entered the shops and emerged laden with food, bottles of vodka and links of sausage, wrapped around their necks. Nearby, one soldier in a truck, waved to a pretty young girl standing in the square and beckoned for her to come over. She reluctantly obeyed and the soldier, thick in the neck and shoulders, picked her up like a toy doll and sat her down next to him. He began to drive rapidly around the square, and as the truck went faster and faster, screaming people scattered to safety. Andrew had held Stefan on his shoulder at the far edge of the crowd, and a good thing that he did, because the truck started to careen wildly and Andrew darted out of its path. Stefan was trembling; they were both unhurt, but several people were injured. At the end of the demonstration of muscle flexing, filled with a vulgar display of arrogance, Andrew was spotted by Dorovitz as he started to leave. However revolting, it was good to be seen as a supporter. Stefan's cheek was tweaked by this dreadful man, and he introduced himself like the polite little boy that he was. Andrew had made the proper impression on Dorovitz, and though he wrestled spiritually with lying, and playing the fool, he knew it was needed. Andrew thought, "How can I be so close to this monster, our enemy, yet it is the smartest thing I can do to save lives?" He had portrayed the pure, innocent peasant to the hilt, and hoped to put it behind him when he reached his sanctuary: home.

THURSDAY SEPTEMBER 21, 1939

Nazi troops intensified the artillery bombardment of key points in Warsaw, and initiated "The Heydrich Plan" which involved the deportation of 600,000 Jews from Danzig and western Poland to central Poland to be concentrated in urban ghettoes. In the United States, Franklin Roosevelt was working at keeping America out of the war by repealing the Neutrality Act which provided embargo on arms sales to belligcrent countries. "Our acts must be guided by one single hard-headed thought -- keeping America out of this war," the president said. Allowing arms to be sold on a cash-and-carry basis would be "better calculated than any other means to keep us out of war."

Andrew and Stefan had returned from Pinsk, slowly avoiding the main road because of all kinds of human traffic. After succeeding at being seen with Dorovitz at his side, Andrew was anxious to get away from even the outskirts of the city. Little Stefan shook with fear as he watched the tanks, and their giant guns, as they slowly clanked along the road. At one point, Andrew tried to shield Stefan from sight of the bodies of executed Polish soldiers lying in a ditch near the road; the little boy started to cry; he worshipped the Polish soldiers, and he kept asking over and over "tell me why Tata". All Andrew could do was weep silently and hold the child as close as he could. They had reached the end of the day's journey. It had been filled with terror and fear, yet Andrew felt that the trip was worth the danger just so he could appear with Dorovitz. Andrew felt that the hatred was behind him as he once again returned to the refuge of love in his home.

FRIDAY SEPTEMBER 22, 1939

Britain began gas rationing. Germany rationed bread and flour. Bialystok and Lwow fell to the Soviets. Many of the Polish officers were captured by the Soviets and deported to Russia where they were liquidated a year later in the Katyn forest near Smolensk. However, all of these tragedies were matched on a smaller scale in Polesie, food was made scarce, and peasant life became harder.

Andrew and Stefan had sadly returned home and fell into bed, only half coherent with the story of his day. However, in the morning he told Marianne the whole horrible sequence of events. She began to live for the day of revenge. The enemy was in sight in front of their house on the road, and the people who passed by in an endless stream, changed from fleeing peasantry to military conquerors. Marianne knew that there was no sanctuary for her family where the road was filled with Russian troops. These men in uniforms, with a megaphone mounted on the truck yelled "We have come to help you."

Stefan had asked his father "Tata, aren't these the soldiers and tanks we saw yesterday? Aren't they the ones who were killing Polish soldiers?"

133

"Yes. We saw them yesterday. Now we all know the bad things they can do."

That morning, they were scheduled to meet in the marsh again. They slid out the door of the house, now cognizant of "observers' ; to any one of them, this family resembled poor potato -digging farmers carrying loads of pulled plants into the woods for compost. Actually, once they reached the hidden paths in the wood, they gathered with the others. Wladek Pasternak's anger had gotten the best of him; his face was beet red. He had heard of the Russian atrocities in the region and from the wireless, across the land of his beloved Poland,. Marianne realized that the Bolsheviks had never imagined the depth of the fervor of the native Pole for his love of his homeland. Wladek said, "The Soviets are proudly reporting that near the village of Iwnovo, armed local Ukrainian Communist peasants gained control of the rail link between Pinsk and Brews. In the northeastern part, Communist Byelorussians connected with the Red Army, blindfolded and then shot 300 Polish soldiers."

When he stopped for breath, Marianne spoke to him as harshly as she was able and said "Please, all of you landholders flee the country immediately. This may be your last chance."

Wladek, however, quietly answered "This is our land. There is more to life than escaping. I choose to die honorably on my property."

Barbara said: "No need to worry. We have a better chance to survive after we build the Liberty Zone. We are too valuable to the regulators with the harvest and all. They must believe that, or surely we would have been massacred as they did other landholders. So what is there to live for except for the larger family here in Polesie? That's our connection to the whole. Wladek and I are staying."

Florence Makowski spoke. "Surviving on our land is not enough. We must live for the next generation. While the Communists and Nazis are destroying, we are building, expanding the family, sustaining the continuity of love of home, country, and God."

These people were proud men and women. They all knew that death was certain for landholders and others in professions of leadership. Adam and Florence Makowski were the largest landholders in the region, Magdalene, who was as beautiful as she was intelligent and Luba, the healer, represented all that is good, and therefore were probably doomed.

They all moved slowly toward the Black Madonna in the center of this grotto, hidden deep in God's woods. They knelt before the icon of the Blessed Virgin, and prayed as they had every morning since the beginning of their vigil, for the many that were lost, for the safety of their families, and for Poland to continue to have a soul in the face of impending evil.

The small group of patriots knelt before the Blessed Mother, and determined their course amid the maelstrom that surrounded them. This was the very instant that they decided to move everyone into the forest, rather than to use it for a sporadic sanctuary and storage place. They had, momentarily, found an inner peace. They loved being Polish, Catholic; however, now they were defenders against the barbarians of the east.

MONDAY SEPTEMBER 25, 1939

Warsaw was captured by the Nazi forces following massive bombings. As the city was being destroyed and captured, deep in the forest of Polesie, another was being built. The Liberty Zone people were constructing secret passages into the forest, and off the road to Pinsk. Everyone in the Grotto settlement worked late into the night. Some trusted families, newly recruited by the Makowskis, and Magdalene, worked together with the Pasternaks to harvest bushels of wheat, rye, potatoes, and cabbages by day, hiding them in underground covered pits by night. Andrew and Stefan created forest passageways, by marking trees and rocks along the way during the early morning hours. These markings were known only to the inner sanctum of the zone. Each of them was connected by a hidden entrance behind the Ludwig's, Makowski's' and Varya's homes, all of which were designed for a quick escape. These routes were secretly completed, and carefully hidden from watchful eyes. Wladek Pasternak became the nominal leader; his house was unprotected and very visible from the side of the road facing the vast fields, diagonally across from the Ludwigs. And it stood alone next to the abandoned homes of the four families who had left.

Marianne, curled up next to Andrew, in bed, was awakened by gnawing worry. Dorovitz had not been heard from since the rally welcoming the Soviet army into Pinsk. Too many questions surfaced concerning trust in these unconscionable people.

As usual, she listened to the sounds coming from the road, and this morning it was too quiet she thought, although she heard the clip-clop of horses outside their house. She awakened Andrew and the children. He opened the window curtain just enough to view who was outside and saw that Tomas Dorovitz was in the field, accompanied by several large men on horseback. Dorovitz casually walked toward the house with his usual burning cigarette in hand. He looked like the NKVD trained, Communist mercenary from Estonia that he was, complete with muddy trousers, dirty boots, a bulky sheepskin jacket and a red arm band. He was carrying a Soviet-made rifle cradled on his arm. Andrew dressed hurriedly, and scooted the children out to the yard in back of the house. Marianne had to keep her ragged peasant guise and look as subservient as she could. He knocked loudly. "Open up" he demanded. Andrew slowly unbolted the door, opened it widely and said calmly, "Tomas, how are you? What can we do for you?"

Dorowitz had come to inspect the "Ludwig" house, and to see if Andrew was really what he said he was. Dorovitz stalked into the house, followed by four or five surly looking dirty soldiers or bodyguards. He demanded water and the use of the stove from Andrew for tea. It was 6:00 A.M., and this boor had arrived for a surprise check on his personal Polish peasant worker.

After Andrew brought him water, Dorowitz filled a tea pot with his own tea leaves which he produced from one dirty looking pocket, and without an invitation, sat at the family table. His soldiers went about the house, inspecting every part of it for some sort of contraband. Dorovitz was, in his own eyes, holding court with the subservient Polish peasantry. Marianne sat huddled on a chair by the fire, and tried to ignore the soldiers staring at her. Dorovitz told them that the four empty houses down the road, occupied by the families that the Pasternaks had helped leave, would soon be full again. He leaned on the table menacingly and vividly described the fate of the four families.

Marianne felt real terror inside; however, she choked back the tears, wanting more than anything to kill the ghastly man, who was arrogantly bragging about his triumph, in their home. This menace felt as deeply about the deaths of his fellow man, no more than someone did stepping on an ant. She knew that to keep Andrew in the clear, they both had to appear submissive and stupid as they pretended to agree with him while acknowledging his superiority.

Dorovitz however, had turned his attention to Andrew, and seemed to have a need to qualify his visit to a lowlife to his companions. "He repaired a roof for me in half the time and then didn't even charge me for it; he fixed my windows and welcomed our soldiers in Pinsk." he said as he gestured towards Andrew who was serving his tea.

The soldiers at this point were all focused on Marianne; even though she was dirty looking, and in raggedy clothes, she was still a fine looking woman, particularly to men who had been on the road for a long while. Rape, in the Soviet system, was a form of reward, she knew, especially of Catholic and Christian women. She became very frightened.

Dorovitz poured the tea into the tin cups. "I hope I did not offend your wife when I told her about the awful business that we are in, but I am obeying my orders from Moscow. Religious and ethnic cleansing is a must here before the implementation of Sovietization."

While Dorovitz drank his tea, he boasted about a Soviet attack on a Polish naval squadron stationed in Pinsk, a base used for patrolling the Pripet marshes with motor launches. The soldiers had refused to surrender. They were all killed, since they decided to fight until they ran out of ammunition.

Marianne sat expressionless, afraid to speak to this gross man. He went on to explain that hanging people as examples, promotes hatred and fear. He implied that anyone who left before the harvest would be treated in the same way, since the army was hungry.

Dorovitz continued with his loud soliloquy. Andrew could only mutter that he couldn't kill anything, it was not in his nature.

At that point the soldiers, full of tea, went outside, turned their backs and urinated in Marianne's garden. Tomas, framed in the doorway in the early morning light, changed his tone radically; this time the information was not threatening, but a warning; he justified it by saying that he trusted Andrew because his wife did. He confided in him that within the next few weeks, local regional Revolutionary Committees, loyal to Moscow's NKVD, called the List of Workers would be formed to keep law and order in towns, villages and cities. Although this takeover would resemble the democracy that the world press wanted to report, in reality it was a Soviet takeover. Dorovitz said that he would be in control of the area and would, hopefully, report only to Comrade Khrushchev. Dorovitz looked around again, still afraid that he could be overheard and spoke quietly.

"You are still a Polish Catholic, and therefore, you are a suspect. After annexation of this territory, the NKVD is in control, even if I am in charge. They will set guards on this road and place our regional headquarters here in Zamolina. We will need to remove Wladek Pasternak, from here, while watching his wife, since they helped Mayor

137

Kowalski and the four families who left at night and now are hanging as a payment. Kowalski is dead. Loyal families will move in to regulate this region, and to set up crop quotas as they assess the production capabilities for next year. Welcome them."

He continued, "We need peasants to harvest the land, but rumor has it that guerilla groups are forming to defy the State. My men will take care of Pasternak. Believe me, he will get the message, but first we need everyone here to finish the harvest."

Marianne was stunned. Inwardly she prayed, "Please God, let Wladek return home."

Andrew sensed that Dorovitz wasn't yet finished, and thought a sympathetic silence was the best he could offer. He knew that like most insecure self-aggrandizing people, Tomas would say more. He explained that Poles are officially the enemies of the people, and from now on, he was listed by the Revolutionary Committees, and would be ordered to relocate providing homes and land for the loyalists and regulators. All land holders, teachers, army officers and potential leaders would be separated and assigned to NKVD agents.

They needed, he said, to remove all the obstacles to their cause. From somewhere deep in his black soul, Dorovitz felt kindness to these good people, even pitied them a bit, so he admonished them to stay away from the Pasternaks and Makowskis and Bolshevik Ukrainians because they were different. The List of Preferred Socialists, he pointed out, would eliminate all "clean hands" in the first three to six weeks. After that, Sovietization, would begin in mid- November, then every Pole would be deported to Siberia to prepare to fight Nazis and build armaments.

Marianne and Andrew stayed silent while Dorovitz continued to ramble on about what was to come. "Make sure you have goods and supplies to give the soldiers and regulators horses, cows, watches, sausages, and lamb, anything of use. The Red Army troops will spare your life for any of these items, since the Polish zloty will have no value. In the coming Communist regime, anyone can be an enforcer or an informer. There will be registration and carefully monitoring of coming and going. Over two million will be evicted in less than twelve weeks. Remember you are quota, property of the state. I have checked on you... Your record is clean, except that you are a Pole and a Catholic. The people who are in charge of this region are more interested in proving who they are, by how many Poles they can eliminate in the shortest period of time, and whose loyalties they need to achieve power."

What Marianne and Andrew never understood at this time or later in their lives, was why this arrogant minor official was telling them this. Was he told to so by his wife? They never knew.

He went on to say that Kowalski's place next to Pasternak's will soon be inhabited by a worker's committee administrator from the NKVD ranks. Their goal was to extricate the entire intelligentsia of eastern Poland in the four to six weeks before winter, and Ipsek Forst was to be the administrator, He would be ruthless to prove that he was a pure revolutionary. He worked for the NKVD under Vishinsky; and would be useful for about six weeks, and then, he too, would eventually be executed. "Stay away from him." he warned

Dorovitz was running out of time as his men were mounting up, so he hastily told Marianne and Andrew that there would be a local list of victims, or enemies of the state, and fortunately they were not on it. Anyone listed, initially by the Nazis and given to the NKVD, would either be Polish patriots or anyone with relatives in western Poland.

"Obey every order, every bullhorn, and if you do not respond, you will be shot. They are on a campaign to cleanse the Eastern part of Poland of intelligent leader"

Marianne continued to wonder why these revelations of inside information? She didn't trust Dorovitz, and she still questioned, at least inwardly, his motivation. He waved at his men in the yard, as if to say wait a bit, and told Marianne and Andrew, even more rapidly to mind their own business, and to do the same activities at the same time every day. He told them to appear filthy, eat like you have no manners, and become the invisible peasant. Marianne, at that moment, realized that he knew more than he was saying about them, why else the advice. Then, uncharacteristically, he smiled, like a small boy who had followed his mother's orders. Then the truth of the confession came forth: "My wife trusts you. That is your triumph. All of our lives are temporary. Who will endure?"

Dorovitz turned to look at Marianne; had her disguise been so bad, she thought, that he saw through it? "What do you think, Marianne *Ludwig?*

The emphasis was on the last name. Her fright was somewhat lessened.

"Your husband mentions you all the time. And he is the only person in the world I trust. You have a good family, and we may need each other. I am as fearful for my wife and children as you are of yours. Ilana trusts Andrew. She feels that somehow you will survive this war. You are on your own after today, as I can't help you anymore, and we are all fortunate that Andrew came to my home before our house crumbled away."

Dorovitz finally admitted that he had been there to check up on them;

"You have a great deal to do, Andrew. Marianne, stay out of sight," he said. "You know too much and I think that behind the torn dirty, over-stuffed sweater is someone like my wife, a very smart woman who does not betray her husband."

Andrew spoke his mind to Dorovitz, offering him some solace. "We don't have a big home, but there are beautiful mornings, and we have a forest behind us. Someday, you may want to bring your children and Ilana to see it."

His meaning was not lost on Dorovitz. He knew, if needed, here was a place for his family.

Dorovitz took off his wristwatch, as if his wrist was sore, and casually asked Andrew and Marianne if they knew of a man named Dumblosky? They said they did not.

"I cannot really help you with him" said Andrew

As he started up the path, he turned, and hidden from the soldiers' view, handed Andrew his wrist watch. "Use it at the right time. Peasants do not have watches. Do not tell anyone how you got it except that you earned it working for me."

When Dorowitz was at a safe distance, Andrew and Marianne, stunned by all this information, none of which was good, clasped their hands together and started to cry. They wept for their native land and for Wladek Pasternak and the four families that had perished. They wept because the worst was yet to come.

Andrew began to pray, and curiously he started by praying for Dorovitz, who was guilty of crimes contradicting all natural laws of humanity , dignity and respect for life. He was a traitor to his honor, to his faith and to his homeland. Yet Andrew prayed for a man whom he pitied. He also prayed for the salvation of the Polish intellectual class, soon, he thought, to be gone from the earth. He prayed for those who

140

would be forced into slave labor and for those who would perish. Then Andrew asked for God's help in the creation and construction of the 'Liberty Zone" where they could do God's work in feeding the needy, while opposing the evil forces around them.

Marianne, listening and praying with him, had tears streaming down her cheeks. She had come a long way from the elegance and intellectual stimulation of Krakow to this thatched farm hut, barely furnished with a wooden table set in the middle of it, and a broken down chair by the exposed hearth, a ruse necessary for survival. While there was still time, she had to warn Barbara Pasternak, and hope and pray that Wladek would only be bruised, yet would be returned alive. Then all of them, Magdelene , the Makowskis and the rest had to move away from their homes into houses in the woods, disappear from view and assume the guise of the uneducated peasantry when necessary in public.

The warning would have to wait, however, until Dorovitz and his accompanying band of roughnecks were finished with the village. Marianne could see from the side window, the villagers gathering in the square as people do in times of trouble. She thought that the tragedy of the four families hanging from the trees, had caused them to come together to mourn the deaths in their own private way.

Dorovitz by this time was mounted, and leading his squad into the town. They were all heavily armed and now included women as well. They followed behind him like so many rats following the "*Rattenfänger*" towards Janow to seize and destroy it as liberators.

As soon as the last truck pulled out, Andrew, Marianne and the children traveled the hidden secret passageway through the woods, and wound around it to the Pasternak's house. They went through the rear door only to find Barbara, sobbing, crying and talking to herself, while kneeling, crumpled on the floor. When she saw Andrew and Marianne, she screamed "They killed him!" Marianne picked her distraught friend off the floor and held her tightly, wiping away the tears as fast as they fell. She told Barbara to calm down enough, to tell them what happened so they could see what could be done.

"It happened so fast!" she said. "I looked out the window and saw four cars with Russian flags draped on each side and guards with machine guns, and a line of soldiers behind the cars. They banged down the door before Wladek had a chance to move, then they dragged him out. I begged them to take me with him, but they punched me and threw me to the ground when I began to follow him out to their car. The soldiers searched the house after that, confiscated rifles and shotguns and took our silverware, all of our money, watches, anything they could. I tried to stop them, but they just laughed at me and hit me again. I pray to God that Wladek is alive."

Marianne told her to keep the belief that Wladek was alive and sent Andrew to warn the others. She told Barbara of Dorovitz's visit and the news that Wladek had been taken. She had to believe that they would keep him alive as a message to the rest. However, Barbara was sure that they shot him.

"You don't know that," Marianne replied.

Little Maria, this time, after seeing all the upset, crying and screaming, and with actions expected from someone older, walked to Barbara and simply held her hand, which caused both adults to start weeping again.

Marianne took the beaten woman to the forest where Andrew had placed the carved Virgin in the center of their new "zone of Freedom" .Barbara stared directly at their Black Madonna while Maria and Marianne knelt and prayed for Wladek's return. They spent the night in the forest, nestled in one of Andrew's run -down huts with the Blessed Mother looking down upon them.

During the night, Marianne awoke to see Barbara in front of the Virgin, praying aloud for her husband's safety. Andrew had long been gone to Dorovitz's farm.

THURSDAY SEPTEMBER 28, 1939

Von Ribbentrop, Hitler's representative, and Molotov the Soviet's spokesman signed a Nazi-Soviet Boundary and Friendship Treaty, which was to re-establish peace and order and to assure to the peoples living there, a peaceful life in keeping with their national character. To this end, they agreed upon a Confidential Protocol which included allowance of people of Nazi descent to migrate from Soviet territory; and for the Ukrainian and White Russian migration back to Soviet lands or territories. However, they both agreed as a supplement, that "both parties will tolerate in their territories, no Polish agitation which affects the territories of the other party. They will suppress in their territories all beginnings of such agitation and inform each other concerning suitable measures for this purpose."

Marianne thought that Barbara had spent a whole night's vigil in front of the Virgin, so she and the children knelt too, while gazing up at their own Lady of Częstochowa." Prayer works" she said," "and we must remain strong and confident that Wladek will return soon."

They left the grotto and went to the Pasternak house. They slowly crept closer, hopeful that no one was there, when from behind, they heard Wladek saying: "I knew you both would be here."

His left eye and forehead were badly bruised, as he had been beaten. Blood oozed from the corner of his mouth. Barbara held him and gently lowered him to the ground under a tree and cradled his wounded head on her lap. "Thank God, thank you God, for answering our prayers." she sobbed.

Wladek told of his ordeal, through bruised lips and a very sore jaw. They had let him go to help with the harvest as there was a need for experienced direction. He, however, knew that afterwards, they would try to eliminate him. Makowski and Pasternak had the largest farms in the district, which would yield a bumper crop.

"You must leave Poland," Marianne said firmly. "You must leave this minute."

"It's too late for that." he responded quietly. "They hanged the four families that were our neighbors. There are NKVD patrols everywhere. I saw the execution of twenty –seven human beings,"

He struggled to speak further because of the hours of questioning and beatings that he had endured. The interrogators wanted to know whom the Soviets could trust in this region, and any information of a secret group that they were sure was preparing partisan actions. When they asked him for the amount of the harvest, he had remembered Marianne's proposal to hold back fifteen percent and lied about the actual amount. He assured them that each acre would provide the needed quota to feed their armies.

By this time, Marianne had given him water, and Barbara had wiped away most of the blood; however, his eyes were darting about in panic, still, even though he knew he was safe. "God help us all." he said:

He told them that what happened after the beating was worse than the physical abuse he had suffered. The NKVD had taken him into the farmlands nearby, where the landowners owned large amounts of acreage. Each man had been identified as an enemy of the people, and, therefore, was a target of NKVD retribution. In actuality, Wladek realized, these farms had been designated as a gift for the regulators ; he was dragged from the car and forced to watch the NKVD soldiers gain entry into each house, drag the inhabitants out, ordered them to kneel, so that they could receive a bullet to the back of the head. He was not allowed to look away. This style of execution had been handed down from the Tsars of Russia to the current leadership.

As Pasternak described the scene, he started to weep silently. "How insane can one be? God, help them."

Marianne and Barbara wept along with Wladek, who said that despite the pain of the event, these animals had to be stopped.

Marianne assured him that he had to leave his current home so he would not be a victim, and that he had to hide in the forest. They would need to work hard in the coming weeks before the new regulators arrived and take more from all of them. They had to plan to hide part of the crop and move trusted families into the center of the forest. They would, she continued, disguise the peat cutters' shacks. She repeated to them that these could be heated by burning the local peat, which would leave the trees standing and would not produce the wood smoke of a hearth. If asked about the fires, they could always say it was the drying of the peat for fuel. Whatever had to be done, it was needed almost immediately; therefore, she asked Wladek to be the first governor of their own nation.

"You are the perfect person," she said. "The Soviets fear you most because you are an effective leader, and the good and decent people respect you. They will need you to lead them in the construction of our sanctuary in the woods. "

Wladek could only nod in assent. And then he passed out.

There was no more time for words.

SUNDAY OCTOBER 1, 1939

The wireless brought the bad news to Marianne: the Nazi troops had devastated Warsaw. Hitler had arrived and attended a victory parade. Marianne had nightmare after nightmare now. .She would awake with horrific images of Ludwig, Joseph and Stephany facing advancing Nazi attacks, SS guards and tanks. There was no word on the wireless of anyone's family, and even worse, she worried about Janow and Anna and Jan Zamolenski, she wondered if the NKVD had taken over Zamolenski's estate

Marianne was raised as the kind of person who needed to take action in the time of crisis. She worried that others would resent her presence and ideas; however, these moments were crucial to survival and

144

therefore she needed to act without thought of the consequences or of the feelings of others. On this Sunday morning, she needed to contact the Zamolenskis, and to hear from her father and family. She wanted to be sure that they knew of the plan of deportation to Siberia, and also to tell them of the local actions for survival.

She had hatched an idea to organize a local underground Home Army of Polish Patriots. She believed that even as ordinary people, using Polish character that always created the future, and the future belonged to the courageous spirit and goodness of its people, who could be trusted in a time of staggering sorrow; the kind that afforded an opportunity to live through it all... the kind that were honorable and believed in a future, by sustaining a humble spirit of human dignity.

Andrew, was exhausted again, having worked all day and half into the night. Marianne caught him staring   out of   the doorway, worrying about her trying to make contact with Zamolenski in Janow , hoping that somehow it could be put off. She had decided to meet him, as agreed, even in the midst of the turmoil that surrounded them. The trip was now more dangerous than ever, but necessary for the beginnings of a resistance movement on all fronts. Andrew wanted desperately to go with her; however, he knew that he was being watched constantly. Neither of them should be seen with Zamolenski, Pasternak or Makowski. Any connection, no matter how slight, would be considered espionage, and Dorovitz would shoot traitors on the spot.

Marianne convinced Andrew to start the rebuilding of housing deep in the marshy forest while she was gone. They both knew that time was of the essence. She hugged him hard, and after a long goodbye, left the warmth of her house and stood alone for a moment on the silent crater- filled muddy road. She breathed a prayer for deliverance and success, and set off alone, in the wagon, in the dark of early morning toward Janow.

After sunrise, a dirty, slovenly peasant woman on a broken down wagon, reached Janow. The people of the town, she hoped, would ignore this lone ignorant serf. She passed Bolsheviks leading a long, miserable row of thin and bedraggled refugees from Janow, who were removed from their homes, desperately trudging along, faces hidden, dragging their meager belongings behind them. .There was no hope for them, and as Marianne moved along, the once beautiful city appeared gray and dirty, with a cloud of despair hanging over it. This change had been spread all across the landscape of Eastern Poland, which reminded her, in one harsh moment, of all the murders and executions of pain that came with them. She prayed again for safety and for the souls of those lost when she reached the town square, which was now filled with Soviet NKVD soldiers. They were different from the regular Army, wearing red stripes across their hats and collars. Marianne pulled the wagon into an alley several blocks away and decided to head for the cathedral on foot.

She moved away toward St. Stanislaus, passing the railroad station, which now was filled with boxcars loaded with helpless, wailing deportees. Her heart sank as she saw old, emaciated men, young women and children, some with their hands outstretched from the slats in the cars, pleading for release. These people, she noticed, had been jammed into crowded cars with their meager possessions, with no food or water. The stench of human waste and suffering was everywhere. She could not bear to look at this scene, and to do so could have meant instant death from any soldier lined up along the way. On a platform, they had set up machine guns ready to spray their bullets. Marianne thought "Help me God. I am in a Death Zone." She hurried by, head down, eyes averted. As the rattle of the guns sounded, the box cars slowly pulled away toward the frozen grounds of Siberia. "Please God, watch over them." she prayed silently.

A police officer blocked her path abruptly, and asked her what she had seen, so she mumbled a reply in some sort of Mazovian Polish dialect, pretending not to understand him. When he demanded to know what she had seen and what she was doing, her answer became more garbled and obscure. He finally gave up and pushed her on her way. He had more important jobs to do, she guessed, like killing and torturing. Marianne shuffled along, now mumbling to herself, in what she hoped would pass as a dialect.

She turned the corner to the church, passing what had been a statue of the Blessed Mother, now occupied by the new God, Josef Stalin, a red votive light burning at his feet. He was portrayed as the new savior, she realized, but this murderer and earthly devil was far removed from her kind and caring Jesus. The sight pained her, but she moved toward the church, and at twelve, the usual bells of St Stanislaus did not ring. Had these Sunday sounds been silenced as well?

She had to find a waiting place for Zamolenski, who appeared to be late. So she left mass and crept into a narrow alley where she could see the corner on which they had promised to meet. She was behind a wall looking over a break in the rubble. Three quarters of an hour had passed and there was no sign of Zamolenski; Marianne was worried for his life; however, her wait was agonizing; each minute seemed like an eternity. As time dragged on, she focused on dealing with the horror and inhumanity that she had witnessed, and she thought of ways to insulate herself from the agony and still keep her goals in sight. How did one create a Liberty Zone amidst a prison? Maybe God had a purpose for me, she thought, I need to trust him, and as she had the idea, she saw a woman slowly walking along the edge of the sidewalk approaching the corner. She was a raggedy peasant, dirty like Marianne; she was praying; it was Anna Zamolenski!

"Jan is following me," Anna whispered as she walked toward her. Marianne was overjoyed and they hugged each other, relieved that they both were there. "Our house has been taken by the NKVD" Anna said. "At first Jan had driven them off by demanding that General Timoshenko be called, but now we are lucky to be here. Although Jan is under house arrest, we followed our underground passageway from the cellar and out of the estate to the town.

As she finished her whispered news, an old man hobbled into view. It was Zamolenski, dressed as a dirty farm worker. Marianne said, "They will shoot us all if they find out we are here. You should get out of Poland. It is suicidal to stay."

"No, Marianne," Jan answered. "We have been abandoned by the rest of the world. We will die here alone and with honor. We will succeed."

"You are the Polish hard ducha." Marianne answered. Rapidly, she told him of the free zones and the beginning of a home army or vigilante Eskadry. She continued, "We need men like Captain Malinowski. He would be a good leader for this new guerilla troop."

"I hope he can reach us in time," Jan answered.

"We are trying to add trusted families to set up a communal Liberty Zone in the depths of the forest." "Wladek Pasternak," she went on, "has taken refuge in our sanctuary in the marsh land and hopefully he will lead us."

There was little time for amenities, so Jan agreed to supply resistance equipment. In fact, he had hidden wireless transmitters, binoculars and guns, about six kilometers from the town on the road back to Zamolina, marked by a white birch tree next to a large red barn. Then, after he looked around, he stared hard at Marianne and said quietly, "You are our leader here in Polesie."

Marianne did not answer, still hoping that Pasternak would take charge when they finished the sanctuary targeted for Stefan's birthday. Jan felt that although Pasternak was a good man, he was too conspicuous. He should leave Poland. Then he reached into his coat, produced a wrapped packet, small enough to conceal, and gave it to Marianne. It was a letter from her father.

"We could only get it" Zamolenski said, "by secret courier and hidden drop- off spots. I will have a map of drop spots for you soon, for these brave couriers are our only form of communication. Your father is alive. Meet me here on November 27, and I will have maps and drop spots."

"But wait, wait, wait!" Marianne said. "Let me open the letter before you leave. There may be a note for you. With trembling hands, she opened the envelope, thrilled to see her Tata's familiar scrawl. "Indeed, there is a note attached for you, from one battle-worn patriot to another."

Zamolenski tucked away the note to be read later and patted her arm. He said, "Marianne, we are being closely watched. May God be with you! If we cannot make it back in a month, someone will be here to tell you why. You will have the supplies you need. I promise." Marianne said goodbye to her dear friends before they vanished into the rubble and smoke.

Peasants were not expected to be literate, so Marianne had to wait, the letter burning a hole in her pocket, until she got on the road and off into a clump trees, as if to tend to bodily functions. Then she read:

September 19, 1939

My Beloved Daughter Marianne,

The Nazi assaults in Warsaw have been powerful and unrelenting. Those who are still alive face the absolute savagery of constant bombardment daily. No time for details.

Joseph and Stephany fought against a 250,000 man Nazi army - More than 70,000 Warsaw citizens slaughtered. During a tank assault yesterday evening, Stephany was a messenger amid the fighters. , Joseph Kankiewicz, her husband, had both legs shattered by artillery, yet bravely ordered the twelve men and women in his command to continue to fight. A column of Nazi tanks was destroyed, but 12 brave men and women were killed including Joseph. . There is no other option but to fight, not if we believe in resisting evil to the end. This Russian invasion of eastern Poland will be covered up. Do not trust them. Hold them accountable. We expect Soviet and Nazi movement eastward.

Tell Andrew, we have made contact with Father Baron. The Benedictine Monastery is trapped. Father Baron had said, "Tell Andrew that his soul has never left"

My Marianne, my treasured one, farewell. That is not all, "Until all love comes home." If Warsaw falls, we will retreat to the Carpathian Mountains, close to the Czech border to fight another day. That will be our headquarters for our Home Army. I will meet you at the gates of Warsaw, when we have regained freedom.

Your loving father,

Now known as "Zebra"

Marianne was pained with every sentence of her father's letter, but she had to proceed with plans of what must be done. First she felt, she would have to revive the Old Testament credo of an eye for an eye and a tooth for a tooth. She tried not to think of the hideous, grinning faces of soldiers slaughtering and sending innocent Polish men and women to their deaths. She would also have to find a place to put the tragedy of family and friends somewhere in her heart and with a hard *ducha* emotionlessly carry on resistance. The tragedy, including her brother- in- law's death, could be revisited later. There could be no Christian forgiveness for these evil animals and she would try hard to move feelings aside for now and deal with them on their own level.

Alone and dirty, Marianne found the red barn that Jan had described. Under the birch trees where Zamolenski had hidden the tools of resistance, she took an oath to her father and to all the lost souls of the Polish world: "My beloved father, I will let them know the truth and will not fail you. I will cry for the 70,000 dead in Warsaw and for the 600,000 Poles who perished in the western part of the war. The dead do not suffer on earth, only the living do. Father, I have no choice, but to continue the battle. God, please help us all to survive. Please watch over us."

She covered the packaged supplies Zamolenski had left her, with a blanket in the very bottom of the wagon and continued into the pitch blackness. The road to Zamolina would be long and dangerous. She pulled another blanket over her head, and carefully watched the path ahead with the little light that the two lanterns swaying on the wagon gave. She fiercely drove into the night, occasionally smacking the horse to move faster. She thanked God that all was quiet, but for the gentle forest noises, mingled with the soft echo of the horse's hooves on the muddy ground. However, Marianne was frightened and worried about travelers on the road who could become a problem for her. After many tense hours, as she finally neared home, she heard the sounds of hoof beats coming closer and closer. She took out her revolver, determined to shoot any NKVD or soldier who came near. When a horse and rider approached, carrying a lantern, she stopped, pulled the wagon to the side of the road and climbed down into the wet grass. With revolver in hand, she stood behind the side of the horse. A man was riding a workhorse bareback, and gratefully she recognized him. Her relief and exhaustion combined into one moment of joy, "Andrew, my Andrew!" she cried out.

WEDNESDAY OCTOBER 4,1939

Casimir Smogorzewski, a Polish historian and a firsthand observer of the Soviet Occupation wrote an account: *"The inhabitants' belongings were also subjected to strict regulations, inspired by the high principle that one change of clothes and underwear satisfies all legitimate aspirations of the individual. Everything in excess of this was liable to be confiscated. Numerous roving gangs, often consisting of the very scum of society, offered their services and undertook the task of searching apartments by day and night, laying hands on anything of value. Goods assembled in this way were exported into Russia, notwithstanding the recurrent assurance: "We have everything, and you shall also have everything."*

However, the actual condition of the country people was influenced for the worse by the ruin of the natural and necessary exchange between town and country, even more than by the effect of these chaotic measures. The country folk had little enough to sell, and now there was nothing to buy. Clothes, shoes and underwear had become unattainable luxuries, ironware a precious and uncommon commodity. Sheepskin coats - a necessity in that climate, and the cherished belongings of every family, had frequently been requisitioned. In Lida, soon after the occupation, the sight of a wagonload of primitive moccasins - the footgear of the poor - produced a painful sensation. It was, no doubt, intended to be an imposing contribution towards the well-being of the newly acquired province.

Marianne in the depths of Polesie, saw dreadful signs of Soviet occupation everywhere. The sounds of wagons and trucks bound for the Urals of Union Soviet Socialists Republics via Pinsk were traveling on the road near the house day and night. They were carrying property, cattle and most precious of all, a human cargo of men, women and children, headed for the frozen tundra of Siberia, never to return to their homes they loved.

Informers, who had fled from western Poland, were now the New *Regulators*, who were not only new governing officials, but also greedy men and women who could not even be called immoral, because their actions demonstrated no ethical standard, even an evil one. They were an amoral, narcissistic group of individuals whose desire for self-survival passed any call to the needs of the rest of humanity. They were NKVD servants to Polish genocide, and were murdering their countrymen and often their own relatives.

Andrew and Marianne had started their preparations for the new "Liberty Zone". He began to get help and construct the homes deep in the forest. The marshes and wood land continued to be perfect cover, since the new Soviet regulators, and Polish informers were fortunately, ignorant of topography. These people lived as parasites, literally sucking the life out of others and their labors. Andrew, however, who had survived alone in the forest, knew every source of food, water and material that could be used economically for survival. ,

The marshes were very difficult to traverse, and any casual observer would think that there was no way to travel into the depths of this wild looking country side, and hopefully would assume that there was nothing of value buried there. Night travel through the area would only bring disaster; it was easy to get disoriented and lost, as well as it was easy to fall into a swampy muck. It was far worse in the winter when the surface froze. Andrew had carefully mapped out routes, with hidden natural markers observable only to a person who knew where they were. He also had constructed "cold pits" for storage of goods, hidden in the ground. The houses were set in a forest area, so thickly shrouded by trees, that sunlight did not often get in to light it. At night, the darkness felt as if it stretched into nothingness. In the very center of this hiding place, now dubbed the Free Zone, was the Black Virgin's shrine. Andrew's faith was the center of his life, so therefore, this Virgin became the safe haven. He thought that churches had been providing sanctuary since Christ died for us, therefore, we could do the same. This would be a place, not only to hide, but also a place to live without fear, and to continue to teach the children love of peace, the love of home, family and country, to be aware of seasons, holidays, candles, and of sunrise in the morning, and sunset at night. These traditions and the feeling of security and safety, needed to be salvaged in the presence of an enemy that was determined to destroy the foundations of a home, and the faith and human spirit that was inside it.

Near dawn, Andrew and Marianne, after her return, in the dead of night, brought the thirty watches, guns, the rounds of ammunition, the transmitters, the wireless and the medicine from Zamolenski, and hid them in the underground storage space. Marianne often remembered this as a defining moment in their lives, when they both realized that there was no turning back. They embraced tenderly, realizing that the most important possession that they had was each other's love.

Marianne stayed indoors, while Andrew and Stefan, before sunrise, took the cows, sheep, oxen, and the dog Basha into the forest and hid them in an enclosure near the huts. Marianne used Zamolenski's binoculars to peer out of her bedroom window towards the road. To a passerby, it looked from the outside, like a broken window carelessly boarded up by a peasant who could not afford new glass. However, Andrew had put an opening in the rotten looking board so that Marianne could sit in a chair and watch the road.

This morning she could see Soviet guards posted along the road facing the house, stuffing into their mouths any food that they could grab from the meager stash of the emigrants passing on the heavily trafficked road. Marianne started to weep when she saw that the five empty houses, including Kowalski's, were being filled with newly arrived regulators. However, she pulled herself together emotionally, remembering her resolve to focus on survival and not to let the uncontrollable forces effect the clarity of her thinking. She was still, unfortunately, very angry.

Later that morning, Russian soldiers were riding in long, narrow lines, back and forth behind the carts and trucks, whipping the sick and starving young and old, many of whom were marching five abreast following the caravan of trucks and carts, shivering, and shuffling their feet in the October cold. The children were crying for food, and without fresh water, they were forced to drink from puddles along the edge of the road. They had been stripped of all their clothes and their property. They were grim, cold and expressionless. Some were so ill that they were doomed to die along the way, before they even reached Siberia. Marianne wanted to tell each one of them, "You are not being overlooked. There are people out there who are not ruthless, who do not wield clubs, and do not shoot others on the spot."

The need to help turned out to be near disaster for Marianne and Maria. She had to do something, anything for these poor, anguished

152

souls, so against her better judgment and new resolve, she decided to give them some food. She took a pot full of kasha and grabbed Maria by the hand across the field to the road. A sneering Soviet Police surrogate approached her as they reached the edge of the highway. "You have been ordered to stay indoors," he said arrogantly. "Showing help of any kind means death for you and your children. Or would you prefer to join them, you fucking bitch?" Then, he removed his gun from his holster. A fat female officer, a captain, speaking perfect Polish, came up to them and said, "What are you trying to do? He can kill you on the spot. His orders are to move this march on quickly."

"We want to give them food; it is the Polish thing to do." Marianne replied as if she was too stupid to understand the discussion.

"I am not Polish, anymore" she replied. "I am a Bolshevik. See these bastards marching. They are the reason I am here, and they are working for our Socialist cause…liberation! Give them food but I order you not to remember or say anything or I'll shoot you personally,"

As Maria, still a little innocent three year old, handed the bucket to some hungry passersby, Marianne pushed her luck by saying to this officer. "You come from Warsaw. I can tell by your look, Well fed…., upper middle class. What happened?"

"I hate the people of Warsaw. It is over for them, anyway. Listen bitch! I hope you are satisfied. I left because the Poles are a bunch of bastards. The reason that you and your child are still breathing right now is that I do not want to waste my bullets. We are going to need all the bullets we can muster against the Nazis. You are taking big chances with your life. Next time, do as you are told! You have been spared for the moment. Your future depends on what I say to Ipsek Forst, and he will deal with you later. He may have even had "a conversation" with your husband." she said menacingly. "We will keep an eye on you. Now do your shit and go."

Marianne, had heard from the others about the new regulators who were not to be trusted; however, this was the first time she had heard a name. She turned from the guard, shuffling and thanking her politely, as she went toward the road. It was also the first time she had heard the rough language of these people; however, she thought later, it belonged with them and their behavior. Marianne called to a passing older woman. "Here is kasha for the children." The old lady, after a nod from the fat guard, was allowed to break from the ranks, accepted the food. . "God be with you, my child," she said to Maria,

"Z-Bogem," Maria whispered.

As she was ladling Kasha into the old lady's tin pan, Marianne said: "When you have the first chance, run for the forest, there are Polish liberators, Catholics, inside the heart of the forest to save you. Pass the word along. There are people in there who are trying to save your lives."

After the food was handed out, the lines of people continued to move slowly eastward. Some collapsed, some crawled, while those who couldn't move were either shot, or thrown into the ditches at the roadside. Shots rang out with a disturbing regularity.

Marianne held Maria close, as they made their way back to the house and told her she was proud of her foolish little girl with the big heart. She turned back to look over her shoulder at the female guard, who was still glaring at them across the field. She thought, for a moment, that the culmination of all the evil in the world had been absorbed into that one misshapen body.

When they reached the safety of their home, Marianne kissed Maria and said "You have done well today." "What did you do?" Andrew asked as he picked her up and spun her around. "I gave kasha to a tired lady. Did I do the right thing?" Andrew smiled broadly and hugged his little daughter. "That's wonderful, my Maria. Indeed you did the right thing. Never forget to help your neighbors." Much later, as they lay in bed, Andrew told Marianne of his working hard at building this Liberty Zone; he said that he believed that the future lay in the protection of the forest. "I know the way" he whispered so as not to wake the children. "I remember being captivated by nature's gifts when I was a boy. I could escape from the abuse of Brozek's hatred. These Bolsheviks seem like an army of Brozeks to me; therefore I think that our refuge is in the forest's sanctuary."

THURSDAY OCTOBER 5, 1939

The western world across the Atlantic was focused on the 1939 World Series featuring the three-time defending champion New York Yankees against the Cincinnati Reds. As the Yankees swept the Series in four games for the second time in a row, Warsaw was swept by surrendering to the Nazis on officially on October 5, 1939.

Marianne heard on the wireless that on October 4th, bloodied and exhausted, the last Polish unit fought without ammunition against the Russians in the east. Brave men and women had spilled their blood on to the Polish soil. To compound the pain of conquest, men atop of trucks with mcgaphones, bellowed demands in the name of the Revolutionary Committees of Socialists. Those in Zamolina proclaimed loudly:

"Warsaw surrendered Eastern Poland. From the Bug River to Nazi borders is now the property of Germany."

"Russia and Germany are friends and allies; any violators of the proclamations of either government will be shot."

In late evening, the small group of patriots gathered in the forest grotto, with the Black Virgin, weeping and praying for their homeland. Marianne tried to remain cold and strong to the situation: however, she could not. .Finally, with the feeling that acting was better than weeping, they decided to set their" Liberty Zone Creed" on paper, which would be kind of a constitution for them. Marianne wrote as the others dictated, and she added her own touch until they had written the whole document.

Liberty Zone: 1939:

We are proud Polish Catholics who follow the teachings of Jesus Christ.

We believe in the beauty of humanity, goodness, love, and devotion.

We believe that it is a sin to steal and kill.

We believe that all our good works done in Christ's name are done for him.

Our salvation lies in Christ and not in the inhumane acts of Nazis, Soviets and Bolsheviks.

We have returned to God's natural home, the beautiful forest.

We retain our ways and our love of home will endure.

We declare that we have formed a Polish Liberty Zone within our own homeland.

We have much to fear;

We are not the property of the Soviets.

We recognize Zamolenski, the Home Army and the Polish Government in exile.

We shall rise above the war's woes, sorrows and tragedies.

We are together in the whispering forests.

We must prevail.

'*Wieczny odpucynek,*' (May we rest in peace)

155

Wladek Pasternak   Barbara Pasternak   Marianne Krull Andrew
Krull   Adam Makowski

Florence Makowska   Josef Varya   Luba Varya

Solemnly, they placed the document in the Black Madonna, hidden away. They hoped that it would not be discovered during the war; if it was they surely would be killed.

Afterwards, they felt a joined unity as patriots. The deep connection was caused by the love of their God, their country, and each other. For the first time, in this beginning of a living hell on earth, they felt as if all this love came home to them. In that moment, Marianne realized that she did not need to keep her inner turmoil to herself, but with the love and caring of faith, they could stay together, insulated during the resistance.

OCTOBER 7, 1939

S.S. head Heinrich Himmler, a seedy little man, was given power over the lives of others as head of the R.K.F.D.V., an organization responsible for the deportation of Poles and Jews from Polish provinces. He had said earlier: "All Poles will disappear from the world."

He saw to it, that during the first four months of Nazi occupation of Poland, in the area around *Bydogszcz (*Bromberg) 10,000 non-Jewish Polish civilians were murdered. This, the largest town in Pomerania had a population of around 140,000, and as usual to the conquerors of either side, the intelligentsia, in this case, priests, lawyers, teachers and industry leaders were arrested and executed in the town's square by machine-gun fire. Sixteen year old boy scouts were rounded up and machine-gunned to death on the steps of the Jesuit Church. If there was resistance, the reaction was swift and horrible, for every Nazi soldier shot, a group of Polish civilians were randomly selected and executed. In the provinces of Lodz and Warsaw, the SS conducted a total of 714 executions, which took the lives of 16,376 leading Polish intelligentsia and aristocracy, including civil and political leaders. In mental hospitals around Bromberg, around 3,700 mental patients were shot.

The most victimized class of Polish society, however, were those at the outskirts of the Governance: peasants, working class intelligenstia, and clergy were sent to labor camps to finance the war, and four million were never to return to their homes. Many Priests in different towns were summarily exccuted. Himmler's Teutonic efficiency also caused an entire group of bright -eyed Polish children to be medically experimented to produce the perfect race, in which of twenty thousand, only two hundred could be accounted.

SATURDAY OCTOBER 7, 1939

Polesie resembled a smaller version of the tumultuous world where cruel deadly acts contagiously continued to spread across the entire landscape. Although, there were daily reports of death and deportation, and a never- ending stream of small trucks and wagons heading for Pinsk past the Ludwig house, the official government takeover in the east, was scheduled for October 10, 1939. It was formally announced at 7:00 a.m. in Zamolina. The usual men, with the brass megaphones, shouted orders from the top of trucks in the name of the Revolutionary Committees. The Ukrainians were first to be targeted by the Soviets there.

There was a Bolshevik zeal to broadcast atrocities as well as to commit them. Endless announcements were made, from crude amplification systems in the town and from the roofs of the trucks. "Fifty Ukrainian families at the far end of the village have been removed during the night. The rest of the villagers can now rest in peace. You should appreciate that the gangster families who stole your food are permanently gone. Soldiers and members of the List of Workers who will keep you safe, now inhabit the homes of these dirty criminals and wish to live in peace. The land and belongings will be redistributed among the list"

The most disturbing announcement was the direction for the establishment of the Regional Headquarters in Zamolina. . Residents were ordered to stay indoors until the new regime settled in houses designated for their families. Dwellers were to wait for a regulator's visit to account for each food supply, animal stock and property. Once that was done, they were told they had to report the next day at 6:00 A.M. for identity cards.

TUESDAY OCTOBER 10, 1939

As promised, the new government was formally announced at 7:00 a.m. in Zamolina. Although they presented themselves as a "List of Workers, and a new Civil Government, their legitimacy was suspicious to everyone. These people were actually an extension of the Soviet Union, mostly expatriates from western Poland, disguised as local revolutionaries. They had been t rained by the NKVD, prior to the declaration of war, as terrorists. Marianne and many others like her, looked through the excessive transparency and saw the truth. These Soviets were a re-invention of Tsarist and Bolshevik actions which caused decades of death.

Many of these regulators and men in charge were not only physically ugly, but also ill mannered. Mounted on a small platform in the town square was Ipsek Forst, a little man, bespectacled, paunchy with a florid complexion and patches of hair apparently randomly stuck to his scalp. He smiled, exposing yellow- stained, broken teeth. He drew himself up to his full stature and said, "My name if Ipsek Fost. I am in charge. I have been directed by Moscow's authority to immediately take control and possession of all properties in this area as a condition for your continued existence."

Most of the people in this crowd had the same thought as Andrew and Marianne, which was how to survive this tragedy, "We are fighting for our lives in a perilous world. Death lurks in the tall underbrush." Marianne had trouble containing her anger, which was growing with every word from Ipsek Forst.

"By October 15th," he went on, "we should have a final account of property and food stuffs. This will be the time when we will make an example of those landholders who fall short of their production quotas. You understand! Everyone will report to this square at 8:00 a.m. on Sunday October 15th."

Another ugly man stepped forward. He was paunchy, short, and his face was covered with scars from teen-age acne. His shock of unruly, coarse brown hair stuck on his head like a well-used hairbrush.

Forst continued: "This is Isador Hersky, who is organizing new regulators for the region, to conduct accurate production counts and to bring technical knowledge to this area. Together, we will discover which enemies of the people are using the forest for hunting and for hiding food and supplies. The forest is now the property of the Soviet State, and it is strictly forbidden for anyone to enter it. Anyone caught there will be shot. Informants of any forbidden actions will be rewarded with an extra loaf of bread per family." He concluded by rudely turning his back to the silent crowd of villagers, and parted with his comrades away into the center of town.

Upon returning home, Andrew repeated a warning that he had just heard from Dorovitz. "Avoid Forst and Hersky. They are ruthless, crude, barbaric and sadistic." Marianne felt that their speech was direct evidence of this, and that as the people died of starvation, because of the imposed food rationing and exhaustion calculatedly done in the true way of the Soviets, the journalists of the world would believe that people were dying of natural causes. The truth was that many would die a slow death of starvation, exhaustion and frost, caused by deliberate acts to dehumanize and control the population.

WEDNESDAY OCTOBER 11, 1939

In London, the Polish government-in-exile's foreign minister, August Zaleski, consulted with the British prime minister and Lord Halifax, to no apparent result as a commercial agreement was signed by the British and Soviet governments for the Polish timber, now forbidden to the residents, would be exchanged to the Soviets for rubber and Cornish tin.

The forest in Polesie welcomed the first refugees to the newly created "Liberty Zone" when the Ukrainian Varyas left their home and fled through the marked trails to the sanctuary. There was the father Josef, Luba, the healer, and the children Josef, and Justine choosing to hide rather than to be transported to Siberia. Staying out of sight was the only choice at this time. That night on the wireless, Marianne and Andrew heard a report of a lone voice supporting American aid to the war in Europe. Charles Lindbergh, the pioneer aviator, spoke to the American people who were opposed to America's entry into another European war. He said, "Neutrality built on pacifism alone will eventually fail." Marianne and Andrew sat huddled in their old farmhouse surrounded by Russian soldiers on the road in front and lines of people sadly leaving their homes, and they felt far removed from the outside world. They felt forgotten and alone in the center of the Soviet and Nazi maelstrom.

FRIDAY OCTOBER 13, 1939

There was a knock on the Ludwig's door shortly after 8:00 a.m. Andrew looked out the side window at a thin, disheveled looking Russian soldier. "Let me in." he shouted. Andrew opened the door. "Your name Andrew Ludwig?" he asked gruffly. "Yes sir" said Andrew." The soldier announced, "The newly appointed head of the Workers Revolutionary Committee wants to ask you some questions. You are to come with me at once. You all can stay. They only want to see Andrew Ludwig." The children and Marianne cowered in the corner of the room, as Andrew was told to accompany the guard across the field and road to the office of Forst and Hersky.. The trip was motivated by Dorovitz's visit to the Ludwig cottage, the news of which had probably reached the two men by an informer. The question was, why did Andrew merit such a visit? So he was sent for, and as he put on his coat and shoes, Stefan mustered up his courage, and asked the guard if his Tata would come back. The soldier's eyes darted toward the children and Marianne and then answered, "Chances are he will return. Now come on with me Ludwig." Maria started to cry and Marianne hugged the children tightly. Andrew assured them that he would be back.

As he walked with the soldier across the muddy field, he thought he saw an opportunity to make a friend of this apparently underfed and lonely soldier, who confirmed Andrew's suspicion by saying "First Comrade Dorovitz visited you, and therefore you are important."

Andrew was led to the old Kowalski home, now the Regional Headquarters of the Revolutionary Committee's List of Workers Governing Office. The 400 meter walk, with the accompanying armed guard, felt like the road to the gallows. Andrew murmured a prayer, and tried to befriend the soldier. Andrew turned him again and asked with a warm smile, "Will you be based here? You look like a good Russian soldier."

The guard replied that he would rather be in a city than in a mud hole like Zamolina and he told Andrew that he was Georgian, not Russian, and that he had a family once. He had not seen them in years. The soldier was in his early twenties, pale and ragged   Andrew told him that there were good people around him now, in contrast to the danger he might be in the cities.   The man, not much more than a boy was homesick. Andrew saw an opening, and told the Russian that it was safer in Polesie; the people would treat him well, and he then invited him to dinner, He said, "My wife makes wonderful bread, borscht and sausages with mushrooms gathered in the forest."   Andrew added that they had enough for one extra, and that his family would welcome him. The soldier politely answered, "I'll think about it."

The soldier's immediate acceptance would involve a degree of vulnerability; however, this was a chance to exchange friendship, and trust, at a time when life and death depended on how ruthless one can be in exchange for good will. They reached the old Kowalski home, now the newly appointed Workers' Representative Headquarters, a beautiful old wood frame structure, away from the road, distanced from the thatched roof homes of the peasants and workers. The sign on the road's edge, read, in Russian: "By the Order of the First Secretary of the Communist Party of the Soviet Union, Ipsek Forst is hereby Workers' Representative to Administer the Directives of the Workers' Revolutionary Committee

Under the order of Nikita Khrushchev….First Comrade of the Communist Party Polish/Ukrainian Region"

When Andrew entered the main office, Forst, placed his muddy feet deliberately on the desk in front of him. Andrew could smell the body odor of the good Comrade who only bathed every other week to demonstrate his disdain for Capitalistic decadence. His intentions were clear. He was there to carry out the orders of Khrushchev and Dorovitz.

The little autocrat just stared at Andrew, waiting for the peasant to speak first, and to enhance the anxiety of the moment. Respectfully, Andrew told him that he would obligingly follow the rules and quotas. Finally, Forst spoke, saying that Andrew looked like a "good" Polack but, he went on, "Polacks don't exist anymore. Only good Communists will remain. There will be no more landholders, no more bloodsuckers, no more capitalists and no more Poland! " By this time he had worked himself into an unnecessary frenzy and told Andrew that he had to help gather the enemies of the state before winter sets in.

Andrew nodded as he said, "I'll do anything you say."

"But first you must answer this question, "Are you related to the Ludwigs of Krakow?"

Andrew, put on what he hoped was his best dumb peasant look, and replied that they were from Lodz, and Warsaw. Forst pushed on, saying that does not mean you are not related to Ludwig, and answered his puzzled look by telling of the Red Army's possession of Polish government files here and in Warsaw. His manner then became very threatening as he told Andrew the Nazis had co-operated with them to prevent subversive activities in the area, and to eliminate, what he called, dissident elements and subversive operations. He walked toward Andrew, and slowly said that they had their own way of extracting the right answers.

Andrew, hat in hand, continued the guise of the ignorant farmer, and inwardly prayed that Forst would believe him. "I am just a good carpenter and farmer." said Andrew. "I don't look like anyone from Krakow. The war and government are for others. That's all. I am a good Polack. Ask Dorovitz. I do not understand what you are saying. There is nothing in my life except for hard work. Ludwig? Who's he" said Andrew respectfully.

To me a good Polack is one who helps the state to keep order here. "You are telling me that you are not related to Wadeslaw Ludwig?"

"I am not in any way related to Ludwig."

"Do you know who he is?"

"No, Andrew answered, "and it sounds like I don't want to."

Forst turned over the interrogation to his colleague Isador Hersky, who wore the Bolshevik leather coat and smelled equally as bad. Hersky lit a foul smelling Russian, black market cigarette, and blew the smoke into Andrew's face along with a blast of the odor of rotting teeth and terrible breath. He was pompous and strutting, because of his attachment to the Russian secret police. He introduced himself to Andrew, while dragging him roughly by the arm to a window. Very carefully, as if talking to an indigent slow-witted child, he explained the role of the NKVD in protecting the security of Russia in this territory, while emphasizing that they were the only law under the new regime. "Polish citizens have no rights, and their state has been destroyed; therefore, everyone is subject to arrest and imprisonment on the strength of our judgment. I am in charge in this region and have full authority, and I report directly to the supreme command in Moscow. Now do you know Ludwig?"

Andrew shook his head, and asked why Ludwig was wanted.

Hersky, sliding into his best use of expletives explained that Ludwig is a "fucking louse bastard from Krakow" and the leader of the Polish underground against Germany. He went on to ask of Zamolenski outside of Janow, and finally for the woman named Krull for whom our agent Dumblosky is searching. "Any connection to them means immediate execution."

Andrew repeated that he did not know any of them, and that he was just a poor farmer.

Hersky took a different tack and pushed his face close to Andrew's and asked "Why is your name Ludwig?"

"Tradition" said Andrew. "All of us were named after our Father's first name, but the Prussians were here too I got a common first name for a last name. There are hundreds of people named Ludwig, I'm sure."

Hersky nodded, but changed the questioning again, this time about Andrew's army service and rank. Andrew knew to answer with only his years and rank of corporal. He continued to badger Andrew with rapid-fire questions that had to be answered quickly, and buried in the middle of these, was the core of his interrogation. Andrew responded to

162

questions of relatives abroad, of how much land he held, and did he understand quotas and livestock sharing. The driving question was did he know Pasternak, and for how long. Andrew knew that any supposed mistake could be crucial or even fatal. He replied that he had known Pasternak for six weeks, and as he did, he discovered that his outward calm just infuriated the interrogator. When Hersky asked him finally: "Do you think he is a good Polack?"

Andrew's response was "He has treated us fairly for six weeks,"

Hersky hit him with a backhanded slap to the face and roared

"I didn't ask how he treated you, you dumb shit."

He raged on about how he was in complete control, and he didn't care if Andrew worked for Khrushchev or Dorovitz, but that he, Hersky, was in charge, and that the dumb Polacks should answer to him. He continued on about Pasternak not meeting his quota, even though he knew full well that tanks had destroyed part of his crop by rolling over it instead of the road. He went on to describe Pasternak's "education" and threatened the same for Andrew if he didn't toe the NKVD mark.

Then he got to the crux of the matter and asked: "Is your wife's name Marianne Ludwig?"

"Of, course" said Andrew.

"Does she know Ludwig?" Hersky demanded, "And what was her maiden name?" he said, hoping to catch Andrew in a lie, or at least in a statement that resembled one.

"Marianne Kowalska. Her mother died when she was a child.

"Have you ever lived in Krakow?"

"No."

"Andrew, be a smart Polack, tell us everything you know. You are in danger because you are a Catholic, named Ludwig. You will be very carefully watched."

Forst interrupted, "We advise you to become an informant for us, to help punish those who interfere in our creation of a Soviet state. You must report dissidents to us, is that clear? Hersky perched on the corner of the desk, lit a cigarette from the one still in his mouth, and went into a lengthy explanation of the NKVD and Soviet projects. He promised Andrew land rewards in exchange for information, and also implied a threat to his life if he didn't help. He presented a choice of working for quotas home or in Siberia, and described in vivid detail the exchange of the land from gentry into the hands of the people, carefully omitting the bloodshed and violence attached to it.

Andrew waited for a pause and told him obediently that he was only a small landholder who would work the farm to meet quotas.

Hersky said. "Dorovitz doesn't think you are dumb, and you are now warned, since Ludwig is connected to Krull. She did not die in a Krakow fire, no matter what the report was. Now, no one is to share any bread with Pasternak and Makowski until all their food is distributed. You piece of shit. If you know of Marianne Krull and don't tell us, you are a dead man. Now go away!" Forst dismissed Andrew.

"Remember, I don't believe that that you are not related to Ludwig or the Krulls. Get your identity cards on October 15th at 6:00 o'clock sharp!" Forst ushered Andrew out the door.

As Andrew left the office, Pasternak and Makowski were waiting to face Forst and Hersky. Andrew did not look at either man, but kept his head down; he felt that they would know why.

Andrew left with the guard, tormented by what October 15th would bring to them, but especially for Makowski and Pasternak.

On the way back, he discovered that his military escort was named Leopold, and as they spoke of the sticky mud and the need to get home, Andrew asked the guard kindly "Will you join us for dinner. You need people and at least a visit to a family."

"I will" replied the guard, torn by the desire to appear military, and the need for a fireplace and warm food. "If you don't mind, I am off duty tomorrow night and I have to patrol the edge of the forest, first, since I have been ordered to look for secret passageways; that journey will be good cover."

"Good," Andrew answered. "We'll see you at 6:00 o'clock p.m. He trudged wearily home.

SATURDAY OCTOBER 14, 1939

On October 13, 1939, new directives were posted regarding taxes, property and livestock; the Catholic religion was banned; teaching the Polish language in schools was banned; the "zloty" was devalued by 90% on the ruble, and personal property was confiscated. The penalty for noncompliance was death. Meanwhile, in the forest, Pasternak and Makowski dismissed the threats of Forst and Hersky; they were not intimidated. They were supplying the Liberty Zone and the work was hard. Pasternak and Makowski recruited an alliance of trusted families at a time when freedom came at a dreadful price. They secretly distributed sacks of cabbage, rye, barley, wheat and potatoes to the dwellers of the zone, and walked endless kilometers to avoid discovery.

The reality of the Soviet occupation coercively intruded on the feverish preparation and hiding of goods; identity cards were to be issued the next day, quotas, property, and food production registered. The harsh decrees of the regulators could not, however, hold back the ice and blizzards that would cover the area by December which would provide cover for the zone's activities.

However, for now, Forst, Hersky, and the regulators had left the Pasternak's on their own property that was so much part of their home, but probably only until the harvest was over. Wladek was openly and courageously defiant. The Makowskis, on the other hand, were in a small hut, and their belongings had been confiscated, except for very few possessions. They had their huge house along, and all their possessions had been loaded onto Moscow bound trucks. They were "placed" in the abandoned huts of the displaced Ukrainians.

Pasternak had been told to wait in his house, even as Hersky cursed and accused him of a shortfall in food production. He had been warned that this failing would disgrace him publicly in the eyes of the villagers. Marianne had told Makowski of their luck in attaching to Leopold Kabryn, the forest guard, who had taken Andrew to see Forst and that he sensed a good quality in him, so he invited Leopold to dinner. She went on to say that the soldier hastily ate the meal and left quickly in fear of his life; however, they had made a connection with him. The Russian Army was ragged and hungry, so he had accepted the invitation to return for a more leisurely dinner on Saturday night.

Leopold Kabryn arrived at the Ludwig hut for the second time, with the six o'clock gong of the village bell. He crept under the cover of the thick brush at the edge of the forest, taking a longer, safer route, rather than walking through the open field. He was tense and rigid when he appeared at the door. Marianne and Andrew welcomed, but sensed something of a serious and guilty nature about him. Leopold walked slowly to the chair by the stove without saying a word. He warmed his hands together over the hot stove, his hair wet from the cold autumn rain, and he sagged as he sat looking haggard and worn. Andrew and Marianne joined him. Without looking up, he said quickly: "You are not on the list." As relief flooded over Andrew and Marianne, he continued "I will be shot if they find out that I am telling you."

Andrew thanked him, and asked if all of them in the area were safe, and Leopold mumbled "No! Not at all! Forst is insane. He has ordered me to watch you very carefully. He thinks that you are a member of the Polish resistance and are trying to get close to Dorovitz to undermine the Party's cause."

Although Marianne knew that this was the truth, she could not figure out the source of the suspicion. Who had led Forst to this conclusion? Where did he get this idea? However, Kabryn continued "Forst thinks that Andrew would lead him, maybe even by accident, to those in charge of the resistance here in Polesie. He believes that a secret partisan movement is being formed, and that Pasternak is heading it. Apparently, the NKVD's investigation of your backgrounds have some gaps of time in them, which have aroused suspicion .They are both desperate men who want to prove themselves to Moscow before winter."

Leopold said that although he worked on Forst's staff, he was not a murderer. He wanted to live long enough to see Forst banished, and that the NKVD would shoot him if they ever discovered this admission. He spoke quietly again "Many of the soldiers feel that Forst will act recklessly. He drinks heavily and is abusive and unpredictable. He could come after you at any moment. You are not safe, nor can you take any chances since you own a little property and are Poles under suspicion."

"What do you think we should do?" Marianne asked him.

Leopold carefully outlined a plan to these people that he had come to trust very quickly. He told them to keep visible until winter arrived, while soldiers would be too busy rounding those on the list before the real cold and the blizzards began. Kabryn was to watch the Ludwigs; however, he felt that since Forst was behind schedule on his deportations, he might not survive. "The Red Army would take over the administration of the region, then there will be new orders and more butchery will begin again in the early spring of next year."

Marianne's curiosity was piqued, and she asked Leopold why he was risking his life for them.

Leopold sadly answered "I have had a similar family experience. I do not want you to be taken to Siberia. My grandparents died during the reign of terror imposed by the Communists during a similar collectivization program in Russia after the revolution. They were sent to Siberia and never returned. My parents were only 19 and 18 years old then and they escaped deep into the Georgia forest when I was a year old. Your family would have little chance of surviving the slave labor camps, or as they call them "Gulags" in Siberia. They use the free labor to finance the system. They are frantically shipping labor there and you would starve to death, freeze, or die of exhaustion and torture. It would be even worse than the death march. When Andrew spoke to me the other day and I looked into the eyes of your children, I thought about the death march to Siberia. I remembered my father's smile and my mother's kindness and began to weep for them. Afterwards, I wept for all the families who went to Siberia."

Stefan and Marian sat silently listening. The family was seeing a young soldier risking his own life to save theirs. Leopold sat quietly, and he looked sadly at the floor after his long speech. He had spoken of his family with great difficulty. Finally, he said "I hope you will be safe."

Andrew asked Marianne to get the small bottle of vodka from the cupboard. She filled three glasses and gave one to Leopold.

"*Sto lat, Leopold,*" Andrew and Marianne said in unison. "*Nazdrowie*" to all of us. "*Ja was lubie.* We all love you Leopold. You have a kind heart." Stefan, Maria, Andrew, and Marianne hugged him.

"Now let's enjoy our dinner," Andrew said, and for a moment the realities of fear were crowded out by the warmth of a festive family gathering.

Leopold was very hungry and ate rapidly, but he did not speak again. The children finished their dinner and politely excused themselves to play beside the wood-burning stove. Andrew threw two big chunks of dry pine on the fire and it flared up, while Marianne mixed some cherry syrup with boiling hot water and they drank the sweet mixture after the meal.

Leopold had heartily eaten an entire plateful of lamb, mashed potatoes and beets and then mopped the plate with babka. He told them that he had not eaten since he was given two pieces of soft bread and a cup of coffee that morning. After some ersatz coffee, they decided it was a perfect meal hidden away from the hunger, want and strife of the world around them.

Leopold stood and said, "I need to go now, we have curfew at 9:00 p.m. You do not have your identity card. Make sure you get yours tomorrow"

They stood together, looking across the field toward the Forst house and beyond that to the Pasternak's home. Leopold said that it was bitter out there, and the wind was howling and gusting. "Fortunately, the temperature is dropping. The mud will slow all the processes down. Goodbye, Andrew. Goodbye, Marianne. I'll keep a watchful eye out," he added with a smile.

"One more thing," Marianne asked. "Are the Pasternaks on the list?"

Kabryn did not answer but gestured toward their home. His sad silence ended what had been a good evening. Makowski had given up his house; the Pasternaks, however, were doomed. Leopold left by way of the forest.

When he was out of sight, Andrew and Marianne ran to tell Pasternak that he had had been warned of a quota shortfall yesterday. Hersky, from the Beria/Vyshynsky wing, believed in shooting prominent citizens in front of crowds to set examples for not meeting Socialist goals. Andrew was even more upset because he knew in his heart that they would shoot the Pasternaks the next day in front of citizens getting identity cards. Marianne felt that they had to warn the Pasternaks, and get them to safety in the forest.

Andrew set out for Makowski's home, while Marianne went to the Pasternaks. She told Andrew to take the children, and to get the Makowskis to have the Pasternaks vanish. "Do anything to get him and Barbara out." she cried.

Marianne, dirtied her face, put on her rags and traveled the field to the rear of Pasternak's house, to avoid the soldiers standing on the roadside near their home. She hoped the Pasternaks were there, and that she could get them into the forest safely.

Andrew had reached the Makowskis and when he found Florence at the door he said: "I think that Wladek and Barbara may be taken out of their house. Where are they?"

Florence's face turned slowly toward the Pasternak's home. "Adam is with them at the Liberty Zone."

"You and Magdalene should leave to join him. When you see Wladek and Barbara, tell them that under no circumstances should they

168

return to their home. They have no choice but to stay in the forest. Go! Hurry! "

She stared at Andrew for a minute. " I'll snatch Magdalene and the children and join you all. Thank you. We'll see you there in the morning."

"Make sure Adam does not return here."

"*Z'Bogem!*" she cried."

"God be with you, dear friend," Andrew responded softly.

Marianne looked for an opportunity to cross the road to Pasternak's home. She waited until the soldiers were sharing a cigarette and when they became momentarily distracted, she made her way behind some brush to the rear door. She tapped on the back window "This is Marianne" she called. "Open up, Barbara. Wladek, I need to talk with you."

The window was thrown open, and to her horror, a man, obviously Russian, growled. ""Who the hell are you? What do you want? The Pasternaks have been arrested. We removed them this evening. What do you want with the Pasternaks? It is 10.30! , past curfew, you could be shot."

Marianne, chilled from the cold and the news, was terrified. Hastily, she answered, "We pray, sir, every night in Pani Pasternak's vigil. We do not use the front door because I am the cleaning woman."

He answered loudly "Pasternak was taken this evening by the NKVD, with charges of non-cooperation as a large landholder and a food production shortfall. They will be marched to the Village Square. The people of Polesie will be hungry because of him, so he will be punished."

Marianne's heart sank. She mumbled an answer, and at the end said, "I'm sorry, but I need to ask. Is Pani Pasternak with him? She loves her children, and I respect her deeply."

He leaned out the opened window and replied, "They were both taken away! You will see them at the square tomorrow."

"Village Square?"

"October 15th for the registration of all property including stock of goods and identity cards. Anybody caught without them will be punished by death. Pasternaks need to be an example. Don't you agree?"

Despite better judgment Marianne reacted by screaming."No."

The man's suspicion was aroused and he asked "How did you go through the field in the mud without my men seeing you?"

"I crawled along the bushes. I was eager to pray before the village bell rings tomorrow. Forgive me for breaking curfew, but it will be the last time." Marianne, now out of control, began to sob. "Wladek fed the entire village. We prayed for a good harvest. One reason for the shortfall is the war." she cried out desperately. "You need to stop this madness. Sir! Please save Pasternaks' lives! I beg of you. They will have a good spring next year."

"Guilty ones need to be punished. These landholders are sabotaging our plans."

"He couldn't help it. We are in war. Everything stopped."

His stern answer froze Marianne. "I am Colonel Pietrinev, the new Soviet military commander in this region. I am under the command of General Vyshynsky, head of the military unit of the NKVD. We enforce all regulations in this region."

"Sorry to have bothered you, Colonel. I must return now." she said, now much calmer and back in control.

"Consider yourself lucky. I will keep an eye out for you. I will let you go this time, but before you leave, who are you?"

"Marianne Ludwig"

"I am not going to arrest you, this time, but if you are seen near my home, you will be shot. I will have one of my guards escort you to the road."

A guard appeared and led her away. She waited until she was near her house and the guard left her to fall onto a muddy, mossy log and she cried hard. Wladek and Barbara were the finest of human beings and her sadness was unbearable. Marianne brought herself upright to her knees and prayed for God to help the Pasternaks and their sanctuary. They dared to harvest and feed the hungry with secret food supplies that had accounted for the shortfall. She prayed that this Colonel would rid the area of the minor officials and finally for someone to remove him.

Every fiber within her wanted revenge and a painful retribution for what these men had done. She could not reconcile it with the faith that she had lived with all her life. Andrew, she thought, had an easy path, for he believed in a better life after this one if God's work was done on earth. However, did that work include murder, killing, and retribution? She wrestled with her conscience; how could she best use the gifts of intelligence, education and leadership that God had given her in this evil time in history, without breaking his sacred law, given by Jesus Christ, which included "turning the other cheek". Ludwig, her beloved father had inculcated the belief deep within her soul, and there was no way that she could shake the feeling that she would be a doomed sinner if she committed acts of vengeance. Her epiphany came quite suddenly upon her in that dark, muddy place on God's earth.

Jesus Christ had been born into an equally troubled, evil and murderous time. An evil empire had murdered innocent babes at his birth, and the persecution of his followers continued after his death by another equally murderous government in Rome. Marianne was able to see then, even though it arrived through a flash of intuition combined with her studies of history, the concept that God often placed people on earth for a purpose, which they did not always understand at first, but came to a realization later. Hers had arrived. She was, she realized, an instrument for justice and survival. There would be sacrifices along the way, but like Christ, she had to have faith first, and believe that God would provide answers as she followed the path of good and righteousness in the evil world around her. He had sent good soldier Kabryn, she thought, and will provide more help; however, she felt that her lesson was not to lose faith, but also to trust in the Lord , and control her anger, emotions and behavior for His work.

She knelt in the mud, turned her head towards heaven and repeated Jesus' mantra: "Thy will be done", and prayed for strength for the road ahead She prayed for the survival of a people and culture, for her family, close and extended . She prayed for wisdom, and the ability to make judgments.

As she was kneeling there, Marianne believed what she heard from God, not the regulators or the NKVD, who were afraid of people of faith. Then it came to her that one of the nasty women demonstrators back at St. Andrew's had connected the disappearance of Marianne Krull with the emergence of the peasant Marianne Ludwig. She hoped someday to find out. Drained of emotion, she sat on the log for a long while

SUNDAY OCTOBER 15, 1939

At six o'clock, A.M., the bell rang in the Village Square on an awful, grey eerie day. Andrew, Marianne and the children approached it slowly, as did all the other residents of the area. The Soviet hammer and

171

sickle emblem was displayed prominently on what was once fertile Polish soil. Colonel Pietrinev, Hersky, Forst and the regulators stood in front of a growing line of villagers, as identification cards were issued. Each native Pole was given a card stamped with a number, as if it was a ticket to elimination. Soviet regulators surrounded the crowded square, making sure that no peasant would escape without being identified and therefore "perverting justice". They checked each identity card after it was issued, reminding the holder that the punishment for not showing the card would be swift and awful.

When the entire population had received their papers, they were forced to assemble in the square, and face the center of it. Ipsek Forst led the armed guards and forced a pathway to the middle of the gathering. He relished public executions, excited that in no less than a half hour, another Pole of visible influence would be dead. Andrew and Marianne shielded their children and held them tight against their bodies so they would not see what was happening. The little ones started to tremble from fear. They could not see Barbara and Wladek tied to each other by Pietrinev. Andrew wept, however Marianne stared openly at Forst and Hersky, reserving her emotion for her inner core and for mourning later. Forst strode forward angrily, and announced in Russian, "There has been a shortfall in the food production, and that means poor peasants shall suffer even more, unless the evil landholders are separated from them and crushed forever. They will be punished; they will die so their land will be given to the state, and end the secret societies that they have formed. We will track them all down. Such crimes against the state are punishable by death."

He turned to his prisoners: "Wladek and Barbara Pasternak are guilty of crimes against the state and no longer will they walk among you."

Pietrinev strutted to the bloody and battered couple who had survived the night of beatings and interrogation; apparently, he enjoyed this procedure and the public stage on which he was standing. Wladek and Barbara Pasternak were ordered to kneel. They were barefoot; clothing ripped, with the bruises of the repeated blows on their faces. Ipsek Forst untied their hands. All the dignity of a private death and the Catholic last rites had been removed; however, the Pasternaks knelt, martyr- like, in the midst of the people of the village. Marianne was proud of their bearing, and blatant ignorance of subservience to Pietrinev, Hersky and Forst. Their behavior appeared to infuriate Forst, so that he forced Barbara's beautiful face further down toward the ground; He kicked Wladek directly in the face. Then, he pulled his head upright and clamped it between his knees facing Barbara, They both were kept on their knees as Pietrinev told everyone in the crowd to carry their identity cards at all times and to register their property which now belonged to the state

"Although this area is only a small part of the Union of the Socialist Republics, your devotion is to the quota. Should the regulators find any undeclared property, or that a full day's work has not been performed, you will be guilty of robbing from the people. This is a triumph for the workers of the world."

Marianne looked directly at the regulators, who were cheering Pietriniev's speech. He pointed his pistol at the heads of Barbara and Wladek. The Pasternaks had arranged to cry out together at the end, and their unified cry of "Free Poland, now and forever" echoed loudly in the square.

Pietrinev, infuriated, put two bullets in the back of Barbara's head forcing Wladek, still clamped between the knees of Forst, to see his wife's death by murder as his last vision on earth. Her body slumped over. Then Pietrinev placed a single bullet in the back of Wladek's head, his blood spattering Pietriniev's boots.

Marianne wept silently; Andrew cried openly, they shepherded the children toward home, as the regulators stretched the bodies of Barbara and Wladek onto a cart, left in open display in the square as a warning. The best of mankind had been removed because they were patriots who loved their country.

Marianne clutched Andrew's arm, and lifted her head, swearing inwardly that the Pasternak's name would never die. They had served the cause of humanity. They did not break their faith with us "Pasternak's Freedom Zone" is forever Poland."

As they moved toward their home, Marianne could only think of her father's words: 'Is that all?'. The message to her was now clearer than ever, to act accordingly to what rightfully belongs to us----our free soul and mind. We will act in defiance, she thought, and that is our choice and God's will.

THURSDAY OCTOBER 19, 1939

The villagers in Zamolina had been officially registered as citizens of the Soviet Union which permitted travel beyond the town of

Zamolina; however, at all times we are to adhere totally to Communist directives that are posted daily on the village bulletin board:

Effectively Immediately,

All administrative powers have been transferred to the Socialist state and by the security apparatus of the Soviet Socialist Republic.

Effectively immediately Practicing Catholics will be shot.

Children between the ages of seven and fourteen must attend school October 26, 1939.:

At the Zamolina regional headquarters.

Marianne and Andrew decided that she would be the clandestine leader and governor of the freedom zone, while Andrew would be in charge of construction. Both tasks would be dangerous to the whole family, so they decided instead of moving into a forest hut, to remain in the open under the cover of peasants of the land. Forst and Hersky, and anyone else who viewed her daily comings and goings, would see an ignorant –looking peasant woman going barefoot through the mud, pulling a plow or carrying and washing clothes. They would not, she hoped, connect her with Marianne Krull, the educated anti-communist from Krakow. Instead, she resembled the typical feminine piece of property who was too poor to be a thinking person, and too stupid to be more than a reproductive machine and a field worker.

Andrew routinely carried on his daily chores, plowing and harvesting his land. Part of the strategy of their cover was to always be in the same place at the same time, and after a while, the repeated actions would render invisibility to the bored observer. Stefan worked alongside his father, because children's ages relative to the work produced by them, was unimportant to the Soviets. At night, they toiled in the forest to clear space, made pits for baths, designed lookout paths, and constructed hidden dwellings in the marshes. Every night before bed, Andrew and Marianne prayed for the souls of those lost and for the salvation of the living.

The careful storage of food, and Andrew's instruction to families that moved into the Freedom Zone, would provide sustenance through

174

winter and spring. They spent their days not fearing the future because they had been through so much in the past, and they held Wladek and Barbara alive in their memories and hearts. The community in the forest began to grow slowly; information from the outside world began to dwindle as reports on the wireless vanished from Soviet airways. The only information was what Andrew could get from Ilana Dorovitz, who cautioned, "Do as they say. Do not stir the pot. You are dealing with devils that are out to destroy you."

On this day, Colonel Amire Pietrinev was on a rampage. He was yelling publicly about the inability to capture this woman Krull. The obsession with her had come down from Dumblosky, who ordered her elimination. The Colonel did not really understand the bother over one Polish woman, after all what could she do. Pietrinev, connected to Soviet upper echelons Kanganovich and Vyshynsky, was a large man, with a disfigured jaw, left over from the First World War. His cousin was an NKVD chief in Moscow. He had long outgrown the uniform he affected, and it now bulged at its worn- out seams. He littered his chest with medals and considered himself a war hero and savior of the Russian people, because of his work in the revolutionary army in 1917 and 1918. He wore his hat with the red star back on his head, looking like a movie caricature. Negative encounters with this man led to a disastrous result, and like many of his ilk, he was a sadist and punisher of the first order. He emulated his leader Josef Stalin in style, and would summarily execute a man, as his hero did: on a whim.

Pietrinev, was loudly dressing Hersky down in the town square for all to hear, jabbing his index finger at him in front of a small crowd of people. "Why is the school not ready?" However, school reminded him of teachers and teachers led him back to Marianne Krull; he threatened now to exterminate five useless regulators if she was not found. "Dumblosky is coming in four weeks. If we don't have Krull by then, I swear I'll choke both of you with my bare hands."

Pietrinev, the overseer, questioned Hersky and Forst's every move. His "soviet zeal" encouraged the rapid destruction of all remnants of Polish culture; he directed regulators to secure counts; ranted at soldiers to deport Polish patriots; murdered the intelligentsia, and worked toward the surrender of children to the state.

The Colonel's order to get Krull got back to Marianne and Andrew. The word of mouth communication system was still one of the best. A woman overheard the tirade, and told the Ludwigs about it. The woman had no idea who they were.

THURSDAY OCTOBER 26, 1939

"Who will teach me? Will I have to learn Russian?" asked Stefan before his first day of school.

Marianne told him to listen to what the teacher had to say, remember his words, then we'll tell the truth when you get home. Stefan paused and looked at his Mother quizzically and said: "What if I promise that what I learn at the school and what I learn at home are two different things. The one at home is true, the other, we'll see about tomorrow."

Stefan set off for his first day at school, an event that normally would be treated with joy, candy and flowers. Children looked forward to it in Poland, and it marked entrance into the world; however, Stefan's start was a frightening prospect, and was subjecting him to a world of deceit, with everything to lose for the family and nothing to gain for the child. The identity card made school compulsory or Andrew and Marianne would have educated him at home. If he did not attend, they would have been considered undesirable and banished to Siberia.

The Soviet school system attempted to humiliate innocent youngsters. If the child resisted, the family would be deported. Little did the child know, that they would be singled out again and again, denounced for having a heritage and values based on the premise that family, God and country are central to life. Marianne feared that the relentless pursuit of the Krulls, would affect her child particularly, because of the rewards for providing information.

Marianne watched, through her binoculars, Stefan and Luba's daughter Justine walk past a crowd of new regulators at the Village Square. They continued on toward the Old Ukrainian Church, now the official school located next to the soldiers' barracks. The regulators' children, waiting for school to begin, bullied and made fun of the Polish students. Marianne's anxiety increased and she waited until she saw them enter the building before she went back to work.

Stefan and Justine were separated. They sat on either side of the old church quietly and respectfully as they had been taught to do. A small bald man in a rumpled suit entered and stood in front of the assembled children holding a picture of Josef Stalin. He spoke in Russian and looked at the assembled village children with obvious animosity. He asked if they knew who he was. He turned to Stefan, walked over to him and held the picture of Stalin above his head.

"Do you know Stalin?" he asked

"No Sir" replied Stefan.

"Why not

"Are you feeling all right?"

"Yes, sir,"

"Where's your mother?"

"She's at home across the field."

"Does she know Stalin?"

"I'm not sure."

"Put your hands on top of the desk."

Stefan did as he was told, as the teacher hung the picture of Stalin on the wall and got a ruler from his desk. He walked back over to Stefan, who had trustingly placed his hands on the desktop, and slashed the ruler across the little boy's out- stretched hands. Stefan did not cry but just looked up at him. The teacher, infuriated by the boy's stare, took him by the ear and dragged him in front of the class. The teacher then asked.

"Do you pray?"

"Yes sir."

"When you ask for candy, do you pray to God?"

"No sir."

"If you don't, then who do you ask?"

"I ask Mama or Tata."

"Pray to God to send some candy, right now." demanded the teacher.

"Yes sir. Dear God, I hate to ask you, but I need some candy right now. In the name of Jesus, Holy Spirit, Blessed Mary, please do send some candy."

Then the teacher said, "Students, sit down and be quiet. Let's wait a few minutes to see if candy falls from the sky."

Stefan, young as he was, knew that that was not a real prayer... The tall, thin man in the back of the room began laughing, and so did the whole class, with the exception of Justine and a few other Polish children. The new students, who just moved there, kept on snickering and pointing at him like he was stupid.

"So you see. No candy from God," the teacher said.

"Now, Stefan, Mr. Stalin is our leader. He is powerful, more powerful than God is and is always near. God does not exist. I want you to ask Mr. Stalin for a piece of candy. Go ahead."

Stefan obeyed; "Please Mr. Stalin may I have some candy?"

A man appeared at the door and started giving out candy. Everyone was so happy.

"Now, you see students. God did not give you candy, but Mr. Stalin did. Now you know that God does not exist, and you must be sure to thank Mr. Stalin for it."

Stefan was left standing in front of the room with no candy,

"Yes sir."

"Is Stalin all powerful?"

"Yes sir."

Stefan left school at the end of the day, with tears welling in his eyes, very afraid to tell his Mother the story, even though he had promised to do so. Though a child may be right, in school, especially on the first day, they have some guilt feelings and Stefan did not understand fully the teacher's questions.

When Stefan was due home, Marianne went to the window and saw her son, kicking a stone ahead of him as he slowly headed for home. Although relieved that he was home, she saw that something was wrong. The normally ebullient little boy was teary eyed, and stood before her with his head down, as if he had done something wrong. Marianne hugged him, wiped his face and asked about his first day.

"It was terrible, Mama, are you sure you want to hear?"

Marianne encouraged him to tell her, because she would understand the truth. Stefan spent all his stored up tears as he told his mother the story of his day. She gently treated his bleeding and bruised knuckles and hands. He rested his head on her shoulder and they both wept, as he said over and over "They couldn't make me cry Mama."

"We'll show them." she whispered, "You were picked upon because you are an innocent Polish boy. Never forget that all love comes from your home. Do not lose our Polish heart. One day you will understand. As a family, we will pray together, way beyond the teacher, and through this painful experience, good will come."

"Some good came out, Mama, you were right. I will never forget my first day of school, and I was ready for it, Mama. "

MONDAY OCTOBER 30, 1939

On this gray morning, the NKVD took Andrew away. There was a rumor that an insurgent group was being formed. Hersky had grown increasingly frustrated because he did not know the identity of the secret society leaders. He also had not yet found Marianne Krull before Dumblosky's arrival. Two burly NKVD men stood in the doorway. One announced gruffly, to Andrew, that he was under arrest and had five minutes to get ready. Marianne and the children stood huddled, helpless in a corner Maria and Stefan's trembling faces were white. They were terrified. As Andrew was forcibly dragged out of the house, Marianne called out desperately, "We will all go together!"

"You are wasting our time" the man said. "We do not want you, woman. We want Andrew Ludwig."

The children screamed "Tata, Tata" and buried their heads in Marianne's breast. Andrew kept turning back to them, as they pulled him mercilessly along the muddy ground. Forst and Hersky observed it all from the end of the field. Andrew was thrown onto a truck heading eastward, and bounced around as the vehicle swayed. After his eyes adjusted to the dim light, he noticed how the two guards kept their guns leveled at all the prisoners. He tried to prop himself up on his knees to watch them carefully. The other prisoners just stared and shivered for what seemed to be an ugly eternity. Then, one elderly man, sitting alongside Andrew asked the guards, "What is to become of us?"

"You are forbidden to talk," a Russian soldier, barked. Andrew tucked his legs to his chest for warmth, caught his breath, and then looked around at the other men. There was terror in their eyes. They knew that they were marked for eventual liquidation, and who knew what else might come first. Andrew lowered his head and prayed. He heard the labored, panic-induced breathing of the man sitting beside him. Andrew understood the man's fears and wanted to give comforting words to him, for he was equally frightened.

The truck twisted, turned, and finally stopped. "I will not surrender to them." He closed his eyes, took a deep breath and hoped for his faith to be his savior. When they neared Pinsk, the men were escorted from the truck to a makeshift prison, not the small building that had been used by the Polish constable before the war, but a much larger structure, a Catholic school that now served a different purpose. It had become a torture chamber where prisoners would be cruelly interrogated.

The courtyard displayed a startling scene of brutality. Drops of blood stained the ground. Prisoners were shackled with leg chains to the wall. Andrew was numb with disbelief when he saw tormented human beings crammed against the wall, hopeless, terrified, crying out, "Kill me!" More people were outside behind barbed wire. Their sunken eyes looked at Andrew desperately. It was a horrifying sight, but somehow God, they were still alive. Andrew answered by placing his hand over his heart, and then making the sign of the cross to let them know there were other human beings suffering along with them. One woman had an obvious arm fracture, for every time she moved, a sharp splinter of bone protruded through her skin. When Andrew tried to step forward to help the injured woman, the guard hit him repeatedly and shouted "You lousy Polack, you have not seen anything yet. You are going to end up just like them." and then drove him roughly into a long hallway. The guard opened a door and pushed Andrew onto the floor of a narrow room converted into a cramped cell. The walls were of stone and the floor was rough concrete. The guard laughed as Andrew fell into a smelly puddle of urine and feces but righted himself and got up from the floor.

"You fell into the shit box," a voice from the darkness said." They place it in front of the door so it's certain to be stepped into when a new man comes in. It's their joke."

Andrew gagged and threw up, adding to the stench of the box. "I have endured so much. I will survive this too" he thought.

When he was accustomed to the dim light, he saw people lining the walls around him. There were eight bearded, half-naked men, shivering from the cold, scarred, bloodied, and covered with rags , who along with Andrew, were condemned because they were Poles.

The mutilated body of a man lay dead in the corner. A light bulb burned overhead. It was so bright that Andrew raised his hands to shield his eyes. "You never get used to that damn light" a voice called out. Andrew looked at the man who was sitting on a bench against the wall. One of the few still conscious, his badly bruised eye was swollen shut.

180

He leaned forward, feebly gripping the bench and croaked a greeting to Andrew and said that he had been arrested without explanation. No specific charges – just that he was a Catholic Pole, who fought against the Russians in the nineteen twenties. The others were lawyers, doctors, government people and land owners. He had been in the cell for what he guessed was three days, although he said it was hard to estimate exactly in a place where there was no value on time or life, only the promise of a slow death. "Have they tortured you yet?" he asked Andrew.

"No," Andrew answered.

"You are lucky" the prisoner said. "The other seven men in here were first interrogated and then brutally beaten. We are without food and very little water. They beat me as soon as I got here. That hole is full of feces from diarrhea even though our bodies seem to have no fluids left. We get a cup of water every so often, but it has been two...at least two days since I have eaten. I am doing my best to survive. But we will all die, won't we?"

Andrew, sitting on the bench, was stunned by the man's words. A few of the others, all with open wounds, were lying in their own feces, too weak to talk. One man told Andrew, with great difficulty "I have not been fed for three days."

He was from one of the villages surrounding the larger town of Volynia. "Hundreds, perhaps thousands of Polish people have been executed in the region during the first three weeks of the Soviet occupation. The Soviets liquidated the entire Polish community, and took over their homes, land and their property. Our place reeks with the stench of death. God forgive me for not caring to know who they are. I saw this myself," the man said. "Now they want to know are there any more hiding away." He began to weep uncontrollably and whispered with all his strength, "I am going to die and will never see my wife and children again. I am going to join the graveyards of silent human beings. Only God knows who they are."

Later that day, when the citizen guards came to take him away, he asked Andrew to pray for his family. "I will." Andrew replied softly.

Andrew began to pray for all the families. He had always been able to connect with his God and he held on to his faith as the last vestige of normality. As the hours dragged on, Andrew said the rosary, using his fingers instead of the newly forbidden beads. His repetition of the rosary helped keep his connection to his strength of will. He thought of Christ's pain and suffering which resulted in man's salvation. Did he dare think that this was the same for the earthly beings caught in this maelstrom? The entire rosary took about fifteen minutes to complete. He said it at least twenty-five times since the man left with the guards about five hours ago. He sat still for what seemed like an eternity, breathing deeply. He did not know what else to expect in this grotesque world. No matter what, he thought, I will not surrender.

Andrew wondered how Jesus had endured terrible torture before his death, but he also firmly believed that the Christian knows the end result, no matter what happens on earth.

Marianne discovered where they had taken Andrew, from Leopold Kabryn, who could have been shot for what he said. Marianne left the children with the Makowskis, and rode through the night in the wagon. She waited for hours at the railroad station believing that Andrew may be shipped to Siberia. The next morning, she saw Dorovitz near the building used for interrogations. He recognized her and she pleaded for his help, begging him to do something for her Andrew. Dorovitz promised her that he would try to use his influence and went to speak to the commander of the NKVD Soviet troops stationed there.

Marianne brought the gold watch that Dorovitz gave her and offered it back as a bribe for the guard. The Russians love watches so maybe that would work.

Inside the prison, the guards returned for Andrew. "Come!"

He was led into a long hall, then upstairs into a corner room of the school where the executioners had lined up twenty men judged to be patriotic Poles. Andrew endured the usual mockery and ridicule from the regulatory thugs as they took him along with the twenty others to a platform in the center of the town square. Three men deemed "suspect enemies of the people" were standing naked with crudely lettered signs around their necks reading: "Priest"; "Teacher", and "Mayor". Their crime was that they had opposed Sovietization. Andrew realized they were a symbol of what the Soviets feared most: the visible influence of leadership. The Soviets had to punish anyone remotely associated with being Polish in mind, body, and soul, whose presence could unite the good people against the murderers from Pinsk.

The male and female guards, wearing the usual trappings of red hammer and sickle, stood on a platform and ordered the priest, teacher, and mayor to kneel, face down but looking up with their chins flat on the ground, so they could see each other. On command, a water hose was inserted into each exposed rectum and the female guards sat on the

182

prisoners bound hands. Holding onto the hose, as the water was turned on, the three women executioners tightened their grip, and with a flush of sadistic pleasure, shoved the hose deeper into the naked bodies.

Andrew and the others were forced to watch in stark horror as the three men screamed in pain. When bodies, filled with water, contorted and pulsated uncontrollably, the three guards put a bullet into each head. Andrew could do nothing put pray, at least inwardly, for quick death, for the soul of the Ludwig family, and for native Poles now deemed outcasts, who were still inside Poland. The Bolsheviks preferred to murder people slowly, without burying them; however, Andrew and two other men were ordered to carry the three corpses to a site about four hundred meters away, to an open field beyond a ridge, behind which there were heaps of bodies, stacked in a loose pile, like garbage. They were yesterday's living and today's tortured dead.

The ridge was guarded by Russian soldiers and newly hired police recruits from Pinsk, one of whom stepped forward and handed each prisoner a shovel, and ordered Andrew and the others to start digging. Andrew said nothing, he just looked at the fifty or more bodies heaped together. He began to dig. The sweat and tears mingled as they poured down his face. The man next to him said "I hope they just shoot us and leave us here." Andrew gave the last rites, silently, to each corpse he encountered as he buried each nameless human being. Unfortunately, he forgot to do it silently and began to mumble the prayers.

A guard cracked his whip across Andrew's back, then began to whip him faster and harder, "You have no reason to talk or pray. Dig! No talking!" Andrew could only think again of Christ's agony and suffering, even to carrying his own cross; therefore, after falling to the ground, almost sinking into the pit of horror, he slowly rose with shovel in hand, and pierced the earth harder with all of his strength and sorrow.

The guard shouted, "The grave you are digging is deep enough. We have fifty more bodies to cover. Pick up the piece of garbage and dump them in."

Andrew picked up a few twigs and made a crude crucifix, then blessed and prayed over the mass grave .Each prisoner took a handful of dirt and threw it on the burial site, silently praying for the human beings who lay there.

"We are to be next. We might as well be dead right now," Andrew said solemnly before the police returned. As the late afternoon faded, they were ordered to return to the stench of the torture chambers.

Andrew prayed all night, hardly believing it possible that he was still alive. He had no food for two days, and because of his love and overwhelming desire to see his wife and two children, he used a small stone to write on the wall, "Tell my family I love them. Andrew."

Andrew was taken by a guard into another room. He had no sense of time, but thought that his had come when he entered the room and saw two naked men. Andrew was told to step forward. The burly persecutor was sullen and hostile. The other two men stood by as Andrew was ordered to undress. All three were now naked.

A harsh voice roared, "Is your name Ludwig?"

"Yes."

"Some people come out of here alive if they cooperate. Do you know Ludwig of Krakow? He's a leader of the Polish Victory Service, the underground."

Andrew answered "No, I don't know him."

"Do you know Marianne Krull? You have ten minutes to decide if you know the whereabouts of Ludwig or Krull. Ten minutes ago, these other two animals had ten minutes to reply. They are still uncertain. Their time is up. Watch what happens."

The man next to Andrew was held by two guards and pulled straight up. The main interrogator poured gasoline on his genitals and set them on fire. Andrew numbly stared at the sight of the man doubled over, gasping and groaning. The NKVD persecutor laughed. "You have a choice, either the hose or the schmuck. Which do you prefer? Ludwig, you have five minutes to tell us the whereabouts of Ludwig and of Krull."

Andrew remained motionless. He thought "God please give me the courage of these men. I hope I can be as brave." The moaning of the wounded man filled the room. The interrogator growled again. "You have a minute, Krull. Or is it really Ludwig?"

"I don't know Ludwig in Krakow. I don't know Krull," Andrew screamed.

Andrew saw the door open to this room, and wondered what horror was next in store when Dorovitz, who had been an observer of the whole process, calmly stepped forward and pulled Andrew from the room.

"Come with me," he said.

Andrew walked painfully out with Dorovitz. "Here, put your clothes on! They believe that you do not know Ludwig or Krull. You are a strong man. I am sure that you will not betray me."

Dorovitz explained how Marianne found him, and begged for his help. He told Andrew "I promised I would do whatever possible, but I could not be too forceful in my influence because it would be reported back to Beria and Vyshynsky. He went on to say how Marianne had offered the guards the gold watch as a bribe and it worked. "She is waiting for you somewhere along the road back to Zamolina. I gave her food and water. She is very courageous and you are too, Andrew. You should be all right after a couple of weeks."

Andrew, still in shock, said "Thank you Tomas. How do I say thank you under these circumstances. However, I have seen more here than all the horrible and sad times in my life."

Dorovitz answered, "You could have been shot or tortured to death. You are a Polish worker and therefore, an enemy of the people. The next time, when they want something from you, they will torture your wife and children in front of you, worse if they suspect you are related to Ludwig or Krull. Hersky, Pietrinev, and Forst still believe that you are connected to Ludwig of Krakow, and the Krulls. Although you registered your grain and animal stock, they still are suspicious. I believe that there is some informant insisting there is a link. Unfortunately, home is close to the regional headquarters. As one of the workers, show some allegiance to the regulators and then in about two weeks, disappear into the forest. The area will be cleansed of the men responsible for six hundred thousand dead and proclaim Polesie safe for the winter. I can't speak to you anymore."

"Thank you for helping me when there so many in need of help. I am eternally grateful, but how many times does a man die?" Then Andrew asked Dorovitz the question that has been nagging him. "Why did you save me? Why did you do it?"

"I'm not sure," Dorovitz replied. "Perhaps the day will come when you'll be able to do the same for me. I want my children and wife to be saved. One man turns on another to protect himself in this system. "Go! You are lucky today. Your life was spared."

As Andrew trudged down the road, eyes down, his head reeling with images of torture, murder and despair, he thought he could not find a reason for it all. Why do these people want to kill the soul, the mind and all vestiges of normal humanity? Why? Why? Why? He said another prayer for the victims, trying to erase the nightmarish images from his mind.

His body ached and each step was an effort as he stumbled ahead toward home. Then he saw her. Fortunately, seated on a wagon close by the town was Marianne. She rushed towards him; they held each other tight and wept uncontrollably. After a while, Marianne helped her battered husband onto the wagon and as they made their way home, Andrew put his head against her shoulder and murmured "No matter where I am, I shall never feel alive without you."

When they reached home, although the children were overjoyed, Andrew's happiness was hindered by physical and emotional pain; he could barely speak, and fell into bed, into a deep, dark nightmarish sleep.

FRIDAY NOVEMBER 10, 1939

Andrew had lain motionless for days. Without modern medical care, Marianne could not determine whether he had broken bones or was just bruised. His agony and pain was real and every part of his body was affected and although he tried to hide it his cries revealed his suffering. The only medical care he could get was from Luba whose methods were odd and included wreaths of various plants, herbal concoctions, and poultices laced with her own urine. He lay with both legs elevated on wooden logs, and was faced toward the sun at all times. He was fed red beet sugar and water to replenish his blood; however, the best part he thought later was her stories of miracle medical remedies.

Andrew eventually was able to attend a "Freedom Zone "meeting to tell what had happened to him while he was imprisoned. He had to get the experience out and look at it in the light of day in the warmth of a safe haven. It had changed him forever and reaffirmed his deep faith in God and his resolve to prevail against the evil. He believed that the only safe course for them now was to continue to build a network of refugee centers. However, they would need to increase in size and speed of construction. They had an enemy ally in Leopold Kabryn, who had promised to help the Ludwig family. He would try to tell them of Forst's and Hersky's actions. Marianne had befriended him and asked him to find out who was on the secret list before November 15,"

They all had gathered information, crucial to survival about the Soviet List of Workers, who after five weeks of occupation, had murdered ninety percent of eastern Poland's intelligentsia, and removed six hundred thousand people from Polish Lithuania to Polish Belorussia, and who had taken half the property from eastern Poland and shipped eighty percent of the food harvest to Germany and Russia. Forst had given the Soviet Union exactly what they wanted, of thirty eight thousand people under his control; only twenty-two thousand remained.

The immediate survival need of those in this part of Polesie was to feed the thirty-five families now moved into the Liberty Zone. They had worked hard to store enough food to feed at least three hundred families four times a week for a month, and then once a week through the winter. Marianne, Andrew and all the rest were concerned with internal safety and security; how could they know who was to be trusted or who could be admitted. Adam Makowski had organized a system of approval for admission of only one family at a time. His own family moved through local gatherings and assemblies, risking their lives to recruit new families to freedom, such as it was and to safety as well.

They agreed that a series of secret refugee centers was needed under a central leadership. They hoped that by spring there could be a network of sanctuaries for all of Poland. The mysterious Luba spoke up at this same meeting about the coming winter; she said all the signs of nature and the feeling in her bones pointed to a long hard one. "Only St. Martin knows" she continued, "and tomorrow is his day, if he is riding a white horse, that is, if snow falls on November 11th, the winter will be long and hard. If, however, he arrives on a black horse – no snow – the winter will be a mild one."

MONDAY NOVEMBER 13, 1939

St. Martin arrived on his white horse on November 11th. It was a blustery cold day; the temperature was six degrees Celsius and the cold was intensified by a biting wind. Several inches of snow had fallen and then drifted against the walls of the cabins and barns.

The lines of trucks passing the house had diminished some, although those riding them were headed toward an early death. Everyone in the area knew that eventually the weather would stop the transport of human cargo to the Pinsk railroad station; however, it would only start up again in the spring. Marianne was busy getting pertinent information from good soldier Kabryn, and the freedom zone was ready for inhabitants who would move in under cover of snow and ice in mid-November.

The hope, in a land where hope was rapidly disappearing, was that by next year, the trucks would no longer pass, and they could feel safer. Marianne, in the midst of her own household work, and pursuit of information discovered that she was pregnant. Andrew and Marianne saw a new baby as a gift and sign from God. Other people, during this time, had decided that they could not bring a child into a world of evil and the ever present threat of death. However, Andrew and Marianne felt that this birth was divine assurance that they would be able to raise a child in the world of their future, one which they would help create.

Stefan's eighth birthday was approaching and Marianne and Andrew decided to tell the children about the new baby during his celebration. The event was scheduled for three evenings with special cakes, the remaining meat, and finally with the visit of Leopold Kabryn. When the time came, Marianne gently told her children of the new life inside her. Stefan, of course wanted a brother, while Maria wanted a sister, so she could hold the baby and dress her.

Stefan added, "I will make sure he doesn't cry."

Stefan was excited   "Mama, it will be the best birthday that I ever had."

"The greatest gift" Marianne said "besides the gift of faith in God, is love in our home. Ponies, bicycles, dolls are nothing. They are just objects. The forest is full of love. To share this with friends and neighbors is very special."

"Next year we will have a new birthday to celebrate," Andrew said as he wrapped his arms around his two children. "Now let us settle in for the night. It is getting late."

The next morning, Marianne carried a cup of coffee to Leopold who was on guard duty near Forst's home. When she was sure no one was around, she whispered as she handed him the steaming cup, "We are having dinner tonight for Stefan. Come join us."

"If they see me talking with you, they will get suspicious. You and Andrew are being watched. I would love to come for dinner around five. I will try to find out as much as I can by then."

Marianne thought the deportations would increase while the roads were still passable. Leopold muttered that the information was locked up in a safe in Forst's office, and that the list was constructed randomly. They were trying to move as many as possible since the NKVD is purging local Commissars for not meeting scheduled shipments. Any Polish landowner was a target including the Ludwigs. Kabryn added that Dorovitz or anyone else would be powerless to stop them.

Marianne thanked Leopold, who warned her that civilians were now forbidden to fraternize with soldiers. In the future, hidden meetings needed to be arranged in advance. All throughout the day the temperatures dropped as the snow increased. Leopold Kabryn arrived at the Ludwig farm at 5:00 as promised. He had followed the longer, safer path, under cover of the forest's thick brush. A bedraggled Leopold seemed to welcome the warmth of the family hearth, and he said he had briefly seen the List of deportees but he could not read it all. Marianne and Andrew led him to a chair near the fire, where he warmed his feet and then his inner self with a glass of vodka with cherry syrup.

He had come to love the Ludwigs and looked toward them as a safe haven from the cold and harsh weather as well as from the treatment that he got from the army. He told them that there was a rumor concerning the removal of Forst and Hersky; and that Forst was behind on his quota this month for our region. Even the blizzards of winter would not save him, and finally, thankfully, that they were not on the list.

Forst and Hersky were at each other's throats after a falling out; however, the name of Krull kept surfacing into the conversations that he had heard. He said that they all believed that there was a connection between Ludwigs and Krull. When Andrew and Marianne asked what they should do, he advised them to wait for the weather to get worse, and then under its cover to escape to the forest where they should be safe from the soldiers purging the area. He also promised to keep them in touch with the daily news of the area.

Andrew thanked Leopold profusely, who assured him again of help, but cautioned that for the next few days deportations and executions would be accelerated. If the quotas were not met, one official would blame the other. The List of Workers across Poland had caused confusion and chaos, and the army had been put on alert to oversee their progress. In Polesie, Forst and Hersky were to become scapegoats.

Leopold foresaw Colonel Pietrinev and NKVD's army as the new administrators of the region. With Dorovitz and Pietrinev in charge, the butchery would start again in the spring; therefore, Kabryn gave advice as a present to Stefan,that he must disappear from school by becoming too ill. He may want to attend tomorrow and the next day, but then the family needed to vanish as well. He offered to watch the animals which if left behind for a while would also cover the family's escape. He directed Andrew to talk with him once or twice to maintain an orderly routine.

The Ludwigs were grateful to this young soldier who was risking his own life to save theirs.

"*Sto lat*, my friend, Leopold." they all said as he prepared to leave.

"*Nazdrowie*" he answered. "If it snows hard for the next ten days, you will be okay. I will let you know when it is safe to go. This is the end of a perfect evening. "

TUESDAY NOVEMBER 14, 1939

Andrew went to the village very early in the morning to invite Leopold to come that night for charcoal potatoes around the fire; he also asked if there was more information about potential deportees. Leopold whispered a quick agreement and Andrew returned home and told Marianne that Leopold understood, and would try to get the needed information before nightfall. Andrew was leaving for the forest with a goal of building five hideouts with Varya.

Meanwhile, Marianne met with Magdalene and Florence. They huddled together to discuss a way of bartering with the Jewish merchants from Pinsk, since the merchants were involved in two economies, one for the State, the other for their self indulgence, since they had access to supplies in which the regulators winked and looked away.

Magdalene and Florence decided to drive to Pinsk with an empty wagon to barter for food and anything that would survive the existence of bare needs.

By early evening, the Ludwigs had not heard anything from Leopold. Stefan and Marianne built a fire behind the house and when Andrew returned she put raw potatoes into it. She poked at the wood while they anxiously waited for the arrival of Leopold.

At six fifteen, Leopold arrived, out of uniform for the first time, dressed in a peasant's sheepskin coat and fur cap. He sat next to Stefan, on a snow-covered log. Marianne , used to evenings in a drawing room by the fireplace sipping a liqueur, saw both of her children, in the snowy outdoors dressed in the heavy fur trimmed coats, and rabbit skin hats with fur ear covering, and thought how far removed they were from Krakow and the glow of family warmth she remembered.

However, warmth and love was here too, although the conversation often focused on much higher stakes. On this night as roasted nuts and almonds were shared along with the charcoal potatoes right from the fire, Marianne was reminded of other family meals in her past, but thought that potatoes never tasted as good. .After eating, and while watching the fire, it was time for Andrew's story, as a way to celebrate Stefan's birthday in its simplest warmth of family and fire.

Andrew was a gifted storyteller in the old Polish tradition, and the one Stefan always requested, Andrew had first heard in the army. Stefan loved to hear the same story repeatedly, remembering every detail, and if his father left, a part out Stefan promptly corrected him. Andrew began the story of a timid young Polish villager who drank too much in a local inn and took a bet from his friends to go into the local haunted cemetery and hammer a nail into one of the wooden grave markers at midnight. Tradition told that a terrible fate awaited anyone who desecrated the resting place of the dead. By the time he arrived he was panic stricken and wanted to turn back, but his friends had followed him to see if the bet was to be paid. They teased and laughed at him whenever he slowed down or looked back. When he entered the cemetery, the moon slipped behind a cloud plunging the graveyard into complete inky darkness. The wind was howling, bats were flying as the man fell over a wooden cross onto the earth of a fresh grave. Hurriedly, he hammered the nail into the cross. His friends were hiding behind a stone wall nearby making ghost noises and howling. The young man tried to get up and run. As he tried, there was something, or somebody holding him back and stopping him. He kept screaming and running assuming that a dead man was holding him back by grabbing his cloak. He fainted from terror, and when his friends came out from their hiding place to merrily explain their little joke, they found him on the ground and saw that in his panic he had nailed his cloak to the grave marker.

As the fire dimmed and the snow began to powder the branches, Stefan and Maria were put to bed. Leopold told the Ludwigs the news that lay heavy on his heart; that it would be unsafe to stay beyond the sixteenth of November—exactly two days from then. He was certain an execution would take place on the next day since Pietrinev was raging about Forst and Hersky's lack of matching the quotas set. He suggested that they leave when the temperatures, which were rising, went a bit higher so that there would be no tracks in the snow when they left. .

The last bit of information was that the Makowskis, Magdalene Kozinska and the Varyas were on the deportation list. He suggested that these families leave as well.

Leopold Kabryn, good soldier and now a good friend, hugged Marianne and Andrew, and wished them well; As soon as he was out of sight, Marianne went to the other families and told them to leave immediately, that night for the forest shelters. Marianne and Andrew lived too close to the NKVD headquarters to leave without being seen, so she told her neighbors that they would wait until the expected executions would occur using them as cover.

When Marianne reached her own house, she found Andrew packing clothes, food, and medicine to take into the refuge. He had built a little "pony cart" from the old wagon, which was originally designed for hauling peat in and out of the marshes, and was just the right size for navigating the now frozen trails into the forest. Hopefully, the melting and refreezing of the frozen ground would obliterate their trails. When the cart was full he hid it in the barn ready for a quick departure.

WEDNESDAY NOVEMBER 15, 1939

In a bitterly cold winter start, Stefan Ludwig attended school, and although Marianne had been told to stay out of sight, she was desperate to know if Jacob Dumblosky had arrived. Andrew took the cart filled with family goods into the woods. He left the cow and the other horse behind, Kabryn would watch them, and their presence would allow observers to think that the family was still in residence.

Marianne could see people and troops entering and leaving the village square across from the house. Every once in a while sporadic shots would echo across the field. She could picture even the sudden executions of anyone who displeased, offended or insulted a regulator. The shots would bring unwanted images of inhumane treatment to her mind's eye, and she sat huddled in the corner of her house peering out the window feeling fear leaving, only to be replaced with an increasing anger. Her anxiety for the future included a need to get started on the resistance movement. Marianne was a natural leader and more and more she was forced into a leadership role. She was strong enough, but her pregnancy was bringing uncontrollable mood swings which she felt needed to be placed under control for the success of a great cause driven by a rational love of country and home...

Marianne had downplayed the personal danger that she was in, and that the mood of the times was courage and self sacrifice but simply that it was the right moral thing to do. Few knew, of the surrounding neighbors, how the local regulators were obsessed with finding her. The only reason they wanted her was to lead them to her father now head of a military resistance movement. Her only crime, she knew, was to have resisted demonstrators at the school and to be Ludwig's daughter.

THURSDAY NOVEMBER 16, 1939

Marianne and Andrew awoke at seven in the morning to the sounds of two shots from across the field. Marianne grabbed her binoculars and saw Forst with Dumblosky. The time to leave was now. Hurriedly, they assembled the family; each member had a rucksack stuffed with goods including food and a pistol in each one of the parents' sack. Andrew led the way onto the rutted paths into the forest using the unfriendly appearance of the snow, mud, chilling winds and dense underbrush which actually was an advantage and good cover for an escape. There was something beautiful about the children holding the old harness that they used to keep them connected, as they trudged through the stormy weather. They wound through the wooded marshy area, being careful to avoid the many pitfalls that the wintry swampy land provided, and finally reached the entrance to the Liberty Zone, now named in memory of the Pasternaks. The tall thicket at the bottom of a shallow ravine reached by the path at the bottom was submerged in a frozen combination of mud and ice. Andrew had been able to take the small wagon and horse through, the day before, but a larger wagon could be in trouble if it approached a thick brush. There was a slit in the thick brush, which led to another path directly to the sanctuary, the Blessed Black Madonna and their new home.

Andrew went directly to the icon, now dressed in the white coat of winter and crossed himself as he said a quiet prayer of thanks. Against what looked like a bank of earth were some dead tree branches, which when Andrew pulled on them revealed a door which he opened, and led everyone inside a little hut with wooden walls and a thatched roof. There was a small fireplace and chimney already loaded with *"torf"* or dried peat. He lit it and its unique smell, and quick combustion gave heat and warmth to the room. They lit a lantern, and felt as if they were safely tucked away in a forgotten part of the world, shielded from the dangerous one outside

Andrew was joyous when he reconnected to the "bounties of the forest": the world of his boyhood. The houses, somewhat resembling the Roman catacombs, were ready for thirty-five families that would be coming soon. This was to be their place..... Pasternak's Freedom Zone. All love comes home, Marianne thought, and these are the good, loving and faithful. It was a quiet spot offering what life should mean to all of them--- a chance to choose their own values and live on our own terms.

SATURDAY NOVEMBER 18, 1939

This day marked the birth of the Pasternak Freedom zone -- Pasternak Strefa Wolności or as the inhabitants later shortened it to "*w Pasternaka*". Moscow now owned and controlled the country. Poland had lost its sovereignty, except here in the woods of Polesie. Marianne thought "They may occupy our land but they have not dimmed our passion. Truth will live on as will the hard ducha that aches deep inside us." They knew that they had to be ever mindful of the long dark days ahead, but there was no turning back.

One hundred and fifty people had arrived "*w Pasternaka*". Although some were scarred both physically and emotionally, they had survived the orgy of destruction and horror.

The Grygas, Rygalas, and Pilats, last to arrive this morning, appeared wet and cold and half starved. Makowski had begun the "free market exchange" for an underground economy by trading a cow in Pinsk for additional tools which he had brought there. The last of the four families from the original settlers, the Pilats, emerged from the brush, flushed and tired. They greeted everyone with a gentle, "God be with you." Andrew and Marianne answered, "Joy be with you." These poor, hungry farmers worked for Wladek Pasternak, and they brought knowledge of the terrain and could be trusted.

At the end of the day, at an evening vesper service held by flickering firelight, Casimir Pilats, marked by scars from beatings and torture by the NKVD, administered in front of his weeping family, spoke to the others. He was the only survivor of Makowski's six guards and their families. "No more hiding, it is time to draw the line." he said.

Marianne had emerged as the leader of the "Freedom Zone", trained well by her father; however, she had to tread carefully in a society where men were still the heads of households and where women were considered less enfranchised. She knew that she could not appear authoritarian, even when she was sure she was right, and that she had to step cautiously, even in these times, in the presence of deception and the unsavory nature of the world around and the obvious deceit of those men and women who are falling in lockstep to harm all men with a soul.. She responsibly asked Casimir, with his experience, to take care of gathering intelligence, along with his wife, to oversee the security of the perimeter and entrances and exits to the area. Both of them agreed readily, and appeared to feel energized and optimistic about the task. What Marianne kept to herself was the knowledge that the search for her had been intensified, and hopefully there was no one person that could identify her. And it was everyone's duty to secure Pasternaks Liberty Zone as the center of economic, barter, and health needs for the trusted citizenry. In sharing their skills, they designed an auxiliary economic system outside the imposed, centrally controlled redistribution system of quotas, shortages and misery.

The women, along with the men, faithfully believed in what they were doing, but true to their character and intellect, were building a humane system of survival. For instance, Florence Makowski, albeit self taught, initiated her "health care system" to provide medical aid to those in need and life saving techniques in a brutal society.

The Rygalas, Edmund and Susan, had just arrived as well, and set about increasing the numbers of hidden huts. They were followed by Alexander and Patricia Gryga, farm laborers on Pasternak's land with five children ranging in age from five to thirteen; all their property, food and money had been taken away. They took on day-to-day management of the sanctuary. The members were trying to increase the size of the compound, with the idea of accommodating at least five hundred people. Justina Varya was the last to arrive with her parents, Luba and Stefan, and her two brothers. The four of them took on path and passage maintenance to keep them resembling just natural useless trails.

When the families had assembled, they wept as they carried their pitifully few things to share. They brought a little cocoa, tea, some meat, sugar and salt. However, as a group, they could share goods and clothing, as well as be sustained with emotional support. The Lukasz's came with a pair of shoes to give to the Nowaks. The Nowaks brought three sweaters to present to the Swiederskis and the Kazmirs. The Witoszs, expert trappers, brought with them knowledge of the forest's richness, and along with Andrew, were ready to teach others how to forage for food

Marianne's plan was to create a network of "freedom zones" along secret trails deep inside the forest from Polesie, north to Vilnius, and west down the road to Brest Litowsk, then southwest by next spring. Adam Makowski, would carefully select those in charge of each zone, and would connect them with secret codes and routs, but only with good, trusted people, and as Andrew would always utter: "where there are good people, there is hope." There was a profound sense of silent heroes of Polesie and the true reason; love of home and country.

The danger was the presence of informers and oppressors. Adam Makowski, like Wladek Pasternak, lost all his property and of the five original landowners, only he remained alive. He had provided goods and materials for the construction of the original huts and enough provisions for a large number of people. .

Andrew said as he started the makeshift service: "This is the day that we can say our prayers openly. When the priests return, Christ's message will be sent among the people, as it has never been before. I shall dedicate today's services to Father Zajac and Father Baron and to all the priests who suffered and gave their lives so that we can be free to say our prayers in the pure air."

Andrew peered out at the anxious, gaunt faces. As they became silent, he looked at the homemade altar, decorated with green pines, boughs and candles, and small hand carved triptych nestled at the bottom of the altar. His own sacred carvings had been placed in the center of the large forest in the middle of winter's winds and snow, surrounding the carved Black Virgin. Andrew, for that moment, stepped back into his seminary training and presented a homily as he was reminded of his friend Father Baron. Andrew started to pray in Latin. The ragged congregation answered with fervent intensity. Martyrs like Father Zajac and Father Baron cultivated the soul. Love and love alone was their guiding light for a peaceful and eternal joy. Though Andrew could not practice as a priest, they were all comfortable when he led them in hymns, prayers and portions of the Mass.

Andrew asked Adam to lead them in the Polish National Anthem. They stood with locked arms singing *"Jeszcze Polska Nie Zginela.* "Poland is not dead whilst we live." with voices echoing through the whistling forest.

The emotional moment sent tears of release, and Marianne rose to speak to the little congregation who still stood with arms linked together in a kind of symbolic statement of unity. "This place matters to all of us, and is our future, the center of our existence. We have peace of mind, joy, pride here, where exhausted families are not hunted or haunted in an empty place of the world, but are alive in our sanctuary. Our faces tell it all. I will take pride in preparing for our future"

As she began to speak of Wladek and Barbara, her voice cracked and she started to sob. "Wladek and Barbara promised to celebrate Stefan's birthday, and we all want our children to reach their birthdays. These little boys and girls need to grow up to be adults with love of faith and courage. This is our ultimate purpose and reason for living"

Marianne looked at her son's shining face, and the faces of the other innocent children in this group. She realized, as she saw them, that they were actually culturally deprived. The Sovietization was based on control of mind and indoctrination and this enclave was a unique spirit of courageous people, rarely, if ever found in one place. She vowed to herself to prepare these young boys and girls to have a tomorrow, a next season of candles, and another day to pray. She knew they would all need to get busy to start a "Freedom School" as soon as possible, never to lose the human spirit that always remains supremely beautiful. How else would the heart and traditions of a free Poland be passed down to youngsters during these terrible times in a history of evil and betrayal? To this day and beyond, each moment in their lives is not the end of a journey, but a shining light beyond the marshes of Polesie.

Kettles of hot kukri, a soup of yellow mushrooms, potatoes, and lamb, and kluskie, basha, kielbasa and kapusta were all brought forth after the service and shared along with two grilled lambs and babka baked with sugar and honey. Finally, satisfied with food for both the stomach and the spirit, they returned to their huts in the earth.

They had journeyed from stylish homes to crude farmer's houses and now to buried huts; however they were safe in the strength of knowing they all had a chance. As always, Marianne, however, was cautiously enjoying the momentary security; but she was focused on the historic push for freedom of the mind. She often thought of her father and the resistance movement. For her, retreat to safety was not enough; there had to be some recompense, some accountability for these oppressive peoples who were inflicting great pain and suffering and she thought the leadership had a duty to rid the evils.

She approached Adam Makowski privately. .She carefully told Adam that the next step had to be taken separately from the security of the enclave. She vowed to see Zamolenski soon. "The Home Army" she continued, "knows the horrors of the Nazi and Soviet Occupation, and we need to try to stop the deportations of millions to the slave camps where their chances of surviving the war are"O".

Adam said: "I am not sure what I am agreeing to, but I will help."

Marianne, sounding a bit like an evangelist said: "Every Polish life that we save is a victory for us. Bringing back our priests to the churches is another, and while the enemy is still killing everything near and dear to us, we must feed and clothe the needy. I do have a plan in mind. " she concluded cryptically.

FRIDAY NOVEMBER 24, 1939

For six days and nights, the work to expand the sanctuary continued at a feverish pace, Andrew, Stefan, Rygala, and Pilat excavated ten more huts, two additional Russian baths, and three fireplaces. There was room now for many more people. Animal traps were set by a group of boys under the direction of Rygalas, Pilats, Varya and Makowski's sons, who managed to catch a wild boar, five deer and twenty-seven rabbits for the week's supply of meat.

The onset of winter was fierce, as the temperatures plummeted below 6 degrees (20 degrees F) for the first time. The varying temperatures brought snow one day, followed by slush and ice the next. Marianne's secret plan was to meet Zamolenski in Janow on the 28th; however, if there was an unexpected warm, sunny day the ground would become a quagmire of slush and that would make travel on foot or by wagon almost impossible. If, however, the frost in late November hardened the slush to ice, a traveler could be frozen into it.

Over one hundred refugees arrived in the sanctuary this day. They were asked to pledge allegiance to Poland. Marianne acted as an instructor for safe existence, including procedures created to provide a protective invisibility. Hersky, Pietrinev, Dorovitz, the informers, and the regulators were identified as the enemy; the objective was to avoid them for the protection of all those hidden in the forest. Children had to be taught how to respond to interrogations and to use identity cards. This crash course also demonstrated how to use Russian to avoid confrontations, which would also be helpful for bribing regulators and soldiers. For example, "JA WAS LUBIE" is I love you in Polish, and if you substitute *cie* for was you get... I *like* you in Polish. They were taught how to act, and how to stand mute when confronted by the regulators, and how to move from one village to another, without disclosing anyone else's' identity. Magdalene Kozinska gave instructions for the underground economy with the Jewish merchants for exchanges of food, clothing, tools, cigarettes, vodka, watches, medicine and coal. Florence Makowski helped them learn how to pronounce Russian words and Stefan Varya assisted with spelling.

They all were pitifully poor; therefore, any goods, no matter how small, were a godsend. Each of them had something that people could use. If a cup of milk was needed, it was worth traveling a long distance through winding passages in exchange for bread. Babies and children could die of malnutrition without the precious essentials of milk, bread, honey, and meat. To protect foods from spoilage and rodents, it was kept in pots and pans outside the huts. They created a central distribution center of the collected crops and forest harvests, so that the needy could be fed.

Money however, was a larger problem. The Zloty was gone, replaced by the Russian ruble as legal exchange. The idea was to collect a stash of valuables for use as bribes or in case of medical emergency; 29 gold watches in a pot, which Marianne and Andrew brought with them, were buried beneath a tree. Magdalene Kozinska was the banker.

Vodka became another commodity used for exchange after the discovery was made that Adam Makowski's sons had ability to make it with a still, moved from their home. Since Russians loved their vodka, it became almost priceless among the Communists, who valued their drink as a part of their life. Under no circumstances, did anyone dare to divulge the existence of Pasternak's Sanctuary or as was sometimes called Fern Cathedral. It had to remain secret. Except for an extreme emergency, recruiting and scheduled exchange of goods was to be done by Magdalene: her code name became "Vistula."

Marianne and Luba insisted that each person have at least fifteen minutes in the hot steam baths, hidden around the enclave. Some were hidden more than others were. Saturday retreats in the baths were a respite from their hectic, often confusing life in the hideout for married couples and lovers. Although the steam and hot water was often a stimulant of passion, it helped keep the cleanliness of the huts separated from the rampant dysentery and typhoid of the outside war torn world.

The community gathered at night around the central fire pit, where very often Magdalene Kozinska began to teach the children to read and write. Florence Makowski, taught preventive health measures. In the center of the enclave, others would relax with good food, some sugary syrup water for the children and Makowski's vodka. Hungry faces clustered around the fire as Andrew passed the babka, and the Pilats, Rygalas and Grygas produced bowls of hot potato soup, borsht and kluskie. They had a greeting song for all joyous occasions, *"Sto Lat! Sto Lat….."* May we all live to have one-hundred years of happiness.

Andrew, a natural teacher, attracted children, and he would point out the mysteries of the forest and its wildlife to them. He explained

All Love Comes Home

that the deadwood supports an immense colony of small life, and that a crack in the bark is a place for spiders to nest, while in a log's center, black fungus consumes the heart of the wood. Eventually, Andrew said the termites would follow the thousands of soldiers and workers to build cities."On a smaller scale it is what we are doing here," he said.

Andrew helped others to adapt to their life in the wild. Many of the men had now begun to grow beards, but a shaven face was cleaner and safer. "Nothing is more painful than to have to strip icicles from your beard." he said. "If you are crawling in the snow and the ice thaws and you get soaked, the worst problem is having parts of the body dripping wet with accumulated thawed frost and water. The important rule is to keep your clothing and your animals as dry as possible. Otherwise, when the temperature drops rapidly after the frost and ice have thawed out, there is not sufficient heat to dry them, so you can freeze to death. Let the regulators keep their beards, but we must be clean-shaven. Tell the city types that they look great in beards as they send pictures back home to Moscow." he laughingly added.

In the winter chill, sleds and skis were as valuable as fire, food and water. For safe and fast travel in the face of strong winds, blizzards and frozen marshes, they could make the difference between life and death; therefore, Andrew began to get men to build sturdy sleds, skis and snow shoes stronger than those that had been confiscated." Let the Soviets travel in their own way" he said," We need these sleds for our safety. The best ones are made of hickory and oak and put together entirely with rawhide lashings," he told his fellow carpenters "There is not a screw or nail anywhere. This design gives them flexibility that withstands any amount of strain, while sleds rigidly constructed of steel, without joints, made by nails or screws, are likely to break when they are exposed to solid rock or ice. Also, the rawhide lashings make repairs easier if a part should break." As the winter started to set in, they hurriedly prepared the necessary tools for survival.

SATURDAY NOVEMBER 25, 1939

Andrew made skis, a sled and snowshoes for Marianne to travel to Janow sometime during the next three days. Her trip remained a well-kept secret as a precautionary measure. Florence Makowski had warned Marianne about frostbite, and she was given rules for its prevention, including proper hygiene and extra clothing for protection. She had stressed the importance of slits in the pants to avoid total exposure when, as she said: "nature called." If the temperature fell suddenly and in Polesie, it could drop at once to minus 28 C below zero, exposure of any

200

body part could result in frostbite, and she was admonished to eat regularly including kasha and water, or death would be the result. Marianne was told to keep her clothes dry, and to avoid exposure to the cold. She was given a bottle of water, which when emptied could be filled with snow, kept next to the body to melt to keep a constant supply of water on hand.

Magdalene Kozinski was a sharp trader and peddler; she returned from Pinsk where she had gone on a foraging expedition. She knew that under the Soviet system, the black market would flourish, and although trade with it was dangerous it was essential for a steady supply of medicine and other needs. Dorovitz's headquarters were in nearby Pinsk, the center of Muscovite activity there and deliberate barter with the Jewish merchants, could result in personal disaster. However, she operated in this horrific pit with skill motivated by her tragic experience at the hands of the Bolsheviks. Behind her concealing peasant attire, there was a very attractive woman that never showed. She smuggled goods in her undergarments and with Adam Makowski, brought food, canned milk, fruits, sugar, and syrup for the children. She traded vodka bottles with Pinsk merchants, who sensed that vodka that mysteriously reappeared in a continuous supply had to have a lofty political connection, and to keep its supplier alive was worth more to them than having her arrested or shot. Magdalene loved the vodka as a monetary coin, and it gave her access to all kinds of goods.

"I headed directly into Pinsk" she told Marianne "with Makowski and flirted with the merchants. Although some people issued dire warnings about the penalties, I pulled out a bottle of vodka, with another one hidden between my legs while Makowski remained outside with a gun strapped to his leg.

"Look" I said to a Jewish shop keeper "If you want to survive, a case of vodka equals supplies for fifty lives." Magdalene stood holding the bottle aloft.

The stout Jewish merchant grumbled loudly, as he tried to lower the barter price. But she told him, "*Ja was lubie* "in Russian. "I can assure you of a guaranteed supply."

He walked with her into the back room, which was fully stocked with coffee, cans of fruit and sugar. Then he supposedly jokingly said, "When you're arrested, will your sources continue to supply me with a case of vodka each week?"

"No!" she said "I am your only source, as long as we love each other."

"We have a deal," he said.

"I got a pound of sugar and coffee for three bottles of vodka. In addition, for three more bottles, I got ten cans of fruit. But that was not all" she went on to tell Marianne. "Adam and I went to another merchant further down in the market. I repeated the same message. This one asked me, "Why haven't you been arrested for exchanging goods through the black market?"

"He opened the door and showed me his secret room...a secondary supply of canned goods in back of a building reserved for the regulators. He thought I might be a mistress to someone important, someone in the know! Therefore, he could be arrested and possibly disappear with no explanation for not cooperating. He finally made the transaction, clearly convinced that the merchandise saved his life and those of his well-connected regulators. He wanted to continue doing business." "Frankly," Magdalene told Marianne later, "if it meant feeding my two daughters here I would do anything! Vodka between my legs was only a seductive promotion. The real value was the transaction. I got my goods, and he got to dream. That's a fair exchange, don't you agree?"

She had found fur boots for Marianne's journey, which when aged and scuffed, could be those worn by a peasant. Adam had filled Andrew's little cart with food which was being stashed away. "I could have done better if I had had more time," she said with a satisfied smile.

"You have your fur boots, and food. What else will you need?" Magdalene asked.

"As much courage as you have." Marianne answered.

SUNDAY NOVEMBER 26, 1939

The next morning, the sunlight made the tree branches look like glass needles. The families had been in the forest, but they had to stay focused on the dangers outside. A small group had gathered inside the Ludwig's hut. Andrew was going to Dorovitz via Janow to see if he could get information about coming events, hopefully he could see Leopold as well.

After Andrew left, Marianne met with the other emerging leaders of the "Freedom Zone", in her hut. Any knowledge of retribution of any kind could be fatal to Andrew, after his last encounter with the NKVD.

202

They were being watched when visible. Adam Makowski, Magdalene, Florence and Casimir Pilat had become a kind of council for the little hidden village. What none of them realized was that in their quest for survival, they were practicing democratic communism, which had been perverted beyond recognition by the Bolsheviks. At this time, they wanted revenge and retribution and their feelings ran high with an almost uncontrollable anger burning in each breast. Adam wanted to kill them with no regret, and hunt the beasts down one by one----Dorovitz, Pietrinev, regulators, and officials. "Only then will they begin to believe in us." he said.

"Only the conscience of a few good people will be able to restore Poland to an independent and humane society. There are not many left who are capable and have the integrity to lead and die for our country. The Communists have eliminated so many potential leaders and intellectuals. The rest are in prisons or dead. It will take a long, long time and even more suffering." said Marianne who now was the leader, a role which she did not relish because of the danger to her family and unborn child; however, she was the voice of reason and could encourage others to take a sound course of action.

The established, hidden settlement provided a safe haven, at least for the moment; therefore, Marianne envisioned the creation of a resistance force, inspired by her father, both recently and from her childhood which would strike fear into the regulators and stop deportations. It must be a secret counter insurgent organization. She told those present that it was imperative for her to see Zamolenski to start defining the targets, and to gauge the possible effectiveness of the group. She needed to convince her friends that a rag tag army could fight a system of terror that they were facing. She also knew that they all wanted to do something-anything to counter their feelings of anger, hate and helplessness.

Marianne suggested, and she had spent sleepless nights planning this all, that they start by making a list of men and women most dangerous to them. "At the moment, it would be better to let them execute each other .The survivors of their own purge can be attacked next spring. In the meantime, we know there is a prison holding the intellectuals and potential leaders outside of Pinsk. If we are to save a thousand lives by the end of the year, we should free those tortured souls. That's where our future leaders are."

Casimir and Adam questioned the danger and the timing. Adam looked at Marianne and spoke softly, "That means we have only two weeks if you mean by the end of this year."

Marianne had been brewing a response to the Bolsheviks inwardly for weeks, and she realized that planning action and resistance was the best medicine for these suffering people. She also had to present her ideas as if they were rationally planned and could be successful in execution. She had carefully worked out the starting points. Florence and Magdalene were asked to create identity cards for the prisoners, while Adam and Casmir were in charge of drawing a map and floor plan of the target. They all promised to do as asked, and for the first time Marianne noticed, they left with their heads high and a vision in front of them.

MONDAY NOVEMBER 27, 1939

Andrew had returned home late the night before, worn, exhausted and somewhat defeated. His trip to Janow went badly and cost him the family horse. He finally sat, at early dawn, and told his wife the story. When he reached Zamolina, the wagon got stuck in a slushy part of the road. He pulled and tugged on the reins and the horse, but the wagon sank further and further into the mire. He looked up and realized he was near the headquarters of the local "leaders"; and he hoped that they would not notice him. However, Colonel Pietrinev arrived roaring loudly, "You dumb, Polack. Can't you see that a wagon will never make it in this snow and ice? How dumb are you?"

Hersky appeared and added "How does Dorovitz find you so useful when you can't even cross your field? You are the one who needs help."

Andrew looked at them as if he did not understand, and as he did, the horse and wagon pulled out of the slush. As he turned to go, Pietrinev called," I want to talk to you. Hersky and I have to know if you are interested in helping us."

Andrew kept his head down and replied "As I told Dorovitz, I just want to be a good farmer, carpenter, and good citizen. That is it. Dorovitz is waiting for me and I need to go. I'll see you when I get back."

Pietrinev grabbed the horse's halter and stopped Andrew from moving; threateningly he said "Stay! We learned a lot," he confided." Just this week I accompanied Hersky's secret police to conduct a "removal" of two small Polish settlements west of here."

He launched into a story of his trip on snowy roads to trick local villagers and send them off to deportation stations and camps. As he told the story, albeit to a captive audience, he puffed up, making a case for his own prowess and his pride, in the destruction of the lives of others They had been falling behind their schedule of "relocation" .and he didn't know why, until they discovered, and he emphasized how smart he was, that the villagers were posting warning sentries and leaving before the Russians arrived. He gleefully recounted, how clever he was to order the headlights of the trucks turned off to surprise the settlement. Before this, the peasants had been sleeping clothed and escaping on the first warning shout. He emphasized, Andrew thought, his devious cunning instead of his initial stupidity of approaching stealthily with lights blazing. This time they were successful in rousting out the villagers, limiting their provisions and loading them into trucks, Resistance meant death.

His story continued with a detailed description of how families, separated from each other, were   pushed into crowded trucks. He was not aware at all of his self-portrayal as a sadist. Hersky continued the victorious saga relating how mothers were cutting their children's throats rather than letting them be taken. He also added that some houses were burned to prevent hidden families from remaining; however, the idea was to use many for regulators coming in later. The goods that the families brought for the journey were confiscated anyway." We only took 150 people out of 400. The rest ran into the forest as if there was safety there."

At this point Andrew got very frightened; someone had given information to the NKVD.

"We didn't have time to chase them," Pietrinev continued. "Someone is spreading a rumor that living to the end is better than surviving in Siberia. We got far too few people for the amount of time it took. We need to have a more efficient method next time. "We need to get as many out as possible. Our goal is two million people in the following six months", Pietrinev boasted.

"If we are not able to deliver, it will be death for all of us," Hersky declared.

"Remember when you were dragged out for interrogation and torture and   Dorovitz rescued you? He did the right thing. A few months ago you were seen with Zamolenski, by Dumblosky, who never forgets a face. When he comes here in a few weeks he will want to talk to you; you know what I mean."

205

Andrew shuddered inwardly at the threat; Hersky went on to say that Andrew could help them. "Someone, he continued, "is organizing a resistance movement. We want to know who it is. Keep your eyes open."

Andrew played to the "dumb Polack" to the maximum, "I am a good farmer. Perhaps the best way to help you is for my family to meet your food production quota for next spring's harvest. Dorovitz believes it is very worthwhile for us to be here. You need people who know what they are doing. Otherwise those people in Moscow will take their anger out on you. Dorovitz understands. Why don't you?"

Hersky grunted angrily and turned his back, while Colonel Pietrinev said "Those bastard Polacks! They hold on. What makes them press on?" He stomped off with Hersky, back into their building.

Andrew thought that his next worry was the man who never forgets a face. Soon after, he got moving on the road where he saw Leopold Kabryn and saluted. His returned wink indicated that everything was all right with him. Andrew was able to follow a convoy of Soviet trucks, tires fitted with snow chains, whose tracks made it easier for the wagon's journey through the snow and ice. He followed them to the nearby railroad tracks, and there he saw a row of cattle boxcars at the station, closely guarded by sentries and the newly replaced Pinsk police. Soldiers, warmly dressed in winter gear and carrying fixed bayonets, milled about while shabbily dressed children, men and women gazed out of the tiny openings of the car hungrily. The packed human cargo had been forced to be without woolen underwear, coats or blankets, as another load of precious humanity was snatched away and herded like cattle to Siberia. The sight was becoming all too common, he thought, as he continued on to the other side of the town to Dorovitz's home.

Andrew drove up to the armed guards at the gates of the house; he could see Dorovitz at the window as he was stopped by one of the soldiers. After being required to identify himself, he was allowed to pass and go upstairs.

Dorovitz welcomed Andrew warmly, slapping him on the back like an old friend, and he led him to the back store room at the rear of his quarters. Two entire rooms were filled with canned goods of all kinds, including peaches, potatoes, meat and peas.

"The landowner who was living here had been stockpiling food for a long time," Dorovitz said with a grin. "He guessed correctly what was coming. How could he have known that when the war started, he wouldn't get a chance to eat any of this?"

The landowner, Andrew remembered had a wife and several children. Now, Dorovitz possesses their property and their lives. "Pity, we are starving out there. I know I could be shot for saying this to you" Andrew said.

Dorovitz stared at Andrew and added flatly, "Everything is going to the Russian war effort; although times will get better it will be a long war. No one deserves their food more than you. Go on, take some. I owe you money anyway. Help yourself. Next time, don't mention the scarcity of food, since you are right, it is a crime to blame it on the Soviets. Share some of the food with your neighbors. I know they are hungry. Besides, you came here for the food anyway, didn't you?"

"I worked for you as a friend," Andrew said "but I can't take another man's food. I believe that is stealing. We don't need it."

"Andrew, you can't be innocent all your life. Share with your neighbors." Dorovitz changed the subject "The weather looks bad. I hope it does not snow heavily tonight."

"How many people will be deported for work duty in Siberia?" Andrew asked quietly. "That is not right, Dorovitz!"

"I could have you shot for that remark," Dorovitz snapped back. These people are needed for different reasons first; Stalin needs a million workers in Siberia and Kazakhstan in the next year and a half. Life is hard there and the weak will perish; therefore, the need for Polish, Ukrainians, Lithuanians and Byelorussians, will run into the millions .We are at war with Finland and many of the men from Siberia are sent to fight the Fins, while others are needed in the coal mines and industrial plants for the war effort. My task, here in Polesie, is to ship out as many people per week as possible. Two million Poles are scheduled to be deported by harvest of 1940. It doesn't matter where they die, here or in Siberia."

Andrew, at this point in Dorovitz's diatribe, was afraid for his life. He wondered why he was the target of this explanation which sounded, to him, very much like a self-rationalization on the speaker's part.

Dorovitz went on "Khrushchev, who works for Stalin, wants Poles to provide space for the Soviets and its regulators, and he wants to keep all Catholic Poles out of the Communist system. The only way to do this is to eliminate all anti-Communist activity, and few are as good at it as Poles. You are a Catholic?"

"Yes, but I have no politics and I am no threat to anyone," answered Andrew.

"Poles are stubborn Catholics. We are atheists. Stalin doesn't want the Catholics anywhere; therefore, the NKVD is ever on the alert for anti-communist Poles."

Dorovitz paused, drew in his breath and leaned closer to Andrew, "When this is over, we will meet in the end whether before or after death as a Catholic Pole, and a Communist. My wife Ilana quietly struggles with her conscience and morality. She is more than aware of the consequences in our own world. She is expecting total destruction of our family and fears for her children. You have a promise of hope, and I live in fear. Listen very attentively to what I am saying."

"Yes, I understand." said Andrew not really sure of what Dorovitz wanted.

" Andrew" he continued, " Last week, I heard that a NKVD agent used the wrong code of entry at the former Zamolenski home, which now houses the Russian high command. He muttered "Zebra", and after intense interrogation he was shot and the origin of "Zebra" was gone with him. . The NKVD then confiscated a letter which never reached its destination, and it was in wet pieces, so little was left of it; however; they think it was intended for someone at the Zamolenski house. The only legible part said "........daughter, Vistula, continue with the dream. An unlit candle gives no light. Only when it is burning will it shine bright...Zebra." "Zebra is alive in western Poland, and someone is connected to him. This information has led us to believe that a resistance movement is starting here."

Andrew tried to understand if he was reading this message correctly. It appeared to be too artfully presented and too calculated. "My God," he thought, "he knows of Marianne's father. "

"You have had a long month, Tomas. Ilana and your children are important." said Andrew, who realized the risk that Dorovitz was taking by giving out information that could be beaten out of a captive.

"We have barely begun." Dorovitz put his arm confidentially around Andrew's shoulder and dropped his voice to a whisper, "It will be exceptionally hazardous to all, and who will live on to say that my causes are more or less important than yours are. I am willing to take part in Stalin's plans to march all the Polish citizenry to Siberia. We are in this together. I trust you. We may need each other someday."

Dorovitz's words were fast and quiet, "Do as I say. When you get back, immediately donate your horse to Colonel Pietrinev. They will be confiscating it anyway. Work horses are precious to the Russians; therefore, they need to acquire as many as possible. Let the guards see you doing the same chores each and every day, and get special permission to travel the main road during daylight hours. I'll sign your card saying so. Make sure your wife is visible doing her outside work, they are watching her as a suspect, but Hersky is not sure of whom she might be. As long as you work for me, he has certain rights, but not to kill you. You will live if you stay disciplined to daily chores, remain silent, and you and Marianne do not vary your routine. Donate the horse, volunteer some barter, be ready to escape into the forest. They won't go beyond 2 kilometers into it. They will find you invisible if your routine is worthwhile to them, and your wife will not be noticed except as a field hand. The six hectares of land you own is too large by Russian standards. Allocate it, and all necessities, even to the smallest things. I have said enough. You get the message."

"Yes! "Andrew said.

Dorovitz told all of this to Andrew rapidly, like a naughty child confessing his actions to the priest in the confessional, and as if Andrew could give him some sort of absolution for his actions.

Andrew thought- what kind of salvation can this man hope for? Did he observe his own days of Atonement on Yom Kippur, or was he desperate enough to wish for some sort of atheistic or divine retribution?

Andrew replied simply. 'I will look out for you and Ilana; somewhere inside each of us there is a soul. I am not political, and therefore, I thank you for your kindness to me."

"You're welcome Andrew." Dorovitz replied. "You have been given more information than most. Remember, remain unnoticed. You have touched Ilana's heart and I felt the influence of your peasant wife."

"I will do everything in my power to help save as many lives as we can---including yours and your family. I have to go now Thomas" said Andrew and he left with a quick goodbye.

His journey home with his horse was sad as he knew it was for the last time. When he arrived in the town square, Andrew took the traces off Sasha and slowly walked to Colonel Pietrinev's headquarters,

He tied the horse to a rail, told the guard it was a present for the Colonel, and personally pulled the wagon slowly away towards home.

TUESDAY NOVEMBER 28,1939

Despite the falling temperatures, Marianne decided to see Zamolenski. Andrew knew of the life threatening conditions in the forest and out of doors from his own past, whereas Marianne had only seen winter from indoors and from the ski slopes of the Carpathian Mountains.

Marianne was lying next to Andrew and they held each other close in their hut in the woods. She decided, as warm and tempting as it was, she nevertheless would leave six hours earlier for Janow than she had planned .She wanted to get started on a fighting vigilante group that would cause fear for the enemy, more than that she envisioned a prison escape before year end to expand and collect these guerillas into the network of Freedom Zones. Deportations would be starting soon again, and maybe, she thought, if we cannot stop them, she could save some lives. She could see a network of Freedom Zones slowly building and connecting across Polesie which would expand the Home Army into Warsaw.

Marianne was possessed with these thoughts, and at the same time, she realized that sharing them with Andrew could result in torture and death for him. He had told her of Dorovitz's warning and the loss of the horse, and she was angrier than ever. Her fear for her own safety was subjugated to the desire to continue the resistance to the Bolshevik menace. However, the situation dictated that she remain hidden from the regulators as a leader, and her role as the dirty peasant was necessary for her survival. The stress of her existence and the balancing of her roles as wife, mother, leader and insurgent were mollified only by her actions. The more she did for her cause, the less was her personal anxiety. She said to herself, "Women make the best guerillas, if only to protect their children." Therefore, she pushed forward with her plans.

As Marianne looked out the window at the violent gale, she thought too, of Magdalene Kozinska who had delivered the promised boots to her the day before. Magdalene had journeyed round trip to Pinsk and back, twenty kilometers in below zero temperatures. She went into the store where she had left a case of vodka the week before, which bound the merchant to her and bartered for the precious boots. She threatened that his involvement on the black market could be tragic for him if the right person was told. "I'll never be too far" she warned, before turning around, doggedly toward home with conviction and courage against the icy elements.

Andrew mapped every leg of Marianne's journey; he was uncomfortable with her traveling alone, but could not go with her since he had to make daily appearances around the farm near Pietriniev's headquarters. He helped her spread a salve made from the buds of aspen trees for chapped lips. She was outfitted with crafted wooden skis, homemade tin stoves, filled with nuts and moss, matches, food for the journey and a bottle of water. She was bundled in layers of pants and sweaters, a sheepskin coat, a rabbit-fur hat with earflaps, a scarf, a pair of fur gloves and a blanket poncho over everything else .

Her most important piece of equipment, however, was a map that Andrew had made of the trail, which he had marked earlier in the year. The Soviet curfew from 8:00 P.M. to 7:00 A.M. would cover the morning part of her travel. Marianne picked up her rucksack filled with food, barter, and a loaded pistol, said her goodbye to Andrew, hugged the children, promised she would be back soon and set off into the icy black forest.

Her feet crunched through the deep snow while she faced a howling gale. She had trouble keeping her balance and footing and could barely drag herself along with the wind gusts forcing her to stumble and occasionally fall. She finally started moving from tree to tree hanging on for her life. She was strong now from all the farm work, although she worried about her pregnancy and the bitter cold. Marianne reached a more sheltered part of the trail, then was only able to worry more about losing Andrew, freezing to death, losing the baby, and being captured tortured and killed by the NKVD. At home there was support; however, she was alone here with her terrors, the forest and the cold. Ludwig's voice started to echo in her mind: "Is that all?" Over and over she thought of it and the real meaning of the statement: there was more to live for and to do, so on she went, a lonely figure bent into the icy storm.

As sunrise came and went, her eyes strained from the constant glare, and her shoulders ached with pain. Her legs felt very heavy. When she felt exhausted, Marianne began to recite the rosary, fully believing that her faith would re-energize her and it did. Every half hour she would say more prayers to the Black Madonna, the Holy Mother, and the Virgin Mary as she pictured each in her mind. Finally, she reached a larger trail along the forest. The snow continued to fall and the drifts remained high; as Andrew had predicted there were no patrols. As a small village came into her view at the edge of the trail, and as she turned to look at

211

the small clump of houses, she slipped and slid into a ditch and was trapped waist deep in icy slush. "My God," she thought "How am I to get out?" Try as she might to crawl or climb, she slid further and then started to panic. She could feel the bottom of the ditch with her feet; however, there was ice water surrounding them. Marianne was weighed down by clothing, slush and her skis, but she found a branch near the edge of the ditch and with a strong effort, buoyed by panic, pulled herself to the edge and to safety.

She took off the frozen outer layer of clothing, lit the two fires and huddled under the blanket; she sucked the rock candy and massaged her legs vigorously, doing exactly what Florence instructed last week. After an hour, her stiffness had abated, and even her cheeks were warmer. Each piece of her protective equipment had worked so well, she thought: the fire cans, the vodka, the protective covers, the hot potatoes and chestnuts; the horsehide for double protection, the rosary...how important they all had become! Her clothing was still wet, but she decided to go forward anyway, praying it was dry enough. Andrew's map showed a pile of wood under the snow about an hour away, and she found it.

Marianne cleaned as much snow off it as she could, found some dry wood, sprinkled vodka over it and set it on fire. No longer afraid, she huddled under the blanket near the fire. She talked to only herself, and then she realized that her fire, while warming, might draw unwanted company. She hastily dressed in the now dry clothes, but when she started to put out the fire, she turned to see a tall man in a heavy sheepskin coat with knee-length leather boots and a cavalry style fur hat standing there. Flanking him, were five men and a young woman standing silently. They approached slowly, looking curiously at her; they were wearing red and white armbands as they came closer. These Polish Nationalists were obviously remnants of those lucky to have remained alive. They did not appear to be cautious, as the leader in the fur cap approached her and asked "Who are you, Pani?"

"I am Marianne Ludwig" she answered and she started to weep with joy and relief. The leader put down his rifle and the others followed suit. These were really patriotic Polish people. Each one said politely, "Dzien *Dobry*," The leader introduced himself as Stanley Kulakiewicz, Lieutenant of the frontier force commanded by General Orlik Rückemann. "We have made a strong effort for Poland. Most of us were either shot or taken as prisoners of war to Russia. We escaped. What are you?"

Marianne felt ludicrous in her homemade suit, blanket and skis. She explained briefly her trip to Janow and the importance of her work, the need for sanctuaries and resistance fighting, and she said that perhaps her fall into the ditch provided this opportunity to meet with people of the same idea. All of the Polish resistance fighters, whatever they did, needed to unify. She continued "You are lucky that you survived the brutality. You talk boldly and passionately and we need your kind of heroic leadership which will be a real threat to the Communists." She suggested that they meet at this place on her return that night, to which they readily agreed, having heard somewhat, of the work she was doing. They said how pleased they were to meet her. Marianne desperately wanted to know if anyone of them knew the whereabouts of Jan Malinowski, the cavalry captain, who was bound for Pinsk with a small band of soldiers.

The leader replied that he knew him and indeed he was still alive. Marianne was overjoyed with the news and told them it is urgent that they be in contact for an ultimate mission. Then she made a request that they get rid of the armbands which were much too obvious. Marianne said they would meet again that night, then waved and skied off on the morning snow.

WEDNESDAY NOVEMBER 29, 1939

Hours later, she crept into Janow. In the heart of town, a crowd gathered of Polish Christians, Ukrainians, Lithuanians and Jews trying to escape Nazism in the West. There were also regulators and Russian soldiers who were united against Polish Catholics. Marianne feared for her life and tried to look neutral, impoverished and as invisible as possible.

She finally worked her way to the corner of a building in front of the cathedral to meet Zamolenski. It was heartbreaking to see St. Stanislaus Cathedral no longer a stirring place of joy but rather a pathetic symbol of fear. Big red posters of Stalin and Khrushchev, Beria, Vyshynsky and Kanganovich were hung in the entrance. A fence surrounded it with stone-faced guards encircling the cathedral. Barbed wire blocked the entrance from all sides. St. Stanislaus Cathedral had been transformed into a prison! Before the war, it stood for God, family, and country, but now, it smelled of death. It no longer lit Janow. Marianne started to weep as she shook from the cold. People passed by in silence.

213

Zamolenski was standing in front of her. He was expressionless. He hugged her. Marianne asked where Anna was. He said that Anna was sick, back in the house now shared with the NKVD and regulators. Their possessions had been confiscated, and they only survived because the NKVD thought that they are connected with the Polish peasants and the Nazis. Marianne begged him to join her in the forest of Polesie, but this brave veteran refused, saying it was too late for them. However, although she didn't understand, she said how proud she was to be connected to him; however, their time together was growing short, being seen could again be a death sentence. They thanked each other, vowing to keep resisting, but Marianne really was getting frightened for her father. Zamolenski told her that her father was part of the Home Army, a newly organized Polish resistance force fighting against the Nazis. He had escaped into the Carpathian Mountains. Zamolenski pulled a crumpled paper from his coat telling her that this letter from her father had been delivered by a courier system over three hundred miles. He continued to tell her that Ludwig was still alive.

Afraid of drawing a crowd, and knowing she could not take time to read the letter in public, since peasants weren't supposed to be able to read at all, they hurried to the end of their conversation. Marianne told Zamolenski of the five fighters she met in the woods, and asked when they could meet again.

Zamolenski spoke quickly about this man he also knew called "Eagle" who was brutally tortured by the Communists who cut off his right ear; however, he had not revealed Zamolenski's connections to Ludwig or to Marianne Krull, nor to the government in exile. He had a transmitter, ten guns with ammunition, watches, vodka, cigarettes and some warm clothing, and with his knowledge of where the sentries are posted and their schedules, Marianne should escape successfully. "I can assure you; the name "Eagle" will not be forgotten, "said Zamolenski.

Zamolenski and Marianne decided to try to meet again March 20, 1940. Then she told him of the new Ludwig that should arrive before then. Zamolenski was overjoyed and whispered that he hoped it would be a boy. Marianne wished Anna well and said goodbye to him.

She walked to the appointed corner and there was "Eagle" waiting. His head was covered with a fur hat, a slit revealing only his eyes giving him an eerie aspect. However, she climbed up on the wagon, sat next to him on the front seat, as he said, "We will have no trouble leaving since the guards do not like to patrol in this weather. You can lie down in the wagon. I will head towards Zamolina and the place for your meeting, near Zamolenski's sheep barn. You are safe."

Marianne thanked him and sat in the back of the wagon, anxious to read her father's letter; however, she waited until she was well outside the town, maintaining the image of a tired looking peasant woman napping in the back of a wagon. Finally she unfolded the letter, which had been written on the 24th of November. Her father, with the care of the scholar, had detailed all the atrocities that he had encountered with the hope that Marianne could preserve the history until either freedom or a new generation arrived. There was so much information that she had trouble taking it all in. He wrote:

"My Beloved Daughter,

I hope this letter will reach you finding Andrew and the children alive. As long as I still live and with God's guidance I have decided to engage in a life and death struggle against the Nazis and Soviets

The mass executions, deportations, and resettlements make Poland the bloodiest place in this century. So far as we know almost five million Poles have perished, or are dying -over half a million by military means, another quarter million by mass executions, three and half million have been deported to concentration camps by the Nazis, and another three quarter million killed in Soviet's gulags. Who will be left? We can expect to have more than one out of three Polish citizens disappear by the end of this war.

What began on September 1st, 1939, will bring further suffering and death. Poland's geographical location finds us in the center of two belligerents. However, the saddest news is personal and typical of Polish families in this time. Joseph Kankiewich, Stephany's husband, fought in Warsaw. He did not turn his back, but held his ground brick by brick. He was independent in spirit, one of the many in Poland before the war who had no doubt that these two evils needed to be stopped. He only fought Nazism as he gave his life for this cause. Unlike the Nazis and their seemingly endless manpower, there were no re-enforcements for Joseph. I want my grandchildren to know that Joseph Kankiewicz held fast to his beliefs; he will be forever remembered in the streets of Warsaw

The other tragic news is that your sister Stephany has been captured; she was a courier during the Battle of Warsaw, one of the many beautiful Polish women that fought for our country. After the battle, they were tortured for information and then were placed in trucks

215

and trains bound for the labor camp in Dachau, Germany. We estimated that two hundred women were deported. We do not know if she is still alive, those who have returned tell of horrible disease in the camp.

Marianne, no matter what the method, the Polish people are being methodically killed off. History will prove me right; however, there are those who believe that it is only one country conquering another. Thousands more were herded onto trains bound for concentration camps in Germany.

I escaped from Warsaw, and then traveled to Krakow, leaving one city of terror to enter another one. The entire faculty of Jagiellonian University was arrested by the Nazi SS. All one hundred and eighty four were sent to Sachsenhausen Concentration Camp, near Oranienburg, Schoenhausen

I am somewhere in the mountains of Karpathia. If Nazism and Communism are not stopped, the dignity of the individual will not be restored. Unfortunately, I may soon have to close my eyes for the last time, my legs are fractured, and my bruises are healing. I was dragged out by some loyalists. My body is broken but my mind and spirit are still alive. I wish I were there to hug you, give you a broad smile and ask you, "Is that all?"

Goodbye, my beloved daughter.   Our hopes and journeys continue.   We will not fade away, die, or withdraw, but we'll rise again to have a tomorrow, so the ideals do not die before the Ludwigs. Tell Andrew, I love him. Bless Stephany and Joseph in heaven. May their memory forever and ever remain a sword to be a Ludwig.

Farewell, my love, we shall meet again, tomorrow! Be vigilant far beyond!

Your beloved and devoted father,

Ludwig

Marianne cried and started to shake uncontrollably in the back of the rattling wagon. Her sorrow turned to anger, and then to rage. However, dressed in her winter clothes in the back of an old wagon in the middle of rural countryside what could she do? "Stephany!" she thought, as all the images of the torture and death that she had witnessed came roaring back to her. She vowed revenge once again, and riding along the rutted road, exhaustion took over and she fell into a troubled sleep.

216

NOVEMBER 29, 1939

When she awakened, the wagon had come to a halt and a man was staring down at her over the wagon's side. "Are you Captain Jan Malinowski?" Marianne asked trying to stay calm. Eagle's eyes welled with tears.

"Yes, I am. I contacted Zamolenski. He told me all about you. You and your husband have given us hope. I am very happy and privileged to be in your presence and will never let you down. That I promise."

Marianne jounced and bounced in the wagon as Captain Jan led the horse quickly over a field. She had hatched a resistance plan of guerilla warfare while traveling over the last several weeks and was excited about the opportunity to start it. She knew she needed fighters skilled in combat, since most of the "home armies" were manned by civilians easily beaten by the trained military. Her plan was to use the hidden Freedom Zones as centers for liberated prisoners and soldiers for sanctuary as well as for the development of an armed resistance force. She even had chosen a name for this guerilla force: *"Trumpeter Eskadry"* or Trumpeter Squadron which would become part of the evolving Polish Underground Army.

Jan stopped the stopped the wagon at an old rotting barn, and a small group of patriots appeared out of the woods. Marianne explained to them, after they had settled down by a fire, the creation of the Freedom Zones, and then launched into her plan of attack, and by this time her anger escalated her into an evangelistic zeal. "You will be visible heroes, The "Trumpeter Eskadry" for Poland, like Gideon's Army in the Bible, will be a new symbol of hope, courage and patriotism, to keep fighting as long as we are alive."

"Zamolenski is in no position to lead; he is too close to those living in his own house; so he decided that I should be the leader or overseer of this group. Right now the winter will give us time to plan a clear course of action. Our goal will be to cause chaos and fear for both the Bolsheviks and Nazis, with careful resistance movements. Then too, these actions could cause a world awareness of the plight of Poland. We need to resist the temptation for immediate violence. We are not alone. We must gain others to help." She suddenly stopped talking, and waited for a reaction from this small band of fighters.

Stanley Kulakiewicz said "We can't wait."

"We need to be seen as an independent group in saving lives, and not part of a government. The Soviets have made the punishment very clear, deadly and massive in scope. We need to find people who truly love their country. " she concluded.

Stanley questioned what they would do first, and Marianne outlined the plan to connect with a newly formed Home Army in western Poland. She went on to explain that underground fighting had already started there, and she was connected to it by her father's code name "Zebra." She emphasized, as she spoke, the need for carefully planned action and safety. She had been identified and was a wanted woman. Random acts of sabotage would not work, she continued, and the problem was more complicated because of her connection with the Soviet offices in Janow through Leopold Kabryn. They needed, she said, to be independent and effective.

Marianne could tell that this small band of patriots was listening to every word, and hoping for a solution better than the one they found wandering randomly through the forest. She was a natural leader, a trait her father had seen in her girlhood; people listened to her and usually took her advice. Marianne viewed it as a gift, which could also be a curse to her existence; however, she pushed on with her design for a network of Sanctuaries. The Soviet prisons were filled with good people that they could trust. It won't be easy, but they would need to find a way to get them to the sanctuaries. Marianne explained carefully, that the first of these Freedom Zones was now established within the forest near Zamolina, and that they hoped to extend to more than twenty by March. She outlined the connections with Communist administration leader, Colonel Pietrinev, Hersky and the regulators of the region, and even more importantly, Andrew's part in learning information from Polesie's Communist Secretary Tomas Dorovitz, of Pinsk. "We will need to begin with a small group of fighters while using every tool at our disposal."

They talked for a few minutes and shared stories of escapes and torture, and their mutual hatred of the oppressor. The six men were young Polish officers who escaped into the forest when the NKVD was separating officers from enlisted men. Stanislaus Kulakiewicz and his fellow officers had been told it was safe as they were pushed into box cars; fortunately, he and six others broke away. "One got shot and the rest of them dodged bullets, vowing never to forget the deceit of the Russians and how they riddled with bullets the bodies of men with their hands tied. Those who escaped vowed to fight for freedom.

Monika had been sitting, staring into the fire, and as if she was in a trance spoke slowly about the execution of her father and mother by the Bolsheviks. Her father had been a timber trader and he and her mother managed the trading at Zamolenski's estate in Baronowicz, As soon as the List of Workers took control, her parents were tortured to reveal her two brothers' military units. This torture had been done publicly in the usual way as they burned her mother's face and inserted the hoses into her father. Her parents' bodies were torn to pieces; she was stripped, raped and left naked to hug her dead parents and scrape the blood off the ground in the village square. Monika had started to sob, and then told them of the terrible nightmares, when she could sleep, and how desperately she wanted revenge, retribution and satisfaction.

Jan Malinowski continued his story with difficulty, often lapsing into a struggle for emotional control and for the next word. . He had been captured on the way to see Zamolenski, after he had met Marianne the first time; he then met Monika's two brothers in a prison camp near Pinsk. He had promised that if he survived the planned escape that they would return to Baronowicz to try to help their parents and Monika get out of the country. Eight men made a break for freedom; however, Monika's two brothers were shot. The rest fled to the forest, while Jan hid under the railroad track bed. That saved his life. Malinowski took the baggy trousers, shirt, and shoes of a dead railway coalman who had been shot, dressed him in his uniform and hid near the station. Jan wanted to get to Baronowicz. On his way through the rail loading area, he found a young girl who was semi- conscious, wearing tattered rags and makeshift bandages. She was barely alive; he still had a piece of fruit in his rucksack which he had carried along with him. He fed her some of it and learned later that it was the first bite of food she had had for the last three days. That is how he met Monika who told him then, how she was arrested after her father and mother were tortured and killed.

Their escape was miraculous and demonstrated how desperate men in desperate times do desperate deeds. They waited for a passing Police guard, tripped him, took his revolver and clothes then pushed him naked under a moving train. They searched for several days for others in their same situation, and then they met with five men of the Citizen Guard at the edge of Janow. Jan Malinowski's continued, "Marianne, I heard about the Citizen guard directly from a former one who escaped. It was organized immediately after the Polish officers surrendered to the Soviets across the Brest-Litowsk borderline. As part of the List of Workers government structure, they were to kill the intelligentsia, and maintain order. It was quickly expanded by incorporating armed

219

Communist sympathizers; their name was changed after the military takeover, when their armbands became red. The Polish high command, including two generals, was arrested and shot. The Citizen Guard is the enemy of the Poles.

"Monika Wisniewska, the five others, and I were surprised one evening as we sat exhausted, against the barn wall at a Ukrainian farmer's house; we had taken off our coats and washed the dirt off our faces, after having traveled two days and two nights. The Ukrainian farmer kept glaring at me, then covered his eyes with his hands and wept. We were confronted by NKVD agents, who first bayoneted four of the five men and forced the other to kneel. They shot him in the back of the head. Monika and I were stripped and ordered to dig a pit. Monika stood there, digging naked, while the men made lewd comments, but she shut her eyes and continued. We were made to carry the five corpses to the pit. They were not done; they tortured Monica with cigarettes on her nipples and buttocks. While she screamed and pleaded to be shot they just laughed; then one cut off my ear. Monika and I begged them to kill us as an act of mercy."

"Wouldn't you rather be burned?

"Just kill me, please!" said Monika. "They grabbed her, gripped her roughly and threw her into the pit with the dead soldiers. They cut my buttocks and threw me in on top. They thought we were dead but fired three shots anyway, then left. I was still alive, barely conscious, and buried with the dead. In the darkness of the night, the farmer dug us out. Monika and I were gasping for life."

The farmer murmured to us, "I'm sorry, I had to obey." His head sank lower and lower. "My God, I'm so sorry."

Marianne wept with them until the end of the stories. They were all cold and exhausted and crawled toward the fire for warmth; Jan volunteered the group as the armed security and protection for the Sanctuaries. Emotionally sapped, cold and exhausted, they crawled toward the fire for warmth and slept.

At dawn, the wagon, two horses containing the germs of this resistance force, journeyed back toward Zamolina; however, on the way back they saw a village in the distance. They took great care to skirt it and stopped to see what was going on as they heard gunfire and shouting. Regulators were collecting more booty from the already strapped and starving peasants; it appeared as if they had leveled new quotas and were demanding even more. The poor people were dragging every kind of necessity including fuel, food, lumber, livestock and clothing to become the property of the Soviet Union.

Monika was angry and disheartened at the sight and decided to stay behind and after the regulators left with their stash, would encourage, cajole and convince these people to take refuge in one of the Freedom Zones, which they could establish about five kilometers within the forest. Jan Malinowski offered to stay with her and get the area organized and protected. They decided that communication between the new Zone and Marianne's could be done by courier

She thought, on the other hand, that they would be better off if Jan went with her, while the others stayed. After connecting him with Adam Makowski and Casmir Pilat, she would send him back. Marianne stressed the need to tell these people that help and food would be on the way, and they could start with the supplies already in the wagon. "Please," she begged, "let them know the choice is only death in Siberia."

Marianne was a worrier, who had trouble separating worry from planning for the future. She and Jan started back on foot, and she was hoping for a moment, on the way, to propose retaliation by freeing the prisoners. She knew that time was of the essence and that she needed Jan and his companions to join the newly formed "Trumpeter Eskadry": Jan, not surprisingly, was as anxious to get started as she was. As an experienced soldier, he knew that on New Year's Eve the Russian guards would be ill prepared for any kind of action. There would be no system for defense, and Jan believed, that there were weaknesses in the prison security. The guards were inexperienced men who would value their own safety ahead of their supposed cause. Marianne hoped that any freed men would be added to the different resistance forces. She told Jan of the coming plan already in place and they agreed to do it.

They walked the rest of the way silently, as it became difficult to talk in the biting cold and snow. Marianne thought of her father, the loss of her sister and brother-in- law, and about the fate of eastern Poland. Her thoughts turned from worry to grief.

They arrived in Zamolina chilled, but at least with some confidence for their own futures. While Marianne returned to the warmth and security of her family, Adam and Florence Makowski took Jan to their hut, as Florence proudly announced that the zone, by the next week, would have four hundred or more people, and he would be needed to maintain a secure transfer and vigilance. They all agreed that this

Christmas, a celebration and statement of faith could be done openly with joy within this conclave.

Dirt had often bothered Marianne; dusty houses, dirty Russians, unwashed peasants and grime were her enemy in many ways. She always wanted everything cleansed. On her return home, she hadn't bathed in two days and was covered with smoky cinders, mud and dirt. She felt tired and filthy. Andrew, ever her protector, had anticipated the need and built a wooden "hot tub" in the sanctuary near the hut, and had filled it with soothing hot water. He undressed her, slowly removing the dirty clothing and carried her into the tub, after massaging her aching back, then down to the tips of her toes. "I love you" she told Andrew who pulled her close and caressed her in a moment of passion; however, though she tried to respond, exhaustion took over and she fell asleep.

"Is that all?" she thought as she drifted off, secure, warm and loved.

DECEMBER 15, 1939

Although the entire population in the ever expanding Freedom zone was aware of the inevitable arrival of Dumblosky and the NKVD in Zamolina, they approached the holiday season with a sense of purpose and direction. Production of goods for barter had begun, including candy and vodka; daily life had started to settle into an almost pleasant challenge and routine. Often, the family of workers would start the day by kneeling in front of the Blessed Mother icon and praying, then arms linked, they stood proudly and sang "*My Cheher Boga.*" We want God to bless our spot. These good people would then work tirelessly to expand the enclave by creating shelters, building roads and performing the maintenance necessary for a large group of people living closely together.

Florence Makowski, Carol Pilat and Patricia Gryga were tough, strong-willed women who were sent away each day into farms and villages to listen to the local gossip and put their own lives at risk while saving others by recruiting new families. Their goal was five hundred souls rescued into the forest, who would take a loyalty oath and band together with them for freedom.

Daily life in the forest resembled that of a medieval community; Andrew had constructed shared ovens in a hidden cellar under one of the huts and a small mill for making bread. Magdalene Kozinska oversaw the creation of rock candy from sugar, grain and fruit syrup. She had

222

Gene Fisch

obtained the sugar by trading with a merchant and continued as the chief negotiator for supplies.

Marianne spent about an hour each day recording the events, on whatever paper she could find, and then carefully folded it into the compartment of the Madonna icon, praying each time for success and protection. Others were busy as "hunters and gatherers", returning to the early customs of their forbears, including hunting game, gathering berries and other forest bounties. During the late fall, as much as possible was cached away for winter; however, during this cold season trapping and hunting became a major activity. Every bit of the animal caught was used; fur, meat and even the bones for making soap.

Marianne's plan to liberate the prison was kept a close secret. There were several reasons for the concealment, including leaking facts which would result in someone's death; however, she wanted to protect Andrew from holding information in the presence of Dorovitz, so he needed to be kept out of the plans. It was hard for Marianne to keep anything from him; she even felt guilty at times. Adam Makowski, Casimir Pilat, and Captain Malinowski had scouted the prison. They watched the guards coming and leaving from everyplace that they could. Casmir carefully noted the way the guards changed shifts, what greetings they appeared to use, and how they traveled.

Adam and the others agreed on a completed plan of attack; however, their worry was Marianne. How could a pregnant woman lead them? She said that she felt she could do it; however, there was one condition: that Andrew must not know anything about her leading this liberation.

Her determination spoke for itself, so the four of them focused on the plan ahead. They started with a courier system to notify the places of sanctuary for the released prisoners, Jan Malinowski had a schedule of guard changes, and gate openings and closings .He had counted twenty nine guards who were watching about three hundred men. The last chore was to manufacture new identity cards, including a replica of Pietriniev's signature for those freed. They knew that timing was crucial and that the winter blizzards provided perfect cover for the attack; all that was left was to make sure that there was more room than ever in the newly created linked Freedom Zones.

Marianne desperately wanted to get word to her father, that not only was she all right but also about her involvement in Freedom Zones and The Trumpeter Eskadry. All mail was censored, and if any letters sent by courier were captured, they could lead right back to her. She really wanted to know if he saw the dire events of the past year. Ludwig was her sounding board and her heart. She needed his wisdom desperately, so she wrote a letter which she planned to send through the courier system with Eagle:

December15, *1939*

My Dear Zebra:

We, in Poland, have been orphaned by the rest of the world. Who on this earth can say that one person's agony is worth more or less than another's? Who speaks for universal suffering?

I believe Germany will expand beyond present Poland and the Soviet Union will solidify its borders stretching from Finland to Poland. In November, my path was in one direction...a network of citadels armed with remarkable people. In the New Year, the road divides in two directions. One is to instill the spirit of living and the other is to save lives. Both are noble causes for humanity's sake. Do not worry, my dear father. I may be exhausted but my mood is still vibrant. In early March, a new life will begin in our family and we will prevail.

I want to hold you and have you rest your tired head on my shoulder, remembering always that we will fight together for as long as we are alive. I remember in my childhood the promises I made to you. –I love you, my dear father. We barely have time to breathe. Thank you for your inspiration. With passion, all love comes home.

Vistula

There was a solemn end to their meeting after Eagle agreed to take the letter. They had no intention of backing down to anyone; this small, ferocious angry band of Monika Wisniewska, Stanley Kulakiewicz, Paul Mikewa, John Urbanek, Mark Jablonski and Walter Mazur were ready. Though conscious that everything might end disastrously, they were devoted to their cause, for there was little choice. Makowski and Pilat shook hands with all the rest. Malinowski carefully placed the letter inside his coat lining, "Count Zamolenski will bless our mission." he said. "I believe he will, for his last words to me were, "For every Soviet regulator killed, one hundred will be shot. And for every one coward, there are a hundred silent heroes. "

Marianne added that soon they must begin planning for Zamolenski's escape; however, the first task ahead was the freeing of the three hundred Polish soldiers two weeks after Christmas.

CHRISTMAS EVE DECEMBER 24, 1939

Christmas in war and peace stops the clock temporarily for all Christians. The world is forgotten, and the focus turns only to the birth of a Savior. Before she was able to celebrate, Marianne had one chore to finish. This time she was back in the farmhouse, at her post with binoculars watching the road. She was searching for Leopold Kabryn. She needed information from him and was ever fearful that disaster would strike him suddenly. The quest, this time, was for ink and signatures for identity cards.

Finally, she spotted the good soldier sluggishly moving along the road eastward hidden behind the snow banks. .She took the path along the edge of the forest until she found a very gloomy Leopold Kabryn sitting on a log. He looked depressed and sad and probably was very homesick. Marianne touched his cheek and he said quietly, "Have a nice Christmas. I wish I could spend it with your family, but in fifteen minutes I must return to duty."

Marianne knew how much he wanted to be home and told him: "I know your heart is in Georgia. I wish you could be with us this Christmas for one day; however, you are giving me the greatest Christmas gift of all.....trust and allegiance. Your parents will indeed be proud."

He smiled warmly, a man who was still a trusting young boy inside the big soldier's uniform and said: "I know you are up to something."

He brushed the dripping snow from his forehead, dug deep in his pockets and gave Marianne samples of Colonel Pietriniev's handwriting and signature, radio and telegraph transcripts of messages to Vyshynsky, including one which related that Vyshynsky was complaining about the sloppy security precautions at the Pinsk POW prison.

Colonel Pietrinev had dismissed the precaution and answered: "We will send more guards in February to double the present number. It is quiet and everything is at a standstill. We don't have the trucks. They are all heading to Finland."

Marianne thanked Leopold and gave him a bottle of vodka, babka and a gold watch for barter. He said "I'll watch your home. Rest assured, I won't betray our trust,"

She assured him that he was taking the right action in helping others. Leopold sat in front of her, like the youngster he was, seeking approval; his heart was home in Georgia which motivated him to reach in Pietriniev's desk. He really wanted to go to his adopted family but he could not. As the silence of the day was broken by the village bell, he said: "We must go. Have a blessed Christmas and New Year!" Marianne held tightly to the papers and the container of ink as she walked into the forest depths toward the sanctuary altar, where the Christmas celebration was to be held.

The families had gathered around the altar containing Andrew's carved Madonna which he had crafted at the very beginning of this journey; he had painted her veil green and the baby's robe orange. To the unknowing eye, it looked like primitive art and really not worth very much as it stood, a spot of color in front of the white snow- covered trees. Marianne loved the Madonna because of her faith in God, her faith in Andrew, and for the faith in her actions. Symbolically, it was the home for all the history of the evil doings as they went on. She had been hiding the records of their battle there, always accompanied by a prayer. Andrew had conceived the hidden compartment without telling her, when he had seen her writing on every scrap of paper that she could find. The Madonna presented safety in this ugly world, where possession of one's own written ideas could mean instant death.

The gathered families stood quietly as Andrew lit forty-three candles, one for each day since November 17th, the beginning of their journey of suffering. They would remain as beacons in the dark until the year end, January 1, 1940, the start of a new season. Cruel as the wounds of the past were, they felt that they would survive as long as the eternal light of freedom shone in their free zone. They all knelt close to each other on this "*wigilia*", then blessed themselves and finished with a quiet prayer. Marianne and Andrew felt the absence of the Mass deeply and vowed to celebrate Christmas with a priest offering the sacraments as soon as they could find one for their enclave. They crowded into one of the larger huts and enjoyed the traditional meatless meal of mushrooms, fish, and greens for the traditional "*wieczerza wigilijn*" or large supper. One by one, started by Andrew, they stood and sang "*Chcemy Boga do panowania*" (We want God to Reign). There was Christmas joy in the sanctuary

226

As the music and dancing began near a warm fire, Andrew, sitting with his children on a log, thought that the perfection of Christ's love is found in the peace within all of us. One should not fail to see it. It seemed to Marianne, as well, that all the love and care in the area had come home to settle in this one small part of Polesie. As she looked at her family, she prayed that this love would spread like a ground covering across the land.

The reality of the situation returned, as Adam Makowski came over and told her that the identity cards would be ready by December 31st. Marianne told him that she was overjoyed; however, inwardly she was terrified of the approaching time line . There were only six weeks left until the deportation of Poles would begin again as soon as the roads were passable in February, March, April and May of 1940. They would do their best to slow down their schedule, but only effectively if the released three hundred prisoners could join the battle. Gone were the days of the winged Hussars, the elite Polish cavalry; all that was here was a makeshift little army taking on two giant armies. However, they all were undaunted and knew this as the only choice.

Marianne wished with all her heart to share these ideas with Andrew; however, the drawbacks outweighed the desire. Andrew was at peace with himself, and although he knew vaguely of the Trumpeter Eskadry, he didn't know of the coming attack on the prison, and if he did, he would never agree to a "mother- to- be" storming the gates and going into a dangerous situation. The Pasternak's Sanctuary, for Andrew, was a haven for reason and for the soul – not a secret command post. Andrew was a non-violent man. Marianne wished she could bring back a priest to help them all restore their spirituality.

When all the food had been stored away, and the fire put out, the tired folk went back to their earthen huts in the forest, Marianne and her family returned to their tiny hut. They had traveled far from the elegance of Krakow, to the house, to the cottage and now to a hut, but they knew as they wished each other Merry Christmas, that the true home was where they were together.

.DECEMBER 30, 1939

Daily life in the sanctuary began to resemble a tale of the great hero Janosik, the Polish Robin Hood, who reportedly   robbed the rich to feed the poor, while living in the forest. Marianne sometimes wished that they had his reported supernatural powers: a magical resistance to arrows, bullets and wounds protected by a special herb he carried in his

227

pocket. Preparations were being made for tomorrow's attack on the prison. Florence and a few other women were working by candle light inside Adam's hut. They were industriously forging identity cards, and had completed two hundred and eighty, by exact count, of the three hundred needed. Adam was excited when Marianne arrived and said that they had about eighty more to make. They had dried and tested them and were satisfied with the result. Marianne, after examining the cards knew that they felt right, and thanked them all for their long hours of careful work.

She traveled on to Casimir Pilat's to look at the map and blueprint of the prison, which showed   seven building structures, three sentry posts and a heavily guarded entrance. They had decided to attack on the next day at 8:00 PM: New Year's Eve.

Marianne met Jan and Monika and the others to start the journey under cover of darkness. Jan had drilled details and positions into everyone; to the point that they did not have to think about their task, but could react to any situation while the attack was in progress. The small band of guerillas, disguised as muddy, smelly Russian peasants, was made up of six men including Jan, and his nephew Paul,(Gem), Stanley Kulakiewicz,   (Sabre) ;Walter Mazur, (Oko the Eye) John Urbanek,(Copernicus),and two women   Monika (Karpathia) , and Marianne (Vistula). Each one of the little band had seen the worst of men in the worst of times; each had witnessed personal Bolshevik atrocities. Each one had a different motivation for revenge. Paul had seen his little brother and sister brutally murdered as was his pregnant Mother, who had been bayoneted while pleading for her children's lives; his father was burned alive. Paul had witnessed their deaths and was put in a makeshift Bolshevik prison. He escaped from there with Jan Malinowski. The others had been Polish soldiers, mistreated by the Bolsheviks, who had managed to escape. The freedom fighters all took on code names, just in case of interception and interrogation, which were also so silly-sounding to eavesdroppers that they would not be connected with any military insurgent group.

DECEMBER 31, 1939

They reached the prison at daybreak, hoping to keep watch and to get sleep during the warmer hours of the day. They looked at the building, which seemed impregnable from a distance; however, Jan said that if they could destroy the machine gun nest located fifty yards in front of the prison's entrance gate, they would have a chance to infiltrate, disarm the three towers, and evacuate the buildings.

Marianne watched the snowfall in front of the huge gray prison. From the sanctuary in   Polesie, the prospect of liberating the prisoners seemed far more possible than it did in front of this giant old building. She watched Jan and the others approach the task as if it was an army exercise, fully confident that they would succeed. There were three hundred men locked in this compound whose only crime was to be born Polish.

The hours dragged by as the snowy gray day turned into the blue gray color of the early evening in Northern Europe. As the darkness grew, there was no turning back for this little band of patriots fixed on the execution of the plan. The snow would cover movement to their targets; they had to wait for eight o'clock.

They lay face down in a snow bank, two hundred yards from the gate, each gnawing on a half- frozen loaf of bread. Marianne, lay silently, wondering where her strength would come from, and whether or not she would survive to see her family again. She was taken aback, too, at her own strength these days. She had stood naked, at home,   looking down at her newly muscled body and wondered where that came from; what had happened to her soft girlish frame of the past. Weeks of manual labor had hardened her. Therefore, she felt confident, that at least physically, she was up to the task ahead. She had to keep her hatred of the Russians in check so that the resistance plans were a result of cool logic and not unleashed misdirected emotion.

They all counted upon surprise; an escape attempt or an attack would not be launched so close to Pinsk on New Year's Eve, and even if there was a glimmer of expectation, who would be executing it? The Bolsheviks counted on the weakness of a starving peasantry; however, Jan and his well-fed, disciplined squadron were ready and had assigned tasks to execute on a tight schedule.   Paul (Gem) was to crawl to the nearest sentry, once they were inside the compound. The others carried maps with clearly defined escape routes to the forest. Each one of them had committed the secret pathways deep in the forest, and where the rifles, ammunition, food, and medicine were hidden, to memory so that no evidence could ever be found.   Once the prisoners were freed, each member of the group would lead a pack of escapees to a spot on the map.

They had decided that after the machine gun nest was taken over, Jan and Marianne dressed in gray coats resembling soldiers, would approach the gates with arms linked along with Monika who would look like a whore seeking business. With vodka in all their hands, they hoped that the guards would think a New Year's Eve party had arrived at the prison. The others would enter under cover of the distraction to kill anyone in their path.

As they talked, the weather worsened, and turned into blizzard-like conditions, Jan thought that chances for success had improved with the wicked weather. Apparently, with the snow, the road from Pinsk to the prison gates was too treacherous. The second shift would not be able to get there. The guards inside, he believed, would be doing a double shift and would start to grouse and complain about food, the weather and their lack of relief.

As they readied their entrance, Marianne checked the revolvers attached to her waist. She and Jan had to get near the machine gun nest and put on the Russian uniforms stolen from somewhere by one of the squadron. The rest of the group was focused on the entrance gate, and they got as close as they were able to, while avoiding the mined areas.

There were three guards in the machine gun nest, which was placed by a gated entrance on the road. It was a small shed, with no cover in the front, and with the blizzard having taken a fortunate turn, anyone approaching would be hard to see. The men were bored, tired of looking into the snow, and believing that no one was going to enter the area. One was smoking a cigarette with his back to the road; the other two were hunkered into what shelter the cover of their position provided. Jan, Marianne and Monika decided to brazen out the approach. They swayed down the road toward the machine gun nest, arms linked, singing a loud off key version of the "Internationale" the Bolshevik anthem. In the dim light of evening and the blowing snow, they appeared to be fellow soldiers. Jan grunted in drunken Russian, something about how their car was capsized, and he waved his bottle of vodka in the air. As two of them put their arms around Monika, she shot one, with a gun, silenced by an old wet towel; Marianne shot the other as Jan stabbed the third. Their war against the Poles was over; there was no time for rejoicing. They quickly cached all the Russian rifles, ammunition and supplies for later retrieval.

"Ja *was lubie*", the three apparent celebrants shouted as they continued to approach the gate. Two guards cautiously walked forward. One held a flashlight and aimed it at them. As Marianne and Jan leaned on each other, Monika opened her coat, as the light hit her, revealing a low cut transparent blouse which did nothing to hide her swaying breasts. The diversion was successful; one opened the gate as the other approached Monika with his best male swagger. The rest of the squadron was able to slip inside the gate as the second guard came toward the vodka and Monika. "Good, come over. You have permission" he said. Those were his last words. He was shot as was the soldier groping for her chest. She put a bullet at close range into his open mouth. The Trumpeter Eskadry quickly changed into the dead soldiers' uniforms and helmets. Each tower's guards needed to be quickly and silently dispatched.

Jan and his five men left Monika and Marianne on guard, and tower by tower approached, then silently killed the warders. Marianne and Monika remained outside each tower keeping a look out for any guards moving from building to building; however, the cold conditions, they realized, were keeping the men indoors. When Jan and his company were finished successfully with their grisly work, they met Marianne and Monika outside of the last tower. There were four barracks filled with prisoners, each one with guards. Jan and the others had no trouble dispatching, as they said, of the drunken tower guards who were fat, lazy, dirty and dozing. The Eskadry entered the first barracks building, leaving one member to keep watch outside the door. The alarm system was now disabled in each of the towers, since Eagle had cut every wire he could find. Remaining silent was the key; they had planned for them to guard the seven barracks until all were freed and then to let the prisoners out.

Miraculously, no sentry or soldier survived the attack long enough to call for help. Marianne and Jan were counting on the hold up of relief guards, although some of the Russians quartered next to the barracks were easily shot. Each building housed somewhere near eighty to a hundred men, crammed onto stacked bunks. Many often awoke in the morning to find the bedmate next to them, dead from dysentery or exhaustion.

All the prisoners were half-naked, cold and ill, some shivered uncontrollably, and others could barely hold their heads upright. As each of the barracks was taken, the inmates were cautioned to remain quiet, and in their place in the bunks.

The vodka worked as an entrance ticket to each barrack and as a ticket to Hell for the guards. As the guards came to the vodka, in nearly all the cases, one of the Eskadry gunned them down. The roar of the outside wind and storm covered the slight sound of the gunshots. At first, the prisoners were very skeptical of the rescuers, who were clad in Russian uniforms; after all the scams and tricks of the Soviets, most of the prisoners fearfully huddled together on the bunks.

"We are Poles," they were told, and when the time came to leave, they were instructed to grab any clothing, guns, ammunition or supplies to take with them. Marianne found a few men who were stronger than the rest and who were obviously educated, and she asked them quickly if they knew where there was a central office to the prison, so any records could be either burned or taken with them. The five or six men knew where to look and the rest who were freed took off to find anything that they could, including wirers and transmitters.

Finally, the exhausted "Trumpeter Eskadry" watched a steady stream of haggard tired men walk to freedom. They still needed to be guided to the sanctuaries in the forest. There was no time for thanks or talk, as they fled; however, the look of gratification and salvation was very evident on each face. Many shook the hands of their rescuers and oneyoung man called out in his weakened voice "I will always remember this as the best day of my life. We can't thank you enough.". Three hundred or more prisioners were now free; It was 12:15 A.M. the start of the New Year 1940.

In the hour that followed, seven separate processions were triumphantly led through the forest passageways of Polesie. A Trumpeter Eskadry member led each man to an assembly area at Pasternak Sanctuary so they could be treated, fed, properly clothed and given their identity cards. They eventually could start their own sanctuaries further away. Fortunately, for Marianne, Andrew was at the farmhouse near the village square, after she told him that she would be helping out a sick friend. . When Marianne arrived, he was asleep with the children on either side of him in the bed.

Marianne looked at her sleeping family, and silently walked to the little altar in the house's main room. She was torn with conflicting thoughts, and it never occurred to her that her brave deed of providing freedom to all the prisoners was as dangerous as it was. Her actions now were all a blur in her memory, and there had been no time for doubt or fear. The right thing had been done; Tata Ludwig's words from long ago, or so it seemed at the afternoon meetings, were the first that she thought of: "In all systems of human life, everything depends upon the good or evil of men and women who manage the governance." The good was evident and visible, but had she committed mortal sins? Marianne totaled them up, as she crossed herself at her little altar. She had lied to Andrew, and she lied and cheated to get into a prison where she committed murder. How could God forgive her? She thought that there were no confessionals, no priests for comfort, no masses and no communions left in a world where her children were expected to be raised to be atheists, with only Josef Stalin the evil father. Where, she thought, is the substitute for the church, and finally she started saying quietly "Forgive me father for I have sinned", as if God himself was her priest. Marianne decided to listen for His voice in the early morning light, and a revelation struck her. She had been listening to the voice of God all along. She had been sacrificing for others, holding out hope and consolation to so many, including these poor prisoners that had just been saved. Maybe God was working, through her; however, just to be safe she started acts of contrition "Hail Mary Mother of God"........Andrew found her that morning asleep on the floor by her altar.

"I love you, Andrew." she said as he looked at her. "I am home now."

"I love you too, with all my heart. I hate to do it, Marianne," he said "but I need to go. I must see Dorovitz. "

Marianne was now very afraid for Andrew's return. She looked in on the children, still blissfully asleep on the large bed and hugged Andrew. "Be careful," she said.

Andrew whispered "God willing, we shall have a family of five very soon. It makes everything worthwhile. What a New Year". He pulled on his heavy coat, gave Marianne one last hug before he left the house. Behind the shed, he harnessed the horse to the wagon and took off into the early morning darkness.

Marianne fed the children when they awoke and took them into the sanctuary, quite still afraid for their safety in the farmhouse as well. She went to Florence's house, where the children happily played as the women told her of their raid on homes that the regulators had seized. They decided to take back some of the clothing that was stolen; therefore they carefully watched the eight homes, and as soon as the new occupants left to steal more property somewhere else, the women hurriedly entered the houses and seized everything that they could including boots, coats, pants, parkas, and sweaters. The regulators could not report the thefts because they never had reported the confiscated property to their authorities, but kept it all for themselves. "They are common thieves" said Florence, "Could you imagine the look on their faces when they returned to empty homes?"

Marianne laughed with the women, and took her children to the hut in the forest, as she worried about Andrew's return from Dorovitz. All the recent retaliation was sure to bring some kind of repercussion from the local government. Would they intensify their search for her, for the Eskadry, for the thieves of the regulator's goods, and for her father? Only when Andrew walked through the door did she feel more at peace.

SUNDAY FEBRUARY 15, 1940

While Andrew slept soundly next to her, Marianne passed a fitful and uncomfortable night, partially because of her pregnancy, and because she had the nagging sense of something being wrong. She still was wrestling with her conscience, wondering continually if the freedom of so many men justified her taking lives with her own hands was the reason, or if she was more fearful of terrible reprisals. The danger was sure to come; rumors fly even in this isolated world. She knew that the Trumpeter Eskadry was a target for destruction and the events seemed so far from this little reality of warmth and comfort. Andrew was undaunted, secure in his faith and in his contributions to the Freedom Zone by working for Dorovitz.

The sun rose and Andrew was up and readying for the trip to Ilana and Tomas Dorovitz. He had gained their trust, and had established himself as a man of spiritual integrity, honesty and principle, who would be available to aid Ilana's children in the future; however, she was still a regulator and still an enemy. This morning, he opened the door, took a deep breath of the cold air, and asked Marianne if she needed him home now that the baby was so close in coming. In light of her own anxiety, she told him to go and that information was needed more than ever. With a hug and kiss for Marianne, Andrew set off to harness the horse to the wagon and ride off to Dorovitz.

Meanwhile, Marianne still pictured the discovery and capture of her as the leader of both the Trumpeter Eskadry and the Sanctuary movement, and then pictured a horrible NKVD execution in front of her children. She simply had to have more information on the local Russian activities. The brave patriots, she thought, have endured for nine months, while the eastern section of Poland, the main bridge to Europe, still occupied by Soviet regulators, remains obscure to the world press. Every inch of land was stained with blood. One million Poles had died in the last months. This fact strengthened Marianne's resolve. All patriots wrestle with the conflicts that they face. When does the love of country and its way of life, overcome the personal inner turmoil? Marianne, as leader of this underground, had to keep sight of the fact that it was opposition to a force which was trying to crush the Polish spirit that kept them fighting.

Intellectual rationalization, even for a just cause, could bring some peace; however, now, Marianne felt that her ignorance of coming Russian actions, particularly in the spring, would bring harm to all. Therefore, she decided to take action herself, and once started, there was no stopping her. The children were safe with Florence and the women in the forest Freedom Zone, so she was able to set a course to find out what the Soviets across the road were up to. The formation of new sanctuaries was now out of her hands, and even though she was regarded as the overall leader and organizer at this time, she had to let Monika Wisniewska form an enclave where newly released prisoners were given aid. Makowski, Pilat, Kozinski, Grygas, and Varyas were building methods for organizing Sanctuaries across Polesie, and for developing a communications network, couriers, and an economic system of barter.

Marianne took out her binoculars and focused them on the square and the NKVD headquarters once again. She was on the lookout for actions taken by Pietriniev or Hersky; she wanted in some way to talk to one of them, as well as to Leopold. As the day moved on and the two men she was watching were walking outside the office building, Marianne dressed in her peasant worst, shuffled along the road to the village square. She had on a bulky old coat covering her obvious pregnancy, wispy strands of hair protruded from her large babushka, which extended over her forehead to cover her eyes. She tried to keep, what she thought was the dull- witted peasant look, and carried an empty wooden bucket on the pretense of getting water from the village well which, if anyone asked, would not be frozen over like hers was supposedly at the farmhouse.

She wanted to get Pietriniev's attention without arousing suspicion; she was really hoping to see some warning signs issued from the mouth of this bullying braggart. She abruptly got her wish. Colonel Pietrinev was standing near the well. He was not wearing his old rumpled uniform, but had adopted the NKVD uniform of royal blue and crimson red, which would distinguish him from the "simple Red Army" and certainly with the array of medals across his chest, he would stand out above the "mere" or "average" soldier. His attire reflected his belief that he, and all the others of his rank and organization, was superior to anyone who was not one of them. He had lost, in a trade for his position, friends, neighbors and his family, and above all the compassion for humanity; his campaign belt stretched across his paunch and chest and there was a holstered gun on his hip. The focus of the Russian government at this time was in Finland, and Pietrinev was fearful of repercussion, once attention was turned back to the east in the coming spring. He was angry, his usual temperament, and worried. Like all bullies, he had to kick the bottom dog; he looked at Marianne approaching the well, who appeared to be a shuffling, ignorant, inferior peasant woman, and he decided to exercise his authority, as if it needed to be tested on a regular basis.

"Get me water," he commanded in Polish; for he would show his superiority in choice of language, after all, peasants don't understand Russian.

Marianne nodded and dropped the bucket down into the well, poured water into a cup; she glanced at him as if waiting for a thank you. None came. She mumbled a comment about the weather and still received no response. Pietrinev, looked at the "stupid" woman, and curtailed his impulse to kick her, because he was visible in the square to the regulators, and he was aware as well, that this woman's husband worked for Dorovitz. He actually hated the peasantry, and in his present black mood, this woman was annoying him just by her presence. He looked down at her as water splashed on his boots and created a bit of mud from the step, upon which he was standing.

"Women like you serve only one function bitch!" he roared as the water spilled. The porch stairs and path leading to it were filthy from mud and debris.

"You will return for the next two weeks and sweep this area."

Marianne played her role, grinned stupidly, picked up a broom from the porch and started to sweep, thinking that she would be at his door, daily keeping an eye on what was happening. For the following weeks, Pietriniev raged on, inside the house and out, but Marianne heard nothing about the prison break. She was more and more uncomfortable as her pregnancy progressed toward childbirth, but she kept sweeping daily. During one of her last days there, she saw Leopold Kabryn, in his dull khaki uniform on guard duty; he nodded slightly so she knew to slow down on her way home when she passed him. As she headed for her house across the road, she stopped by Leopold and grabbed her back as if she had a spasm; he whispered quickly, "More sentries and road checks are being placed along the road to Pinsk. They are looking for saboteurs and will search the wagons; even worse, a secret cavalry unit will be working for NKVD and Dumblosky will arrive in three weeks with his executioners. He will go village to village, unannounced, to publicly execute ten villagers, at a time, to extract information to help Pietrinev and Hersky find the leadership of the Trumpeter Eskadry who they regard as the most dangerous criminals to the state." He then said ever so softly, "I want to see the baby when it arrives". Leopold glanced at her as she left him, apparently, to observers, disinterested in this poor woman.

Next morning the loudspeaker trucks rolled on with the ominous announcement: "There is a band of saboteurs operating in Polesie. Death will soon come to them; anyone who can inform on this enemy will be rewarded."

Andrew had been returned from the Dorovitzes late in the evening; he told Marianne of the sense he got there was something very wrong with Ilana and her family. She was a lonely woman; an island in the midst of a destructive world. She could not trust a single person; however, he thought, she was starting to trust him. When he talked to her privately, she was very tense. She asked him if he knew anything about the prison escape, and as if programmed to say so, said it was extremely dangerous to the people of Polesie, at a time when Tomas was trying to expand food production in the spring. The other part of Poland, she said, was to be relocated and the NKVD would fill the empty homes and jobs with loyal Soviets regulators. "You are protected," she told Andrew. "If you know anything about the prison break… you can trust me; let me know about it now."

Of course, Andrew really did not know anything of the prison break;

"You, Marianne and the children, can be saved only if you tell me everything. What I am saying now is very important. Dumblosky boasted that he knows the leadership of the Trumpeter Eskadry, but he is keeping it a secret from my Tomas and Pietrinev. That will save him, but not them. He has murderous intentions. Please be honest with me to stay alive." Ilana had said all that she could.

Andrew had known what she meant. She started to weep for herself and her children and their souls, while Andrew had promised to look after them; in return she would look after his family now. Andrew understood her message well.

FEBRUARY 26, 1940

In light of Ilana Dorovitz's warning about the intensified search for the Trumpeter Eskadry, and the increased quotas in the spring, Andrew cleaned out the farm house and took all extra food, the weapons and other goods to the hut in the forest. The family was staying in the house near the square, awaiting the birth of the baby. Moving out would have caused suspicion, particularly since Marianne had been sweeping the Colonel's porch and path daily.   The news of Dumblosky's imminent arrival was the most threatening, since he knew Marianne and her father from Krakow. She didn't know if he would recognize her; however, there was too much of a chance that he might. She wanted to have her child and then disappear into the woods as soon as possible. Today, she still had to go sweep, but movement was difficult, because she was due to go into labor any minute.

With both hands, she leaned heavily on a chair and raised herself to a standing position. As she struggled to get dressed, she thought of several ways to execute Dumblosky. In her mind that word was better than "to kill" and the idea gave her strength. If she only knew what lurked in the minds of Colonel Pietrinev, Hersky, and Forst. She sent Andrew off to Dorovitz, over his objections. He wanted to see his child born; however, this too was growing more important on a daily basis, and he could get home on time. Her children were staying with the Varya's as was the usual custom in Northern Europe, for little ones did not know where babies came from. They came home to find the little package from "under the cabbage leaf" or the "gift from the stork."

Colonel Pietrinev was waiting for her on the steps. She said simply "Good morning, my commandant" through the scarf partially covering her face.

"What do you know about the Trumpeter Eskadry?" he asked gruffly.

Marianne replied "Colonel Pietrinev, I live at the edge of the forest. I know only what is posted and what I hear on the announcements."

"Your husband works for Dorovitz. He must have information that I don't."

"My husband works for Ilana Dorovitz for extra bread and candles- Nothing else."

The Colonel went into a long angry declamation of the people, and an accompanying lecture on the need to increase quotas, and how Marianne, after her baby was born, would have to pull the plow. He had discovered her pregnancy, but to this megalomaniac, the important thing was that she had to be still able to sweep. She half listened as she swept and he talked on and on. When she heard that he was upset, because a troop of cavalry was given to Dumblosky in order to find a "Trumpeter Eskadry", she listened intently. He was angry because as a full Colonel, a war hero, and a former cavalry officer who was in charge of this region, he felt slighted and ignored, and probably had some fear of reprisal from Dumblosky, who would be there in two weeks.

Marianne finished her sweeping, and headed toward the house. Two weeks was so little time for her to prepare, and then there was the new baby. Almost at the same instant, as she was deep in thought, her new child decided it was time to enter the earth, so she rushed into the house. She was in labor, but it was early yet and she hoped and prayed Andrew would arrive soon. She lay on her bed, her pains still bearable, counting seconds between some erratic contractions, and suddenly there was Andrew. Marianne called out, "My love, please fetch Florence and Luba now. The pains are coming faster and I fear this little one will wait for no one". Without pausing a second, Andrew ran off.

When Luba arrived, she said confidently "You will have a beautiful child. Don't worry". She had delivered many babies and quickly took complete charge of the birth. The new baby's clothes were kept warm near the fire. Andrew was sent to the shed to do "something". When Florence arrived, she prepared the cradle for the baby and set out a washbasin to clean the new child. Luba told Marianne to push hard as the pain cut through her, and after what seemed like an eternity to Marianne, Luba delivered a healthy baby girl whose first cry echoed in the little house. The baby was washed and wrapped in new clothes and handed to Marianne. Andrew was summoned and when he arrived Luba told him "You have a daughter, a beautiful little girl". Andrew kissed Marianne tenderly, who was by this time exhausted. With great joy, they named her Alexandria.

Florence stayed with them for several hours, then left Andrew and Marianne to care for the new life now lying in Andrew's hand carved cradle. Marianne thought, as she gazed lovingly at her new little daughter with the bright eyes and patch of dark hair, "Is that all?"

MONDAY MARCH 4, 1940

As Marianne and Andrew's baby daughter grew, so did the Freedom Zone; there were nine hundred people within a network supplying medicine, clothing, food, and most meaningful of all, a haven of love and trust. The released prisoners had started new sanctuaries from Ratwyn, to Zamolina to Janow and to Brest-Litowsk.

Marianne was staying in the forest more and more. Her presence at the farmhouse was only to assure the observers that there was still someone living there. Moments of peace came to her in the little hut with Alexandra nestling to feed at her breast, and Maria and Stefan playing near the blazing fireplace where the potatoes and chestnuts were being charcoaled for the children. The neighbors often joined them, cooing over the new baby. Andrew sat whittling something out of wood, usually for one of the children; he glowed with quiet pride, bordering on reverence, believing his family was reason enough for living. Life here was settling into the life of a normal Polish village and except for the unusual setting and the surrounding turmoil of the outside world, that is what it was.

Jan arrived at their door, greeted them warmly, then up and handed Marianne a letter. He was pleased to relay the news that Ludwig was alive. Marianne thanked him and wished there were some way to show her gratitude to all the couriers who had hand carried it. It was the first sign of her father in two months; in the flickering firelight she anxiously read Ludwig's note, which had been hastily scrawled on a scrap of torn paper.

February 15, 1940

My Dear Vistula,

I know each family now lives with pain. . Polish people, Catholic, Jewish, men, women and children are being murdered daily by the Nazis. Property has been confiscated and the owners of it shot. Both of us share the goal of diminishing the death toll of the Poles. I am happy that your child is to be born in late February. May you have a healthy baby that brings you much joy. Acts of rescue are noble, but be careful, my daughter, and know that this was not the future that I saw for you.

Devotedly, with all my love,

Zebra

Marianne sat and wept, as she now always did when she thought or heard from her father, quietly, and alone. Her emotions were running in many directions, including love of father, family and country. If all love comes home, she thought, there needs to be a home of any nature, emotional, spiritual, and lastly a safe haven. Her children were the only motivation to continue on the right path to assure them a future.

Later that Monday morning, the leaders of the sanctuary met as usual; however, this time the need for action was immediate. Marianne wanted to see Colonel Pietrinev as soon as possible, to find out about the deportations to Siberia and then to plan the expansion of sanctuaries to accommodate thousands of people. Magdalene Kozinska found a group of women, expert hagglers, who were dealing with supplies from Jewish merchants from Janow to Pinsk. Andrew warned them that additional roadblocks and checkpoints would be placed, because of the "black market" that Monika's peddlers were successfully using. They are also seeking out vigilante saboteurs. He had gotten the information from Ilana Dorovitz, and added that everyone at the Sanctuaries should avoid sentries, and to be sure their identity cards were absolutely clear and in order.

Andrew, traveled to Dorovitz's later that morning, and Marianne after settling the children at Florence's hut, went to see the Makowskis, Pilat, Jan Malinowski and Stanley Kulakiewicz, who had copied Andrew's detailed homemade maps of the road from Pinsk to Janow, showing the railroads, the fishing and hunting sites and the landmarks. The hidden campsites, where the Trumpeter Eskadry could sleep for the night and where ammunition, wireless, transmitters and other supplies were secretly hidden had been marked with a Christian cross.

Marianne had a lot of time to think over the last month, with the new baby. Moscow had given Dumblosky of Krakow, his own military unit to drag out and kill ten villagers in each town as a reprisal for the prison break, and, she was told Zamolenski is an important target for execution. Marianne knew that she, not Zamolenski, was a major target and that her capture would guarantee success to Dumblosky's survival. The Zamolenskis were the first that needed help; however, Stanley and Jan were going to Zamolina to insist that they go into hiding, no matter what. "If he resists we will drag him here" Jan said sharply, "However, the roads are frozen, slushy, covered with ice in spots and although that slows down the Russians, we cannot move rapidly on it either."

Marianne had been thinking for a time about seeing Pietrinev again; if she played dumb enough, she could get permission for weekly visits to Pinsk, supposedly to gather additional farming supplies for the increased spring quotas. Her hope was that Dumblosky would stop and question her on the road where she would have her Eskadry along to take care of matters, and short circuit the plan of executing villagers. She told her friends that she would be getting in and out of Pinsk as well, under the guise that Dorovitz had told her to do so.

Jan's face was etched with concern "We need to be there with you on Friday morning." he said.

She finally told them that she was wanted by Dumblosky, and maybe if he saw her going this route weekly, he would stop her and try to make the connection with Marianne Krull. The major problem was using the small band of resistance fighters to take on a cavalry unit. There would be no luck of a covering snowstorm this time. Jan told her and the others agreed, "We need to move fast. We are left with one choice after that; take and release the trains."

THURSDAY MARCH 7, 1940

Marianne, as a child, had once done "shows" for her father in the house at Krakow; he delighted as his little girl danced and acted all the parts in the plays that she had written. She would pull the curtains between the dining room and the parlor and surprise Ludwig with tales of Polish folklore and legend. One moment she was a goddess, or an earth mother, in the next a fairy spirit. She loved to act and hoped that now, for Pietrinev, she could give the performance of her life. She was still playing the role of a poor, ignorant, peasant woman, muddy shoes, straggly hair, dirty, grimy and bordering on stupid. Marianne kept her head down and looked at her feet when talking to "superiors". Her major matter was feeding and caring for the new baby. The good mothers of the sanctuary stepped forward and solved the problem for her. Even though Marianne had three children, women who had borne nine, ten or even twelve, considered her a novice. They found substitutes for Mother's milk when Marianne was away or not able to get back to feed the child on time. They had some goat's milk, and one of the Mothers was still able to wet nurse Alexandria.

Jan Malinowski insisted that Marianne be armed if she was going to continue to put herself in harm's way. He had taken a Nagant, M 1895, complete with a suppressor, (silencer) from a dead Russian soldier, along with its holster. It was a nasty weapon, gas sealed using 7.62 mm shells and it fired seven shots when fully loaded. The gas seal allowed the exploding cartridge gases to have greater power, when sealed in the firing chamber, and it was able to penetrate a wool coat and uniform accurately at about thirty yards. This gun only weighed two pounds and was ten inches in length with a 4 and one half inch barrel; therefore, Marianne would be able to use it easily. The NKVD had adopted this brand pistol and used it primarily for executions. The only object shared by the former Tsar of Russian and his family and the murdered millions of innocent peasants was a bullet in the back of the head from this weapon.

Ironically, years earlier, Ludwig had taken her to the local "hunting and shooting club" that he belonged to. It was a throwback to the Prussian "Schützen Verein" and it was there, that the little girl learned how to fire a rifle and a revolver in the shooting range. This gun and holster was fitted, by Jan, around Marianne's waist on a belt. He cut a long slit in the furrow of the right side of her coat, so if needed, she could grab the weapon easily and use it through her overcoat.

As she left her house, by the side of the road, she went into her "tired peasant woman slouch" and shuffled her way to the bulletin door in front of Pietriniev's headquarters. The Colonel, as she had hoped, came out to confront her. He noticed gruffly that she was not pregnant and with all the charm of an ignorant Bolshevik asked: "When did you lose the baby?"

Marianne, did not miss a beat, and told him of her beautiful healthy daughter Alexandria LUDWIG. She emphasized the last name and grinned at him.

"I am only interested in how much we can produce. You should be planning for spring if you want your child to live through summer." he said with even more lack of grace.

Marianne looked down at her shoes, and said softly "Oh sir, my husband has forced me to come into your presence and ask for a favor that would increase our spring production. He told me to ask you directly, not to tell anyone else, and he said that you were the only one who could approve our plan." Marianne, was gagging inwardly at her own tone, but continued, "I am asking you directly if I may schedule our oxen and wagon to ride into Pinsk every Friday. With all the checkpoints, it would be a mistake if the same person did not make the trip. It would be more efficient if the guards know me. Besides, I hope you will be generous on the seed allocations. Many plowing tools have been reassigned elsewhere. My husband says that you will not make your quotas if we do not have the tools. We will live only if we make the quota; otherwise, we will be starved to death. The rest will die in the cemeteries of Siberia and Dumblosky's execution squads shall threaten all our lives." She finished as if she had memorized her speech.

"Your husband should concern himself with making the quota. You need to worry about helping him. Your son and daughter need to dig with their hands and eventually I will get my own military unit."

243

"He is concerned about our future and how we increase the harvest in partnership with Dorovitz."

"What do you mean by our results? Partnership?" he growled.

"My husband Andrew exceeded last year's quota when things were really bad. Now, he will do even better. I promise. He is a good farmer. Give him the tools and seeds, and he will do very well for you."

Marianne continued: "Andrew says it is like the fisherman who goes to sea. Without a good boat, captain and crew, plenty of hooks and bait, the partnership between the captain and fisherman will never make their quota to feed the village. Give him an extra supply of seeds and tools and he will produce a lot more for harvest. I am to go to Pinsk every Friday to make sure we get our share. We can do this; Dorovitz and Andrew are on your side, not Dumblosky's. He is in more trouble than you know."

Marianne wanted him to believe how stupid she was, and therefore separate her name from that of Marianne Krull. " Why should you worry about Dumblosky; you should worry about me, Colonel Pietrinev," she continued "we need to remember the produce quotas."

"I expect you to gather supplies for the village each Friday. Next time, work with my administrators."

She gave him a silly grin and told him seriously that he could rely on the farmers to produce more if they had enough plows.

Pietrinev would allow the weekly transports only if he saw all the peasants toiling on their knees in the mud at the crack of dawn. He told her to report what she sees and find out what Dumblosky was up to in Zamolina and not to worry about the local authorities. However, he said it in a way that puzzled Marianne; did he think her that stupid that she would tell Andrew to ask Dorovitz. Therefore, she just smiled and backed out the door.

Dumblosky in Zamolina upset her greatly. She thought: "Did Stanley Kulakiewicz and Jan Malinowski reach Zamolenski in time? Oh God! God! God! I am afraid for Zamolenski. He is defenseless and trapped." She retrieved her children from the other family and crawled under her comforter in her hut, keeping Alexandria warm and close. She waited silently, anxiously praying that Jan and Stanley had rescued them and managed an escape. "Oh, my God, please help them!" she prayed.

As she waited for Andrew's return, Marianne envisioned men dragging Zamolenski out of his house and putting a bullet into his head, from the same kind of gun now hidden in the space under her bed. She kept thinking that if she had known sooner, maybe the guerilla fighters could have rescued him and taken on the cavalry at the same time.

After seeing the worst in her mind's eye, she started to pray, still conflicted with carrying a gun, and obsessed with having to take a human being's life. She concluded with the thought that Dumblosky could not be human at all. "Dear God", she prayed "let me never become paralyzed with fear, nor too dazed to act, nor too weak to resist the Dumbloskys of this world. If he dies before me, I cannot help but rejoice to be the woman who plunged a knife into Poland's symbol of betrayal." As her anger rose, she continued to tell God that integrity was the best defense in the world. Dumblosky had to be evil, for when he was given freedom in Krakow, he turned to the Atheist Communists, and tried to start deadly civil strife in the streets. He failed. "However, dear God", she prayed, "how can I ever forgive his committing not only one murder but thousands of them." "God, she went on "I have a plan to take the right course of action before either of us dies." She then prayed for strength and forgiveness to do what needed to be done, and in her heart, she knew that the souls of Jan and Anna needed prayers too.

Marianne told Andrew, when he returned that night, that Pietriniev had agreed to let her go to Pinsk every Friday. Andrew, worried, asked her how she did it. She told him the story, and about her fear for Jan and Anna .Her night was filled with ghastly dreams of a screaming, dying Poland and of its people being forced like lemmings over a large cliff into the boiling sea. She awoke early, and left the children with a sleeping Andrew. She had to get her wagon and horse registered with the authorities before tomorrow's journey.

As she shuffled to the regulator's headquarters, she looked up and there on the top of the steps, saw shiny cavalry boots, which struck her as odd, as they were attached to the usually disheveled Colonel Pietriniev. His uniform was stained and crumpled, as usual, but this time there were red specks up and down his pant legs over the freshly cleaned boots. Marianne looked up at him and among the grease spots and medals on his chest, there were more bloodstains. He glared at her and asked why she was there, and while explaining to him about the registration of her animal and wagon, it was all she could do to keep from shaking. Whether it was rage or fear wasn't clear at the moment; however, it got worse as he spoke using the top of the porch as his platform.

"Dumblosky has been to Janow and he is coming here next." he said. "I too, just came from Janow, where Dumblosky made maybe one hundred peasants kneel down, then shot them yesterday afternoon. I was given the honor of having peasants clean the blood from the ground."

Marianne couldn't even imagine the horror, and the fact that this man was still wearing the blood of those killed. She desperately wanted to run, but prayed "Please God, let me slowly walk away."

She pictured Jan and Anna Zamolenski executed with the others, and she said to Pietrinev. "No one is safe, my Colonel Pietrinev."

By the time Marianne reached the house, tears were streaming down her cheeks. Fortunately, she went into the farm hut to gain her composure before heading back to the forest sanctuary. Pictures of Jan and Anna, lying, bleeding on the street, with their blood running over Pietriniev's boots, filled her mind. She was sitting on the edge of her bed as she heard the hoof beats in her yard; when she got to the window she saw soldiers, on horseback, winding their way toward the farm. There were maybe twenty armed men riding up to the house, some dressed in the NKVD uniform and others wearing the tan of the Russian army. Two of the NKVD troopers came to the door, and at first they were very polite. The larger of the two said "I am Captain Drevnovitz."

He was a big man, square- jawed, with a beak-like nose, his face reddened by the cold wind. He took a deep breath and spoke in a heavily accented Russian voice. "We just did our duty in Janow. And we were told that you are Marianne Krull!"

"Tomas Dorovitz knows who we are." she said.

"Where's your husband?"

"He is at Dorovitz's farm getting it ready for spring planting."

"Have you seen any partisans - Polish or Ukrainian?"

"No, I haven't."

"Are you sure?'

Marianne told him that no underground partisans would come to a house so close to Colonel Pietriniev headquarters. The resistance was not the reason for this visit of this band of soldiers who answered to Dumblosky. They wanted to know if she was Marianne Krull, and that they would execute ten villagers a day until they found her.

246

Marianne was fearful that someone had turned her in; however, she knew that if they had any hard evidence they would have arrested or shot her on the spot. She pleaded ignorance to the knowledge of Dumblosky, and said that she only knew the officials of this region--- Dorovitz, Pietriniev, and Hersky. The guard indicated how powerful he was, and postured around the room, threatening her physically and offered rape as a method of wresting the truth out of her. Marianne, stood up to him, and quietly told him to do what he had to do.

"Then do what you must" she said. "Dorovitz will hear about this. I can't believe he or Pietrinev knows you are here. If either of them thought that Marianne Krull was in this region, they would kill her."

The NKVD officer continued to rant about the Trumpeter Eskadry. "No one knows when Dumblosky's unit will strike again. Only Dumblosky knows. We have to search your house."

Marianne knew he meant to destroy the inside and take what he could. . She had to be punished for defiance, so when the two men finished their search, the cabin was in shambles. They had opened drawers and emptied the contents on the floor. They also pulled apart and slashed the bed covering and the fern-filled pillows. They flipped the table, looked into the crevices of the wall, and shook the beams. As she watched, she said: "We are too poor to be of any threat to you. Dorovitz will hear about this."

"Your house is off the road and close to the forest," the commanding officer coldly observed, stepping back outside. "I don't see any openings. No secret passages. I'm sure the dogs could sniff it off if I unleashed them. What do you think?"

Marianne answered him flatly, "I would not lie. I told you that we are only 500 meters from your regional headquarters. Does Colonel Pietrinev know you are harassing me, particularly since my husband is working for Tomas Dorovitz? You can get in trouble for this." she repeated

The guard hoisted one foot onto the door step leaned toward Marianne and looked directly into her eyes, "No matter how much you lie, Dumblosky knows who you are. You are Marianne Krull. He doesn't want Pietrinev or Dorovitz to kill you. Others have failed. He wants to be the one to get the credit. Dumblosky, himself, wants to kill you. You get the message?"

After the soldiers had left, Marianne tried to clean up the mess, find a way to continue to live in the house, keep her children safe, and yet continue fighting. She trudged into the forest, retrieved her children and waited for Andrew to return. When he did appear later than usual, he looked upset and haggard. Andrew was a man who glowed with care, faith and fortitude; however, now he looked broken. He sat down heavily on a stool, and looking at the earth floor of the burrow, told Marianne that Ilana told him that Anna and Jan Zamolenski were shot last night, along with one hundred others."

Marianne took hold of Andrew and held on to him and cried, "Oh God! I knew in my heart. I was too desperate to tell you first, but I am too much of a coward."

Marianne and Andrew huddled together in the dark night, knowing that her next journey to Pinsk or the next one after that could bring disastrous results. However, since they were considered property of the State by Pietrinev, they had to continue.

FRIDAY MARCH 8, 1940

The phrase "Marianne Krull- Dumblosky knows who you are" kept echoing in her head. Marianne rose out of bed in the burrow. A bit of morning light was coming through the little space in the front that Andrew had kept as a window. Much as it offended everything within her, she did not wash, and walked barefoot on the dirt floor to keep her ankles filthy. Marianne was playing the dirty peasant to the edge. She hated it. As a child, she disliked dirt, dust and grime; as a mother and wife she cleaned, scrubbed and polished. However, the necessity of disguise kept her filthy. She focused on the journey ahead for today and was really frightened of it. All that Andrew knew was that she was going to Pinsk for supplies, and no more; if he realized that she was using herself as bait for this executioner he would not have let her go at all. . She knew that Dumblosky was somewhere in Pinsk this morning, so her best hope was to lure him away for the kill. She had contacted the Trumpeter Eskadry, and they would connect with her as well. Marianne counted on Dumblosky's need to succeed in the eyes of the Bolshevik leaders, and certainly the capture and execution of the notorious Marianne Krull would be a figurative feather in his cap or a notch in his gun.

Marianne never could figure out how her notoriety grew, for she really hadn't done very much to start this manhunt. There were other vigilante freedom fighters that eventually formed the largest underground resistance force during the war; however, she thought that targeting of this woman was the only course of action they had to find and eliminate a scapegoat. Yes, the Trumpeter Eskadry had emptied a prison, but in the Bolshevik scheme of events, that release meant nothing. These men would eventually be caught or starve to death, or so they thought. The Bolsheviks, during their own revolution, not only freed prisoners, but revolted against their fellow soldiers. Morality was not the consideration, but the elimination of this woman, whose face and force had become mythical in the smaller sphere of Polesie, became very crucial.

Marianne, instead of thinking why she was the target, focused on the need to eliminate Dumblosky's execution squad and save thousands of lives. She dressed quietly, so as not to awaken Andrew, and strapped her gun and silencer around her waist, then put on her baggy coat. She had a flashing thought of the Bolshevik vision of Marianne Krull, more like Joan of Arc and less than this shapeless dirty woman.

She nudged Andrew, kissed him gently and whispered, "Darling, I must leave shortly. Get up."

After a prayer of thanks for another day of survival in this torn world, she took the children to Florence's, and although she thought to take them along, she realized that their going on the journey would raise suspicion. After all, children of Stefan and Maria's age were expected to work, and babies like Alexandria were handed over to old women, who were no longer useful for physical labor. Andrew knew that her first trip to Pinsk would give the opportunity to learn more of the Communists' doings. Marianne could read the official bulletins wherever posted, listen carefully to the undercurrent and gossip and pass the information along to the Home Army, which would get it to the Polish government in exile.

Eventually, she climbed the little old wagon, with its single horse and started out on the road to Pinsk. She had led the horse first to the farmhouse, where the wagon was kept and when the road was fairly clear, she set out to Pinsk. She was stopped along the way by the usual guards and officials who were checking papers. They signed passes and identification, and her assumed look of a sleepy peasant woman, got her through to Pinsk with no incident.

She parked her wagon near the town square, read all the posted notices and registered to get Zamolina's seed quota for spring planting. Marianne was on the alert, however, for the presence of Dumblosky; he would certainly recognize her, despite the disguise, after seeing her at her father's house so often. She hoped that he would come to Pinsk alone to confront her, backed up somewhere by his killer cavalry unit. They probably would rape her, she thought, before an execution, the way Russians had always done to women in their terrifying past. "Oh, God," she prayed, "Keep me safe!"

The latest bulletin boards had been posted with complete indifference to needs of the people who could read them, designed only to appease appearances, as if there was sense to the governing body. A small crowd had gathered by the bulletin board that was filled with the latest Soviet and Nazi triumphs. Marianne was saddened. Soviet soldiers and regulators, however, stood gloating, pleased with the outcomes. Then, she saw a posting of the names of the one hundred men and women, "enemies of the people" who were shot in Janow, omitting Jan and Anna. It was all she could do to show no emotion, when she was feeling sorrow and rage.

One post bragged that Finland would soon surrender to Russia after a long struggle. The war in Finland ends soon. "What is the world doing?" she thought silently. "Nothing!"

As Marianne turned away from the bulletins, to walk to the end of a line of people waiting for their seeds, she saw a vaguely familiar-looking peasant couple shuffling along. As they approached, she realized that it was Karpathia and Eagle. The three of them walked to a sheltered doorway. To the entire world, they looked like simple Polish peasant farmers talking about crops and complaining about the lack of rations. They had received the message and had arrived to help her.

"We don't have much time to talk" she said, "I am sure Dumblosky knows I am here. I am going to try to get Dumblosky out in the open with his cavalry and I am fairly sure he will take me to the edge of town, in the woods to be shot. He could then return with a body, and blame the killing on someone else, while privately taking credit for it at his headquarters. Hopefully you could attack his cavalry. Pray for me!"

A concerned Monika asked, "What happens if they don't take you out of town?"

"Wait until they separate a bit from Dumblosky. Kill them, and run into the forest. Raping women is their soldier's reward, so I am counting on them leaving town. They don't leave witnesses."

Marianne could not believe what she had just said; some strength and courage had over ridden her fear, and she hoped she wasn't taking a very foolish chance with her own life and that of her family. She got on

250

the end of the line at the Registration Building; the square was fairly crowded now with traffic and people. As the village clock struck nine, a man in the N KVD   black leather coat, sauntered up to the line of farmers and smiled at her .He waited until she got her seeds and followed her to the wagon. She tried to act naturally and ignore him; however, he eventually pointed at her and yelled "Bitch" and as he did, three men rushed towards her. One of them was Dumblosky. Marianne would recognize that ugly dirty, smirking animal anywhere. They took the wagon reins and two of the men took her by the neck, pushed her face first against the ground and told her not to shout or struggle.

"Marianne Krull," said Dumblosky, needlessly loud.

Marianne remained silent, praying that they wouldn't find the gun at her waist. Unfortunately, they rapidly tied her hands behind her back and tossed her like a sack of flour into the wagon bed. Dumblosky, now mounted, leaned into the wagon and said "You need to answer some questions for us in private. Think about it bitch; think what we can do to you if you don't cooperate. And don't scream; there are other uses for your mouth."

On the outskirts of Pinsk, the wagon was stopped near a large field with the cavalry unit remaining a distance from it. Dumblosky pulled Marianne out and half walked and half dragged her to a small grove of trees even further away. "I hope your father is dead, you dumb whore" he said as he slapped her hard across the face. "You are Marianne Krull, are you not?" he yelled as he forced her to kneel in front of a large tree.

"Listen, bitch. I have waited a long time to slit your throat," Dumblosky snarled, as he casually lit a cigarette.

A horrifying minute or two passed. He continued, "Are you commanding the Trumpeter Eskadry?   Where is Wladeslaw Ludwig hiding? They are organizing a Home Army of civilians; tell us where he is and who is leading this Trumpeter Eskadry."

He walked over to Marianne, and just as casually used her neck to put out his cigarette. She screamed in pain, so he hit her.

Dumblosky muttered then hissed. "Shut –up Krull!"

Frantically, Marianne pleaded. "I don't want my children or my husband to know what I am doing. The fact is they know nothing." Then as if a switch had been flipped, she changed her tone and using every bit of her acting ability to appeal to this boor's male ego: "Why don't you let

251

me be the whore you want me to be? Then I'll tell you everything-who is commanding the Trumpeter Eskadry and where Ludwig is. But you must keep it to yourself, so only you know the location of the Home Army HQS and Trumpeter Eskadry. Only you, Dumblosky, need to know!" Her seductive tone got his attention and she continued "I can do wonderful things to you with my mouth and I can take on all three of you at once. Have you ever done that? "

Marianne could see his lust as his pants bulged.

"All right, you really are a slut."

The three agents slid off their leather coats; however, Marianne said "You need to untie my hands so I can stroke two of you while I suck on the other"

One of the agents, a little fat man, jumped forward and without orders, released her hands. While she rubbed her wrists, she told the men to drop their pants so she could see their manhood. Dumblosky's lust, driven by his rage and feeling of power, was out of control. She had succeeded. They unbuckled their belts

"Dumblosky, how big is it?" she said as she shot him in the crotch. She had gotten the gun, while they were undoing their pants, and then after Dumblosky, she shot each man in the same area. As they fell to their knees, hidden from the sight of their cavalry, Marianne walked up to the NKVD men and shot them in the back of the head Russian style. When she reached Dumblosky, he tried to stand, but her bullet found the artery in his groin, so he fell down on his side. She told him that she was indeed Marianne Krull and put the gun to the back of his head as he held his bleeding crotch. "May you rot in Hell, you arrogant bastard, this is for Jan and Anna and everyone else you killed."

Dumblosky had circled the remaining cavalry men around Marianne's wagon and horse. She was lying now on the ground, waiting for one of the soldiers to approach and see what was keeping Dumblosky and his henchmen occupied. She lay still, hoping he would get close enough to get a shot off when he drew nearer. Sure enough, one cavalry man started up to the tree clump, in which they were hidden, to see what the results were, and Marianne rested her pistol on the ground near the dead bodies of the three would- be rapists and waited. She lined up the man in her sights, hoping the range was close enough, when a shot rang out and he fell off his horse. Monika was standing behind Marianne, with a rifle, as the rest of the Eskadry opened fire with a stolen machine gun, on the remaining cavalry. Most of all of the men fell, except for one who knelt with his hands up to surrender. Jan walked over to him, put his rifle at the back of the man's head, and watched him start to blubber and beg for his life. He was told that he could live; however, he had to give up his shoes, start running and report the death of Marianne Krull and Dumblosky. The panicked soldier did as he was told and when out of sight, down the road, Monika led Marianne back to the wagon, which surprisingly survived the onslaught.

They had all retreated to the tree grove; however, time was short, more soldiers would be on the road and Marianne had to get home.

"We did it! We pulled it off! Unbelievable!" they called out joyfully..

Her Trumpeter Eskadry suffered no casualties, while they destroyed twenty Russian guards. Eagle gathered the Soviet equipment, horses, ammunition, guns, clothes, and food. The little band sank to their knees, and thanked God for watching over them.

"We need to go." Eagle said quickly. Karpathia and John Urbanek hurriedly mounted the horses and Stanley Kulakiewicz tied the others onto one line and they rode off into the woods, after unceremoniously dumping the cavalry bodies into a nearby ditch.

The return home was uneventful and Marianne produced her passes and showed her seeds for planting at each stopping point. She thought of how she needed to keep away from the farm house and Pietrinev; however, would he even believe that Marianne Krull was dead? She knew she had to remain apparently ignorant of the whole affair.

However, she did tell Andrew, who was horrified at what happened. They prayed as usual, and Marianne decided to keep her diary to record the day's events, in case something happened to her. She wrote, on this night, in the burrow: "Off in the distance is where our future lies. We are home, we are safe, and I look forward with great expectations towards having a future. I love our home more than I can ever say. Most of all, I love what's inside our home."

Dumblosky and the twenty executioners are gone forever. Deportations and starvations are days away that could kill thousands more, as we struggle with a Soviet nightmare assaulting our home. If we are to ultimately succeed for individual justice and freedom, a huge part is borne out of our hearts, our Polish Catholic nature that is on a pathway to truth. It is the power within, our home. I am confident that we must deal with the enemy on every level, and then if we must, we'll die honorably as Polish patriots. It is the accumulated sum of individual courage that will prevail. In the balance, lies the whole future of who we are and our free Sanctuaries."

Wearily, she folded up her worn paper collection and put it in the compartment in the Virgin and crawled into bed next to Andrew. She continually reminded herself, as she did each time she added to the collected papers, that it must not ever be found, or they would all be doomed; however, the record was necessary for all of them, so that someday the world would remember and realize what happened.

MONDAY MARCH 18, 1940

Marianne had recovered from her Pinsk ordeal and had even made the trip one more time. Her body had taken a beating, and the sleepless nights following it, caused her to be very tired. She was wrestling with new internal demons supplied by the external ones of the NKVD; there were so many concerns and choices, that at times she felt overwhelmed. Marianne was a mother first; however now she realized that so many more people had become her children, and she was desperately trying to save as many of them as she could, using subterfuge, stealing, lying and murder to protect her own young and those of Poland. These actions conflicted with her own moral fiber; however, once she attached to Nature's plan of Mothers protecting their young by all means necessary, along with her strong faith in a God using her as an instrument, she felt somewhat better intellectually.

Marianne made a slow journey from her hut to the village bulletin board, usually carrying the baby. She had moved into the hut and usually, under cover of darkness, would travel to the farmhouse, and then be seen leaving it to go to the town square. The muddy peasant woman and child, would sneak a bit of vodka to Leopold Kabryn, friends, and then listened, keeping abreast of what the regulators were mumbling, grumbling or boasting.

Andrew continued his work at Dorovitz's farm and was doing double duty, keeping up with chores at the Sanctuary. As Spring approached, Marianne had an uneasy feeling that some new horror or action was on the way, so on this day she took Stefan, and Luba's daughter Justina to work in the fields behind the farmhouse. She told them "You and Justina have an important job to do. You are our eyes and ears."

'We know." Justina said and she and Stefan went off into the high brush, near the road, settling in a thicket of trees. The frost from the pounding night rains was beginning to thaw and just after the children settled into their lookout spots in the trees they saw a steady stream of trucks stretching along the roadside, eastward toward Russia. The heart wrenching, soul-stirring cries from inside the vehicles echoed in the early light of dawn. The screaming came from the crowed trucks where families had been separated by sex and age. Seated on the bumper guards of the truck, and crudely tied on by ropes were several children being used as human shields against resistance fighters. Their mothers were frantically screaming in anguish, pain and for help which would never come.

Stefan counted thirty-five trucks, two military vehicles and twelve guards on horses. He and Justina ran back to the farmhouse, and found Marianne to tell her of what they saw. They were afraid. Fearful of being tied to the front of a truck, they both started to cry. As usual the Mother's protective instinct took over, and she hugged the two badly frightened children and told them it would not happen to them, while inwardly she vowed that this barbarism needed to be stopped no matter how often it was repeated.

That night Andrew returned from Dorovitz, to the hut, mud and dirt filled in the lines on his face and it was streaked down his front and into his boots. He looked worn, tired and very depressed. "Nothing has changed." he said. "Dorovitz told me that three and half million graveyards for the Poles alone are expected to be dug in Siberia in the next eighteen months."

They sat silently for a long time. It broke her heart to hear about good people being hurt, but it strengthened their will. She planned to have the Eskadry make a definitive move to charge this enemy. Meanwhile, all they could do was pray.

WEDNESDAY MARCH 20, 1940

The Sanctuaries now were extended from Pinsk to Janow, from Stolyn to Mozer and to Kovel in southeastern Polesie and to Kamiln, Koswiske, Sarny, Ovruc and Vilnius in the north. They reached beyond Polesie to Poland's territories of Ukraine, Byelorussia and Lithuania. Marianne was gratified finally with some good news. The escaped prisoners had spread the ideas and ideals of a Polish Sanctuary and built many more hidden enclaves in the forests. However, she knew that even these were not enough; millions of people were being moved to Siberia, or being executed. Would there ever be any peace, she thought. As Marianne waited for Andrew to wake up, she restlessly plotted the next attack by the Trumpeter Eskadry.

As a rule, they rose at five o'clock in the morning to use the early light of dawn, and to move back to the farm and appear to be still living there. There was no word in the neighborhood of Dumblosky's or Marianne Krull's death. Therefore, as Andrew headed for Dorovitz's farm once again, Marianne took the sleepy children to Luba's, placed Alexandria with a "wet nurse", to whom she kept giving supplies. This poor woman, Sophie, had lost her own child soon after its birth so she had enough milk for another baby. Eventually, the little one had no problem nursing with the surrogate mother. Marianne then, dressed as always, in dirty farmer togs, headed for the village square, desperate for news of the day and particularly of the demise of Marianne Krull.

She walked across the field and before long was working on plowing it with a primitive version of the farm tool, which still had to have the mud cleaned off the blade by hand. Some of the poorer peasants used a wooden "stick" version, causing slower and unsuccessful production. Some had lost their horses, so family members took turns pulling the awkward wooden contraption and in light of the increased quotas, the work load to the farmer soon became nearly impossible. Marianne finished the furrows on her field this morning, stopping every so often to clean the blade and water the horse. She kept looking across the field for some glimpse of Pietriniev who often stood on his porch, making fun of the peasants who plowed and worked the fields. She saw him, finally, and when she finished a furrow, she tied the horse up and walked over the road. He was leaning in the doorway of his building, and after a deep draw on his pipe, he looked at her and then chuckled, showing his mouth full of yellow broken and stained teeth, " My trucks are on target sending labor to Siberia. "But Ludwig", he said "there seems to be an empty space in the field over there. Why haven't you plowed it?"

"Colonel" she said mustering up all the syrupy tones that she could force out, "Don't be offended; you do remember, no doubt, my opinion of farming. More plows make for more potatoes and cabbage. When will you allow me to have more tools?"

"You have no choice but to make your quota on the hectares you were allocated. Dorovitz knows that."

"But did you know, she continued," that there are those in Moscow angry that Polesie is not meeting its export quotas for the Nazis? Dorovitz knows we all live in an area filled with potatoes and cabbage ready for sauerkraut, and potato pancakes ready to be exported to Germany. Your task is to get more out of our six hectares. Next Friday, when I go to Pinsk you should sign off for another cart and more plows."

"Dorovitz says so?" he inquired.

"Andrew told me it came straight from his mouth."

He agreed, and Marianne was delighted that there was no mention of Dumblosky, only of the connection to Dorovitz. There was still no word of anything about the Sanctuaries, or Trumpeter Eskadry. A while later , she finished her plowing , put the horse in the barn, and headed back through the secret passageways to the sanctuary, where she met the Trumpeter Eskadry, who had arrived with an extra horse laden with rifles, ammunition, bombs and food. They were planning for a Friday attack on the truck convoys at the source and at the railroads where they will transfer the prisoners to boxcars. That way the human shields would be removed. On the following Friday they would first hit the truck storage depot in Hrodna, and then two hours later the railroad center outside Wilnious and then railroad tracks to Pinsk from Wilnious."

Stanley Kulakiewicz, was worried about the guards and security; however, the decision was made to blow up as many trucks and trains as possible and then to move hurriedly into the depths of the forests.

They had assembled a crude informational packet for those who escaped from the trains and trucks, written in the proper dialects of each area, and twenty former prisoners were to spread out and distribute them

After meeting places were determined, the main resistance unit, the Home Army, needed to be notified. A short letter was written in the usual "invisible ink" of urine between the lines of a birthday greeting. The recipient only had to heat it to get the letters to appear. They included no names or places, but just enough information to allow the government in exile to know what they were doing. They were operating on a small scale and only through communication of resistance efforts across the land, could Polish Catholic lives be saved. Some Polish Jews had joined the Bolsheviks and were promised great rewards as regulators. Others had long fled the country. At this time, the faithful Catholics were the target.

The Eskadry each went off in a different direction, while Marianne returned to the hut and collected her children. She hurried to the midweek gathering in the center of the sanctuary, and joined her neighbors by a central fire. Andrew had lighted the candles around the icon of the Black Madonna for an evening vesper service. As Catholics, in the absence of priests, they were now denied the sacraments including communion. They could however, give thanks and continue to pray as they did on that night.

Magdalene had been able to buy supplies to build the Sanctuary's first vodka distillery. Andrew discovered that Polesie's cabbage mash also could be transformed with a little extra processing into vodka. The two tradeswomen, Magdalene and Florence, anticipated that the vodka production could blossom into a viable exchange for food, medicine and clothing.

"This year," Magdalene proudly proclaimed, "I expect to sell more than 100,000 cases of Freedom Zone Vodka."

Andrew Gryga, Varya, and Adam Makowski built a vodka distillery inside the enclave. Bushels of potatoes were put away for the Sanctuary before the Soviet invasion and occupation. It was constructed for three treatments, after which a liquor of 75-80% alcohol content was produced, and then could be watered down and used as currency in the emerging black market economy. Vodka was to become the most trusted medium of exchange since the ruble was the official currency with value on the black market. The Polish zloty had been reduced to ninety percent on the ruble, and with ten watches and the help of Jewish merchants in Pinsk, Hrodna and Wilnious, Magdelene and Florence were able to build the citadel's vodka distillery.

Casimir had to taste the very first batch; he dipped in a ladle, had a taste and proclaimed "Very good!"

Gryga became the tour guide to vodka production. He explained "After the potatoes and cabbages are washed, they are dumped into a large eleven hundred liter kettle where they are boiled before the fermentation process. Later, the liquid goes through a 200-liter copper pot that Adam and I built, then it has to circulate three times through a 5 meter cone carved by Josef Varya and Andrew out of wood from a piece of a tree trunk, so that it reaches a 85 percent alcohol."

His presentation was stopped when everyone wanted a taste. Magdalene as the trader supreme, sampled a bit more of the vodka, and then described why and how she did it. " I am going to tell how I am needed and loved. What makes vodka so popular is its versatility. The Jews don't drink, but they had been the dominant distillers, distributors, and retailers in Poland. Communist red tape and quotas made it harder for them to get back into business. Now they can't manufacture it, but they know the market. Just as long as the Russians are drinking it, the regulators will sell it. Bolsheviks will pay extra for quality, there's no doubt about that. Drinking vodka has a premium value compared to saving lives.

"Once in Pinsk" she continued, "I asked my merchant friend Pan Cohen "What is a ruble worth?"

"Whatever the market bears," he answered. "I handed him a bottle of Vodka from my coat pocket and told him we all can have worth in our own way if we work together."

"Pan Cohen agreed; he was only too glad to accept."

"This is a tragedy for all of us in the quest of having a future. How much is a case of vodka worth?" he asked

"I'll buy as much as you can make," he said to me.

Andrew acted as the sommelier and said "Magdalene, your artistry gives vodka a new dimension. A most elusive quality: smoothness. Last week, she was still tweaking the taste profile. The latest version is full-bodied with a pleasant warm sensation when swallowed and just a hint of fragrance." Then he added seriously that it may account for one hundred thousand lives saved by harvest time!

Later, back at home, as Marianne thought of the camaraderie and friendship of that night, and the hope that was present, she wrote it all in her diary including the "vodka recipe". She saw her world now, symbolically, anyway, as a vodka funnel. In the warmth of the bottom, there was love, and care, and faith, distilled into this home and sanctuary, while at the top, the cold world spun crazily out of control. Ironically, hope for the future hinged on the success of seven or eight people and a lot of alcohol. She tucked her diary away and crawled into Andrew's arms.

FRIDAY MARCH 29, 1940

The Friday of the planned attack was cool to start and Marianne began her usual routine in the early morning. The fields had been plowed and planted, so all that was left was the weeding until the seeds sprouted. Today, she climbed out of bed, after Andrew left for Dorovitz's farm, and took the children to the usual surrogate parents. No one asked where she was going, since they trusted her so as a leader. They were more than happy to do their part by watching her children, and she felt secure with the little ones there; however, later in the spring they would have to appear in the field to work, as was the Bolshevik decree.

She traveled to a ditch on the road to Pinsk, riding an extra horse that Jan had brought earlier carrying arms and munitions. As she rode along, dressed in her peasant pants, this time, muddy boots and a long coat, surrounding her revolver, she felt as if she was galloping very far away in time and distance from her home in Krakow, where she first learned to ride in an elegant stable, with a riding instructor. She finally tied the horse in a convenient clump of trees and took a green tin box containing a wireless transmitter and receiver out of her saddlebag. Marianne scrambled down a small rise into a ditch along the road, where the deportation trucks were expected on the way to Pinsk. There was a haze that drifted slowly over high grass to the forest. Jan Malinowski had gone over every bit of the plan of attack; however, it still traveled back and forth, over and over again in her brain. "What if the number of guards were doubled around the perimeter of the truck compound in the city of Hrodna? What if there was an information leak? What if an ambush?

The road from Pinsk to Hrodna was 17 kilometers long. Her job was to alert the Trumpeter Eskadry as the trucks rumbled back from the railroad station to refuel and start out again. The Bolshevik Motor Pool was in sight from her vantage point in the ditch; the six other band members had stashed ammunition and explosives deep in the forest near this spot. Her radio was to be used to forward information on the movement of the trucks, and at about six o'clock A.M, they started up the road from their drop- off point of the railroad station. The Eskadry members had spent the last several days watching the route from the forest and observing timing, arrivals and number of guards. When the trucks had left the night before, Eagle and Jan had buried explosives and detonators around the circumference of the Motor Pool. The guards were relaxed, lazy and sleepy, so no notice was taken of the stealthy intruders. The plan was to explode the bombs when all of the trucks were refueling and the guards watching, then to use grenades or a machine gun, to blow up the trucks and ignite the gasoline pumps.

As Marianne tried to get a clear view from her ditch, she heard the sound of an approaching motorcade of trucks. She ducked low, hiding in what cover she could find, as the vehicles went by. The trucks reached the compound and she could see with her binoculars that some of the guards wore the red and blue of the NKVD, while their underlings wore the dull khaki of the common soldier. They all were armed. . She twisted the transmitter handle, and whispered "They are there!"

She waited for what seemed like a very long time, until finally the ground shook with a series of explosions. The crude homemade bombs tore the compound apart, and as the soldiers rushed to the perimeter, two machine guns opened a crossfire. Men fell everywhere. Monika and Stanley were at the back of the compound, shooting at the Russians, who fired wildly at them amid the noise smoke and confusion. More shots rang out. Marianne could not see who was firing at whom but prayed her friends would stay safe. As if by signal, the firing stopped, and she could see her comrades standing near the compound. Eagle ran in and threw grenades at each truck; eventually as he fled, there was only a huge fireball left.

Shortly thereafter, the Trumpeter fighters, all seven, gave thanks to God as they held the horses behind a thicket of trees. They told each other that by a combined count, thirty-two trucks and twenty-five Soviet soldiers would never again be used to murder Polish citizens.

Marianne had just arrived to meet them, still clutching her green transmitter. She looked at them and Monika and said, "Everyone is safe!"

Eagle insisted that they get moving, as they had only two hours to get to Hrodna. The night before, the same seven vigilantes had wired inside the town, well-placed explosives in the heavily guarded railroad junction, and in the water tower about a mile away. They found that the guards there, as well, were lazy, inattentive and often fast asleep. Twenty of the soldiers, who were freed from the prisoner of war camp, armed, wearing red and white arm bands, were prepared to strike at this target. They were waiting to lead about three hundred men, women and children to the freedom of designated Sanctuaries.

Marianne and the others waited in the forest at eleven fifteen, as a procession of trucks was coming closer to Hrodna. Their canvas tops were rolled down. Each truck was crowded with Poles tightly packed shoulder to shoulder. "Most of them are from Brest," Oko told Eagle. "The regulators said that they would take them this far. Their plan was to ambush this part of the convoy, free the prisoners, then to continue into the town of Hrodna and free those locked in waiting railway cars."

At a bend in the road, the trucks slowed, as they lurched forward. The difficulty in attack was the extermination of numbers of armed guards; Eagle, however, counted twenty-four…. five on motorcycles and nineteen scattered around the trucks.

The men in the arm bands were hidden alongside the road to secure the passageways for the escapees to rush through the woods into Sanctuaries, they too were fully armed with the guns stolen from the prison.

Eagle was about 50 meters away, watching the twisting column, ready to fire into the trucks' windshields as they slowed to navigate the bend in the road where the first part of the convoy had slowed causing traffic congestion. He fired at the windshield of the first truck and it stopped abruptly. As the guard on the passenger side stepped out, he was shot immediately by Eagle, and when the other trucks were forced to stop, the Eskadry opened fire on all of them. The Poles inside the beds ducked to the floor boards and waited as one by one the drivers, guards and motorcyclists were leveled by machine gun fire. Years later Marianne could still picture Monika poised behind a machine gun extracting revenge with every bullet. The suddenness of quiet occurred for only one moment, when the captive Poles began to scream in terror.

"Poles, save yourselves!" cried the Trumpeter Eskadry, as they galloped on their horses alongside the trucks and opened the rear gates. "You are free! Follow the men with red and white arm bands!"

The people in the trucks got to the ground and crawled across the road to the shallow ditches where the men in red and white armbands, who now had retrieved as many guns as they could, led the freed Poles to a thicket of trees.

The trucks were blown up where they had stopped, once all the people were cleared from them. The whole operation took just fifteen minutes. The Trumpeter Eskadry suffered no casualties. Jan Malinowski turned to Marianne and told her that he believed that the element of surprise for any attack was now over, although the railroad guards in Hrodna were still not aware of reprisals. He said that in the future she would need to be protected and take less of a risk. She just nodded, and rode along toward the railroad station, thinking that that wasn't possible.

However, the element of surprise was still effective at the railroad station. The horseman and one new motorcyclist, "Gemstone" stopped at a park near the railroad station, and detonated the preset explosives. As explosions echoed, the water tower fell, spilling its contents everywhere in the area. The guards and police started to seek the causes of this disaster, and ran hurriedly around the station.

A large section of the rails had been blown up. While Jan and Monika kept up fire at the police and guards, the red and white arm banded liberators led the frightened people off the trains and into the adjoining park. "Follow the men in the red and white armbands. They will save you." shouted the voice from the bullhorn.

They had opened the heavy doors of the box cars; the captives streamed out of the dirty, stinking cars as Eagle called to them, "As long as we are alive, Poland is not lost. Follow the armbands to safety." At least six hundred people had been in the boxcars and cattle cars.

"You have a choice. There are free zones. Join us. Be a liberator!"

They finally rode rapidly away, as the refugees from the trip to Siberia followed the liberators through the streets and to freedom in the woods. The Trumpeter Eskadry knew that the columns of trucks wiping out the spirit of a nation, during the last days of March, had been slowed. Over nine hundred lives were saved; however, there were over half a million perished or deported before them.

Marianne, separated from her little band, rode doggedly home, hoping to arrive there before Andrew did. When she reached home, she put the horse in the barn, and after hiding her weapons, now including a stolen rifle, she huddled with her family, and then before bed, wrote down everything that she could remember, from the rapid and exciting events of the day. She closed her eyes, blew out the candles and fell fast asleep.

The next morning, Andrew was off to a good start. Since his ground was furrowed and planted, he lent his plow to Josef Varya for his five hectares and then to pass it on to three other farmers. The prescribed quota was to produce ninety-five bushels of cabbage and two hundred bushels of potatoes for each hectare of land, ten percent of which was kept for the villages while the rest was for the Soviet state.

As Marianne sank her hands into the rich muddy fields and clouds blanketed the dark skies, her thoughts drifted to the liberation of hundreds of Poles who were led to the Sanctuaries, but also to the many more still oppressed. The trucks heading eastward toward Russia's gulags passed daily. And then she thought, "That is the way indecent things are, but we must go on. Time is dangerously short," she muttered to herself.

TUESDAY APRIL 23, 1940

Andrew passed a newly mounted sign on his way to Dorovitz's farm, proclaiming in bold red letters: *Workers of the World Unite...May Day Celebration. Thursday May 1, 1940.* Andrew noted the event and for a fleeting moment wondered if they all would be required to go. However, his thoughts as he drove his horse along the road, were of Ilana Dorovitz and her own struggle with her daily life in the shadow of the depravity and destruction witnessed on a daily basis which made her life joyless. As the devoted wife of Dorovitz, she strove to keep her six children protected from the effects of the mass murders he was directing. Ilana confided to Andrew that in her heart, she was horrified by the terror. He sensed that she was afraid of the future and particularly that of her children. She kept repeating this theme every time he saw her. However, as her despair and the accompanying depression grew daily; she and the children were captives in their own home, forced to live with the ongoing endless slaughter of their fellow man. Andrew always listened to her patiently, and sensed a moral, spiritual and intellectual need from this educated and once elegant woman, who now was trapped in the household of a corrupt, greedy, and murderous husband. She confessed, to Andrew, that at some point, she would have to face judgment for her participation in these events, not only by family, but God himself.

Ilana was Jewish, as was her husband who had abandoned the faith of his ancestors a long time ago and had assumed that his wife had done the same. Andrew's patient responses to her questions, and his spirituality drew her to him as if he were a father confessor. There was a lot of the Rabbi in Andrew, she felt, for he could understand her feelings. Jews did not seek personal confession as do Catholics, he had once thought, but do seek Atonement during worship. Andrew was sorrowful for those who had their faith in God removed for any reason, and therefore would be removed from God during life and after death. Ilana, who was raised in an Orthodox faith of centuries which separated men from the women in the temple, had been separated now from her attachment to her own faith as well. Dorovitz had simply assumed she would carry on his own brand of Bolshevik atheism, and although this assumption was far from the truth, Ilana, who kept her belief, had nowhere to turn but to Andrew, a priest without a frock, for comfort. For this reason and this reason alone, she confided in him more and more, assuming that information would be kept private and confidential. Andrew on the other hand, felt almost guilty about revealing information that he gathered from her to others, as no priest would do, with material garnered from the confessional. He realized that it was necessary in order to save many, many lives, and now focused on what would become of her children in the future, and how he could help them. To Andrew, a life represented a soul worth saving, regardless of the situation. He finished thinking and searching for solutions when he arrived at the Dorovitz farm.

Marianne, too, was more concerned at this moment, with the salvation of imprisoned countrymen. For the past three weeks, in the darkness of night and in the secret passageways during the days, the Trumpeter Eskadry had completed eleven more "insertions" as they started to call them. They had coordinated their efforts with the Polish underground of western Poland, and with its own command of the Polish government in exile in Britain. Convoys in Brest, trains outside Lwów, regulator food supplies in Baranowicie, were attacked and in Valynia and Wilnious, railroad tracks were destroyed.

Marianne had an idea that if disruption of the coming May Day celebration were to happen, perhaps the world would be alerted to truth, as she carefully placed her writings into the Virgin Icon and went off to meet with Jan Malinowski and Stanley Kulakiewicz. She wanted to find a way to stop funeral trains on May 1st.

TUESDAY   APRIL 30, 1940

The Varya family was considered by all the inhabitants in the sanctuary to be the wizards of the forest. They were loyal, trustworthy and skilled at many facets of life. They built secret passageways, shared tested health remedies, and they were the only Ukrainians in the Sanctuary.

Marianne asked Luba and Josef if she might take Myron, their fifteen year old son to Pinsk for the May Day celebration. Polish and Ukrainian patriots need to be united, she told them. "I understand" Josef answered. "Myron is going on fifteen. He will be forced into the Soviet army, shot after harvest, or captured by Ukrainian partisans that are a problem every Ukrainian boy will have to face. I would so much like him to live the life of a Polish citizen, loyal to Poland."

Luba continued," Myron needs to go with you. It will be a life lesson." Marianne asked him to be ready at four-thirty the next morning for the trip to Pinsk.

Andrew rode off to Dorowitz's without knowing of Marianne's planned trip to Pinsk. She picked up Myron very early in the morning before sunrise, since she had one errand to run on the way. The children were safe with Luba; however, she was worried about the fate of her young Ukrainian passenger. They drove out of Zamolina; along the road, the wagon passed the checkpoint where the Russian patrols appeared to have increased in number, as gunfire echoed in the distance.

Jan Malinowski and Stanley Kulakiewicz were masked by the usual brush at an assigned meeting point past the checkpoint three kilometers down the road. They paused there as if in need of a necessary road side stop. Myron was told to hold the horse and yell if anyone approached, as Marianne exited into the small cluster of trees. When she squatted as if urinate, Malinowski, appeared, and squatting also, warned her that the tracks outside of Pinsk to Kiev, Smolensk and Moscow had been mined. Stanley had placed explosives all around the tracks heading to Stalingrad, which could be detonated once the trains were in sight. When they stopped, liberators would attack and escort the exiles safely to the forests. Trains were scheduled to leave after the May Day speeches and ceremonies. The message was given quickly and curtly, and the two men disappeared back into the dark forest. Marianne pulled up her skirt, ignoring her gun strapped to her waist, and appeared on the road as did any peasant woman using the woods as a stopover.

Myron drove the wagon along the rough road into Pinsk, and halted it on the perimeter of the town, near a road leading to the Market square, where the celebration was to take place. May Day parades, as a show of might and force, were important to the Russians; therefore, soldiers in armored vehicles, moved along the wide street into the town's square, as units marched between the armored vehicles. The event drew most of the military to the center of town, leaving the outposts thinly guarded. Jan had planned this day well; Marianne looked at groups of soldiers and police standing on each corner. Crowds of people lined the streets, waving red flags and cheering the troops. The event looked like a victory parade and a joyous celebration, to the townspeople, of the Bolshevik success in the area; however, in reality, they were the regulators from the surrounding regions taking part in a propaganda parade, and distributing an extra ration of bread. In celebration of May Day, two loaves were given, rather than the customary one per household. Marianne and Myron played the role of happy peasants, and after showing their identy papers, they acted thrilled when they got two loaves apiece.

Dorovitz, the man who had already ordered boys beaten, girls burned, and soldiers strung to trees to die, and to date half a million Polish Catholics deported to Siberia, appeared on the steps of the beautiful old church in the square. His murderous presence on this sacred spot, seemed to be a deliberate act of disrespect, and it filled Marianne with additional sadness. He looked over the crowd, "These are special days! They are meant to make our lives easier." he said. He spoke of scheduled resettlements, declaring that a significant portion of the workers had to feed the Soviet state and regulators.

Dorovitz continued his rant, announcing that Pinsk will be the first to operate new trucks that just arrived. That meant more jobs for the workers. The trucks, he said, were a gift from Moscow.

As he was speaking in the square, hundreds of people were waiting, ready to be packed into boxcars and cattle cars at the railroad station. Their destination was Siberia. They were brutally packed, boarded and driven into cars posted with a large "P" for Polish Catholic, "U" for Ukrainian, "L" for Lithuania, and "B" for Belorussian.

The regulators continued to yell, berate and abuse the hungry and desperate people, until they were finally locked into cattle cars, while watching for attackers, since the Trumpeter Eskadry had a significant effect on these trains and convoys earlier in the month. Thirteen trains were halted in April, and many more trucks destroyed.

Marianne hurriedly rushed Myron back to the wagon, as Dorovitz was still speaking, for she had spied a long line of people headed for the railroad, and she needed to escape before the explosions started. As Myron slowed his pace to stare at the line of hapless people, Marianne pulled him along. "It is our duty to help those people leaving for Siberia. I hope you will soon see some of them at our Sanctuary. Perhaps they will be the future brave soldiers like you."

As they got to the wagon, there was a loud explosion and black smoke appeared on the horizon. As Marianne had feared, when they turned back toward home and away from Pinsk, the minute the bombs were detonated, an increased watch would cover the roads to and from the city. Eventually about three or four kilometers out of town, they were stopped by a troop of mounted men, carefully searched and roughly treated. Myron was pale with fright; however, Marianne knew how to play the role these men were seeking.

"What's your name?" a guard demanded.

"Marianne Ludwig. This is my neighbor's boy, Myron Varya. Here are our identity papers."

"We know who you are. Your husband works for Dorovitz," he answered with a trace of bitterness in his voice, and he turned toward the slight figure of Myron, who by now was shaking with fear. He obviously was not a member of the resistance, nor did he look big or old enough to be a rebel.

"Ukrainian?" he was asked. "Do you know of any violations against the state?"

"No."

"Do you know of any incidents of violence or saboteurs against the state?"

"No."

"Why did you go to Pinsk then?" the man demanded. "What did you get in Pinsk?"

"We went to celebrate May Day. My neighbor wanted to thank Pan Dorovitz for giving her husband a job." Myron replied.

Another guard searched the wagon, but found nothing that could be considered a violation. "You give me no choice, but to search you. There are people who hide money and watches in secret places. If I find any violation, you could be shot." he said as he grabbed the four loaves of bread and shoved them into his coat; fortunately he stopped with the bread before he reached the pistol that Marianne was carrying.

"Go! You are lucky to be alive. We'll keep our eyes open for you." the guard warned. They were free to go, and as they left they knew that there was a line of people and wagons waiting to have their bread stolen too. As May Day drew to a close, Marianne had to take the wagon to the farm house; then she walked with young Myron to his home. He had had to absorb all the events of the day, although he had been spared some of the murderous spectacle. The slight boy was still not over his loss of bread, and the harsh treatment of people by the regulators. Marianne hugged the boy when she brought him home and picked up her own children. There was nothing more to say.

WEDNESDAY MAY 14, 1940

On this day, two bits of news had reached Marianne. None of it good- She had lain awake praying that no member of the Eskadry was injured or dead. For the past week, the band of Freedom Fighters had traveled the main road, avoiding Russian checkpoints and cavalry. They had endured rain, barbed wire, and armed guards. She now feared for their lives.

Early that morning, she took the baby to her "nurse" without awakening Andrew, who by now was suspicious about her trips and odd activities. He never let on that he suspected anything, realizing the danger caused by his connection to Dorovitz. Marianne meanwhile walked through the wooded path and the peaceful dawn seemed far from the war- torn real world, and just for a moment she remembered what life could be like. Children going to school, good food, the solemnity of a high Mass on a holiday all were very distant in a dim past.

She reached a spot, a distance from her shack, and unearthed a green radio transmitter from the base of a tree. The old green metal box was dirty and rusty, but the radio was wired to work. She cranked it, realizing that the Pinsk explosions of train tracks would not be overlooked by Dorovitz, and that reprisals would be forthcoming.

Marianne put on ear phones attached to the green box. Several minutes went by and finally she was able to reach Eagle who was just outside of Lwów, the largest city in eastern Poland. He told her that there were now, seven established Eskadry campsites nearby, stocked with caches of guns, ammunition, radios, loudspeakers, plus medicine and food confiscated from the Russians, providing protection for several more Sanctuaries. Lwów and Brest-Litowsk were considered military fronts, by the Russians, and Mongolian troops were stationed there as the frontline defense against the Nazis.

He continued "We have been in action for the last six days, since Pinsk, salvaging human cargo from trucks and trains; however, the fear of continued ambushes has kept some of the Russian trucks off the main roads, and they have been using smaller back and farm roads."

Marianne asked if there were any reprisals.

"We know the army is chasing us. Pietrinev and Dorovitz have put a high price on the Trumpeter Eskadry. We don't know if they believe Marianne Krull to be dead either."

"You need to be extra careful." she said.

"I hear you. After an attack at Baranowiczie's truck depot, we fled to a high ridge. Two or three Russian battalions stormed out converging on the Ukrainian section from three directions. The civilians did not resist. It was brutal. They were massacred, men, women and

269

children. All the buildings and homes were leveled. I believe two or three boys escaped into the woods."

She thought of the killing of innocent Ukrainians to create hatred of the Jews as a group because they were the most closely connected to the NKVD and against Poles because of the conflicts of the past.

"Were any Poles killed?" she asked

"We don't know, but that's not all. The NKVD sent Polish labor crews and forced them to bury the dead, to make Ukrainians in general angry at the Poles. Funerals are sacred to them, and the Ukrainians will not forget the Polish faces burying the dead without Orthodox Christian last rites."

Marianne told him that maybe they should retaliate by killing two regulators for each Pole executed. Then she asked "Are there any Ukrainian resistance or guerilla activities?"

"There is one band called Banderivtsi that outmaneuvered the guards and split up Russian forces near Valynia; they are part of the Ukrainian Insurgent Army, and although unfriendly to Poles, they have caused considerable Russian and NKVD casualties. Stanley Kulakiewicz suddenly took over the microphone and asked. "What do you think we can do with them?

Marianne asked him to see if the Ukrainian guerillas could attack the Communists and NKVD, and distract them from their own attacks. She added that they should let everything settle down for a while, and find out if there are reprisals, and where. She suggested that they come to the interior of the forest for a while. The Eskadry wanted to know if they could contribute to the Sanctuary, and Marianne told them that the people were starving for meat, as their diet had been reduced to wild mushrooms, cabbage, potatoes and bread. She signed off hurriedly and re-buried the radio in its cache under the tree.

As she headed back to pick up the children, she figured that the Russians would rather have Ukrainians kill Poles, and since the Sanctuary's black market economy was heavily dependent on an autonomous Jewish economy separate of the Communist economic system, it would be to their benefit to let the Communists attack the Nazis. It was also terribly confusing, particularly since they had so little information of world events, so she focused on matters at hand.

She wondered how Ilana Dorovitz was getting along living in her two worlds. What was inside her mind, and how conflicted was she?

How could she establish a value system to her children, while remaining faithful to her husband's politics? Why was she willing to share with Andrew her deepest Soviet secrets? Marianne could not forget the look on Ilana's face when she warned of the school being targeted by NKVD. Would she also give Andrew information about Soviet intentions? Marianne guessed that one day, when the events got worse, she would appear, or be rescued to their sanctuary. Marianne believed Ilana wanted to give something to life, unlike her husband who wanted to take from life. Ilana had the advantage of Andrew's guiding presence, which she had welcomed into her home. Marianne thought that it all hinged on keeping her children alive.

Marianne was filled with ideas, that morning, and continued on to Myron Varya's home of mud and logs. She wanted very much for Luba and Josef to allow their son to work with a Sanctuary security defense. Josef replied without hesitation, "Of course. I was worried for a time that as Ukrainians, we might not be included in your plans." Marianne assured them that this was not the case.

"We agree. Myron will join you -first thing tomorrow."

Marianne continued on to the wooden hut of Adam and Florence Makowski, and asked if their son Matteus would help guard the Sanctuary. Adam replied that although Matteus was only barely sixteen, he would be drafted into the Russian army right after harvest, as will Myron Varya; therefore, , this was an excellent idea.

Matteus hugged Marianne and proudly declared, "You have helped us and given us strength. The real enemy is out there. I am ready to do my best."

Marianne spoke seriously to the youngster, "We need everyone to save lives and our country; you and Myron will have to be the first line of defense to keep our Sanctuary safe." "Perhaps" she continued "Adam, you and Casimir could join us, and also have Josef Varya come to our security gatherings. Tonight we can meet at seven, and we have a lot to talk about."

Marianne gave hugs all around and headed home, after she picked up the children.

MAY 11, 1940

Andrew and Marianne began and ended each day concerned with hope rather than with the struggle at hand. While they both wanted happiness on earth; and they believed in life after death, they felt connected to a spirituality that few in the surrounding outside world could understand, now that it had been rejected. Andrew carried his faith and connection to God like a torch in the darkness, and while he worked with his hands at the Dorovitz farm, he was building a relationship of trust with Ilana Dorovitz. Andrew continued to be aware of her inner struggle about her family's very existence, which was facing elimination either by the Soviets, reminiscent of the deadly purges of older Bolsheviks prior to the War, or by Nazis because they were Bolsheviks' ruling intelligentsia. She and Tomas were slowly separating emotionally and intellectually from each other. Although Ilana was aware of the barbaric methods used against innocent people, she somehow had a remarkable capacity for shutting her eyes to it all. Andrew told Marianne that she truly felt pain. She knew that every choice, in her husband's world, was a struggle between good and evil, and that if evil was necessary for enhancing his power, it was right. Andrew was not sure whether Ilana Dorovitz's cooperation would continue. She remained defensive, but Andrew saw some hope. Perhaps even as the wife of a mass murderer, she might have considered a life hereafter for her and their six children, only if she eventually confessed her sins.

Andrew told Marianne that Ilana had revealed all that she knew of the coming events to him, and had hinted about an upcoming military development, but couldn't seem to bring herself to tell him the details. She, however, told him the truth because she feared losing him as a spiritual presence, or even as a kind of father confessor, and because of her children's future, if this very secret operation reached its end. "Mongolian troops, with dogs, are going to be unleashed from the Maskowski estate to find the Sanctuaries, and to find any guerilla bands that might be there as well," she had said to Andrew under her breath, as she brought him some water in the field.

Andrew foresaw, therefore, that the forest dwellers would be in danger. She did not give a clue as to whether the death of Marianne Krull had been reported. When he reached home, Marianne took all this information in, and thought of the challenge of the life and death struggle that lay ahead. She asked Andrew, on today's journey to the Dorovitzes, to try to find out a time when the Mongolians would be starting their search. She knew that they too could live off the forests. She kissed Andrew good- bye and prayed for his safety, so grateful to have this good kind soul working with them. He smiled, and bounced to the wagon, and waved as he drove off.

Marianne turned to the task; whenever these Sanctuaries would be attacked was not really as much of a concern as their continued protection was. What an immense undertaking! She felt that this fight was her destiny, and she had to plan for the inevitability of attack. She went out to find good soldier Leopold. With the boys set as look -outs, plus information from him, at least a defense could be organized. She wanted Leopold to join them for he did not belong to the enemy with whom his family had experienced twenty years of death and destruction. She found him on lonely guard duty, and after a quick check to see if he was alone, asked him to supply information of troops in the area. She emphasized that their lives were in danger, and asked if he could join them when the need for him to escape arose. He agreed, thinking that he would save more lives if he stayed where he was, and reported to the Sanctuaries regularly.

Marianne then found the boys, that she had recruited, and even added little Stefan to the group. She asked them to be the eyes and ears of the Sanctuary, look- outs, and to avoid suspicion by appearing to be trapping small game, or running farm errands for their parents. They were to look out for Ukrainian Nationalists and Soviets. The boys, as boys will, knew all the hiding places and paths of the woods, and had seen enough to be aware of the danger. They had grown up far too soon.

Marianne gathered the inner group of Sanctuary residents to try to find a way to fend off the expected intruders. She met with Makowski, Pilat, and Varya, and told them of the Banderivtsi. They agreed that these insurgents could be a danger to their own Trumpeter Eskadry, since Ilana Dorovitz had informed Andrew a cavalry troop, with dogs, would occupy Adam's old estate. They decided to wait for the expected occupation and then burn down the estate, and the grounds to eliminate the danger. Adam readily agreed saying it was only a house and not a home.

The last decision was how to deal with Stephan Bandera, the guerrilla leader, for there was the chance that the Banderivtsi might attack the Sanctuaries and use them as sites for their operations. They agreed it would be better to join forces with them, and that they would ask Josef Varya to join Bandera and try to make a deal not to attack Trumpeter Eskadry, or any of the Sanctuaries. Since Hersky and Pietrinev would probably start massive executions using the Mongolian troops, perhaps even in Zamolina, and more than likely the Ukrainian section could get hit the hardest. Therefore, they all decided that all the Ukrainians including Myron, Josef, Luba, and Justina should move into the Sanctuaries.

273

Decisions had to be made for the young boys now doing guard duty. Marianne suggested that Matteus join the Trumpeter Eskadry, to keep continuity, and if possible Myron would join the Banderivtsi as a Ukrainian partisan.

Josef Varya took the responsibility of infiltrating the Banderivtsi. All Marianne could think of on her way home, was the recurring theme of a Mother's protection of her young, and nest, because it is her home where all of her life and love is centered. The sanctuaries were more than just a refuge; they had become an extended home and family, which now was the focal point of the homeland of the Polish people. This movement was the center of love of country, each other, and of their maker, in a cold tumultuous void. These Sanctuaries must be defended at all costs.

<h3 style="text-align:center">SATURDAY JUNE 15, 1940</h3>

Marianne lived in daily fear of discovery, and with it, the loss of the Polish heritage and faith. Her family was now living in the forest with the other refugees, and sometimes on a summer evening, like this one, the horrible world conflict seemed to be just a noise in the far distance. The children were running among the trees, and someone was playing polkas on the accordion in the warmth of the setting sun. The Black Madonna was framed by red and white roses blooming around it. Andrew had used a Polish flag as a makeshift altar cloth. Marianne thought it a beautiful symbol of the faith that kept them steady. Andrew, who had been busy playing with the children like a great boy in an improvised soccer game, came trotting over, and she asked him:"Ilana?"

Andrew answered, "Ilana is not completely sure, but in the next week or two, the NKVD will be building a dog compound, and bringing in a cavalry squadron to Adam's old estate."

Adam, who had been struggling as the self-appointed goalkeeper, was leaning on Andrew breathing hard, "We must make it difficult for them to threaten the villagers, and patrol the woods. If the dogs sniff out the Sanctuaries, we are lost. It is not a question of if, but when? We must attack them Timing will be crucial." he said as he caught his breath. "If the forests are filled with Ukrainian partisans and Mongolian troops, Catholic and Christian Slavic families are as good as dead!"

Jan, Magdalene, Josef and Stanley Kulakiewicz saw this small conference and joined them, all seated on the warm ground. They told of Soviet propaganda posters that they had seen showing Ukrainians hanged by Poles, and although the true hangmen were the NKVD, the intention was to confuse the populace while polarizing and churning up ethnic anger. They were also posters: *"All Jews unite with the Bolsheviks against Poles and Ukrainians."*

Although Marianne said that they had to neutralize the propaganda, they all realized the immediate threat of the cavalry and their dogs. Stanley said, "The Mongolians in full force can be lethal. We do not have the numbers or the resources to take on a well-armed force of more than forty men. For every Polish fighter, we can kill five, possibly six Mongolians. Our support is not well armed. The best strategy is to strike first before they reach full strength and target those who have the capabilities to destroy our Sanctuaries and that could mean horses, dogs, tanks, and low-flying planes which they used in an attack on the Banderivtsi near Lwów."

Josef Varya had been missing for the last week; He appeared to have been bruised and cut badly, when he arrived and sat down painfully. He said that he had good news and that he had waited for the right moment to tell them. He found the Banderivtsi.and they agreed that they needed to keep the Ukrainian Nationalists out of local business and would unite with them against the Bolsheviks as a common enemy. Bandera's forces, therefore, had temporarily made peace with Poles."We do not have to worry about the Ukrainians attacking our Sanctuaries and fighting Trumpeter Eskadry. I am just so lucky to be alive." he added.

"We, even as the lone Ukrainians, feel that we are part of the family here, so after we talked about it a week or two ago, I went to Galicia to talk to the Banderivtsi. I followed rumors, whispered information, and gossip to try to find them. On one road to what I thought was their camp, I was seized by one of the NKVD patrols. They stopped me about twenty miles from Kalusz, Galicia. First, they inspected my identity card, and asked me one or two questions about my intentions. Knowing that I was a Ukrainian from Zamolina, they asked me if I was going to join the Banderivtsi. I told them that I was just trying to find a job in Lwów. Then they started to beat me. I kept repeating, "I am Josef Varya of Zamolina! I am hungry, and my family needs food." Two soldiers grabbed my feet, flipped me upside down, and hung me by my ankles, until Hersky, the same KGB officer from here in Zamolina now living at Makowski's Estate walked in.   I will never forget his face "

"Are you are making contact with the Banderivtsi, or maybe the Trumpeter Eskadry? You have little time to tell us. Where is Bandera?"

My silence angered him. "It is now a war between us. This is only the beginning for Ukrainians. All of you will pay".he said, and he walked away. They tied a noose around my neck and left me dangling from a tree to strangle slowly. I pretended to be unconscious, and after they left, I was able to get free. I gathered my strength and made it to Kalush where I met the Ukrainian Nationalist representatives. All I had to do was show the raw flesh on my neck and they knew I was really a Ukrainian."

Josef continued, ominously, that the Ukrainians would leave them alone, and he finished by saying that he and his son Myron would be honored to lead the attack on the canine unit at Makowski's old home, since he was the foreman there. "I want to look straight at Hersky's eyes and end his miserable life." he said finally.

His tale sobered and momentarily silenced them all. Marianne waited a moment, and then told them that the Mongolian troops were on the way, and that Leopold Kobryn told her that dog pens and cages had been placed in Adam's old farm. The Mongolian units, as Jan Malinowski had surmised, were being prepared to reinforce the campaign against Bandera, and were scheduled to start moving in within the next few days. The boys had been watching closely.

Young Myron, filled with adult responsibility, told everyone that he had seen Mongolian troops, followed by tanks, and more trucks passing Matteus' old home. A few days ago, he said, men on horseback stopped by Matteus' farm several times to rest their horses. He reported that they wore green and blue striped coats.

They agreed that this moment should be remembered as a life changing turning point. As the fire dimmed, and the children were sent off to bed, shared vodka added a glow to the warmth of the companionship and sense of family. Adam and Jan returned from a check on the status outside the village. "This is it!" Adam said, "The dogs have arrived, and there are horses in the barn. We need to act soon and burn the barns down. We probably have a day and a half or so before they are fully settled in. That may be enough time to make a plan. I will help Myron, Matteus, Adam and Josef with their observation posts tomorrow morning. Andrew should go to Dorovitz tomorrow and see if there is anything that could change our plans. I suspect that they have twenty men in one barrack plus the NKVD people and maybe four officers in the home. If we surprise them I think that we will have the usual success, since we have the advantage of knowing the layout of the farm."

"We need to find out if there will be a password to get into the compound, and we must create a diversion to protect the villagers and farmers still left in Zamolina from NKVD reprisals." he concluded.

They decided to finish the plans for the attack the next day after finding whatever information that they could. What had started out as a warm friendly summer evening turned into a tense night of planning a battle.

MONDAY JUNE 16, 1940

The night that passed before the raids was sleepless for all involved. The Varyas had decided to remain in their farm home for two nights, one before, and one after the raid and burning of the farm. Appearances were most important, as all of the farmers could feel eyes on them at all times: Were they working hard enough? What would the quota be? They were forced to repeat their daily activities as if everything was right with the world, which it was not. Andrew decided to stay at the Dorovitz farm for the next few days so that he would be less visible at home. Marianne, with her children safely in the sanctuary, remained back at the old farmhouse, trying in vain to sleep as she reviewed the plans in her mind. Repeatedly she pictured the coming attack, and when she envisioned the end, she always was left with a sense of terror, and a bad finish to it all. She prayed that they had not miscalculated their approach, and that she would be forgiven if her plan and conception failed.

In the early morning, she decided that she needed to see Leopold who was standing guard across the roadway. The only difficulty was that she had to pass Colonel Pietriniev's home and headquarters. As she did, the disheveled Colonel appeared on the porch and grunted at her for being late to the field work.

"You are late this morning. It is seven- thirty. Damn, how do you expect your child to be fed if there is no bread on the table?"

"Colonel" replied Marianne sweetly,"We are not living by bread alone. We work hard, and your region will meet or even exceed quotas. My husband is staying overnight at Dorovitz's to make sure he has an increased crop. The additional tools that you graciously got for us made a big difference with the Ukrainians and Poles. We are your most productive workers, and I believe Dorovitz is pleased."

Pietrinev only nodded vaguely. However, Marianne pushed on, "We all saw these new Mongolian soldiers, and you should know that

277

they are thin, hungry and smell badly. From what we know, the Russian soldiers need to be more worried about them than they are about Ukrainians or Poles, for they are desperate men, ready to snap at any moment. They could start killing the NKVD troops in the middle of the night. Then you will have an uncontrollable problem on your hands."

"What do you know?" he replied foolishly. "The Mongolian troops are not based here; only one cavalry unit is coming to hunt in the forests."

Marianne inwardly thanked him for the information and said: "I may not know anything but I remember what happened to the experienced officers just two years ago. They were condemned and executed by the NKVD. Dorovitz fears inexperienced officers with the Republics' soldiers, and since the Mongolians are here, I would look over my shoulder. There is no loyalty. They will only fight and kill to get the next meal. . If I were Russian, I'd go to bed terrified, for these troops have guns. Along with the Ukrainians, I'd fear the gunmen from Mongolia."

As always he had a sneering answer: "They are here only to keep the scum away."

Marianne replied "Good day Colonel" and kept on her way towards Makowski's old place. When she passed Leopold, who stopped her ostensibly to check her papers, she slipped him a large piece of babka and whispered, "I need information. What is the latest password for the NKVD, and how many troops are stationed at Makowski's old compound?"

As he looked at her papers, he said, "Hersky, five NKVD agents, six regulators, and Mongolian troops are based there, and none of the Russians want to be close to them. The NKVD brought the Mongolians in to watch over the Russian soldiers. However, someone has to watch the Mongolians so they have a larger elite NKVD group of mercenaries from Latvia, Estonia, and Russia guarding them."

"How many troops and how many dogs are there?"

"About twenty-five mounted soldiers, and maybe twenty dogs. You would be doing the Russians a favor by shooting them all. The password is the Ukrainian word ZAMOSC. Hersky's joke- It means mass executions."

"Of the Ukrainians?"

"Yes!"

278

Marianne folded up her identity papers, and put them in her big coat pocket as she whispered "Thanks!" to Leopold. She reached Makowski's farm, passing the beautiful old home with its carved façade, and counted the buildings in the farmyard. There were five workers houses, which included the attached barn, one overseer's larger house, all with thatched roofs. The house was occupied by Hersky and four officers. On the other side of the road, in the fields now covered with tall grass waiting to be mowed for hay, there were three wood and sod buildings, used alternately as barns, housing for day laborers or even pigs. The livestock was shared by Luba's and Florence's family. No one noticed the dogged peasant woman ambling home.

She continued to the woods until she found Florence, Luba, Magdalene and their children Eugene, Veronica, and Justina, who were all familiar with the forest as they had helped build a secret path that leads into Pasternak's Sanctuary. Marianne told them of the coming attack on the old farm, now a compound, and asked them to help form a bucket brigade after the fires broke out, and while doing so, loudly proclaim that good people ought not to kill.

"We will need to save a few regulators' lives so they can tell their superiors.We want to leave an impression that we are peaceful." Marianne turned to Luba, held her by the shoulders, looked at her and warned not to be anywhere near her old home tomorrow, because she was sure that the Ukrainian section would be attacked by the NKVD, blaming it all on them. The women hugged each other, trying to hide their fright. None of them had been involved in any violent behavior. These were peaceful, devout, loving women. Marianne, however, was beginning to be hardened to the actions that needed to be taken, realizing that she had to give strength of belief and morality to this group of women, now cast in new roles. She asked Magdalene to bring a nice bottle of homemade vodka to the guards, and then explained that the bombs would detonate early in the morning, and to be on watch for the fire and explosions so they could start bringing water. The women watched Marianne stride purposefully away, looking little like the ignorant peasant woman she often pretended to be, and instead like the trusted leader she really had become.

Marianne often wondered what life would have been like had the Russians and Nazis not invaded. Would she have been content to be a mother and housekeeper, or would she have continued to teach? She knew, however, that life would have been wonderfully fulfilling and most of all, there would be an absence of the fear that she lived with on a daily basis. She found Josef, Myron, Matteus,, Adam with : Jan Malinowski,(Eagle) and Monika Wisniewska (Karpathai), Stanley Kulakiewicz, (Saber), Paul Mikewa(Gemstone), John Urbanek(Corpenicus), Mark Jablonski(Orion) and Walter Mazur(Oko).The Trumpeter Eskadry looked fierce, now that they were armed and ready, and even their code names, which they often viewed as silly, made sense today. Going and liberating a prison was very different from fighting an enemy on your own home grounds.

Adam had drawn a crude map of the farm buildings with approximate distances to and from the buildings. The biggest challenge would be the placement of bombs on or in the buildings, and then the escape from the farm yard to safety. The boys knew the land well and even had discussed how to hide as they would get nearer the yards. Hopefully, in the early morning, the guards on patrol would be sleepy enough not to be too careful. The rest of the band would wait until just before sun up to ostensibly report for farm work, carrying the tools of the trade.

Josef would drive a wagon to the gate, give the password, and tell the guards that he had vodka for Hersky, and give a couple of bottles to the guards. He would park the wagon as close as he could get to a house, and walk out to join the other "peasants" for work. However, after it was over, he was to take Luba directly into the forest for safety. If some dead Mongolian soldiers were dressed in peasant clothing and left for the NKVD to find, it would certainly cause confusion. If it were at all possible they decided to do that as well. Once the farm buildings were in flames, the women and their buckets of water would arrive and start to try to save the buildings. With all the planning complete, the vigilante band of patriots settled in for a rest, and some food.

Marianne was confident that her children were safe deep in the forest; however, she was worried about Andrew at Dorowitz's. What reaction to this attack would affect him? She guessed that he would be all right and at about 2:00 A.M., dressed in a dirty red shirt and muddy trousers, smeared her face with mud, strapped on her pistol and walked to where Florence and Magdalene were waiting for her on the edge of the farm property. Each now was armed with an automatic rifle; Magdalene greeted Marianne with a salute and said "Look at the Amazon Warriors ready for action". It was all they could do to stifle giggles at the remark and also upon seeing what each of these gentle women had become.

They could see Josef and his wagon approaching the gate, and as he did, the guards were intent on its contents. Meanwhile, two of the

Eskadry crawled nearer, with rifles. Josef left the wagon near a house so that the ensuing explosion would also detonate the wagon. He left to get his farm tools, he told the guards, and joined, however, the waiting riflemen, Orion and Saber who armed him as well.

The area emptied of patrolling guards, who were sleepy or wanted more to drink: and as if on cue, a violent thunderstorm began, complete with high winds and pouring rain. Karpathia, Matthew, Monika and Ludwig arrived at the regulators' homes. Hopefully, Matteus and Myron had placed charges at the rear of the buildings.

Fortunately, the dogs began to bark at the thunder and lighting, which removed suspicion of intruders and the noise, masked the attack better than expected. The explosion, when the bombs were detonated sounded much like a thunder clap, and when the buildings' fires triggered the explosives in the wagon, there was a burst of machine gun fire which came from either the Mongolians or from the Trumpeter Eskadry; the women lying outside the barnyard couldn't know who was firing. As the soldiers and guards were picked off one by one as they ran through the yard, Josef headed straight for Hersky's house and shot him at point blank range as he exited. A bullet to the heart ended his miserable existence. Eagle and Saber took the clothing off three soldiers and two officers and, as planned, dragged the now disguised bodies closer to the regulators' homes. They had fired another round into the masked gunmen and some of the soldiers.

The whole scene took on a Hellish appearance: the wagon exploded and the yard resembled one huge fireball. The whole attack took less than twenty minutes, however, while the barns and homes were burning, the women ran to the well in the farm yard center with buckets and formed a line to try and douse the flames. Minutes later, men, women and children swarmed from the edge of the village to join other families in a large bucket brigade. Florence wiped the blood off the faces of two regulators, and then helped three more surviving women regulators get on their feet and walk to the field away from the flames.

Florence was sobbing, "Too awful," Magdalene sighed "When will this all stop?" she said to the surviving five regulators, who joined her by sobbing as well. Magdalene Kozinska said "I'm so sorry. Everything done in war is mad, mad and cruel. Totally revolting! It doesn't have to be this way."

"I understand," an older regulator murmured back. "You are a decent woman. "

281

As she spoke, she saw Colonel Pietriniev and a small band of his soldiers arrive. The surviving regulators went to him to explain what happened. Marianne and Florence walked away to the bucket brigade and turned just in time to see all of the seared and burned regulators shot by the Colonel, who galloped over to the fire fighters and shouted "Go away! Return home! Those not found in their homes will be hunted and shot."

Marianne chose to return to the forest Sanctuary as did the other women; the exception was Josef and Luba who had decided that the Ukrainian faction must appear to have been in the farmhouse when the attack occurred.

TUESDAY JUNE 17, 1940

The remains of the farm, and the barnyard, were still smoldering, later that morning, sending wisps of smoke into the spring air; the bodies of soldiers and the executed regulators lay where they fell in an obscene pattern of death. The small band of saboteurs had headed into the forest to the sanctuaries. Marianne waited, while Andrew was still at Dorowitz's, in her field by the house near the road, ostensibly working the weeds in the rows of green spring sprouts. She was worried about the Varyas; some internal mechanism churned at her stomach, and she felt that they were in some sort of danger. They had fled earlier, she thought, into the forest; however, she wasn't sure if they got there safely. She kept chopping at the weeds, harder and harder, releasing her anxiety and fear, as if the stubborn weeds were the NKVD and the regulators.

She did not know why she looked up from the furrows, but when she did, she saw Justina running across the field, and as the child drew closer, Marianne saw that she was sobbing hysterically. Her clothes were covered with blood; she was shaking uncontrollably. Marianne, half hugged, half walked and half stumbled with the child and took her into the house, She held her tightly and tried to clean her up as best as she could. Justina took long gulping breaths and as soon as she quieted down, she would start sobbing again. Marianne soothed her, held her on her lap and finally she was able to speak. She blurted out: "They shot Papa." and she started crying again. Marianne's premonition was right; something terrible had happened to the Varyas. Justina finally got the whole story out; Pietrinev arrived at their doorstep earlier that morning. They wrecked the house and barn, and ordered everyone back inside. That's when the killing began. "They shot Papa," Justina sobbed again.

282

"They pushed him on the porch, forced him to kneel then shot him in the back of the head. They left and went to the Ukrainian homes in the area and shot the oldest man.

I ran here because my Mama collapsed, and she needs you. Myron is with her now. Would you please help us?" she pleaded. "They said they would kill more of us each time a regulator or soldier is shot."

Marianne took Justina's hand and walked her quickly across the field. Josef Varya was lying on the porch of his home, face down on the steps; his left hand held out from his body was clutching a rosary. Slowly, Myron came out of the house and began to speak, "Pietrinev told us to leave the body here for two days as an example to others," he said. "He wants the Poles to look at them. He said more of us would be killed if we tried to bury them. My Papa was praying when they shot him."

Marianne stood in silence, and then was shocked to see Stefan coming out of the house holding Luba's hand. Myron held his Mama protectively with Stefan at his side, whose eyes were swollen from sobbing; she had hoped that her son would have been spared this, but Myron had run into the forest looking for Marianne there, as Justina had run to the farm house. Stefan returned with Myron, and sensing the terror, went right to Luba, almost as if he was Andrew offering comfort in prayer.

Luba said "It was our home, and Josef dared to make it known to the Bolsheviks. He wanted me to tell you that." In a soft voice, nearly a whisper, she said, "Thank you. They won't let us bury him. Josef had insisted on going home that night, and not to the forest, since he thought it would be better if the Ukrainians were in their houses when the attack was over." Marianne was heartsick. He was a good man, who died a martyr, she thought. Marianne took the rosary from Josef's cold hand and placed it around Luba's neck. As she began to finger the beads, Justina began to weep again and said: "I cannot forgive what happened this morning. It will never leave my mind."

"None of us can forget. Justina will be alone without her Papa." Luba said sharply. "I have no man in the house except for Myron but his eyes are already towards Galicia."

Marianne offered to stay with the family for the next two days and until Josef had a decent burial; however, Luba sent Myron and Justina into the forest with her, then said that her place was with her husband.

A burial finally took place, behind the icon of the Black Madonna in an unmarked grave. Andrew officiated, and they all prayed that someday he would be laid to rest with the moving music and haunting chants of a proper Ukrainian Catholic service.

Myron, at the end of the service, told Andrew and Marianne. "I promised my Papa that I would let you know. I will join the Ukrainian fight as a true patriot. Be assured that Pasternak Citadels is safe as long as I am alive. Now I must leave. My Papa wanted it that way." They all watched as he went off to the unknown war of Banderivtsi

Andrew stayed at home that day, and after the funeral, took Marianne into the forest away from the Sanctuary. He often found peace, and talked with God, as he said, deeper into the forest, often in spots that he believed were untouched by man. That morning, Andrew spoke about Ilana Dorowitz and her dread of Stalin ruling the world, and Roosevelt aligning with him, and about her fear of the approach of the Nazi forces. The regulators, she pointed out, are trying to starve, deport and inflict even more torture on Catholics, Poles, Ukrainians, and Lithuanians. Colonel Pietrinev vowed to satisfy Moscow's demands, and Tomas Dorovitz predicted total annihilation of anti-Communists within the Polish and Ukrainian population.

Andrew went on to explain that they had exceeded their quotas, but since harvested food was the "property of the state", whatever Trumpeter Eskadry and the Sanctuary's' members could hide, would help them survive the coming winter. Ilana had also told him of the shift in focus on those deported. The Trumpeter Eskadry actions and disruptions caused Dorovitz to turn his attention away from the Poles and toward Lithuanians, Byelorussians, and Ukrainians.

THE SUMMER OF 1940

The weather all across Europe, that summer, was cooler than usual, and in the wet marsh land of Polesie, the crops flourished. The good people of the sanctuaries worked the fields from early until late, believing that they were being watched at all times. Late at night, a crew would assemble at the back edge of the field and harvest some of the crop, carefully leaving enough for the Soviet quota. These bundles of grain, corn and vegetables, were secreted away in caches in the Sanctuary. As far as the regulators knew, they never existed. The potatoes would have to wait until later in the fall, and even some could be left as winter potatoes.

As their labor continued, the Soviets started to widen the road, removing brush, long grass and even crops growing in the adjacent fields. They created a space of three hundred feet on either side using wasted looking prisoners for their labor force. This process reduced the fields often by as much as two hectares which would reduce spring food production as well. This all was done to lower commerce in the black market, and to target resistance forces.In this case, Pietrinev saw the Ukrainian Banderivtsi as the new enemy; trees had been removed so they couldn't be used as cover for any operation.

The black market was becoming more difficult to use as distribution of food and supplies were drying up. There were checkpoints and thievery among the soldiers which made it more dangerous to transport bulk products. Russian troops had been ordered to shoot anyone without authorization of food quota and supplies, on the road leading from Brest-Litowsk to Pinsk. Vodka was currency for the ruble. Three bottles of vodka was traded for one pound of butter; five bottles for a pound of canned ham.

One gloomy late summer day, a constant light rain watered the crops as increased NKVD surveillance patrolled the now widened road, watching and listening, ready to shoot workers on any whim.

Marianne had slogged through the mist with the children, to visit Leopold. She found her friend, who hurriedly explained that Pietrinev viewed the Banderivtsi as the new enemy, and that the Russians knew exactly which Ukrainians to pursue and which to execute. Today they would be taking Polish workers from the field to bury Ukrainians, and he believed it would be best if Andrew took off. Kabryn explained why the NKVD would want Andrew. "The Soviet build-up is centered around the town of Kovel in southeastern Poland close to the Russian border; mostly Ukrainians live there. Pietrinev knows very little about them, and whether or not there will be a strong resistance; therefore, he decided to eliminate a possible growing partisan menace before winter. The orders from Dorovitz are for the Soviets to seize the Ukrainians in their stronghold. Stephan Bandera's band of guerilas is the target." he continued quickly, "They need Polish labor to bury the dead, and they will have the Ukrainians witness the Poles burying the corpses, which will inflame an already tense relationship so the Ukes will start to kill all the Poles and Jews. Then the Russians can unify the Poles and Jews against the Ukrainians as the enemy. For them, Bandera killing Poles, Jews and Russians, would hasten hatred towards Ukrainians. If they take

285

Andrew, he will return, but it would be best for him to hide and stay out of sight."

Marianne thanked Leopold for the information and grabbed the children by the arms and rushed home. Too late! Almost as she got there, Russian soldiers were approaching Andrew, who was working on the weeds in the rows of vegetables. The sight of the NKVD uniforms and automatic rifles was brutally menacing. The men pointed their guns at him, and demanded his papers, which he.supplied at once. His quiet strength and lack of fear always seemed to set the men in authority off. These soldiers had been commissioned as part of a special NKVD unit assigned to execution squads, who reported directly to Dorovitz and were malicious, hateful, well fed and unemotional. Andrews' papers were examined carefully and then handed back. Marianne and the little ones were terrified.

The soldier in charge nudged Andrew with his rifle barrel in the direction of a truck, from which he had come. "Get in there," he said. "Your husband will be joining other workers."

As they marched along pushing Andrew ahead of them, he had a certain look in his eyes, one that Marianne had seen before, as if to tell her "Don't worry. I'll be back." He had been taken away again. Each time, it seemed to Marianne, that he had less and less of a chance to return. "Tata will be back. He will be safe. I promise." she told her children. "Your Tata is strong and brave, and he loves you all. Let's pray. We all love him so," she said gently.

Marianne was stuck at the old farmhouse with the children; she would be observed and needed to keep up appearances of her daily work. Ordinarily, she could send the children to be watched, and leave to go to their Sanctuary in the woods. However, today, she could not appear to be missing. Cautiously, she returned home, but was ready to leave at a moment's notice. She pictured Andrew in a pool of blood, as she kept up her vigil waiting for his return; however, after a while she decided it was a lost cause for today. After dark she returned to the forest's safety.

Special NKVD units were assigned to Kovel even before Andrew arrived there. That afternoon, smoke began to billow in the street, with great blue-black clouds drifting into the sky. Andrew heard people screaming when the truck stopped at the edge of town. The truckload of Polish men was released and led down the road toward the town. "They're killing Ukrainians." screamed a man running by. "God's curse is on the place."

Andrew felt that he again had arrived in Hell; this is what it must be like, he thought. Tortured cries could be heard everywhere, as people were being rounded up and taken into a large red brick trimmed building in the center of town. This stately building with twin towers holding the traditional Ukrainian red onion roofs was now surrounded by a large, high stockade fence. A crowd of people had gathered along the edges of the street as line after line of prisoners was led inside. From a loud speaker, a faceless, horrible voice announced, "Regulators, Jews, Byelorussians, Poles, and Russians, Go back! Go to your homes! We're only killing Ukrainians. We're only killing Ukrainians!"

Andrew and the others were forced to line up against a building inside the courtyard behind the fence. They were told to dig a huge pit across the yard. As they dug, they feared it was for them, but the guards kept hurrying them and saying that they needed space for the new Ukrainian arrivals. The NKVD guards were dressed in summer bloused shirts, waving their Nagant revolvers about casually. Andrew thought that they looked and smelled as bad as usual. When the pit was completed the Poles were lined against the fence to wait and watch as each prisoner, men, women, young teenagers and often a child were led from interrogation rooms in the building to the wall, until there was one long line, and then several NKVD stepped forward and shot them in the back of the head.

Andrew realized that these were villagers, like him, who had been brutally tortured, starved, and interrogated, bleeding, deformed, and blinking at the bright light. These were neighbors, friends and compatriots whose only crime was to live in the wrong place, at the wrong time, and to know nothing about Banderivtsi. The mass murder was completed methodically, and unemotionally. Andrew alternately wept, and prayed for each tortured soul. When the entire line had fallen, the Poles were forced to carry the bodies and throw them into the pit, and then to stand against the fence and watch as the next line was brought out. The procedure was repeated until the men could hardly stand. Outside the fence, women and men were screaming names of their loved ones, hoping vainly for an answer. The bodies had no identifying papers, but were just tossed into the pits.

A few years later, citizens begged the Nazis to allow these bodies to be recovered, and eventually they were permitted to search through the remains for parents, husbands and children. However, in this time, to the NKVD, they were just so much dead meat. A solider repeatedly told Andrew's line "It's time for the burial detail!" Andrew was placed next to two elderly men, and they were ordered to carry the corpses. The first body that Andrew handled was a woman who was badly burned. One of the older men who bent over to take hold of her legs, screamed when her lips moved. A soldier shot the woman in the mouth. Blood splattered on the old man who jumped back in terror. "Get that Uke into the pit. If you don't hurry, you can go with her." a soldier commanded

They worked feverishly, piling bodies on top of bodies. Andrew blessed himself repeatedly, and then said a prayer over each body he handled, while trying to block out the faces of the dead, especially those of the children. Occasionally, there was a pistol shot when a soldier found someone alive, but as the removal continued, there were fewer shots. Finally, the only sounds heard were the commands of the NKVD, the labored breathing ring of the burial squad, as they carried bodies to the pits. It went on late into the night when the NKVD soldiers set up powerful spotlights. Andrew was so tired that he could hardly move; however, he continued to carry the corpses by their legs to the grave. The ground at the edge of the pits was slick with blood. Inwardly, he hoped that the silent prayer he said for each person, would do as the last rites for their souls and he knew, as he prayed later, that they would go to a better place with God. The process went on for a long time before the dead were at rest. Andrew was sick to his stomach; his body was trembling, and he stared at his hands. Then he looked with disgust beyond the tall, well-fed soldiers in the shadows towards Dorovitz's home.

Several days later, a fretful Marianne, took her sleepy children to Luba's house in the forest, and hurried to her tree with the hidden transmitter in its green box, very early in the morning. She prayed for it to work; her fingers turned the knob harder and harder. "Eagle, this is Vistula. Please acknowledge." She stared at the green box. Nothing! She hoped and prayed for Andrew's safety yet again. The minutes passed into a seesaw of hope and despair until she finally heard Eagle'voice "Yes, yes, I am here." and as she said, years later, at that moment, God touched her on the shoulder and she knew her Andrew was alive. Eagle was on the other end, his voice hidden by static; however, he was there.

The first words were "You can stop worrying. Your husband is safe. "We'll get him home safely before we have to attack again," Eagle said reassuringly.

Marianne answered, "Oh Eagle, I am so relieved. Where did you see him?"

"We followed a group of slave laborers from Kovel to Sorny, along the road to Pinsk. They were so thin and frail, down to skin and bone, but we saw him. Your husband is alive. We counted 98 men," Eagle continued. "They were very weak, but your Andrew will come home. We are prepared to whisk him away, but we do not want to disclose our identity. He is a strong man. He's only about ten kilometers from Pinsk. They are dropping off the workers village by village, and then executing them as murderers of the Ukrainians. "

He told her that Andrew was at the last of the line of those who were made to complete this grisly task; they were not destined to survive to tell the tale of the NKVD executions, but in the sense of the perverted Soviet logic they were to die as enemies of the state. He went on to tell her that the Russians were reinforcing Polesie's regional headquarters. Russian troops had replaced the Mongolians, Pietrinev tripled his armed guards and the road from Pinsk to Zamolina was heavily fortified. "We will not let anything happen to Andrew. Be very careful" were Eagle's words to Marianne. She pleaded, "Please take all necessary steps to have him return to me. That is all I can ask. Bless every one of you." They say their goodbyes and Marianne shuts down the transmitter.

Early the next morning, after deciding against telling the children about Andrew's return until it happened, a storm with hard rain pounded at the hut door. Marianne looked out and to her alarm, a shadowy figure was stumbling toward her; it was Andrew. The waiting was finally over "Children! Children! It's Tata!"

His cheeks were sunken and his face was chiseled with heavy lines of fatigue. The ripped clothing, drenched by rain, barely covered him, but he was home. Miraculously, they were sitting in the mud and rain, Marianne's head on Andrew's shoulder. It was as if the heavens were crying too, and its tears were blending with their own.

OCTOBER 15, 1940

After telling the whole sad story, Andrew, weary and aching, managed a weak smile, then murmured with a heavy conscience, "If I only had the courage….if only…", but then he stopped abruptly to stare at his bruised hands, that had touched the atrocity of defenseless and innocent lives, whispering from his sense of guilt that he bore witness to in Kovel, "Perhaps, just maybe," he mumbled, "I could have prevented the tragedy…. if only I convinced Ilana how terribly wrong her husband was. I am so ashamed; I must clean my hands from the blood on them."

He looked at his hands and then stumbled out of bed to the wash basin. After a short time, he returned and sat next to Marianne who told him that he had to rest for a few days. The Soviets and its regulators had desecrated the nation, but only God knows how far they have pierced the hearts of it. Marianne went on to tell Andrew that Ilana and Tomas were in the midst of struggles of their own......one against the soul of their home, and the other, the destruction of the spirit.

Andrew was ashamed of his connection to the Dorovitz family, because of his love for the people in the sanctuary. "Now I have to face Josef's widow Luba whom I regard as the soul of Zamolina. Oh dear God, she will soon know that my hands placed Ukrainian corpses into pits of horror." he said.

Marianne reminded him of all the good that they had done, and how many lives they had saved. "You saw firsthand terrifying and awful events; however, you kept your dignity as a man—your heart and conscience remain strong. Tomas Dorovitz is a madman bringing the sorrow and injustice from his political life into his own home. We must connect to Ilana's heart and need for salvation and repentance. That's what is meaningful. We have no choice, but to be close to her. We have a responsibility to save lives, not take them away. Regulators and Soviets rely on agitation and chaos to unify group against group. We are acting with a simple sense of justice, and we all can judge what is right and admit to it passionately." Andrew kissed Marianne gently and said "One does not know what death is unless one has touched it. My darling, your heart is in the right place. Our fight is not finished."

Later on that day, Andrew and Marianne gathered with the regular inner core of the Sanctuary.

Andrew felt he had to find a way to tell the others, including Luba, about the bloodbath that he witnessed. He spoke in his quiet fashion of the torment and torture of the Ukrainians, and the resulting blame on Poles followed by the execution of many of them. Luba's composure cracked, when she heard this, and she completely lost control of her emotions as she shook her fist in the air and shrieked, "I detest them. Those regulators deserve the same fate that came to the Ukrainians. The Nazis should get to them and end their miserable lives. They deserve a slow painful death."

The general feeling of this small band of patriots was to kill Dorovitz, Ilana, and their family. Jan Malinowski wanted revenge. He looked at Marianne and Andrew and said, "We are focused too much on

Ilana and her information; what use is it if it happens anyway, and furthermore is ignored. Tomas Dorovitz is behind terror perverted with horrible lies. Those bastards! We should kill them."

Marianne waited for a quiet moment amid the angry shouting and told them. "Ilana is our protection. I believe she would take a bullet to save her children, and that means she has the courage to return the human spirit to her home."

The buzz persisted, but Andrew stopped the whispering and Marianne continued:"Ilana is a witness for all of us. She suffers in her own way, and I believe she will never stop suffering for what her husband has done and is doing."

Andrew looked at Luba and said with his quiet strength. "Although the NKVD ignores the cries of the hungry, tortured, burned and maimed, they have lost their soul. We can judge them, but the final decision is God's. Jesus taught us 'Judge not lest you yourself be judged', and even with the atrocities that we live with, God's purpose, whatever it might be, must be seen to. There will be more deaths, for Tomas believes and supports the need for them. Ilana still keeps, at least privately, her religious beliefs. Although they are different from ours, she still sees a need for atonement and salvation and that living cannot be based on hatred and guns. The responsible act is to save her children's souls. Dorovitz is only living to travel from this Hell to his next one. We, meanwhile, are saving ourselves. Let us pray that the Ukrainians did not die in vain and will find peace in God's world where only he knows why they died so painfully. Let us pray for them and for Ilana since she will always suffer from what Tomas Dorovitz has done and is doing."

They all found a quiet moment as Andrew bowed his head, and took the hands of Marianne on his left and Luba on his right; all of them joined hands then, and prayed silently in front of the icon of the Black Madonna. When done, they blessed themselves and sat quietly in the forest as if waiting for a word from their Heavenly Father. A great sense of peace, in the midst of this tumultuous world, settled on them suddenly.

Magdalene was the one to break the silence by saying, "We need to pray for the soulless; not all of whom are Bolsheviks. Some are just thieves. Others have a soul. The regulators know Stalin's will, just as we are ignorant of God's. We trust in him; they cannot trust in Stalin." "I wonder", she went on "if Stalin is indeed their new God? If this Nazi Blitzkrieg will crush eastern Poland and beyond into Russia, these regulators will be punished by the next soulless army; they will be blamed for worshiping Stalin. They will suffer then. They are now in constant fear of the Nazis and Ukrainians. Ilana is not alone"

Luba took Andrew's hand and said "I have no man in my house here in the dark burrows of the forest, yet this Sanctuary is my angel of life. Rest in peace, my husband; as a mother I believe that; saving the lives of Ilana's children is the right path, and while the winter approaches we must concentrate on survival and feeding the hungry."

Marianne felt that the gathering had reached a conclusion; however, just to provide some closure and a direction to the future she told them "We are not living by bread alone, but on determination, discipline, and truth. Not everything is dark. We are hungry and empty in Zamolina. We must save all our children, keep faith and learning in the middle of this madness. Dorovitz will continue on his evil path. Ilana will cling to her Judaic values to save the souls of her six children. We, too, will continue to stand firmly...at the roots of home. We must put an end to any discussion of killing Ilana."

Marianne took her children and Andrew into the forest to forage for mushrooms and nuts for the winter; at last she felt some relief in this task as it was done by the family for their home.

MONDAY NOVEMBER 25, 1940

Rumors of a massacre of Polish officers in Katyn Forest in April or May of 1940 only reached the interior of the Pasternak Sanctuary by November. Close to twenty two thousand Polish officers, policemen, and intelligentsia lay massed in several large graves in Katyn forest. They had been imprisoned, starved, and tortured and were taken by the truckload to the woods where they were executed, one after the other, by a single bullet to the back of the head. The guns used were not always the usual NKVD Nagant, but German 7.65 mm Walther PPK pistols as well, which originally were imported to lessen the strain of repeated recoil on the executioner, but were used later as supposed "proof" that the Nazis executed these men. Methodical executions were carried out day and night, the sounds masked by heavy machinery, and without the prisoners being aware that the man in front of them was being killed. Giant pits were excavated and filled with corpse after corpse. The entire operation was kept top secret, and no evidence appeared until three years later. However, rumors of the event spread underground slowly. Two men, Stanislaw Swianiewicz, and Józef Czapski survived the massacre; Swianiewicz was imprisoned in Smolensk, and more than likely the tale of the horror spread throughout the countryside and into the sanctuaries.

The world, including the Nazi invaders, was entirely unaware of this evil process. Ethnic cleansing was paired with the execution of the finest minds in the country.

Marianne heard of the massacre on Friday, the twenty third of November 1940, six months after it occurred. She felt as if she was hit in the stomach with a great force; for a time she was devastated by the news, repeatedly picturing the individual executions of the finest Polish men. However, she soon returned to the fight at hand, realizing that only prayer and inspiration for continued opposition could help the dead soldiers and leaders.

She had started her usual Friday trip to Pinsk, and after being stopped, searched and humiliated, as usual, she brought sad news home. When she received her two loaves of bread which according to new Russian regulations should feed fifteen families, on the way back to the wagon, she heard the whispered rumors of the massacre from villagers who lived closer to Smolensk. She continued on her way when she saw a sign on a post that read:

Germany occupies most of Western Europe –

France, Belgium, Czechoslovakia, Netherlands

All young men 16-20 report for military duty.

Mobilization of eastern Poland is ordered.

Tomas Dorovitz Commissar

Marianne filled with horror, and images of executions, starvation and approaching tanks spinning in her head, headed for home. The journey, accompanied with the usual stops for checks, identity papers and inquisitions only increased her anxiety. She parked the wagon near the old barn, led the horse to his pasture in the woods, and knowing her children to be safely fostered, headed once again for her "green box's hiding place" and tried to reach the band of resistors. She knew where some of the Eskadry were; Eagle must be located near Kosiv on the northwestern part of eastern Poland, formerly Polish Lithuanian territory, whose population was suffering and anticipating a famine. .He was distributing captured food, from hidden caches in sanctuaries, to villagers under the Polish flag. Food was scarce. Bread was a luxury item available only a few days a month. Meat was almost impossible to find. The sanctuaries continued to be shelters.

Marianne was saddened as Eagle told her that brutal NKVD reprisals were being leveled at Polish and Lithuanian groups. If they found hidden food, they blamed the Trumpeter Eskadry for telling them about it; those who had it were killed or deported to Siberia. Brutality raged on. "Everything around is being destroyed," Eagle said. "The Soviets burned several villages in Polish Belorussia because of suspected guerilla activity. Not one building was left standing, and the NKVD forbade the inhabitants to remove any furniture, clothing or food from their homes before they were torched. Equipment, and especially farm animals, was dragged out of the barns, and several peasants were shot when they tried to protect their herd. The atrocities of murder and rape got worse and worse; Belorussia, an anti-Communist area is rapidly diminishing in population."

In the limited amount of time that they could stay on the air, Eagle recounted atrocities in Gorodek, where when food was taken from a supply depot at the Soviet regulators' station, the NKVD arrested local school boys and threatened to have them whipped unless they disclosed the identity of the Trumpeter Eskadry; when there was no result their parents were forced to beat their own children. When no one admitted to the crime, ten boys were chosen at random and then shot by an NKVD firing squad.

Marianne stared at her green box, disheartened by this news; she felt that all of these acts, including the rumored massacre, needed world attention. However, in the case of Katyn Forest, all that was known was only hearsay; in a moment of inspiration she made a decision. The trumpeter Eskadry could possibly find evidence in Katyn forest, and even if the world leaders and press did not acknowledge it, which she hoped they would, at least the people of the land would know it to be truth in light of NKVD propagandistic lies.

She talked rapidly to Jan, because air time with this wireless could bring about discovery for both of them. She told him of the rumored massacre and she said that the evidence of Katyn Forest murders needed to be exposed.

Jan replied. "If the massacre of the Polish Officers did occur, and the cover- up was to be revealed, the mystery would be removed, and the world would know the true character of the regulators."

"Jan", she answered quickly, "Do you think that you could start by looking for the missing soldiers in Katyn Forest, and find proof there of who was responsible? I'll try to find a way to get the information out to those who need to know. "

"We'll start right away."Jan replied. "The snowstorm will make travel and search harder, but we'll go from Kosiv to Smolensk, and then to Katyn Forest. We will try to bring back evidence of the shootings."

Marianne added that there must be some kind of route to the place of execution, maybe guarded and maybe covered up; she told Jan to see what he could find.

He said that he would do his best and get back to her; meanwhile, she should keep up appearances to everyone in her area, and whatever the need, do not mention or discuss Katyn. If the regulators or Dorovitz thought there was any knowledge of this slaughter, the reward would be instant death.

SATURDAY DECEMBER 14, 1940

Winter landed heavily in Polesie, and in the forest sanctuary, only the Black Madonna remained clear of snow, as the faithful gathered each morning to clean up the altar. Kneeling and praying became almost a penance as the icy ground was hard, and very, very, cold. The elderly and small children were kept inside huts, warmed by the peat fires burning all day and night. Food, although scarce, had been carefully cared for, and most were comfortable with their rations. The temperature dipped below zero this morning, for the first time, and Marianne had walked through the snow to meet Jan and Stanley whose figures gradually emerged from the grey blue fog and snow.

They followed her carefully to her "extra" hut, where once the fire was lit, they were able to speak. They came with the news that they had found the victims of the Katyn massacre. "After we talked to you," said Jan, "we gathered our group and headed for Smolensk which is about 18 kilometers from the forest. We tried to find a road or path into the wood; however, as the ground grew more and more frozen it became difficult. We eventually saw half a dozen guards on a roadway which appeared to run into the forest and we took them alive, stripped them naked, and sat them on the ground; their choice was to lead us to the forest or freeze to death. Karpathia encouraged discussion by putting her pistol to the back of their heads, and asked if this is how it was done. They agreed to lead us to the graves. Unsure of whether we were partisans or NKVD, four of them didn't resist; however, six made a break for their machine guns, and were shot on the spot, covered with snow and then we moved on. It took a while to get oriented to the forest, and find our way through the snow drifts; however, we came to an area, Kozy Gory, which was once a resort, where one of the soldiers pointed to a grove of newly planted trees and whispered, as he crossed himself, "That's where some bodies were buried. There are two or more mass graves of thousands." He whispered again. Another soldier, an Estonian, assuming we were going to kill them anyway, like the NKVD, said "I stood guard for weeks. The line of trucks would pull up to the site in the evening, crammed with Polish officers, priests, teachers and leaders; there were so many I couldn't count them well, but I think they brought two hundred fifty at a time. . The NKVD built a kind of sand bag shelter around a cell- like structure, padded the door with felt, with one entrance at the front and another at the back. They also ran loud fans or some kind of machinery, so that what went on in the cells could not be heard. The soldiers and others were taken off the trucks and told to take out their identity papers for inspection. They were lined up in front of the sand bagged shelter, and one at a time, had their papers checked and then were handcuffed. After they entered the cell, they were forced to kneel, and then were shot, once to the back of the head. The bodies were dragged out of the back exit and thrown into a waiting truck, then were dumped into an open mass grave, which after being bulldozed over, was planted with trees to cover up the pits."

Jan continued telling that some of the soldiers doing the killing were Mongolians, and were there to relieve and supervise the tiring NKVD executioners. Vasili Mikhailovich Blokhin, chief executioner of the NKVD, was responsible for seven thousand deaths by himself, which made him the most prolific murderer in history. Dorovitz was in charge of this part of the slaughter, and he was largely responsible for filling the Kozy Gory Sector of Katyn Forest with the corpses of thousands of Polish Officers and civilians.

Jan told how they made the four Soviet soldiers start digging in search of the dead bodies; however, weather conditions made the quest even more difficult. Temperatures dropped to -17 degrees Celsius, and the digging down to the frost line was hard and fairly lengthy. Finally on Sunday, they found the first corpses, piled one on another, all with a single pistol shot in the back of the head. They pulled out corpses, frozen like bricks, hard as concrete. They were able to cut the shoulder boards off the frozen corpses of five Polish officers and to rescue their papers, which identified them as the missing soldiers. They had ignored the older Russian corpses planted there by Stalin as early as 1929. The frozen dirt kept the bodies almost preserved. There was no way to find other gravel pits or to count how many were buried there.

Jan was lucky to find what they did. The four soldiers that they had captured thought that as many as eighteen or twenty thousand might have been buried there; however, there was no accurate way to count, unless one had the papers of all those who were murdered. Most all were shot in Smolensk and transported over a three month period. They got a signed, sworn statement from one soldier that at least four thousand Polish Officers were shot in the back of the head, and he saw Dorovitz sign, and give the order to dispose of the officers interred in the prisoner of war camps in Smolensk. The NKVD methodically emptied the political "enemies of the state" from other camps as well. Among the thousands dead were civilians providing essential needs ...doctors, lawyers, and teachers. He was able to find the burial ground that was dug up, by his memory of the bulldozers covering over the still quivering corpses. He began to cry, and oddly enough kneel and pray as he wept; saying that this ground steeped blood was now a solemn, holy place.

Jan added somberly "We are lucky to be alive after witnessing the corpses of Katyn Forest. We are as good as dead, now!"

Anger, dismay, sorrow and revenge were words that did not accurately describe the group's reaction to mass murder. They felt as handcuffed and as helpless as the murdered men. They tried to think of what kind of evidence could be produced to prove that they were not concocting a tale to pinpoint the atrocities of the NKVD. "We know they were down there, but we couldn't possibly reach them."

They decided on a grizzly proof of death, and took one of the heads of an officer, marked the place of removal and gently packed it away in snow. If this head thawed, it would really increase in the decaying process. They had taken a sworn statement of guilt from one of the repentant soldiers. The other three were shot. The severed head, however, could not be sent or delivered after it left the freezing weather; the Eskadry, including Marianne, wanted to send the head to Winston Churchill through the underground, but with stepped up surveillance this task would be impossible.

Marianne decided to try to get a letter through the underground, signed by all the witnesses, and delivered to Churchill and Roosevelt. Even if the letter were not to arrive, at least the atrocities would be recorded. The truth needed to be told now. The little band huddled around a small stump being used as a table, and in the smoky light of the "torf" fire helped Marianne write in her best "teacher" diplomatic language:

14 December 1940

Somewhere in the Mountains of Karpathia: HOME ARMY HEADQUARTERS

Dear Zebra and Prime Minister Sikorsky

We have found convincing evidence that there was a Katyn Forest Massacre, during the spring of this year, unknown to the allied world, and it was executed by the Soviets. Twenty-seven to thirty thousand Polish Officers and civilians are buried in mass graves in the areas surrounding Smolensk.

The Soviet atrocities and the occurrences in the Katyn Forest area need to be condemned and investigated. We have tangible evidence of Polish genocide, which includes five shoulder boards of the officers, identification papers found on the bodies, and a confession by a soldier who witnessed the mass murder. Tomas Dorovitz was in charge. Who was to blame? Tomas Dorosz? Laverenti Beria? Since it was done under the Soviet process of regulation, every one of them is responsible.

Polish officers were sent to Katyn Forest area near Smolensk, several hundred kilometers northeast of Janow. The NKVD took the soldiers and civilians from prisons, shot them in the back of the head, transported them to the forest area and buried them together in several mass graves. We think that there were between twenty and thirty thousand of them executed in a short time, and then dumped into burial pits. This is murder on one of the largest scales known to man.

Our source, Ilana Dorovitz of the Soviet System, is knowledgeable of the planning and maneuvering by the Muscovite governing body, and has alerted that Stalin has issued a sealed order to the NKVD to broaden the influence of journalists in America so that Roosevelt can justify giving aid to Soviet Union. Obviously, that is a very sinister maneuver. Please do all you can do to make the world aware of the slaughter in Katyn Forest.

From Eagle, Saber, and your devoted daughter---Vistula

Stanley Kulakiewicz hid the letter in the lining of his coat. Sorrowfully, the small troop disbanded, hoping against hope that this massacre would be seen by the world; they prayed, however, deep within themselves, they felt it would too be ignored.

CHRISTMAS EVE DECEMBER 24, 1940

All the families in Polesie were together on this Christmas Eve feeling shielded, at least for the moment, from the death and destruction around them. Christmas traditions are very important in Poland, and particularly in a year that was filled with disasters and Godless government. Families prepare for Christmas days before the holiday; even in the depths of the forest the women cleaned and scrubbed their burrows as best that they could, for they believed a house dirty on Christmas would remain dirty for all next year.

The Ludwig family, followed the Christian tradition of helping others on Christmas eve or *Wigilia;* therefore, at the crack of dawn, Andrew, Marianne, Stefan and Maria left little Alexandra with the neighboring family in the sanctuary, since the weather was too cold for a baby to suffer, and set out on the now widened and empty roads to Zamolina. They were going to give milk and bread to the families in Zamolina that were not part of the hidden Sanctuary, but very much on their minds. Before the Soviet occupation, the people of the small village were friendly, always expecting to help a neighbor in need. Now on Christmas they needed to be helped.

Polish people believed for centuries that no one should be alone on Wigilia, as a reminder that Mary and Joseph were also looking for shelter, and at every family celebration. Poles were famous for their hospitality, especially during Christmas, and in Poland, an extra seat is kept at the supper table in case someone should arrive unexpectedly. They believed, too, that whatever occurs on Wigilia has an impact on the coming year; therefore, if an argument should start, a year filled with trouble would follow. On Christmas Eve morning, if the first visiting person is a man, it means good luck; if the visitor is a woman, trouble could follow; therefore mistletoe is hung over every doorway to insure good fortune in the coming year. The weather was much the concern for the farmers, who believed that the weather on Christmas influenced the weather on Easter and throughout the next year.

Marianne, Andrew and family returned to the ninety huts which were sunken into the earth and had candles lighted in front of them for the holiday. They echoed the warm glow of Christmas that filled the hearts of those that lived there. The farmers had returned from the ritual of the blessing of the fields with holy water, and the placing of crosses made from straw into the four corners. The regulators would not connect the bits of straw in the snow with the faith still held by those who worked this land. Marianne looked over this little hidden community which had plowed the earth with rough hands and shaped it into cultural, economic, and schooling centers. She looked at the lifesaving vodka distillery, bread-making production, and stash of all varieties of wild mushrooms dried with age, sun and smoke. Marianne, as she gazed out over this woodland village, took Andrew's hand and looked at him with awe and thanksgiving. This group of people, survived the year because of his knowledge of the gifts of the forest, and also she quickly realized with her own leadership, a role she never had expected. She and Andrew had helped men and women, accumulate hundreds of sacks of wild onions, mushrooms, dried fish, and game and wolf skins. The children had benefitted too, by an underground educational system including catechism. The teacher in Marianne realized the need for instruction in troubled times to keep their eye on freedom and morality, as well, as giving them a way to cope with the times in which they lived.

Therefore, the Christmas traditions became even more important on this day in 1940. Even with sparsely decorated Christmas trees in each burrow, and the absence of actual gifts, the time brought everyone together, they felt, to celebrate the greatest gift of all, Jesus' birth. The community gathered near their altar, and brushed the newly fallen snow off the Madonna, as they anxiously awaited the sign of the first star which would signal the start of *Wigilia*. Stanley hugged Marianne and whispered that he and Monika had delivered the letter as far as the Carpathian Mountains.

In normal times, families would gather in each home at a table covered with a white cloth and straw. These people represented a surviving, extended family; therefore Leopold, the Grygas, Rygalas, and Luba cooked a traditional meatless Christmas Eve meal of different kinds of mushrooms, combinations of vegetables, potatoes, wild onions and cabbage. The *Oplatek,* a thin sheet- shaped wafer crust was traditionally broken by the father or eldest member of the family and then half was given to the mother. Small pieces were broken off and shared with the others, while wishing long life and happiness in the coming year. This Christmas, Andrew broke the wafer and shared it with Marianne indicating that they were, at least symbolically, the heads of the village family. There was happiness among friends, heroes, and neighbors who had gathered together. After the supper set outdoors in the cold around a fire, the traditional singing of carols (*koledy*) began. They all sang *Cicha noc, święta noc* (Silent Night) softly in the stillness of the night. When midnight arrived, they knelt in the snow, surrounded by the glowing candle lights, praying together to celebrate the birth of Christ. Andrew assured them all. "We are now surrounded by wonderful vitality and spiritual power, beyond the touch of evil. It is a hopeful road for all of us to take when love bears all." Their only sorrow, at that moment, was that there was no priest for Holy Communion.

Magdalene, Florence, and Luba prepared baskets of candy, sweet breads, and berries covered with honey, and gave them to each of the families for the now sleeping children. The following morning, long ribbons of red and white were placed along the altar on the carpet of snow glittering with light and with sparkles of hope. This was the traditional Polish "First Day", a day for families. They would go off together and celebrate the love of the Christian faith. The Second Day was for visiting extended friends and family. On this First Day, however, the Sanctuary gathered as family, led in prayer by Andrew again. .

"We pray today with love...*My Cheher Boga* Poland is free as long as we are alive" he said emotionally, "Thank God for that!"

Stanley Kulakiewicz and Monika Wisniewska came to say good bye to Andrew and Marianne saying that that they must leave to join a sanctuary in Ratwyn. Marianne had written a letter to her father; she asked Stanley to take it, and hopefully it would reach him. She kept the information brief, and in case the letter was intercepted, she omitted her locale and even the fact that she was housed in a sanctuary; however, she signed it: Your devoted daughter---Vistula and then "Is that all?

SATURDAY FEBRUARY 15, 1941

Andrew, in the past few days, sensed that Tomas Dorovitz had developed a need for religious faith, which since his return from Moscow, appeared to have more meaning in his family's daily life. Ilana told Andrew, "I think I am a better human being with Tomas joining us on the Sabbath and even saying Kaddish for the dead"

His religion had to be secret, which was an additional burden. Exposure could mean the end of his NKVD activities and would reveal Tomas as a worldwide conspirator on behalf of the Communists. Marianne and Andrew both thought that the weight of many murders was on his soul and that he, like others, was seeking salvation. Unfortunately, he was caught between two Godless forces, the NKVD to whom religion was forbidden and the on- rushing Nazis who were openly tormenting and exterminating the Jewish population of Poland.

Tomas was a mystery, as he somehow qualified his own conflict between the malicious actions, while having no guilt as he viewed himself as a pure believer. When he arrived at home, Ilana reminded him of his faith as the fulfillment of his life and family.

Andrew felt that the guilt of Tomas' murderous actions was unbearable for her, so that she would betray her state for the sake of her soul, family and faith. Time was running short, and Andrew had resolved to help Ilana with her conflict.

Marianne was hoping that her decision to expose the Katyn Forest Massacre to whatever part of the world that she could, would be successful, but so far there had been no reply or result from her letter.

SUNDAY MARCH 30, 1941

The torrents of spring brought more Soviet deportations to Siberian camps. The massive death totals were spiraling, and the NKVD goal of reaching 800,000 by summer was only three months away. Some of those who were deported would die a slow death within six months or less, while thousands more Catholic Poles were openly executed by the NKVD.

Tomas Dorovitz was actively involved with deportation and murder on a private level whether executing his own native countrymen or deporting people of his own faith. His actions became tinged with an abnormally evil blood lust. Ilana Dorovitz whispered to Andrew one night, "Tomas will be exterminating every opposition in sight. The regulators are obediently following Moscow's orders," she gravely added.

Andrew's goal was to gather information particularly about the Katyn Forest Massacre. She told him, when she hesitated to continue about the local actions of Tomas one night, that there were events that could not be discussed. Andrew took the opening and said "Is one of them the Katyn Forest incident? The rumor is that Polish officers had been sent there but never came back."

Andrew could sense her feelings of remorse, and also that she knew much more. He felt that eventually she would confess, at least in an attempt to get the sins off her mind.

He spoke to her daily, spending his time on the Dorovitz farm which left Marianne to work the fields near Zamolina. The children were now old enough to go with her; Stefan and Maria were expected to work for the quotas, and the baby could be settled down in the field next to her Mother during the hours from dawn to dusk when she worked. When the spring rains made it impossible to be outside, Marianne could stay in the forest and let the children play with the others, and in some small way have a few moments of a normal childhood. Marianne, herself, became tougher, and one day she found a mirror in her chest in the forest, and glanced into it. She was never a vain person, wasting time on make-up and hairstyles; however, the person looking back at her little resembled the cultured elegant figure that she once was. Her beautiful hair was lopped short, her skin was colored by the sun, and when she looked down at her once soft hands, she saw work- worn fingers and dirty nails. Marianne sighed, but she had no regrets; "God leads us into strange places and ways" she thought, and most precious, she had her Andrew. "What a gift!"

During the days and weeks that followed, Ilana Dorovitz, appeared to Andrew, to be a lonely, devoted protective Jewish mother, wondering if the souls of her children could be saved. During the last days of March, she became obsessed with the idea of Tomas being shot by Vishinski's NKVD, as a witness to mass murder. She knew Moscow's nature. Blood had randomly spilled. Andrew would discuss religion and atonement daily with her, as if she could talk her way to a clean soul. He repeatedly asked about Katyn and always received the same answer, about the danger of the discussion of the destiny of the Polish officers.

"I dare not speak about Katyn Forest," she said as she looked out at her children playing with their friends. "Doubtless they will learn about it someday and when they do, they will be saved by coming to terms with truth."

The sight of her six children peacefully playing in the yard, and the discussion of their future pushed her over the edge; she knew that her husband's usefulness to the Bolsheviks was nearly over; she broke down and sobbed "What if they kill them along with us? My husband is a mass murderer. It is our nightmare; it happened because we allowed it to. There is no moral defense of our actions."

Andrew prodded softly: "Was Tomas Dorovitz one of the men who ordered the mass deaths at Katyn Forest?" Andrew asked again.

Ilana's eyes stared towards Smolensk and down the notorious Vitebsk Highway into the dark forest. "I have waited for this hour for a long time, maybe I will be the one to tell the truth".

Andrew said nothing. Ilana was doing all the talking. Andrew, using his training from the confessional, quietly spoke. "For your own salvation, there is no better time than now for you to step forward before more have to die."

"Let me wait until spring." she said. "I fear the loss of my children and my home more than my husband and the state. By the end of spring, we may know how much longer this alliance between Germany and the Soviet lasts, and whether there will be Western support for Moscow."

"Ilana, I bear no doubts and fear the depths of the unknown. Until the Nazi planes fly over the Polish sky, it shall be."

FRIDAY MAY 15, 1941

Marianne was still saddened by the lack of response to her letter about the Katyn Massacre. If only they could make the world aware of the evil intent and nature of the Soviet Union. Marianne found Adam Makowski and Casimir Pilat and Jan in the Sanctuary, and after they told her of the Eskadry raids on trucks and trains which were still ongoing, she wanted to talk about exposing the Soviet evil intent to the world along with the emigration to Siberia. Holland had surrendered to the Nazis, and the threat to Poland from the on -rushing German army appeared to be imminent; therefore, the Soviets were mobilizing, burning, destroying and murdering everything in their path. Now, the army and regulators were told they were no longer fighting for freedom of man, but for Mother Russia. Marianne thought, although very dangerous, the time was right to see Katyn for herself. They needed more answers. No one cared. Marianne believed that if they could get Ilana to the graves in Katyn and get a photograph and a written confession, that maybe this packet would startle and alert the world press.

She had looked at the map, and she told the others that she wanted to bring Ilana Dorovitz to the forest before the NKVD killed all witnesses. Jan, however, emphatically said no. They all had come to respect her leadership, so that he found it difficult for him to offer a counter plan. After a long embarrassed silence, he told her that they had revisited the area again, at night, and found that it would be impossible to return. The NKVD had removed trees from the path to the forest and widened the road. The old resort on top of a hill overlooking the site was now NKVD headquarters, and the three story building had observation posts for the whole area. To further complicate matters, the small trees planted over the grave site to mask its use served as markers for the graves, so that they could be carefully watched.

Jan met a peasant, who still lived nearby, and talked quietly to the old man , who said he had heard a shot or two in the distance, and the sound of heavy machinery, but he also had seen truckload after truckload filled with Polish soldiers go by on the road, only to return empty. He had counted the trucks, and the best estimate Jan could make from the number of men crammed into each carrier, was that 4,000 men had been buried there.

Casmir continued the story by saying that the rumor mill told of over 22,000 NKVD murders; however, no one knew where the remainder of the bodies were disposed of or buried. Some of the underground said that many were dumped in the Arctic Ocean, while others were reported dumped in Siberia. Marianne was disappointed and very upset. What could they do to make this crime public?

She said "Other people in this world need to feel the horror. The bullet holes! The rattle of dump trucks day and night, and a sinister delivery of death! At least four thousand Polish patriots, teachers, lawyers, doctors, and army officers, the finest and brightest leaders lie in mass graves abandoned inside the darkness of the forest."

Marianne finished as tears rolled down her cheeks, and her emotional outburst caused her companions to remain silent again. When she had regained her composure, she spoke once more. "I want Ilana Dorovitz, a Bolshevik Jew, to stand up and confess to these crimes, not only against Poland, but also against humanity; this will be her atonement. I really wanted to make her walk barefoot to the edge of the forest, wearing muddy clothes, symbolizing the long suffering, bearing the pain of a Soviet Union occupation, and push through the mud over to the coffins and place crude wooden crosses into the ground as a memorial; what can we do now?"

Jan, the soldier, and experienced analyst, mindful of Marianne's emotional connection, had an idea. He said "Look at the situation: we cannot go to Katyn in daylight, and even an approach at night with the NKVD post and flood lights would be suicide. However, we have the one head of a poor officer right here in the forest. We need to bring Ilana to it, sign a confession, and to be pictured next to it."

'The first problem will be to get her to agree to come, meet Marianne and have her picture taken with the skull and bullet hole, and then to put her name to a confession. The best we can do after that is send this confession and pictures out. The second problem is where do we find a camera and get the pictures developed?"

Adam spoke up as a sly grin crossed his face. "Did you know that the Nazis brought their personal cameras to record their victories? Did you also know that these cameras were used as barter with the

Russians for food, and drink and whatever else? I just happen to have one. Do not ask me how I got it, but I have a small Leica 35 mm with a collapsible lens, and I have some film with it."

The others looked at him, and although wanting to know how he retrieved a camera from a Russian, they did not ask. The problem that followed was how to develop film, with the portrait photographers' shops and lab closed, and then who would have the expertise to develop any pictures.

Jan suggested that they search the sanctuaries for former photographers and their chemicals, and then worst case, they could always send raw film in the metal canisters that they came in. Marianne sadly agreed; however the Ilana problem still remained.

THURSDAY MAY 28, 1941

Ten days after posing the problem of getting a confession from Ilana, Andrew agreed to make a cautious effort to help her to make the right decision, and save her children. Marianne told him only of the plan to get a statement, and nothing of severed heads and photography. "The only way she can survive, spiritually is to act morally, and I am afraid something will happen to her at any moment. What she loves most are her six children!"

Andrew took a chance and brought Stefan with him to Dorowitz's farm, to "help" hoping that the sight of this child would trigger Ilana to make the right decision. Marianne, however, took the other children to the field to keep at the weeding of the sprouting crops. After a while, she carried some milk to the neighboring houses across the road and had a hard time even looking at the regulators who were walking pompously through the little village. Marianne decided to ignore looks that would come her way. Some smiled, while others stood in silence; as they did, the anger increased just by being in the presence of these loathsome murderers. She thought that in three or four weeks from today, there may be no time left for most of us. We will all be facing death whether or not one was a Bolshevik, or even a plain peasant. The whole land could be overrun by Nazi green uniforms. One regulator walked over to Marianne and said mockingly "You have your priests. It was announced on the loudspeakers! We will open one officially sanctioned church in Pinsk. How do you feel about that, Marianne?"

She answered quietly, and with no rancor "I am not at all happy with the priests coming to a State sanctioned church. However, it's a miracle."

Although she was churning inwardly, yet happy at the return of priests for any reason, she felt that it all was a ploy to gain favor from the United States before it was too late. They were putting forth a false face of religious freedom, only intended for Roosevelt's politics, and to counter the Nazi's murder of many thousands of priests in Germany. Pietrinev, too, was quiet, and Marianne had an uneasy feeling that this sequence of government was coming to an end. Their current reign of terror against ethnic groups to demonstrate supposed attacks on the regulators, would be motivation for America to align with the Soviets. Marianne fully expected the Bolsheviks to run and save themselves, leaving the population in Poland to whatever fate that the oncoming Nazi invasion would hold for them.

Pietrinev walked out his door and directly to her, leaving her a bit startled at his presence and even more by the big smile and outstretched hand offered in her direction. She thought we will never be friends. However, she shook his hand for the first time. "We are catching up," he said, "Thanks to your workers."

Marianne left him as he stared at the passing trucks returning 'loyal Bolsheviks" to Moscow. She took her children to find her good friend Leopold, on picket duty. He was happy to see her, and they sat on a log nearby. She whispered: "You must leave for the Sanctuaries. You will soon see the Nazi troops come marching through here. Soviet soldiers will not survive, therefore, be ready to go on a moment's notice."

"Something's up all right," Leopold said, "But no one seems to be getting too worried. Pietrinev just shrugs it off with a wave of his hand, believing us to be allies. But I will certainly go to the Sanctuaries tonight!"

Marianne and the children took leave of Leopold, and walked back into the forest, where, once settled, Marianne began to worry about Andrew's progress. She tried to reach anyone on her wireless, but to no avail. Then she heard planes overhead. The Russians had no need to fly over; therefore these must be the German Luftwaffe, and their approach meant that danger was imminent.

FRIDAY   MAY 29, 1941

Ilana, not only heard the planes but saw them too. For her family, a Nazi presence meant death to them, because they would be part of the "final solution". The aircraft caused her breaking point; Ilana shed all of her reserve and began to cry with the realization that her entire family could be wiped out in a moment.

"Andrew! I saw the planes," she said after running to him in the field, far from the house. She started to hug little Stefan, and repeatedly stroke his head. She was babbling and sobbing about being Jewish, and a mother, and a Bolshevik, but after a while Andrew realized that she wanted to meet Marianne, and make a full confession. She said she would do whatever was asked and tell her everything, if her children would be cared for after her certain death. She said she knew that this moment would come, and after the shock of the coming invasion, she was prepared for anything. She clutched Stefan tightly to her, and kept repeating "precious children" over and over.

Andrew comforted her, and hugged her as he said: "Your children will survive and reach adulthood, and millions of lives will be spared. It is the most heroic decision you could possibly make. God is merciful, Pani Dorovitz. The cycle of revenge killings must stop, and the War must not be prolonged."

He reassured her about her decision and set off towards home with Stefan. When he got there, he told Marianne of the decision, and although happy at the outcome, he as always, was concerned about the person. Where would her soul go? What kind of forgiveness and salvation could she garner? Marianne was convinced that this was the right path, and she asked Andrew if Ilana had ever considered the souls and salvation of the thousands of people murdered by her husband. Andrew stood firm in his belief that salvation of each and every one was important to God, and that if the will of God had allowed these many sons of Poland to die, their salvation had already taken place. Ilana on the other hand, was the first of these amoral people, that he knew, to turn toward her own faith, and to her own God for forgiveness, and that her confession should be welcomed in the path of faith and not as a result of revenge. He pointed out that the lives of her children were most important. He left the burrow, a solitary figure, and walked slowly with head bowed to the icon of the Virgin; there he knelt and fervently prayed for the souls of the Dorowitzes and wished for them a return to the home of God.

MONDAY JUNE 8, 1941

In the early morning of June 8th, Marianne was tossing about on the straw pallet that served as a mattress in the burrow; Andrew was peacefully sleeping, as were the children. She still wished to get Ilana into Katyn Forest, concerned that any photographed or written evidence would be insufficient. The Soviets were masters of deceit, and cover-ups, and the massacre in the isolated forest would remain masked for years to come, leading to more murders and sacrifices. Marianne could only pray that someone would come forth and notice the warnings that they planned to send.

Ilana Dorovitz was an intriguing enigma; "Was she as closely watched as Marianne suspected she was, and above all could she be trusted?" Andrew had reassured her that Ilana's intentions were honorable and that she knew of the Sanctuary for a year and did not report its whereabouts to the NKVD.

When the sun came up, Marianne woke Andrew, hugged and kissed him hard, as he was her salvation she thought, fed the children, offered morning prayers, and hurriedly took the children to Luba for the day. She had to go to the center of the clearing, near the Virgin where she was to meet Jan, Casmir, and Adam. However, this morning she was taking a circuitous route via her farm and crops. When she got there, she wasn't a bit surprised to see the Russian trucks heading eastward; she glanced at the Zamolina square and there didn't appear to be a soul stirring. There was no sign of military or NKVD guards on the road, and little attention was being paid to the fields and the farms. The rats are leaving a sinking ship, she mused, as she took some water from the cistern behind the farm cottage to put on her small vegetable garden behind the house. Andrew was going to lead Ilana from the farmhouse to the sanctuary, and Marianne wanted to be sure that observers weren't going to be on hand. The area was clear and she started back to the sanctuary, and as she did each time she took the trip, she marveled at Andrew's clever construction of a hidden entrance behind the pig sty near the shed next to the woods. Behind it was an apparently random pile of brush and roots, which a seemingly careless farmer had stacked when he found them with his plow or they had to be cut to clear an area. On the right hand side of the pile, there was a small hole, which appeared to be caused by the haphazard configuration of the roots and branches; however, it allowed a person to crawl inside the pile, and if that man or woman continued forward and turned again right, it led to a low overhang of brush further into the forest. If one was to continue on that path, bent almost in two, it in turn led to a forked pathway. On the left hand side of the path was a small stump, the right hand side was clear of any vegetation. The stump marked the path toward the sanctuary, the clear side led into the marsh and swamp. Marianne hurried along the path

309

toward the huts and then further on the carefully camouflaged marked path to the sanctuary.

Everything was in readiness when she arrived. Magdalene had solved the photography problem; she found a black market entrepreneur who had taken over a studio in Pinsk, and salvaged the chemicals and paper needed for developing photos. He agreed that he would process film, only to the stage of negatives for two cases of vodka. He had succumbed to all of Magdalene's charm and persuasion. She was in at the hut in which they usually met, with Casmir, Jan and Adam. At their feet was a box containing the gruesome baggage of a skull with a bullet hole in the back of it. Casmir had the camera and six rolls of film. They all hugged and sat down to wait for Andrew and their visitor. They were joined, moments later, by former Russian soldier Leopold Kabryn, who was now a resident of the sanctuary as well. Marianne had asked for his help, as sort of an expert on Russian manslaughter and murder.

The use of Ilana's confession was not totally clear to all of them. Once written and photographed, how could it get to where it needed to be for world attention, or at least for someone to take some action? No one knew for sure. Hopefully a picture was worth twenty-seven thousand truthful words.

Finally, through the thick brush, an impressively built woman, who was stout and strong, walked slowly towards them. Her face was muddied. Marianne's first reaction was to be filled with a melancholy sadness, for she was so unlike the woman who saw her at St. Andrew's and expressed gratitude that her children attended school with Stefan. Only a few yards away, with the accustomed Bolshevik paranoia, she looked frantically around to see if she was being followed. She wore high leather boots and a leather coat.

There, deep in the woods of Polesie, unprompted, she gave her heartfelt confession. She had taken Marianne's hand in greeting, but wouldn't let go of it. She still clasped Andrew's hand tightly as well. She took in the small group and began to weep, even though they scarcely resembled a tribunal, she started to confess and pour forth her soul. "You have done what you needed to do to survive in this hideous world that we created for you. I am offering my death for your farewell blessings and for your forgiveness." Andrew clasped her hand to his chest and began to silently pray.

Ilana continued, her voice taking on strength as she spoke, "We were all born with a soul. My husband Tomas lost it, and I went along with a lust for selfish power. We made a mockery of what is right and wrong in this world and our only end, as we see it now, will be tragedy. I am prepared to do what you want."

Marianne said to her, realizing that Ilana feared for her life among this vigilante group, believing all the horror stories that the NKVD had told about them, said "We have no intention of asking for your death, nor would I ever violate your trust. I believe that you will do everything to save lives."

Ilana looked at her, "My dear, Marianne, I have trust in you. Should you survive, I am asking you to give your spirit to my beloved children. Germany will be invading soon, maybe in the next week or two, and before they do, Tomas and I expect to be shot. They will come for my children anytime now. The young Bolsheviks and middle level officers are fleeing towards Moscow, or they will stay here disguised as civilians, to be part of Moscow's resistance organization. Old leadership will be buried among the neighboring graves. Those who come and grieve for their neighbors will spit at ours. I don't want my children to be buried with Tomas and me. It is all over for us. We are the sacrificial lambs of the Soviets' atrocities."

Marianne broke the silence which was then only punctuated by Ilana's sobbing. Andrew held her upright, as Marianne told her "We were treated disgracefully and badly by the regulators which we can never forget or forgive; however, I will cherish your truth and your blessings. The fight is not over for me. I have been fighting tirelessly against the Soviets, and I am prepared to give my life against Nazism. I love this Polish ground on which we are standing. Someone has to bring our cause to light and attention."

Ilana pulled Marianne and Andrew to her in a hug, the others observing, felt as if they were witnessing a sacred moment. The baring of the soul outside of the domain of the confessional or atonement service was a frightening time. Ilana had tears streaming down her face and said again "I trust you! "

Marianne broke from the embrace and brought a few sheets of paper and an old piece of board to her to serve as a writing surface. Ilana looked up, wondering what she needed to write. Marianne explained that a full confession of the Russian extermination of Catholic Poles, intelligentsia and military, originated in Moscow, was carried out on a large scale and also was blamed on other ethnic groups. She then gave

Ilana her father's fountain pen, which she thought fitting for this confession.

Marianne went on to say that names should be included clearly in this incitement of crime against Poland and humanity .Beria, Vyshynsky, Frenklin, Berhman, Stalin, were to blame at the Russian National level and Dorovitz and Pietrinev locally. Ilana had agreed to write that, and swear to the contents. She was also asked to blame her husband for his part in the Katyn Forest murders. At this moment, Jan produced the single skull from its box and placed it in front of Ilana, and said "Someone has to be blamed for this death and the thousand others like it, write about it as well, and we know you will accuse your husband as being one of the directors of this massacre".

Ilana gasped at this poor decayed head, with its single bullet hole, on top of the box in front of her and began to weep. The description of the executions that she had heard could not match the reality of this single, lonely skull, once housing a man's brain and emotions, now reduced to an empty shell with a hole in the rear. This head, she realized, was only a symbol representing thousands more like it. She pulled herself together, and started to write on the paper that she had been given.

" *I, Ilana Dorovitz , being of sound mind and body, and under no duress or pressure , confess that during the Soviet occupation of fourteen million Polish citizens, close to three and half million were mass murdered, -Thousands of intelligentsia were abducted, tortured and killed during the first three months of the War. Moscow's mass murderers covered-up the horror to hide the truth.*

Katyn Forest is now a monument to one of history's greatest modern massacres. More than twenty thousand men and women were executed one time, and four thousand bodies were buried in a mass grave in the Katyn Forest, the rest of the bodies are now lost somewhere in the Arctic Ocean, and to Siberia. NKVD agents executed each person individually with a single shot to the back of the head, using German pistols, not only to be able to blame the Nazis later but to relieve the strains on the arms and shoulders of the executioners. My husband Tomas Dorovitz, I, and the men from Moscow with whom Britain and America are presently negotiating, are the only remaining witnesses.

My husband Tomas Dorovitz told me that Nazi persecutions will intensify in the coming months, Moscow will continue to point at victims for its own safety, saying that the Jewish population, and the Communist surrogates, collaborators, and black market profiteers are at the heart of the problem in this area. As a result over two million Jews will be buried on top of three million Polish graves. Another million or so more are in Siberia dying a slow death.

The allied world of forces of freedom needs to kill as many Nazis and Soviet Regulators as possible, and then let the Nazis and Russians destroy each other. We all will perish as we have lived."

Ilana Dorovitz June 8, 1941 Forest of Polesie

This confession took longer than expected, and Ilana, emotionally wrought, stopped writing for a moment. Marianne gave her a glass of vodka, and the rest of the party watched her in silence. They asked her to make more copies of this letter, which she did. The idea they had was to try to distribute it with an accompanying picture in different directions, hoping that the letter and photos would reach the right person, one who had the power to use this information.

Jan and Casimir placed a large stump in front of the Virgin, and put the skull on top of its container. They escorted Ilana to it, and handed her a gun, the NKVD model Nagant. They had asked her to point it at the bullet hole in the back of the skull for a picture. Ilana said that she would do that, however, when the moment came, her hands started to shake and she began to sob violently. Marianne rushed to her side, and held her up, and then she too started to cry. Andrew came over to both women and held on to them, while he prayed out loud for the soul of the unknown soldier; as he did, the other members of the Eskadry, who had seen so much death and destruction, knelt together as if on cue, and began to weep as well. Finally, Casmir took the camera, and the accompanying six canisters of film which Magdalene had scrounged, and began to take picture after picture in the bright light of the midday sun. The plan was to use five rolls of film to be developed into negatives, and to keep one undeveloped for later use. Ilana was shaking violently as she stood there as Andrew reassured her that this penance would relieve her soul and release her children to a better way of life. "God hears all voices" he said, "Jesus helps us; however, Yahweh the God of the Ancient Hebrews will grant you forgiveness as well."

He began to pray in Hebrew, ancient words meant to calm her, and show her God's love. *"Yivarech'cha Adonai v'yishmerecha. Yaeir Adonai panav eilecha v'chuneka. . Yisa Adonai panav eilecha v'yasem l'cha shalom."*

He had covered his head with his farmer's cap, which he then took off and crossed himself as he said with the same blessing only this time in Polish:" May God bless you and keep you. May the light of God's face shine upon you and be gracious to you. May God watch over you and give you peace." Andrew believed in all spirituality, and was letting Ilana know, at least symbolically, that her children's faith would be nurtured.

It took quite a while longer to finish; each roll of film had to be rewound by hand and removed into the canister in the dark of a burrow. Each roll held 36 pictures and Casimir took every one, and Ilana, by this time, buoyed by Andrew and Marianne, held her ground. When she finished, and returned the pistol to Jan, Ilana Dorovitz turned towards Smolensk, and looked off into the distance at where her home should be. Marianne turned to her and said, "You chose the right course; we will care for your children no matter what."

They took the very weary lady to Marianne's own hut and fed her the wild mushrooms and dried food that they had, and added a bit more vodka, cherry flavored this time. Ilana looked at them all and said: "I can't believe you lived like this, and I know that there is hate in your heart, but what you had, that I did not, was faith and love."

Tears were streaming down both their cheeks. "Marianne", she said "I am not grieving because I have to die for my Communist beliefs, but because I have not shown my children a moral way of life; you have done so much for your people, and I trust my children in your hands. Tomas and I remain to live in our own self-created Hell. My eldest son's name is Aaron, and my youngest is my daughter Myrna who is seven. Tomas and I have decided to leave the children's future in your hands."

Marianne assured her that the Pasternak Sanctuary would embrace them as their own, and that her children would be considered one of an extended family. She went on to say that they would be able to retain their Jewish faith, even in difficult coming times.

"Marianne, there is more that you need to know. Tomas and I knew that Marianne Krull did not die on the road to Pinsk. We know that you and she are one and the same. Even though it is difficult for me to see, in the light of your kindness, the killer and leader that had been reported on the loose. We will take this secret to the grave."

Andrew, Marianne, and the Trumpeter brigade could only bring this broken woman to the edge of the forest, from there she had to continue on alone. At least she had regained a spiritual identity but the price of her political choice was her family. They watched as she slowly walked toward her home, a solitary figure on a lonely road to her doom.

The Eskadry had agreed to deliver the letters to higher authorities with the hope of exposure of the Russian murderers to the world press. They realized the many obstacles in the way of the couriers, and the dangers that lay ahead. Marianne had added one letter of her own to her father, which said very little, in fear again of revealing her whereabouts, hoping that he was safe.

Andrew led her back to the Sanctuary where they carefully placed Ilana's letter, and roll of film into the storage space in the Madonna, who was now know fondly as the Black Madonna of the Forest. They both prayed there quietly for the dead soldier, whose head had now been properly buried, and most for the soul of the lost Ilana Dorovitz and her family.

MONDAY JUNE 15, 1941

On her daily visit to the village square, Marianne heard loudspeakers announce that NKVD forces in Pinsk "defeated a significant enemy element," the Banderivsti, who were blamed for the deaths of six hundred regulators. Roadside bombings near Janow struck Soviet army vehicles killing twenty-six Soviet soldiers, and Pietrinev, still looking like the overweight, dirty, gap- toothed martinet in an ugly uniform, blamed Ukrainians for the attack. "We know that it is the work of their terrorists, and our forces are trying to trace and capture them," he told the slowly gathering crowd, while fondling the pistol at this belt.

The NKVD, desperate for cover on their exit from the area, was killing regulators and Jews, and blaming it on the oncoming Nazi forces. Time was very short for Marianne to gather Ilana's children; her growing fear was that Ilana and Tomas Dorovitz might be killed before long by the NKVD, but also by the extremely vengeful Banderivsti who now supported the Nazi's Crusade in the area. The armed and masked killers were leading attacks against regulators; who they were was a question, because the motives were NKVD driven. The sacrifice of the regulators as the wrathful evil-doers would unite local citizenry in a resistance movement against the Nazis. At someone's whim, anyone could be killed for helping the regulators, or be shot for merely being Catholic Poles. At checkpoints, on the roads, nervous soldiers were killing civilian suspects. Vehicles and convoys were blasted away and hundreds of regulators had been executed along the road from Brest-Litowsk to Pinsk.

TUESDAY JUNE 16, 1941

The announcements and postings in the village square were coming at a rapid pace. When the crowd assembled in front of Pietriniev's headquarters, Marianne found herself next to a young, Jewish man in his early twenties. He was wearing the traditional yarmulke, which covered his whole head, and left his *peyos* hanging down his cheeks. He was reading his *Torah* and swaying to the tune of the ancient Hebrew prayers. Marianne glanced down at his prayer shawl (*tallis*) with the fringes hanging below his black vest. She thought how dangerous his garb was to his presence in the square, and also how he seemed to have the belief in his own faith, even if it too was forbidden in a spiritless society, when he whispered hurriedly, "Fifteen gunmen stormed Jewish homes in Pinsk at about 2 P.M. They arrived in civilian cars wearing NKVD military uniforms, and took hostages at gunpoint. An hour later the bodies lay on the streets of Pinsk. Their hands were sawed off to send a message that the Ukrainians are determined to cut off every Jew, for black market profiteering against the State. The gunmen had shouted, "We're coming after you, Jews. We cannot live without victims." One had to be a fool not to know that it was Moscow's NKVD."

How could they, she thought, protect six Jewish children safely in the Sanctuaries?

Pietrinev appeared on the porch, chewing at a morning roll, dribbling crumbs down his already food- stained uniform front. Marianne wanted desperately to talk to him, and approached the porch before he could speak to the crowd. He then raised his eyes at her, and asked, giving a full view of his broken teeth and mouthful of bread, "What do you want? I am busy."

"The loudspeakers said that priests are allowed to return to Mass, and that services will be held on Sunday at an officially sanctioned church in Pinsk. Can my family go to Pinsk for Mass on Sunday?"

He grunted an assent and mumbled, "Certainly, you will be safe."

"Thank you Colonel." she replied, and walked to the edge of the crowd, while the Colonel, without bothering to wipe the crumbs off his face, turned to the assembled villagers.

He addressed the issue of 3000 Jewish corpses, many mutilated, surfacing in towns and village squares. During the last two weeks, hundreds of men were kidnapped, tortured and executed in Pinsk. "As leaders, we are struggling to avoid killings, but Jewish bodies are suddenly piling up. A string of bombs exploded in Pinsk City, killing nearly 50, mostly Government Regulators. We believe Banderivsti, an ally of Germany, are responsible. We must resist Fascist Catholics and fulfill the same sacred duty that we are dying for here. We will concentrate around Moscow. Starting this Saturday, you may leave for Leningrad without being shot."

The young Jewish man, who had been standing near Marianne, spoke and as he did so, a man standing next to him pulled him backwards by grabbing his shirt. The young man shook him off. "We are behaving like fools," he said. "We are Jews killing our own. When will we find the individual courage to stop?"

He pointed at Pietrinev, with his small prayer book still in his hand. "I condemn the Soviet's horror; we will be used as scapegoats and be turned over to the Nazis!"

Pietrinev listened politely, put down his mug of coffee and shot the young man at close range with his pistol. "Never miscalculate the enemy. The Nazis are coming. We need to stay united. Prepare for it." he said.

The silent crowd did not move; guards cocked their guns expecting more trouble, but none came.

Pietrienev just stood sipping his coffee and staring vaguely at the crowd. He continued to show his ruthless and brutal capacity for cruelty, and his lack of compassion for any humanity.

Marianne headed for home, with the slow realization that the Russians were going to leave a bloody trail of murdered Poles on their way back to Moscow. Yesterday, Jan Malinowski told her that twenty-seven Polish workers, men from Hrodna, were lined along the edge of a trench and shot in the head. A majority had been dumped along the wide road of Vitebsk Highway.

WEDNESDAY JUNE 17, 1941

The Nazis were moving further into Poland and eventually through Polesie, leaving a swath of death and destruction. As they approached, the Russians were leaving. Moscow was rushing to deport Poles, Byelorussians, and Lithuanians to Siberia, as well as organizing brown and green uniformed death squads from Latwia, Estonia, Ukraine, and Russia as a beginning of a structured organization of Communist Resistance movement which would try exhausting Nazi supplies, as well as recruiting innocent civilians to support the Communists against their own country.

People living near villages and towns were warned to escape to the forest. Not only will the exiting Russians be a problem, but German Stukas would soon bomb the highways and strafe the streets leading to towns, while Nazi tanks would start to level villages.

Andrew and Marianne had given up the charade of living in the roadside farmhouse, and moved into the safe hut of the sanctuary. Marianne had asked the Trumpeter Eskadry to do picket duty around the perimeter of the enclave, to which they readily agreed and along with the help of other men and boys, they kept a careful watch for danger or intruders. As the afternoon progressed, she busied herself with the chores, sweeping the crude hearth, gathering peat, planning the simple supper and hanging clothes on the crude wash line hanging between tree branches. She was startled by the sudden appearance of Jan and Casmir at her door, accompanied by a short thin bespectacled man who was wearing heavy boots and a long leather coat.

She had not seen Tomas Dorovitz for a long time and was taken by his changed appearance. He was much thinner and drawn than he used to be, and even though the rimmed glasses still perched on his nose, he was now wearing the tradition yarmulke of the Russian Jew. He was really there, a regulator in the forest standing between the guerillas. He stood stiffly, looking at the ground, remorseful yet concerned with the welfare of his children.

"Ilana wanted me to come in person to deliver a plan to get our children to you" He gently fingered the yarmulke, and said "The two of us are doomed. The NKVD will turn on us, particularly Jews, and blame us for the world to see for the situation here. It little matters anymore that signs of my faith are displayed. I am only grateful that I found it, however late, before I die, although all hope of eternal forgiveness is lost to me."

Andrew had been inside washing when he heard Tomas' voice, and stepped out to the perimeter of the little group standing there. When he heard the word "forgiveness" he spoke: "Tomas, there is but one God, although the paths to him and salvation are different for each person and each faith."

Tomas Dorovitz, sadly continued, he no longer resembled the powerful ugly regulator, but was just a little man, shrunken inside a large black leather coat. He continued:"I ask you to trust me."

Marianne looking at this broken figure had a flashback to the time when he was deporting over a million and a half Poles on funeral trains to Siberia, and to his mass murder of six-hundred thousand Polish intelligentsia, and the theft of eastern Poland's property and wealth. This is the hour of truth for Tomas Dorovitz, she thought.

"I trust Ilana; why should I trust you? Are you seeking forgiveness because you are caught? Until you prove yourself, it is hard for me to feel compassion for you. You murdered millions, and now without shame you are still looking for a way out by suddenly embracing a religion that you never observed, or if you did, you abandoned." Marianne snapped back.

Dorovitz's face was frozen into a mask of fear for his existence and imminent death. Then, as if they all could view the change happening, he looked at peace with himself. Andrew had stepped to him and placed an arm around his shoulders. "Even though you were part of a Godless, amoral society, God has a plan, and will forgive all sins as Jesus did the thieves next to him on the cross. God allows salvation and atonement. Have faith; in this hour, we will care for your children at all costs."

Marianne, however, was less forgiving, "You are a present and future threat to our existence. My children and yours may live through Germany's onslaught, the Communist Resistance Partisans, Ukrainian reprisals, but because of you and your contempt for truth, they may not survive. The magnitude of your crimes has transferred a moral Polish culture into one of death and deceit."

"I was part of the Bolshevik group. There are very few of us who realized what it really meant. The most serious threat to our existence, as Communists, was Christian/Judaic beliefs. Many of us lost them." Dorovitz answered. "I hope it is not too late for my children or for me to try to change my path or to do what's right for humanity. I will confess to the mass murder of Polish Citizenry, all of them Poles, Ukrainians, Lithuanians, Byelorussians, Catholics and Orthodox Christians.

He started to shake with emotion, and could no longer speak. Andrew arrived at this moment with a bottle of vodka and pressed it to Tomas' lips. "Drink this" he said "You will feel better for a bit."

The strong drink helped him to continue his confession: "My greatest fear is that my sins will be rested on the heads of my sons. It's over for us, but not for our children. I believe that they will be safe in your care; however, they must be transported safely to you. The little that

319

I could do to make amends is to have identification papers made for you, your family, and my children. You can go back to being Marianne Krull as soon as the Nazi invasion takes place. Having a German name may help. I have registered and changed the ownership rights of the homes and property in Zamolina in Pinsk. Therefore, when the Nazis arrive, all the Ukrainians, including the Varyas can return home. Adam and Florence Makowski will be able to return to their farm, and I have recorded the old Pasternak home and fields of wheat in their name as well."

He paused for another pull on the vodka, and went on: "I made arrangements for the Soviet warehouse with food supplies to be turned over to you. While you are in church, I will meet your comrades in arms there, to empty it while you are at Mass. I will bring my children with me I will stay behind with them at the warehouse, and they can be hidden in the truck, in case there is trouble between Pinsk and here. I am resigned to my fate of death, and I trust my children to you with love and faith."

Andrew was moved at Tomas' acceptance of his fate and with his reconnection to his faith. He took him by the hand to the Black Virgin, and asked him to pray with him in his own way while he prayed in his. Tomas nodded in assent and silently took a prayer book from his pocket. He took off the leather coat, and put on the prayer shawl that he produced from his other pocket. He approached the Madonna and turned his back to the altar, and began to pray in the Hebrew chant that was thousands of years old. Andrew removed his farmer's hat, faced the Virgin and began to pray in Latin. The onlookers could only kneel to look at these two men, of very different faiths talking to God in the outdoor cathedral that no man had built.

"Yitgaddal veyitqaddash shmeh rabba" (May His great name be exalted and sanctified is God's great name.)Tomas started his prayer, swaying in rhythm to the language as all of his forefathers did;

"Agnus Dei, qui tollis peccáta mundi, miserére nobis. (Lamb of God, you take away the sin of the world: have mercy on us.) prayed Andrew as he crossed himself.

"Yitgaddal veyitqaddash shmeh rabba (in the world which He created according to His will!) Chanted Tomas, and as he did, the two men who were both weeping openly got into a cadence of alternating lines.

Agnus Dei, qui tollis peccáta mundi, miserére nobis. (Lamb of God, you take away the sin of the world: have mercy on us);

"Be 'alma di vra khir'uteh (May He establish His kingdom)"

Agnus Dei, qui tollis peccáta mundi, Dona nobis pacem (Lamb of God, you take away the sin of the world: grant us peace)

"Veyamlikh *malkhuteh* "and may His salvation blossom and His anointed be near.

Andrew could not continue, as his voice broke from emotion into sobs, for only he, of all those there at that moment, knew that Tomas was praying the Hebrew prayer for the Dead. Andrew was moved by the desire of one man who had caused so much destruction and evil and was praying to be accepted back into God's kingdom, to be forgiven for his massive sins. Most Catholics believed that anyone, including Jews who did not recognize Jesus as the Messiah, were doomed to Hell. Andrew, however, saw this moment as God's message, and to thank them for getting another sinning soul back to the house of faith.

Tomas told them after he found some composure, that no matter what happened after Mass, they had to get back to the sanctuary. "Andrew," he said," you will be arrested tomorrow at Mass for the profession of your faith. Do not resist; the arresting officers will toss you into the truck which will take you to the warehouse, where we will be waiting. The loaded truck will stop near here, at your old farmhouse, and our children will move in too. Ilana and I will stay on the truck toward Russia."

He walked up to Andrew first, hugged him and said simply "Thank you. You are a good man." He walked up to Marianne, looked up and down and said "Who could have dreamed of you doing so much. I will see you all tomorrow".and he left with Jan.

SUNDAY JUNE 21, 1941

Marianne could not get the scene of the two men praying in the woods last night out of her mind. Andrew was overjoyed of this return to faith .He could not wait to go to a Mass with what he called a "real Priest", and prayed fervently for this Sunday's mass. "I have been waiting a long time for this moment. We are so close!" he said.

She received word, in a brief letter from her father, that although he was alright, he had not heard from her in months. He also wrote of Roosevelt's new policy of treatment of the Soviet Union, which was to place the United States' destiny in the hands, heads and hearts of its millions of free men and women, and its faith in freedom under the guidance of God. The Soviet Union, therefore, could placate Americans of faith by purging the Bolsheviks in charge, as well as by opening churches to rally unification against the Nazis; however, Marianne was tormented by the fact that her pictures and Ilana's confessions never arrived. She could only hope and pray for it. The entire band of Eskadry and friends were assembled in front of the large old cathedral. Only Leopold Kabryn, Jan and Casmir were strangely missing.

Andrew stepped out of the group, and the two wagons, to enter the church first. He always had felt comforted, connected to God, and safe inside the cathedral. He had long missed the Mass, communion, and the atmosphere, longing for the familiar smell of incense, and the echoing chants of the service. As he climbed the steps in front, a few paces ahead of his family and friends, he thanked God for the opportunity to return to the house of Worship. He was shocked when he got inside; the clean stone floor, normally swept, was muddy and there were horse droppings in the aisles. The regulators allowed the return of the single Priest, but left the large room filled with garbage, and excrement as well as broken windows and dirty pews. Andrew stopped, thinking first that this place was desecrated, but after a moment or two, he regained his composure and looked for the cross. He rejoiced at seeing it again on the altar; God's message, he was sure, was that house and trappings did not make the connection, but only the hearts of the people inside. "I am so proud to proclaim our faith at Mass again, and we are blessed to be here and to be together."

Luba started to cry as she genuflected in front of the altar with Marianne. "Let us thank God that we are alive and pray that we get through it all."

Marianne led the children to join Andrew in the very front pew, and. Luba, Justine, Adam and Florence followed. They all sensed, however, the presence of the NKVD lining the back wall, and also one or two newspaper reporters assigned to cover the great return of the Catholic Church to Pinsk. Stefan took out his rosary, formerly forbidden, and prayed as he had been taught. The rosary had survived the Soviet purge, and since there was no chance of his making his first communion, he had been carefully instructed by Andrew how to use it.

As all the heads were bent in silent prayer, the NKVD were whispering loudly, and giggling with each other. There was no music, no vibrating organ sounds, as a priest stepped forward. He was a slight elderly man who had survived the purge of the clergy. He had on old, well-worn paraments shawl, and shuffled to the front of the altar to start the service. Father Ivan had survived bombings, torture and starvation;

322

His balding head, with only a fringe of gray hair, reflected the light as he started to pray. His voice, however, came forth loud and strong as he said:" In *nomine Patris et Filii et Spiritus Sancti. Amen*" marking the first Latin prayer that Andrew had heard in a long time.

The congregation drank in the Mass emotionally, and responded fervently to each part of the service. Unknown to the people of the sanctuary, the old priest had been instructed to ask Andrew Ludwig to deliver the homily.

Marianne glanced at Andrew who was holding baby Alexandria, and had both of the older children clinging to his side. His face was lighted with an inner joy, as he wept unashamedly at every familiar prayer. The priest walked to the front of the altar steps and announced that because of his own release from prison, and his failing health that he wanted Andrew Ludwig to deliver a homily to the congregation.

Andrew, although unprepared for a sermon, flushed, passed the baby to Marianne, walked to the front of the center aisle, and began his speech. "We are all here for a reason today, and that is to feed our souls after a long time away from the comfort of our church. Jesus taught us to forgive, as he did, and we find it hard to forgive Bolshevik criminality which denied us the practice of our faith, endangered our lives and left millions of Christians dead. "

At that point, three Russian soldiers, with caps jammed down over their foreheads stood in the center of the back aisle, and slammed their rifle butts onto the stone floor for attention. The worshippers huddled in fright, as there was an apparent danger from the Bolsheviks after all.

Andrew remained stoic, and as Marianne thought later, he looked like a saint in the colored sunlight; he said calmly, "That's enough." None of the soldiers had removed their caps, and they leaned against the back wall. They showed no signs of respect or care. One of them leaned on the alms box and lighted a cigarette and then they pointed their pistols at Andrew.

Andrew ignored the threat, however, and words that he didn't know were there, spilled forth repeating a need for forgiveness and to return to the center of their beliefs in an amoral and criminal society. "Jesus …." he continued.

"Louder," said one soldier. "We can't hear you back here. We just came to watch. We want to see how Polacks worship an imaginary God."

".....threw the money changers out of the temple." Andrew went on

Once again, the Soviet soldier complained that Andrew could not be heard; however he went on, "We need to see what is important, which is God's people. Unlike Moses, we live in a promised land, which we love; however, like Moses, the regulators and Soviets must let our people go. It will be foolish to stand still while our country is being ravaged and sacrificed. We have survived so many martyrs who died in agony, executed by the NKVD of this war. Human beings are left in trainloads to die in hunger, and our bravest men and women are slain. The pride of our nation lies in mass graves."

"The people I am facing here are the silent heroes that history does not record. On this Sunday morning, we can rejoice and be glad, because we know how to deal with death through Jesus Christ. . "*My Chcemy Boga*"----We want God in our lives...now and forever. We know that the Soviet character is sinister. We are walking through the valley of death, and we will fear no evil. We have our souls and faith intact. There is more evil coming, but as long as we walk in the steps of our Savior we will be all right."

"The world was not watching us, and to the newsmen seated here: Remember us now. We are the survivors, who were denied the freedoms that you hold dear. This is the first time we can wear our crosses and worship in our own way. The Bolsheviks must hate Catholics because of our unwavering commitment to faith and truth. We are the real victims of this hallowed Polish ground; we will lose this disastrous European War if your President provides food, and supplies to help the Soviet Union in a long world war."

Marianne marveled at Andrew's "sermon" where did he get the courage, she thought; however, he concluded by saying; "We must trust in the Lord, not the Soviets, and while we cannot forgive the government for these murderous and unnatural acts we must forgive those individuals that committed them. Dominus Patria".......

At this point, two of the soldiers stormed forward and grabbed Andrew, while the other one pointed his gun at the rest of the people in the row with him, including his family and gestured them toward the door. He was being arrested for treason, in God's house. They herded the small party, weeping and frightened, half dragging Andrew out of the door of the cathedral, and forced them all into the tailgate of a covered truck with two official red flags and a star fixed on each end. The little old priest was pulled along as well, while fervently praying out loud.

Six very frightened children with a Russian guard sat in the dim recesses of the truck: the boys were wearing yarmulkes, and the little girls had their hair wrapped in babushkas and each one sat on a suitcase. The truck was an old troop transport and on the benches at the back were Tomas and Ilana Dorovitz. Marianne and Andrew sat quickly as the truck roared away from the church. Tomas explained that the priest had been told to ask him to give the sermon, and that this truck was bound for a warehouse to be loaded with supplies for the people in the sanctuary near Zamolina. Tomas told them of at least one checkpoint that they had to pass through on the way from Pinsk.

"However, you will have protection" said Tomas, at which point the soldier in the back, raised his hand to his hat, saluted and removed it. There sat their friend Leopold Kabryn with a big grin on his face.

"The Russian military drivers, who arrested you, are really Casmir and Jan. We didn't want to tell you of our plan because you had to look surprised. We will go to our warehouse, fill the truck quickly and be on our way. Maybe, just maybe, the checkpoint guards will assume that this is a troop transport."

On the short journey to the storage center, Ilana kept holding her children's hands and stoking their heads. Marianne noticed that there was no suitcase packed for Ilana and Tomas, and then before she said anything, thought better of it, and assumed that storage trunk she was sitting on held their things.

A few minutes later, at the warehouse, they all loaded the truck with canned goods, and whatever else was boxed up, including dried eggs, powdered milk, sugar, and flour. They old vehicle was bulging with supplies and people. The Dorovitz children, Aaron, 17; Katya (Tamara) 14; Yari, 13; Seth, 10; Seymour, 9, and Myrna, 7, were to be hidden on their suitcases behind the boxes in the rear of the truck; Andrew, Marianne, Monika and Jan were now given rifles, and the rest of the children were told to lie down on the floor. After the truck was arranged, Ilana and Tomas were to sit on the very last box behind the lift gate. Leopold was now the sole driver, alone in the cab, which had been filled as well with boxes of goods.

Before they pulled away from the facility, Tomas took Andrew, and Marianne aside to talk and tell them that the Bolsheviks who had judged the living and the dead, now too must die. "Now I know," Tomas said, "why Stalin believes you as individuals are not statistics, but a tragedy for Moscow. You are the source of inspiration to the hopes of many. "

Ilana raised her head slowly, "It has been a long struggle, I'm grateful that you will care for my children as your own. You have saved so many lives, thousands of them from execution, starvation, disease and deportations. Tomas and I were responsible for those dead bodies. I will die and go to Hell. My children know that I'm sorry, and that they need to keep, not betray, their spiritual heritage."

Marianne was nervous about time for escape being short and asked if the children had new papers. Tomas said "Yes, from now on they are the Ukrainian Wojceks. We want them to survive as Jews, but that may not be possible."

His face was filled with grief and sorrow; he had thought he found repentance. Tomas was a man who had a romance with evil; he fell in love with self-indulgence, but now close to death, he had freed his soul. "Andrew," he said, "please give Ilana and me your blessing before we die."

Andrew felt that only men of God could give a blessing, and told Tomas that as he turned to the rest; however, Ilana said "Please, you have made a *mitzvah*, by saving so many, and my children, and you are, right now the holiest man we know. Please give us your blessing."

Andrew, bent his head, and as the Dorowitzes knelt in front of him, they were both swaying and praying in Hebrew. Only Andrew, again recognized the prayer *"Yehe shlama rabba min shmayya khayyim vesava vishu'a venekhama veshezava urfu'a ug'ulla uslikha v'khappara verevakh vehatzala lanu ulkhol 'ammo yisrael ve'imru amen 'ose shalom bimromav hu ya'ase shalom 'alenu ve'al kol yisrael, ve'imru amen.* He prayed loudly along, as the rest of the people did, all kneeling and crying in front of this old khaki colored truck, showing its Red Star. "Our *Father which art in Heaven Hallowed be Thy name.....*the Polish words drowned out the Hebrew prayer, which Andrew, weeping openly, again recognized as *Kaddish*; however, this one was for orphans and mourners when they prayed for the dead. Aaron glanced around frightened Katya snatched Ilana's hand, and Myrna kissed Dorovitz's thin beard. There it was: all the love came home, for the moment.

Ilana stood, looked at her children and told them: "Don't tell anyone where you came from; sing *My Chcemy Boga.* Pray for your father and mother. Pray for Pan and Pani Krull that they make it through this horrible war."

"We always will, I promise," Aaron answered. "I will love you both forever." He sensed that this was good- bye, or at least farewell.

Then he stiffly and formally told Andrew and Marianne: "Thank you for giving us a home."

Tomas and Ilana hugged everyone "We will die for our sins, but our children will get a new start in a home and village of love. Be careful." he said. They all slowly climbed into the truck;

The day turned warm and the truck chugged down the middle of the highway. It isn't unusual to see trucks and tanks stall or break down on the roads, because of poor maintenance; every mind and soul that day were praying that the truck would make it home. Right now, all eyes were fixed on the narrow bend ahead.

They anxiously awaited and hoped that there would be no Soviet checkpoint along the road to confiscate the goods and maybe shoot them all. Every turn around each bend in the pitted roadway, brought sigh after sigh of relief when the road was clear. Several miles from home there was one, however. Jan and Casmir cocked their rifles and pointed them out of the flaps at the back of the truck after Leopold had called back about the upcoming stop. Unfortunately, there were more troops than they could deal with, even with automatic weapons and their Eskadry.

Tomas leaned over to Marianne and said quietly "No matter what happens tell Leopold to go fast to your home and sanctuary. This is the only stop between here and there."

Marianne, gasped," You knew of this place?" feeling betrayed, she pointed her gun at him.

"No, no you will be safe, but this is the only way. Once we are off first, tell Leopold to go very fast." He and Ilana jumped off the tailgate and walked around to the Russian sentry, and as he did so, he waved the truck on past them. Leopold accelerated in a cloud of dust, and as Marianne peeked out of the rear curtain, she saw Tomas and Ilana forced to their knees and by none other than Colonel Pietrinev. He approached the couple, now holding hands and chanting their prayer, with his pistol out, He was too arrogant to use a silencer, and the last glimpse Marianne had of them, after she heard two shots as she bounced around the rear of the vehicle, was the two bodies lying on the ground, one bullet each in the back of the head.

The group escaped safely. The children were hardly aware what happened. Aaron and his brothers and sisters had been screened by boxes piled in front of them, Marianne and Andrew's children were lying face down on the floor. Then they all realized that this flight to the woods, with food, and the new lives of children had been carefully orchestrated by the Dorovitzes. - Their final act of atonement was the last stop at a Soviet station that they knew would kill them, giving the truck time to get away. . Marianne moved close to Andrew, who was standing with the little old Priest, both reciting in unison: *Misereatur tui omnipotens Deus, et dimissis peccatis tuis, perducat te ad vitam aeternam.* He crossed himself and continued. : *Indulgentiam, absolutionem et remissionem peccatorum nostrorum, tribuat nobis omnipotens et misericors Dominus. Amen.* They *had* given the last rites to two dead Bolsheviks who were Jewish. Most priests only gave these rites to baptized Catholics, and Marianne puzzled, asked him: "Why?"

Andrew replied softly "They needed to go home. They found love. They asked their God, who is ours too, for forgiveness, and salvation. Jesus helped the Canaanites who were considered non-believers. He saw no difference where a man came from or what he believed. He said: "What you do in my name, you do for me. Tomas and Ilana needed to go home and rest in peace." Then he started to sob against the side of the truck.

Marianne pulled him close. "They are free now"she said.

Leopold drove the truck over the bumpy field on a wagon road to behind the Ludwig's shed. They all worked hard hauling the goods to the forest, where to their surprise another two truckloads had been emptied by grinning Russian soldiers who were sent by Dorovitz, who now chose to live in the sanctuary.

The children, all of them, were brought to the little hut which now would temporarily house eleven people. Marianne, sat them down in front of it, and explained that their parents had been taken to be with God, and watched as the brave children cried silently. It was then she realized that they knew all along of their parents' plan. All the love had come home.

MONDAY JUNE 22, 1941

328

The next day, at dawn, Jan Casmir and Leopold parked the truck near Colonel Pietriniev's headquarters; they opened the gas tank, stuffed a gasoline soaked rag into the open tank, lit it and ran. They resembled three old dirty looking peasants, who sprinted away to take cover behind a tree as the truck exploded. Pietrinev, holding his usual morning coffee, stepped out on his porch to see what was wrong. As he reached the top step, a well-placed bullet from Casmir, took the Colonel's life. He fell into a dirty heap, and the coffee cup clinked down the steps to the ground below. The other soldiers inside were too busy making ready to leave to pay attention to the direction of the shot. The Russians were leaving.

The three men brought the news of the Colonel's demise to the sanctuary; where even after the events of Sunday, had to return to work in the fields and on the farms. Casmir and Jan told them that truck after truck of retreating Russian troops were rapidly heading eastward. Marianne and Andrew brought their expanded family of nine children to the altar place in the wood, and joined the Pilats, Adam, Florence, Grygas, Luba Varya and Rygalas at early morning Vesper service.

Marianne prayed, silently, that one of the photos and Ilana's confession had reached someone of importance, somewhere. They all, she thought, had survived the Soviet Occupation. Andrew led them in a prayer of gratitude, and a prayer for strength to rebuild what was left of their home and country. "We are thankful that we are here today. Our lives continue to be a gift from God. We thank Him for our humanity, our faith and our survival in the heart of Poland and in the hearts of Polish people. The challenge will be to continue to live honorably, not as political victims, not with indignation of life, but with a love of life. One tragedy of the past brought us together, and tomorrow's tragedies may bring us even closer."

Stefan, Maria and Alexandra sat with the Dorovitz children, Katya was holding the baby Alexandra, Aaron was staring solemnly forward, and he turned to Andrew and asked: "Am I allowed to pray with you? I only know my prayers in Hebrew".

Andrew hugged the boy and said "Being Catholic or Jewish matters to some, but to me as long as you talk to God, and trust in him, you will be fine."

Andrew led the boy to the altar and the Virgin and explained that the Catholics believe her to be the earthly Mother of God who came to earth as Jesus, and that Jewish people believe that a Jesus, a messiah, was yet to come. The boy, still wearing his yarmulke, nodded, and asked

Andrew could he sit *shiva* in the sanctuary. Andrew was touched that Aaron felt he could mourn his father and mother in the confines of his new home, and promised him that he may and offered any help that he needed.

Marianne took the other children up to the altar to look at the roses, which were blooming there. Curiously, they had never seen blooms in the house or even in the yard around it. Aaron, turned to Marianne, and took her hand as he was now crying openly, as Andrew had allowed his mourning period, and said "I had a good teacher in my Jewish mama," he said, "but when the next seven days of my shiva is over, may we call you Mama and Papa?" All of the children started to cry at that point.

Marianne assured them that they could and that there was more to learn here among the beautiful flowers and trees. "The future is waiting for us" she said, "and we must look there and determine who and what we are, and how our hearts open and close...the promise of life is before us. The worst is not over, but faith, courage, and honesty will help us survive."

Even the littlest child, who had no understanding of what Marianne had said, nodded in agreement. Aaron solemnly walked to the hut where he sat still and tore the sleeve of his shirt in the traditional Jewish manner. Andrew sat with him, praying that he could help this sad child retain his faith. The boy sat and alternately sobbed and prayed all day. The other children went off to play, and Andrew and Marianne took turns comforting the young mourner.

TUESDAY JUNE 23, 1941

Marianne felt good about saving the Dorovitz children and the Priest; however, she was worried about her father, and the fate of Ilana's confession and the accompanying photograph. Was her father still alive in the mountains? She felt that he was; he often said to her: "You will always be my soul that shall not part."

Andrew suggested that morning that they take the children with them to the old farmhouse and start to get caught up with the work in the field. They hustled them along the paths to the house near the battered road, and started to distribute the tools that they would need. Soon, under Andrew's happy direction, the work became fun. He made it all a happy game. Who could fill the basket with weeds first? Who could clean an area? Who could sing a song?

Marianne looked at the workers, and thought there were no more quotas to fill, no more regulators to obey; perhaps they had a chance to move back to the house. She went inside, and decided she would clean it and make do for the suddenly expanded family. She thought that they had survived the Russians. Then she heard the singing. She looked out her window and there was a tank driving by, decorated with the twisted cross of the Nazis. A troop of men followed, singing at the top of their lungs as they marched:
"....*Millions, full of hope, look up at the swastika;*
The day breaks for freedom and for bread...
.....*Soon will fly Hitler-flags over every street;*
Slavery will last only a short time longer.

Marianne realized that it was not over; it's never over. They had to continue to live in the sanctuary. . It is an acquired 'hard ducha' that makes you more worthy to resist the suffering in a place of honor. She whispered to Andrew, "We can't run where we are, destiny chooses where we are going,"

Her eyes are filled with tears, silently clasping the box. "We have one home, one country. Gone are the homes with all the inherited virtues but not lost to the memory of all, but the most humbly grateful to be alive.

But the loss of it all burns in my soul."

Then a quiet moment, against the silhouettes of the eternal beams of light that faced openly against the Black Madonna portraiture. She and Andrew said a prayer of gratitude that gives strength to our souls, to return of what is left of our home and country.

So,when the home is under the Naxi Occupation, we all wonder how we survived at all? Why did these things happen, and why is my family so lucky to be *alive*? Poland was one giant Concentration Camp, its full meaning under German Occupation.

Marianna and Andrew's choices created the future, and the future, as always, belongs to the courageous spirit that affords us an opportunity to live through it all.

All Love Comes Home

Marianne closed the box, and looked at the film canister, which did land, and cause discovery in what ranks as the greatest mystery of the 2nd War, a place whose tragic fate has inspired one's own sense of being, whose human will outlives the trace of its physical existence.

Marianne leaned back, dozing in her recliner in Syracuse, New York, and thought "Is that all?" What's ahead *is* borne out of heart, mind, body, and soul, not seemingly hopeless, brutally honest, so that this family does not come out of this tragedy as prisoners of mistruths.

Despite all the agonies and humiliations endured in those years, despite all the outrages, she still believed she would be triumphant in the end. It's not the anguish, but it is about the joy of human triumph.

Nazis had arrived.

EPILOGUE 2000

Marianne leaned back, dozing in her recliner in Syracuse, New York, and thought.

The meaning is not lost that the direction of World War II could have been reversed with the terrible truth of hallow mass graves at Katyn Forest... something the world could see and honestly react to a moral truth.

"Is that all?" But there is more to her story. Marianne closed the box, and looked at the film canister, which did land, and cause discovery of the Katyn Massacre albeit two years after she sent it. One of the couriers had been intercepted by the German patrols and the contents examined and used to provide the Nazis with evidence of the massacre and in 1943, they unearthed four thousand remains of the Polish officers slain by the NKVD. The resulting films blamed the executions on the Russians. The bodies were reburied. The Russians brought forth testimony at the Nuremberg trials blaming the Nazis for the murders; however, with a Russian judge on the panel, all discussion evaporated until 1952, when the Russians unearthed the bodies once again and blamed the Nazis. Their film had flaws, and there were questions, including where the exhumed corpses landed. No one knows for sure, however, the truth Katyn Forest Massacre was finally acknowledged by Moscow in 1991.

USSR was responsible for the mass execution of twenty-seven thousand Catholic men and women buried in three mass graves near the Village of Gnezdovo outside Smolensk..

Kanganovich, Stalin, Beria signed the order.

Churchill supported the Soviet denial despite evidence to the contrary.

In 1944, President Roosevelt ordered Captain George Earle to investigate the Katyn Forest Massacre. Earle concluded that the Soviet Union was guilty, but Roosevelt rejected the conclusion ordering Captain Earle's report to desist with a written order. Captain Earle was reassigned to America Samoa for the War in the Pacific.

In November 1945, a court of Americans, British, French, and Soviets tried seven officers of the German Army. They were condemned to death for their role in the Katyn Forest massacre and were hanged.

Prime Minister Sikorski, who had alerted the British that the Soviet Secret Police(NKVD) and the men and women behind the English made pistols supplied by the English used in the mass murder of twenty-seven thousand officers and civilians buried in the Smolenks forests.

A joint Polish/British Commission concluded that the death of General Sikorski and Prime Minister of the Polish Government in Exile during World War 11 was assassinated on July 4,1943 in Gibralter, when the British plane he was aboard fell to the sea sixteen seconds after takeoff. Winston Churchill along with Soviet Ambassador, Maisky and Stalin have concealed the truth under various Commissions Reviews.

A definitive British/Polish comprehensive investigation released in 1991 concluded that the Soviet Union murdered General Sikorski when he raised the issue with President Roosevelt of Katyn Forest Massacre and Soviet war borders regarding Poland's rights.

Two previous attempts to assassinate Sikorski in 1942 and on July 4[th,] 1943 failed.

HISTORICAL POST SCRIPT TO BOOK ONE AND TWO

The darkest times were when Poland's thirty-four million people were entrapped between two enemies before and during WW11. The world turned a blind eye to death when the Soviets' NKVD in July 1939 crossed the border and assassinated over seven thousand Polish intelligentsia.

> *. And whoever captured that moment expressed it best:*

> *A scarlet dawn rises over Polesie and the fog, having torn off the lakes and rivers, gets high up in the sky and spills over fields and meadows with motley colors of a rising sun. The dawn of Polesie will trembleand its golden rays will twine. The heat will sink seeing this beautyand you a quail of Polesie, a crane of Belarus or a swan of Russiawill follow the rising sun.*

Virtually every "Soviet official" of the USSR was hateful and operated within the framework of the NKVD security apparatus—informants, butchers, crossing borders, committing atrocities to polarize and divide one group against another.

Over four million Polish citizens, young and old, were either mass executed, or were herded in box cattle cars into Siberia's slave camps to starve and freeze to death at a time when the Communists were an ally of Germany during a twenty-two month period (August 22, 1939-June 21, 1941). It is quite telling before the war, and of course, in a place in Europe which had the highest death toll ever not reported in the history of western civilization.

Truth remained dishonored by hypocrisy and held in *cold storage* for nearly three generations.

Soviet Union's ALLIANCE with Germany resulted in the deaths of 8.5 million Polish citizens, over ninety-five per cent Catholic and Christian, who disappeared from the beautiful land of Poland in twenty-two months from August 1939 to June 21, 1942 to finance the war by both the Nazis in the West and Soviet Communists from the East. Yet the Democracies of the world were not morally outraged

The walls of Roosevelt's White House, and of Communism and Nazism beckon the emergence of truth. Some people may think it incomprehensible to redress President Roosevelt's greatest failure, and the Bolshevik's evil, and to engage in authentic discussion.

I went back to my own resurrected home with a heavy heart. Marianna's voice in this novel is the remaining connection that is a witness to the evolving truth of the Christian genocide under the 20th Century Soviet regime and the compelling secret of two decades of the worst disaster in all of western civilization. Over sixty million Christians perished before 1939. At a breathtaking level,history has disgraced the moral dimensions of the times and its precious truths. The ugliest kept secrets of World War Two were the unfathomable crimes against humanity from 1939 to June 1941, of Book One. My family suffered, along with thirty-four million human beings, while USSR was an ally of Germany. Particularly egregious, were the actions of the new regulators-citizens of western Poland, the *self-preservationists,* who betrayed their country in time of war andjoined forces with the invading USSR, systematically carrying out mass executions against their fellow countrymen.

It is now acknowledged that statesmen of the world knew of the red-stained earth and skeletons in the Katyn Forest. Also known were the deportations of slave labor to frozen tundras of Siberia where people died a Slow Death, by starving and freezing. These were the best and brightest, forever gone from the land that was once heightened with the light of the rising sun and the warmth of the soul of its people. All the while, the world's statesmen were silent to the blood that flowed through the forests of Eastern Europe. They ignored the gory details of mass murder and the misery and terror in Bolshevik Russia.

The White House and Churchill betrayed a moral nation...Poland; and in the process sanctioned and savaged the human body, mind, and soul with Bolshevik cruelty on a blood stained Poland for two generations.

And here are President Roosevelt's powerful words again, not changed, or fictionalized, but the ultimate hypocrisy of the times.
"This is preeminently the time to speak the truth, the whole truth, frankly and boldly.

Nor need we shrink from honestly facing conditions in our country today.

This great nation will endure as it has endured, will revive and will prosper.

So First of all, let me assert my firm belief. That the only thing we have to fear is fear itself- nameless, unreasoning, unjustified terror which paralyzes needed efforts to convert retreat into advance...... Franklin D. Roosevelt---

For history's sake, it is never too late to hold accountable those who affected world's inhumanity... Roosevelt's decision... to ally with the Soviet Union knowing full well their history of evil during two decades of death, while in the so called "Peacetime", sixty million human beings with enormous potential to foster the good in life were deliberately executed by the Bolsheviks.

When the war ended in 1945, and for two years, following the betrayal of Poland, two hundred thousand more Polish patriots were executed by the invaders from Moscow. With full force of Yalta Betrayal, the population of Poland was reduced to 21million by the end of 1946.

Still to this day, history's greatest mystery remains. Why were the democratic people of Poland betrayed by England, France, and the United States and why did a plundering history desecrate the graves of those who fought and died there?

Of those who disappeared, many were my family's friends and wonderful neighbors, great patriots of the world, who were discarded and forgotten by the cowardly silence of the times in which Christianity was sacrificed to a dustpan of history. This is the acknowledged side of the war ignored by the informational purveyors to this day. I never doubted the whole truth would win in the end.

Gene Fisch

CHECK OUT VIDEO-Gene Fisch, You Tube.com
CHECK OUT WEBSITE: www.EugeneFisch.com